GREGG
TYPEWRITING
FOR COLLEGES

Alan C. Lloyd, Ph. D.
Gregg Publishing Division,
McGraw-Hill Book Company, Inc.

John L. Rowe, Ed. D.
Chairman, Department of Business Education,
College of Education,
University of North Dakota

Fred E. Winger, Ed. D.
Professor of Secretarial Science
and Business Education,
Oregon State College

Harold H. Smith *Consulting Editor*

COMPLETE   **GREGG PUBLISHING DIVISION**

COURSE   **McGRAW-HILL BOOK COMPANY, INC.**

NEW YORK   CHICAGO   SAN FRANCISCO   DALLAS   TORONTO   LONDON

Copyright © 1957, by the McGraw-Hill Book Company, Inc. All rights reserved. This book, or parts thereof, may not be reproduced in any form without permission of the publishers. Printed in the United States of America.
Library of Congress Catalog No. 57-1004

April 1959—RD

CONTENTS

PART 4

PART 5

PART 6

CONTENTS

CONTENTS

INDEX

INDEX

Take a 7- or 10-minute test on the copy below, or type it once and grade your work as though you had typed it at 67 words a minute. Grading scale:

si
1.23

Step 1: Compute words a minute	Step 2: Deduct for errors—		Step 3: Grade the remaining words a min- ute this way:	
	1 error: —1	6 errors: — 9		65 or higher: A
	2 errors: —2	7 errors: —12		60 to 64 wam: B
	3 errors: —3	8 errors: —15		50 to 59 wam: C
	4 errors: —5	9 errors: —18		45 to 49 wam: D
	5 errors: —7	10 errors: —22		

◁ **70** ▷
SS

7-Min.
Writings

			SS
0	53	The error into which most of us fall is in thinking that we will	13
2	55	get a new lease on life whenever we decide to do so. We coast along,	27
4	57	telling ourselves that, when our big chance comes along, one worth an	41
6	59	effort, we will then stretch and make good. There is no mistake that	55
8	61	is worse than this. Once you get the habit of coasting, it's too bad	69
10	63	for you. The habit gets you and keeps you coasting; and there's only	83
12	65	one direction you can coast. To build muscles, you have to use them.	97
14	67	Ambition is seldom wholly dead in any of us; most of us long for	110
16	69	the good things that are out of our reach at the moment. But the way	124
18	71	to get them is not to give up and let go; rather, it's to take a leaf	138
20	73	from the story of the old warrior whose son complained that his sword	152
22	75	was too short. The wise fighter said, "Then step closer to the foe."	166
24	77	All this is worth talking about because you will soon be in your	179
26	79	first position; and the work in any first position is usually so easy	193
28	81	for you, since no one expects much of you as a beginner, that you can	207
30	83	get the idea that you can relax in the job and stop growing. If that	221
32	85	happens, you start coasting, which takes you back down the hills that	235
34	87	you climbed to get where you are. If your work is easy, then that is	249
36	89	the time to push, and push hard while the pushing is easy. Don't let	263
38	91	yourself coast nor stand still; get your muscles ready for the climb.	277
40	93	The climb is not easy, which is a good thing for you; if it were	290
41	95	easy, the ladder would be full of people ahead of you. Sometimes the	304
43	97	ladder of advancement shakes and trembles, and you with it; sometimes	318
45	99	the rungs seem mighty far apart. But it's when the stretching is the	332
47	101	hardest and the climbing the toughest that your strength and will and	346
49	103	heart enable you to reach the next rung that others could not attain.	360
51	105	The relaxing and coasting is for those who lack the drive to succeed.	374
Plus ➡			(START OVER)

GREGG TYPEWRITING FOR COLLEGES presents a new, efficient, and systematic program for developing and using typing skill. This book has five distinguishing characteristics. They are:

1. Copy Control

The instructional pattern has been designed with infinite care to lead smoothly and steadily from the simple to the complex: The copy has been controlled as to word length, vocabulary, thought content, duration, quantity, and number of repetitions, to assure that every drill fits into the simple-to-complex pattern. The sequence of presenting manuscripts, tabulations, letters, and other arrangement problems has been designed with equal thought and care. All material is graded in difficulty to build and to pace the growing typing power of the student.

2. Spiral Organization

The book is organized in Parts, each consisting of 25 lessons. The first Part covers the machine controls and the basic operating techniques. Each subsequent Part provides this balanced program:

> *6 lessons on skill improvement*
> *6 lessons on correspondence typing*
> *6 lessons on tables or business forms*
> *6 lessons on manuscripts and reports*
> *1 lesson that is a test on the others*

The material in each succeeding Part is slightly more advanced and extensive, resulting in steady, easy spirals from the simple to the most complex experiences.

3. "See How" Approach

A special feature of GREGG TYPEWRITING FOR COLLEGES is the use of full-sized models to guide the student's first experience with each kind of arrangement problem. Models are given for all letter styles, manuscripts arrangements, tabulations, business forms, etc. There are more models in this book than have ever before appeared in a typing textbook.

The exercises following the models have also been especially designed to help the student: They are usually in almost-model form, with guides and signals. Only near the end of the course, after the student has had thorough training in arrangement, is material given in unarranged form.

4. Progress Expediters

This book features many teaching and learning conveniences, some new and some refined to a new usefulness. Examples:

New speed scales that tell both how
   much was typed *and at what speed*
Color-guide keyboard charts
Extremely helpful marginal "signals"
Grade-your-own-work progress tests
Alphabetic paragraphs with even lines
Printing one can copy line for line
Previews for all timed-writing copy
Sharp-focus drawings, in color
Precise directions for assignments
Provision for self-timing of work

5. Supporting Training Aids

This book is just one part of a full program of materials. The program includes:

A *basic* textbook (first 75 lessons)
An *intensive* book (first 150 lessons)
A *complete* textbook (225 lessons)

A workbook for Lessons 1-75
A workbook for Lessons 76-150
A workbook for Lessons 151-225

Tapes (recordings that coach the student) for
   keyboard lessons, speed lessons, and accuracy
   lessons
Filmstrips that strengthen learning
Special aids for instructors

The workbooks are especially helpful. They include the stationery, business forms, records, etc., that enrich the training program. Workbooks also provide additional practice materials, reprints of particularly helpful magazine articles, and something new: *study guides* that highlight the most important learnings in each group of lessons, reducing the need for discussion and thereby saving much class time.

THE AUTHORS

Below are the first 2 pages of a manuscript that is to be sidebound. Use Workbook pages 349-350. You may use your visual guide. If you are timed for 30 minutes, grade your work by the colored grading signals in the copy below.

MAKING CORRECTIONS   4

By (Your Name)   7

There is no such thing as a perfect typist;   16
so, we must all learn to correct mistakes.   25
This report is intended as a guide for mak-   33
ing corrections. It is a digest of information   43
to be found in books by Smith[1] and by   50
Gavin and Hutchinson.[2]   55

Technique 1: Erasing   59

A. Be sure your hands and eraser are   67
clean. To clean an eraser, rub it briskly on   76
paper or on fine-grained sandpaper.   84

B. Move the carriage as far as possible   92
to one side so that erasure crumbs cannot   100
fall into the machine.   105

C. Roll the paper so that the error to be   114
corrected is on top of the cylinder. Hold the   123
paper firmly by pressing it against the cyl-   132
inder with the tips of your fingers.   139

D. Erase with light, short, circular mo-   147
tions, blowing very lightly to keep the dust   156
out of the machine.   161

E. Return the paper to writing position   169
and type the correction. Tap the key light-   177
ly. Tap it repeatedly until the corrected   186
letter is as dark as the other letters on the   195
page.   (Grade: D)   197

Technique 2: Realigning   202

If an error is detected after the paper   210
has been removed, erase the error and re-   218
insert the paper for typing a correction: 226

A. Insert the paper and roll it up so that   235
the line on which the correction is to be   243
made is above the aligning scale.   250

B. Depress the paper release and adjust   259
the paper so that (1) the line is straight, (2)   268
the line is the same distance above the scale   277
as in normal typing, and (3) the white lines   286
on the scale point exactly to the center of   295
the letter i or 1.   (Grade: C)   299

C. Set the carriage at the point of cor-   307
rection.   309

D. Type the correction very, very light-   317
ly—so lightly that you can barely see it—to   326
check the accuracy of your aligning.   334

E. Improve the aligning, if necessary.   342

Technique 3: Word Shifting   348

When an extra letter is to be typed in a   356
correction, the whole word is erased and   364
retyped a half space to the left of its orig-   373
inal position. If one less letter is to be   382
typed, the word is erased and retyped a   390
half space to the right.   395

Shifting the word may be accomplished   403
by moving the paper or by holding the car-   411
riage in half-space position as each letter is   420
typed. Smith[3] suggests using the backspace   429
key to hold the carriage in half position.   438
The carriage can also be held by hand or,   446
on some machines, by holding down the   454
space bar.   (Grade: B)   456

-----

[1]Harold H. Smith, College Typewriting   464
Technique (New York: Gregg, 1952), page   472
77.   473

[2]Ruth E. Gavin and E. Lillian Hutchin-   480
son, Reference Manual for Stenographers   488
and Typists, Second Edition (New York: 497
Gregg, 1956), page 5 ff.   502

[3]Smith, op. cit., page 77.   (Grade: A)   507

Allen electric   Allen manual   IBM electric   Remington noiseless

Remington electric   Remington manual   Royal electric   Royal manual

Smith-Corona electric   Smith-Corona manual   Underwood electric   Underwood manual

THESE TWELVE TYPEWRITERS . . .

vary in appearance and in some features, but all have certain similar parts. Find these parts on the machine you will use in this course:

1. The carriage is the top, movable part on the machine. It "carries" the paper and moves horizontally.

2. The cylinder, in the carriage, is the long roller around which the paper moves. The cylinder and the paper turn each time the carriage is returned for a new line or when the cylinder knob, at either end of the cylinder, is turned.

3. The paper bail holds the paper against the cylinder. It is raised or pulled forward when the paper is inserted, straightened, or removed.

4. The margin sets are used to set margin stops so that the typing on the paper will stay within limits.

5. The paper release, a lever at the right end of the carriage, loosens the paper for straightening or removal.

6. The carriage releases (one at each end of the carriage) free the carriage so that it moves easily to the right or left. When you depress either release, hold the adjacent cylinder knob firmly, to keep the carriage under control.

7. The carriage-position scale counts the space across the cylinder.

8. The printing-point indicator points to the space on the scale to which the carriage has moved and at which the machine is ready to print.

9. The carriage return is the lever (manual machine) or large key (electric machine) used to return the carriage and to space up the paper for the start of a new line of typing.

10. The line-space regulator controls the distance that the paper spaces up each time the carriage is returned.

11. The paper guide, against which the left edge of the paper is placed when being inserted, guides papers uniformly into the machine.

BASIC INFORMATION

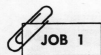

JOB 1

2-column table
Double space
Alphabetize
Column 1
Words: 83

STANDARD REFERENCE BOOKS

Information	Source Book (Title)
Financial ratings	Moody's Manuals; Poor's Manuals
Advertising rates	Standard Rate & Data
Credit ratings	Dun & Bradstreet Ratings
Congress	Congressional Directory
Churches	Yearbook of American Churches
Postal	U. S. Official Postal Guide
Hotels	Official Hotel Red Book
Books	United States Catalogue
Banks	The Banker's Blue Book

JOB 2

Financial
statement
Double space
Pivot to fill
60-space line
Open leaders
Rules
Words: 132

COMPARATIVE EARNINGS STATEMENT
(Years Ending December 31)

Item	1950	1955
Operating Revenues	$65,605,838	$81,960,327
Operating Charges	53,283,067	61,011,682
Net Income before Taxes	$12,322,771	$20,948,645
Federal and State Taxes	3,207,610	6,960,400
NET INCOME	$9,115,161	13,988,245

JOB 3

Boxed table
Draw all rules
Improve spacing
Space after the
alphabet groups
Words: 109

#➤ INVENTORY OF OFFICE EQUIPMENT
Knoxville Office, ~~August 31, 1956~~ *today's date*

Items	Condition			Total
	Good	Fair	Poor	
Chairs, Executive	2	8	4	14
Chairs, Guest	12	2	3	17
Chairs, Stenographic	9	8	1	18
Desks	6	24	2	32
Electric Fans	5	9	1	15
Files, 3-Drawer	6	0	0	6
Files, 4-Drawer	24	6	4	34
Mimeograph Machines	2	1	0	3
Typewriters, Electric	6	0	0	6
Typewriters, Manual	7	2	3	12

JOB 4

4-column table
Arrange it
Group in 3's
Do not rule
Words: 94

NAMES OF THE MONTHS IN FOUR LANGUAGES
(Note the Capitalization)

ENGLISH: January, February, March, April, May, June, July, August, September, October, November, December. **FRENCH:** janvier, fevrier, mars, avril, mai, juin, juillet, aout, septembre, octobre, novembre, decembre. **GERMAN:** Januar, Februar, Marz, April, Mai, Juni, Juli, August, September, Oktober, November, Dezember. **SPANISH:** enero, febrero, marzo, abril, mayo, junio, julio, agosto, septiembre, octubre, noviembre, diciembre.

VERTICAL SPACING

12. When paper is inserted in a typewriter, it is held firmly against the rubber-coated cylinder by pressure rolls above and below the cylinder. When the cylinder is turned, the paper moves around it, thus "spacing up." REMEMBER:

Paper "spaces up" when the cylinder is turned by hand or by a carriage return.

13. Typed material may be single spaced or double spaced or triple spaced. When it is single spaced, typing appears on each line. In double spacing, typing appears on every other line with 1 blank line between the typed ones. In triple spacing, typing appears on every third line with 2 blank lines between the typed ones.

Every typewriter has, at the left end of its carriage, a line-space regulator (¶10) that may be set for single, double, or triple spacing, as the typist wishes. REMEMBER:

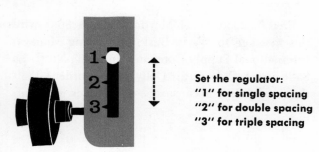

Set the regulator:
"1" for single spacing
"2" for double spacing
"3" for triple spacing

14. The first lessons in typing, like those on a musical instrument, consist of practice in correct fingering. The "scales" of a typing lesson are the lines of drill combinations and short words that give practice in using each new key as it is learned. As in music, fingering drills become easier, smoother, and faster with repetition. So, it is common to type each

drill line at least twice, single spaced, and to put a blank line between drills by returning the carriage an extra time. REMEMBER:

Drills are typed 2 or 3 times and followed by a blank line. The arrow-2 (opposite) reminds you to return the carriage twice, to leave the blank line.	juj juj frf frf juj juj frf frf ₂→ kik kik ded ded kik kik ded ded ₂→ lol lol sws sws lol lol sws sws			

Note that the space is always 1 line less than the number of carriage returns or lines turned up, since you type on the last line you reach. For example, if you wished to leave 6 blank lines at the top of a page, you would need to turn to the seventh line for the start of typing. REMEMBER:

When you want to leave space, do not count the line on which you type as part of the space.

```
1
2
3
4
5
6
7  Start here
```

Another example: A letter signature usually takes 3 blank lines; so, as the arrow-4 reminds, the typist turns the paper up 4 lines and types on the fourth.

15. Standard typewriters provide 6 single-spaced lines to an inch. Typing paper, usually 11 inches long, has 6 x 11 = 66 lines. Government stationery is 10½ inches long; it has 6 x 10½ = 63 lines. REMEMBER:

There are 6 lines to an inch. On standard paper (11 inches long), there are 6 x 11 = 66 lines.

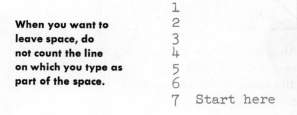

Line 1
Line 2
Line 3
Line 4
Line 5
Line 6

BASIC INFORMATION

This test consists of filling in 7 printed business forms in accordance with the job instructions below. Use Workbook pages 343-346. If your work is graded on the scale on page 307, Jobs 1-3 count as 1 page; Jobs 4-5 are 1 page; and Jobs 6-7 are 1 page. If your work is graded on the quantity of work you complete in 30 minutes, 7 jobs are graded A; 6, B; 5, C; and 4, D.

JOB 1 — Voucher check / Words: 43

To Edward L. Hastings, 831 Warner Building, Washington 4, D. C., for the sum of $53.67 in payment of travel expenses incurred in a trip on the sixth of last month.

JOB 2 — Receipt / Words: 47

For $98.75, paid on account, by Esther K. Stouffer.

JOB 3 — Promissory note / Words: 45

Alexander Wilson promises to pay in 90 days the sum of $500, at the First National Bank of Chicago, to the order of the International Supply Company, Inc.

JOB 4 — Purchase requisition / Words: 33

Mr. Haslett requisitions (No. AD-8-H) 10 new venetian blinds (green metal, with white tapes), to measure 3 by 7 feet, to replace those now in the Advertising Department office. Mr. Gibson approves the requisition.

JOB 5 — Purchase order / Words: 39

W. P. Busk authorizes the purchase of Mr. Haslett's blinds (catalogue number 392-WG-7) from Martin Miller & Sons, 58 Broad Street, Atlanta 1, Georgia. Each blind costs $12. The purchase order number is J-18803.

JOB 6 — Invoice / Words: 44

Martin Miller & Sons send invoice no. 3013 for Mr. Haslett's 10 venetian blinds, at $12 each (less 2% discount in the net amount), to International Supply Company, Inc., 463 North LaSalle Street, Chicago 2, Illinois. Shipment was by railway express.

JOB 7 — Telegram / Words: 60

Fred T. Dodson, of Martin Miller & Sons wires this message to W. P. Busk, Purchasing Manager, International Supply Company, Inc., 463 North LaSalle Street, Chicago 2: "Delivery your order J-18803 delayed 10 days because size of blinds is irregular."

Lesson 223 : *Tabulation Test*

This test consist of the 4 tabulation jobs on the next page. Note that you must plan the fourth table from the information provided. Use Workbook pages 347-348. Your grade may be the average of marks for each table, as scored on the page 307 grading scale; or, your grade may be on the quantity of jobs you complete in 30 minutes; 4, A; 3, B; 2, C; 1, D.

HORIZONTAL SPACING

16. Each time a key or the space bar is tapped, the carriage moves one space toward the left. The spacing is regular and even. All the spaces on which the machine will print are numbered. Every typewriter has a "carriage-position scale" (¶7) with a mark or number for each space.

The carriage-position scale has a mark for each space, and numbers appear every five or ten spaces. There is always some kind of printing-point indicator (¶8) that points to the space on the scale to which the carriage has moved. If the carriage is at the tenth space, for example, the indicator points at 10 on the scale. REMEMBER:

The number of the space at which the carriage stops is shown by an indicator that points to the scale.

17. Paper may be inserted so that its left edge is at 0, 5, or any point near the left end of the cylinder. Planning margins will be easiest if you insert paper so that its center comes at 50 on the scale—a number easy to remember, easy to add to and subtract from (as you do when planning margins), and easy to find on the scale. REMEMBER:

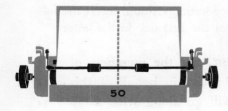

Insert the paper so that its center comes at 50 on the printing scale.

18. If your machine has fewer than 95 marked spaces, however, use 40 instead of 50 as the centering point for the paper (¶17), for setting the paper guide (¶19), and for planning margins (¶¶21, 23).

19. Each typewriter has a paper guide (¶11) that can be adjusted to guide paper into the machine so

that the center of the paper will come at whatever point on the scale you wish. To adjust the paper guide so that it will center your paper at 50, take these steps:

To Set the Paper Guide to Center the Paper at 50
1. Using the space bar or carriage release, set the carriage at 50.
2. Mark the center of the paper, at the top, by a pencil mark or a crease.
3. Insert the paper.
4. Loosen the paper by depressing the paper release (¶5).
5. Checking that the paper is straight, move it so that its center mark is at the printing point (¶8).
6. Restore paper release to normal.
7. Adjust the paper guide: Move it so that its blade edge is snugly against the left edge of the paper.

20. After the paper guide is correctly set to center paper at 50, be sure that you place the edge of each new sheet of paper snugly against the guide. But, REMEMBER:

Note exactly where the paper guide is set (to center paper at 50); and then, if the guide is moved, you can quickly and easily reset it.

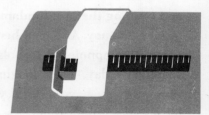

21. Planning margins is easy. Half the line of typing should appear on each side of the center of the paper. For example, when the paper is centered at 50, a 60-space line should begin at 20 and end at 80. The calculation is obvious: Half a 60-space line is 30 spaces; 30 spaces to the *left* of the center (50 − 30) is 20, and 30 spaces to the *right* of the center (50 + 30) is 80. REMEMBER:

Plan margins so that half the line of typing will appear on each side of the center of the paper.

BASIC INFORMATION

The letter below is from John R. Powell, Training Director. It is to be typed in accordance with the job instructions below. Use Workbook pages 339-342. Your test grade may be the average of grades for each letter individually, marked on the production grading scale, page 307; or, your grade may be on the basis of the number of letters you complete mailably in 30 minutes: 4, A; 3, B; 2, C; 1, D.

dear . . . . .

you will be interested to learn that our   **8**
chapter of the american association of na-   **16**
tional advertisers is about to launch a cam-   **25**
paign in support of the annual Secretary's   **34**
Day that is sponsored each spring by the   **42**
national secretaries association. we believe   **51**
that calling attention to this special day will   **61**
do much to popularize the secretarial ca-   **69**
reer, to attract to it increasing numbers of   **78**
superior young men and women, and to   **85**
invite added attention to the equipment   **93**
and training that are fundamental to secre-   **101**
tarial efficiency. As a member of the special   **111**
committee appointed to bolster interest in   **119**
secretary's day, i am looking for sugges-   **127**
tions. do you have any? if you do, please   **136**
let me hear about them. we want to make   **144**
certain that the next observance of secre-   **153**
tary's day is a popular event, and we shall   **161**
certainly welcome ideas on how to make it   **169**
so.   **170**

                       cordially yours,   **173**

JOB 1   Blocked letter
Words: 194

Blocked letter to Herbert J. Mullen, 521 Aldine Drive, Chicago 13. Use *Dear Herb:* as the salutation. Signature is *John,* with no typed name or title under the signature.

JOB 2   Semiblocked letter
Words: 243

Semiblocked letter to L. Richard Shields, Personnel Manager, Scott-Williams Company, 1657 East Nadeau Street, Los Angeles 1. *Dear Mr. Shields* is salutation. Type Mr. Powell's full name and title in the close; do not use a company signature. Add this postscript:

ps: is your los angeles NOMA group do-   **8**
ing anything on a chapter-wide basis to   **16**
honor or cosponsor some kind of secretary's   **24**
day observance in los angeles?   **30**

JOB 3   Full-blocked letter
Words: 237

Full-blocked letter, with open punctuation, to Office Executives Association, Quaker State Building, Oil City 3, Pennsylvania (Attention Special Projects Committee). *Gentlemen* is the salutation. Use only Mr. Powell's title in the closing. Type his name in the reference-initial position. Insert the following sentence after the first one in the letter:

we are confident that the members of   **7**
OEA are already active in behalf of this   **16**
observance and will go along with us in   **24**
supporting this project.   **28**

JOB 4   Semiblocked memo
Words: 192

Double-spaced, semiblocked memo to *Manager, New Orleans Office,* about *Secretary's Day.*

22. When setting margin stops to give the desired margins —

STEP 1: Subtract half the line length from the center of the paper; set the left margin stop at the resulting number.

STEP 2: Add half the line length, *and 5 extra spaces*, to the center of the paper and set the right margin stop at the resulting number. Do not forget the 5 extra spaces; they allow for variation in the length of the last word on each line. REMEMBER:

Always allow 5 extra spaces when setting the stop for the right-hand margin.

23. This table summarizes the margin settings for the lengths of line most commonly used:

COMMON MARGIN SETTINGS
(With the paper centered at 50*)

LINE LENGTH DESIRED	LEFT MARGIN STOP AT	RIGHT MARGIN STOP AT
40 spaces	50−20=30	50+20+5=75
50 spaces	50−25=25	50+25+5=80
52 spaces	50−26=24	50+26+5=81
60 spaces	50−30=20	50+30+5=85
70 spaces	50−35=15	50+35+5=90

*With paper centered at 40 (¶18), settings will be 10 lower than shown in this table.

24. The procedure for setting margin stops begins with centering the carriage.

Royals, Smith-Coronas, and some Allens have "spring-set" margin stops. To set the left-hand stop: (*1*) Press the margin-set lever at the left end of the carriage, (*2*) move the carriage to the desired scale point, and (*3*) release the margin-set lever. To set the right-hand stop: (*1*) Press the margin-set lever at the right-hand end of the carriage, (*2*) move the carriage to the desired scale point, and (*3*) release the margin-set lever.

Underwoods, new Remingtons, and some Allens have "hand-set" margin stops positioned above a special margin-stop scale. Steps for each margin: (*1*) Press the top of the stop; (*2*) slide the stop right or left, to the desired point; then (*3*) release the top of the stop.

IBM's, electric Underwoods, and some Remingtons have "hook-on" margin stops. To reset the left margin stop: (*1*) Return the carriage to its margin, (*2*) "hook on" to the margin stop by depressing and holding down firmly the margin-set key on the keyboard, (*3*) move the carriage to the desired scale point, and (*4*) then release the margin-set key. To reset the right margin stop: (*1*) Move the carriage to the right margin stop, (*2*) "hook on" to the margin stop, (*3*) move the carriage to the desired setting point, and (*4*) release the margin-set key.

25. There are two sizes of typewriter type, called *pica* (pronounced *pie*-ka) and *elite* (ay-*leet*). If you wish to know whether your machine has pica or elite type, type 10 periods in a row and then compare them with the ones in the illustration below. Pica is the larger; it provides 10 spaces to an inch. Elite, being smaller, provides 12 spaces to an inch. Both pica and elite machines space the same vertically. REMEMBER:

There are 10 pica spaces to an inch; there are 12 elite spaces to an inch.

• • • • • • • • • • Pica
• • • • • • • • • • • • Elite

1   2

26. The distinction between pica and elite is not important in the beginning lessons, where directions for margins indicate the length of typing line in terms of *spaces*. But later on, in lessons on letters and manuscripts, the distinction becomes important, as directions indicate the length of typing line in terms of *inches*. When planning the setting of margin stops, the typist translates *inches* into *spaces* and, in the case of elite machines, "rounds off" the figures; as:

CONVERTING INCHES TO SPACES
When Planning Margin-Stop Settings

Number inches in the line	4"	5"	6"
Pica spaces (10 to an inch)	40	50	60
Elite spaces (12 to an inch)	48	60	72
Elite line, "rounded off"	50	60	70

BASIC INFORMATION

UNIT 36
FINAL TESTS

Could you do a typist's work, hold down a typist's job? Do you know enough, have skill enough? This unit contains six tests to help you answer these questions—to answer them *now*, while you may still have time in which to fill in any gaps that may be revealed.

You are allotted the time of 7 lessons in which to take the 6 tests. This schedule permits 1 period in which to preview the tests and verify any details of which you are uncertain, and 1 period for taking each test.

You are encouraged to preview, to study, even to practice these tests before you take them: If the

tests are to measure your capability as an office typist, you should be familiar with the vocabulary, arrangement, patterns, directions, etc., just as the office typist is familiar with these characteristics of *his* work. But note: Do not use or mark your Workbook pages for these tests until you take the tests officially at your instructor's direction.

Alternate plans for taking each test:

1. Your instructor may time you for exactly 30 minutes; you then proofread your work and grade it (the requirements are given with each test) on the quantity of acceptable work that you produced in the 30 minutes.

2. Your instructor may permit you as much time as you need, within reason, to complete the test; you then proofread your work and grade *each page* (each test consists of several pages of work) on the grading scale below, finally averaging the grades for a test mark.

Your instructor will tell you which plan is to be used. He will also tell you whether you are or are not to correct typing errors.

TAKE OFF:	—3 for each major error (top margin, line length, linespacing, correct form, etc.) —2 for each minor error (blocking, aligning, indenting, etc., of each part of a job) —1 for each typographical error	TOTAL TAKEN OFF:	10-9	8-5	4-3	2-0
		GRADE	D	C	B	A

Scale for grading each individual page of production work.

Lesson 219 : *Test Preview*

Lesson 220 : *Typing-Information Test*

A 100-question test covering general typing information (word division, typing terminology, error detection, etc.) is provided on Workbook pages 335-338. Detach these pages and bring them to class. Fill in the answers under the supervision of your instructor.

The office typist does not have time to ponder answers to the kind of questions that are included in this test, nor does he have an opportunity to change his mind. To simulate the same conditions, (1) you are to complete all 100 questions in 30 minutes, maximum time; and (2) you are not to

erase on this test—each page has been surprinted with fine dots so that any erasure will be seen immediately.

(When you preview this test, therefore, be *very* careful not to place any marks on the test pages: You will not be able to remove any marks from these pages.)

Grading the test: Your instructor has a key to the answers. Take off 1 point for each question incorrectly answered; then grade the work on the scale above: That is, 10 or 9 wrong, D; 8 to 5 wrong, C; 4 or 3 wrong, B; and 2, 1, or 0 wrong, A.

PREPARING TO TYPE

Each time you begin a new lesson, take these 9 steps. You should soon be able to prepare to type within 15 or fewer seconds. REMEMBER:

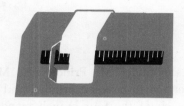

1. Check Paper Guide

Check that paper guide is set so that it will center the paper at 50 (see ¶20).

2. Set Line Spacing

Always start lessons with the line-space regulator set for single spacing.

3. Set Margin Stops

Set them for the line length signaled by the arrows and number at the start of the lesson.

4. Check Paper Bail

Check that the bail is forward (toward you) or up, out of the way.

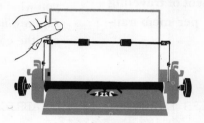

5. Insert Paper

Grasp paper in left hand. Put the paper squarely behind the cylinder, against the paper guide. Draw the paper into the machine by turning the right-hand cylinder knob.

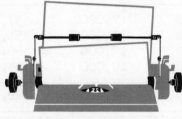

6. Be Sure Paper is Straight

Turn up about 4 inches of paper. Check that it is straight—both the top and bottom halves of the left edge should line up against the paper guide. If they do not, loosen the paper (use paper release) long enough to line them up.

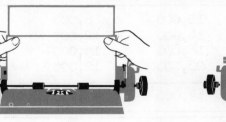

7. Reset Paper Bail

Adjust the rollers on the bail, to divide the paper in thirds; then place the bail against the paper.

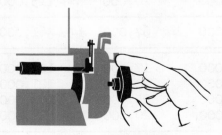

8. Allow for Top Margin

Turn the paper back down (use cylinder knob) until only a quarter inch or so of paper appears above the bail.

9. Take Position for Typing

Put hands on the "home keys": left fingers on A S D F and right fingers on J K L ;. Assume correct typing position, as shown on the next page.

BASIC INFORMATION

JOB 16 2 voucher checks
Words: 85

1. To spooner and moran, 1258 delaware avenue, buffalo 3, new york, for $100 in payment of consultation fee for the month of November, per agreement of May 1.

2. To mr. tracy r. spooner (same address as above) for $85.10 in payment of traveling expenses to new york city, per memorandum of december 3.

JOB 17 Revised table
Words: 222

"Please retype this table," Mr. Prince says. "Make enough copies for me to have an original and one carbon and for each of the four branch managers to have one copy."

He studies the table and then comments, "I think all those zeroes just confuse the real figures. Tell you what to do: Put in a subheading, in parentheses, *Figures in Thousands of Dollars;* then you can leave out the comma and last three zeroes in each figure."

SALES ESTIMATES OF PREFABRICATED HOUSES

Revised December 8,
~~June 30,~~ 19--

Quarter	Chicago	New Orleans	New York	San Fran	Totals
1	12,000	8,000	10,000	7,000	37,000
2	14,000	12,000	15,000	10,000	51,000
3	18,000	15,000	18 ~~15~~,000	12,000	63 ~~60~~,000
4	20,000	12,000	15 ~~12~~,000	10,000	57 ~~54~~,000
1st-year total	64,000	47,000	58 ~~52~~,000	39,000	208 ~~202~~,000
1	20,000	12,000	15,000	12,000	59,000
2	24,000	18,000	24,000	15,000	81,000
3	30,000	24,000	32,000	20,000	106,000
4	33,000	25 ~~27~~,000	30 ~~35~~,000	20,000	108 ~~115~~,000
2d-year total	107,000	79 ~~81~~,000	101 ~~106~~,000	67,000	354 ~~361~~,000
1	30,000	25,000	30,000	17,000	102,000
2	36,000	30,000	35,000	20,000	121,000
3	42,000	36,000	40,000	25,000	143,000
4	40,000	25,000	38,000	20,000	123,000
3d-year total	148,000	116,000	143,000	82,000	489,000
3-YEAR TOTAL	319,000	242 ~~244~~,000	302 ~~301~~,000	188,000	1,052,000

CORRECT TYPING POSTURE

GENERAL BEARING: ERECT, ALERT!

Head erect—head and eyes turned slightly toward the book

Shoulders relaxed

Upper arms and elbows hang loosely—slightly forward

Back straight

Forearms slope upward

Body well back in the chair

Feet apart, squarely braced on the floor

Alongside your typewriter—
At right, the book, on easel or bookholder
At left, your paper and other supplies

 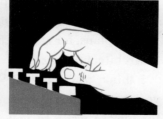 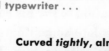 

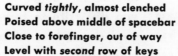

On a manual typewriter . . .   On an electric typewriter . . .

Fingers:	Curved *tightly*, almost clenched	Curved slightly, almost open
Right thumb:	Poised above middle of spacebar	Poised above middle of spacebar
Left thumb:	Close to forefinger, out of way	Close to forefinger, out of way
Heel of hand:	Level with *second* row of keys	Level with *first* row of keys

                 **BASIC INFORMATION**

Your employer is Paul V. Prince, general sales manager for the Corporation. He uses blocked style and this letter closing:

        Yours truly,

        INTERNATIONAL SUPPLY CO. INC.

        Paul V. Prince, Sales Manager

JOB 14 Letter with bcc's
Words: 381

December 8

mr. duncan j. pomeroy, secretary, na- 7
tional association of architects, 425 park 16
avenue, new york 17, new york 22

dear mr. pomeroy: we appreciate very 29
much the interest in our plans for develop- 38
ing prefabricated homes expressed by your 46
letter of inquiry. we certainly have no ob- 55
jection to your publishing in The National 63
Architect any commentary you wish about 71
our plans. 74

as i intimated to you some time ago, we 83
have no idea whatsoever of displacing arch- 90
itects by this process of building low- and 99
medium-priced homes. our prefabricated 107
materials are in a form that permits of in- 115
finite variation, especially for interior con- 124
struction. sufficient leeway exists in the 133
choice of materials for the exterior of homes 142
to enable an architect to construct two 150
homes of the same materials side by side, 159
yet with enough difference in appearance 167
to satisfy most homeowners. as a matter of 176
fact, we are counting on the architects of 184
this country to help us avoid the sameness 193
that has been the bane of the prefabricat- 201
ing industry. 204

within the next two or three months, we 212
expect to issue a booklet prepared espe- 220
cially for architects. it is being prepared 229
with the counsel of tracy r. spooner, whom 238
i believe you know. once the publication 246

date of the booklet is firmed, we shall take 255
space in your publication and similar ones 264
to announce its availability to the trade. 273

if there are more particulars that you 280
would like me to spell out, i should be 288
happy to try to do so. perhaps you would 297
prefer to write to mr. spooner, whose ad- 305
dress is below, since he is the one person 313
who is completely familiar with the tech- 321
nical nature of our plans. again, thank you 330
for your inquiry. yours truly, 337

cc mr. tracy r. spooner, spooner and 344
moran, 1258 delaware avenue, buffalo 3, 352
new york. bcc. mr. gibson, mr. lawrence, 361
mr. beauchamp, mr. taliaferro 366

JOB 15 Letter with display paragraphs
Words: 189

mr. tracy r. spooner [note his address in 4
the cc of the preceding letter] 15

dear tracy: a letter i just received from 24
duncan pomeroy indicates that "the cat is 32
out of the bag" and that word has got 40
around about our prefab plans. this is what 49
mr. pomeroy said: 52

the ominous news that your organi- 59
zation is planning to enter and de- 66
velop the prefabricated-homes field 73
has come to my attention. can you tell 81
me whether it is true? 86

if it is true, can you tell me any- 93
thing about the scope and nature of 100
your plans, for release to The National 108
Architect magazine? 112

i think, tracy, that it would be wise for 121
you to write mr. pomeroy without waiting 129
for him to write to you. give him enough 137
information to stir his curiosity and perhaps 147
to stimulate some degree of enthusiasm. if 155
you do write to him, be kind enough to 163
send me carbons of your letters, will you? 172
yours truly, 174

PART 1

PREPARE TO TYPE; INSERT PAPER . . .

Follow procedure on pages 5 and 6

PUT FINGER TIPS ON THE HOME KEYS . . .

Left hand on A S D F .
Right hand on J K L ; .
Left thumb close to hand.
Right thumb out, over space bar.
Fingers curved slightly for an electric, tightly for a manual.

TAP SPACE BAR 10 TIMES . . .

Use the right-hand thumb.
Use a bouncing-off stroke.
Keep other finger tips close to their own home keys.

RETURN THE CARRIAGE . . .

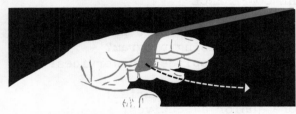

On a manual typewriter —
Raise only the left hand.
Place the forefinger and the next one or two fingers against the carriage-return lever.
Flip the hand, to toss carriage back to the left margin stop.
Zip hand back to its home keys.

On an electric typewriter —
Stretch the little finger of the right hand over to the carriage-return key without moving any other fingers.
Bounce the little finger off the carriage-return key.
Zip the little finger back to its home position on the semicolon key.

TYPE F's AND J's . . .

Take your time between strokes; but once you start to strike a key, use a quick, darting stroke. "Peck" the keys of a manual machine, "tap" those of an electric. Only the striking finger should move sharply; the others spring up just a bit. Where space is shown after the groups in the lines below, tap the space bar once. Type the line twice, as it is shown here. Keep eyes on the book, not on the machine.

	Left			Right			L	R	L	R	
Strike F and J with forefingers.	fff	fff	fff	jjj	jjj	jjj	fff	jjj	fff	jjj	Return carriage.
	fff	fff	fff	jjj	jjj	jjj	fff	jjj	fff	jjj	Return it twice.

JOB 13

Display manuscript
3 carbons
Words: 341

ITINERARY AND TRIP PLANS

For Mr. Gibson, December 12-16

SUNDAY, DECEMBER 12

11:20 p.m.   Leave from Central Station (12th Avenue) on Illinois Central.
Roomette 12, Car 117, of Train No. 17, The Night Diamond.

MONDAY, DECEMBER 13

7:00 a.m.   Arrive Union Station, St. Louis. To Jefferson Hotel.
9:30 a.m.   Call sister. Call Mr. Strauss to confirm Thursday luncheon.
10:30 a.m.   Limousine to airport.
11:30 a.m.   Meet Mr. Prince, arriving on American Airlines Flight 181.
12:30 p.m.   Luncheon in suite at hotel. Start of conference.

GENERAL AGENDA FOR THE CONFERENCE

1. What to do about the nitrogen headlight bulb problem?
2. Changes needed in newspaper advertising program?
3. Expand dealerships in automobile supplies and services?
4. Tighten up general credit policies?
5. Bonus plan versus general increases in salaries?
6. Program for developing more junior executives?
7. Must we use Fair Trade prices on standard merchandise?

TUESDAY, DECEMBER 14

Still at Jefferson Hotel. Conference continues.

WEDNESDAY, DECEMBER 15

Still at Jefferson Hotel. Conference continues.
6:00 p.m.   Dinner party at home of Kenneth Fairmont (president of Fairmont & Gordon, dress manufacturers), 309 Park Place. Formal.

THURSDAY, DECEMBER 16

Still at Jefferson Hotel, but check out before 3:00 p.m.
11:45 a.m.   End of conference; others leave for transportation.
12:30 p.m.   Lunch with Mr. A. I. Strauss, president of Strauss Brothers
(nursery stock), if confirmed on Monday.
2:55 p.m.   Check out of hotel.
3:15 p.m.   Limousine to airport.
4:50 p.m.   Leave St. Louis on Delta Airlines Flight 762 to Chicago.
6:01 p.m.   Arrive at Chicago Midway Airport. Met by Mrs. Gibson.

LEFT HAND

Forefinger . . . . F
Second finger . . . . D
Third finger . . . . S
Little finger . . . . A

RIGHT HAND

J . . . . Forefinger
K . . . . Second finger
L . . . . Third finger
; . . . . Little finger

Space Bar . . . . Right thumb

SPACE BAR

HOME-KEY PRACTICE *(Each line 2 times)*

	Left		Right			L	R	L	R
FOREFINGERS	fff	fff	fff	jjj	jjj	jjj	fff	jjj	fff	jjj
SECOND FINGERS	ddd	ddd	ddd	kkk	kkk	kkk	ddd	kkk	ddd	kkk
THIRD FINGERS	sss	sss	sss	lll	lll	lll	sss	lll	sss	lll
LITTLE FINGERS	aaa	aaa	aaa	;;;	;;;	;;;	aaa	;;;	aaa	;;;
ALL FINGERS	fff	jjj	ddd	kkk	sss	lll	aaa	;;;	fff	jjj

Leave a blank line (return carriage twice) before you start a new line of drills.

WORD PRACTICE *(Each line 2 times)*

aaa ddd add add add aaa lll all all all

lll aaa ddd lad lad jjj aaa lll jal jal

aaa sss ;;; as; as; fff aaa ddd fad fad

a as ask asks asks; f fa fal fall falls

l la las lass lass; f fl fla flas flask

a ad add adds adds; s sa sal sala salad

Return the carriage without looking up.

PHRASE AND SENTENCE PRACTICE *(Each line 2 times)*

a dad; a lad; a salad; a lass; a flask;

Space once after semicolon.

dad asks a sad lad; a sad lass asks dad

dads ask a fad; a lad asks dad as a fad

Your employer is J. T. Gibson, general manager of International's Chicago office. He prefers blocked form and this letter close:

> Very cordially yours,
>
> INTERNATIONAL SUPPLY COMPANY, INC.
>
>
> Manager, Chicago Office

It is *December 7.* Mr. Gibson has just now been asked by Paul Prince, International's general sales manager from New York, to set up a conference in St. Louis with Mr. Prince and the managers of International's branches in San Francisco and New Orleans.

JOB 7 Dictated telegram
Words: 48

jefferson hotel, st. louis. please reserve 9
three-room suite and three singles for de- 17
cember 13 through 15. wire confirmation.— 26
j. t. gibson, international supply 33

JOB 8 Dictated night letter
Words: 78

f. i. beauchamp, international supply co., 9
800 gravier street, new orleans. paul prince 18
has called meeting of branch managers for 26
december 13 through 16 noon at jefferson 34
hotel, st. louis. your room reserved. bring 44
full data on nitrogen headlights problem. 52
please confirm. 55

JOB 9 Duplicate telegram
Words: 78

c. a. taliaferro, international supply co., 9
135 post street, san francisco. (duplicate of 15
preceding message) 55

JOB 10 Dictated night letter
Words: 92

mr. paul prince, hotel statler, boston. 8
conference arranged december 13 through 16

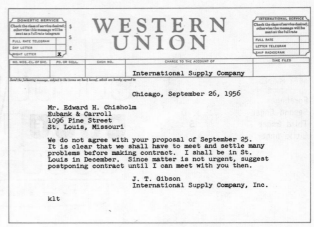

A night letter is one kind of telegram.

16 noon at jefferson hotel in st. louis. beau- 25
champ and taliaferro have confirmed. your 34
suite reserved in company name for decem- 42
ber 13 through 15. will you be coming 50
through chicago or flying directly from new 59
york? please let me know your arrival plans. 68

JOBS 11-12 2 form letters
Total words: 154

Mr. Gibson gives you these addresses—

mr. edward h. chisholm, eubank & car- 7
roll, 1096 pine street, st. louis 13 15
mr. a. i. strauss, president, strauss bros., 9
1430 olive street, st. louis 4 15

—and asks you to airmail to each the following letter, which he dictates:

dear mr. ——: i shall be in st. louis for a 10
staff conference during the week of decem- 18
ber 13. the conference will end a little be- 27
fore lunch time on thursday, december 16; 35
and i shall be free until i leave for my plane 45
about three o'clock. 49

is there any possibility of our getting to- 57
gether during that time? if so, please let me 67
know at once or leave word for me at the 75
hotel. i am sorry that my trip is so sudden 84
and my stay so brief. 88

WARMUP REVIEW *(Each line 2 times)* ◁ **40** ▷

        aa ss dd ff jj kk ll ;; a s d f j k l ;
        ddd aaa ddd dad lll lad fff fad sss sad

NEW STROKES *(Each line 2 times)*

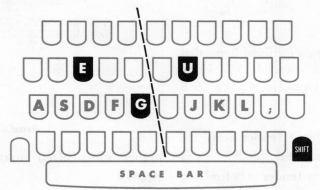

LEFT HAND
D-finger reaches
up, to E.
F-finger reaches
right, to G.

RIGHT HAND
J-finger reaches
up, to U.
;-finger reaches
over, to Shift.

        ddd ded eee ded dee dee fee fee see see
        ee deed ee feed ee seed ee seek ee jell

        jjj juj uuu juj dud dud due due sue sue
        uu fuss uu full uu dull uu lull uu juke

        fff fgf ggg fgf egg egg jug jug dug dug
        gg guff gg gull gg gulf gg gaff gg glad

Leave a blank line
(return carriage
twice) before you
start a new line of
drills.

**Use the little finger of the
right hand to depress and hold
the right shift key when you
wish to capitalize a letter on
the left side of the keyboard.
Use a 1-2-3 count:**

ONE *Depress* shift key while you—

TWO *Tap* the letter key. Then, quickly—

THREE *Return* little finger to home key.

        aaa ;;; aA; aA; sS; sS; dD; dD; fF; fF;
        Ada Ada Sue Sue Dee Dee Fae Fae Gus Gus

WORD PRACTICE *(Each line 2 times)*

        lull lull dull dull full full gull gull
        gale gale kale kale dale dale sale sale
        fell fell jell jell dell dell sell sell

SENTENCE PRACTICE *(Each line 2 times)*

        Sue sees us; Della feels as sad as Dad;
        Dale fed us a salad; Gus sells us eggs;
        A gull sees a lake; Ed juggled a glass;

Part 1
LESSON **2**
Unit 1

Plymouth, 172,400 and 592,778; Buick **131**
Special, 165,800 and 534,990; Chrysler **139**
Royal, 160,391 and 480,018; Hudson Wasp, **146**
153,787 and 417,239. **150**

JOB 4
Requisition
Words: 74

"Please prepare a requisition for some items that
we shall need by January 2," says Mr. Van Horn.
"All items are for stock replacement. We shall
need—"

50 of item 35P15930 Front fender sets **8**
for (last year) Ward convertibles **14**

40 of item 35P15931 Rear fender sets for **23**
(last year) Ward convertibles **29**

75 of item 35P17001 Front fender sets **36**
for (this year) Ward convertibles **43**

90 of item 35P17002 Rear fender sets for **51**
(this year) Ward convertibles **57**

50 of item 35P16222 Bumper guards **64**

50 of item 35P16718 Rear-view mirrors **72**

50 of item 35P16719 Radio antenna **78**

Checking in the files, you find that the last requisition was no. 12AX-96437.

JOB 5
Dictated memo
Words: 169

"Send that requisition to Mr. Gibson, the manager
of our office," says Mr. Van Horn, "along with the
following memorandum—"

do you think that you or our purchasing **8**
department in new york could bring the **16**
necessary pressure to bear on the ward **24**
motor company to obtain more uniform **31**
quality on the paint jobs on the replace- **39**
ment fenders we get from them? **45**

we have noticed a variation in the color **54**
of these jobs on different shipments, par- **62**
ticularly in blue. Not only is the paint an **71**
off color, but the finish is also different—a **80**

Requisition

higher gloss often marred by off-color **88**
streaks. **90**

our customers are constantly complain- **97**
ing that replaced fenders do not match the **106**
paint on their ward cars and trucks. we **114**
have informed them that the ward motor **122**
company makes every fender that we sell. **130**
surely it would be to their advantage, as **139**
well as to our own, if they would rectify **147**
this condition. **150**

JOB 6
Fill-in form or table
Words: 67

ANALYSIS OF SALES PERFORMANCE
Period: October 1 – November 30

Salesman	Budget	Actual
Brody, J. B.	3,500	3,750
Casper, Charles	4,000	3,925
Dodds, Edward	2,800	3,150
Gaines, Alexander	3,200	975*
Holman, William	3,500	3,825
Jackson, Thomas	2,200	2,780
Lewis, Franklin	3,200	3,225
Norris, Parker	3,000	3,320
Rheems, Jorge	1,800	2,450
Klein, Robert	2,800	3,175
TOTAL	30,000	30,575

*Was out for six weeks

WARMUP REVIEW (*Each line 2 times*)

```
aa ;; ss ll dd kk ff jj fgf juj ded aA;
jjj uuu ggg jug aaa jag sss sag lll lag
ddd lad fff fad eee fed ggg leg kkk keg
```

NEW STROKES (*Each line 2 times*)

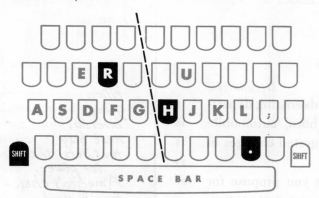

LEFT HAND
F-finger reaches
up, to R.
A-finger reaches
over, to Shift.

RIGHT HAND
J-finger reaches
left, to H.
L-finger reaches
down, to period.

```
fff frf rrr frf fur fur far far jar jar
rr rear rr rare rr rake rr rage rr rule

jjj jhj hhh jhj her her had had has has
hh hash hh hush hh herd hh heel hh heed
```

Use the little finger of the left
hand to depress and hold the
left shift key when you wish to
capitalize a letter on the right
side of the keyboard. Use a
1-2-3 count:

ONE *Depress* shift key while you—

TWO *Tap* the letter key. Then, quickly—

THREE *Return* little finger to home key.

```
lll aaa lLa lLa kKa kKa jJa jJa hHa hHa
Jeff Jeff Kerr Kerr Lars Lars Hugh Hugh
```

Space once after
a period following
an initial or
abbreviation.

```
lll 1.1 ... 1.1 Dr. H. Hale Dr. H. Hale
Dr. K. Dale; Dr. J. Judd; Dr. U. Leeds.
```

WORD PRACTICE (*Each line 2 times*)

```
ear fear hear rear; ell fell jell sell.
use uses used user; age gage rage sage.
```

SENTENCE PRACTICE (*2 copies*)

Space twice
after each
sentence.

```
He sells fresh eggs.  Ed Kerr has a red
jug.  He sees a real deer.  A judge has
flags.  Sashes are fads.  Her dad fell.
```

Your employer is Norton Van Horn, manager of the Automobile Department. He prefers blocked form and this letter closing:

    Yours very truly,

    Manager, Automobile Department
Norton Van Horn/URS

JOB 1

Dictated memo
Words: 177

December 6

To mr. a. t. lawrence, advertising department. From norton van horn, automobile department. Subject: suggested changes in advertising copy.   8 16 25 29

i think that the layout you propose for the magazine advertisement is just fine, larry. i heartily agree that recognizing cars by their front and rear views is now a national pastime and that we would be wise to capitalize on that interest.   37 45 54 63 71 77

i am wondering, however, whether the pitch in the copy might profitably be altered to appeal to the two strongest buying motives we find in our customers: 85 93 102 109

1. the urge to be out front—that is, make a customer proud to have a ward.   117 124

2. devotion to family—that is, let's stress that a ward is a family car.   133 139

i am no advertising expert like you are, larry; but just the same i have tried my hand at writing some new copy along the lines i have mentioned. it is enclosed—for what it is worth.   148 156 164 173 176

JOB 2

Advertising copy
Words: 83

Showing you the handwritten material in the next column, Mr. Van Horn says, "Please type this ad as attractively as you can."

You use display type (page 246) for the two banners and justify the paragraph in 6 lines. You space out the final signature line.

COMING...

3" x 3"
front view of car

3" x 3"
rear view of car

...GOING

When you come right down to it, you're going to be looking at the new Ward-International first and last when you next buy a new car! It's the car that sets the standards...for style ...for power...for economy, too! America's choice for the right family car!

THE WARD-INTERNATIONAL

JOB 3

Unarranged table
Words: 61

Mr. Van Horn gives you the newspaper item below and asks you to arrange the information in it in table form. Use a full sheet.

DETROIT, Dec. 5—For the third consecutive quarter, Chevrolet has led the automobile industry in total units sold. The late summer found Chevrolet dealers moving 255,750 cars or trucks, making a total of 723,476 for the first nine months of the year. Ford followed second, with 225,891 for the summer quarter and a nine-month total of 680,514.   7 16 25 33 41 51 60 68 70

The Ward-International was a strong third, with 200,587 for the summer and 632,604 for the first nine months.   78 85 93

The figures were released at the annual Safe Driving Conference, meeting here at the Book-Cadillac Hotel. Figures for other makes of car were as follows: 101 109 118 124

WARMUP REVIEW *(Each line 2 times)*

```
a; sl dk fj fgf jhj frf juj ded l.l A;La
kk ee gg keg; ff uu rr fur; aa ss hh ash
dd uu ee due; jj uu gg jug; ll ee dd led
```

NEW STROKES *(Each line 2 times)*

LEFT HAND
F-finger reaches up, to T.
D-finger reaches down, to C.

RIGHT HAND
K-finger reaches up, to I.
J-finger reaches down, to M.

```
fff ftf ttt ftf tar tar rat rat the the
tt tuft tt tart tt that tt test tt Tess

kkk kik iii kik kit kit kit it it is is
ii like ii dike ii hike ii tike ii Ilka

ddd dcd ccc dcd ice ice ace ace act act
cc cite cc cute cc kick cc tick cc Dick

jjj jmj mmm jmj jam jam ham ham hum hum
mm mute mm mate mm mite mm mice mm Mike
```

WORD PRACTICE *(Each line 2 times)*

```
ace race lace face; ike mike dike hike.
use muse ruse fuse; ust just must gust.
ime time dime lime; ist mist list gist.
ack rack hack sack lack tack mack jack.
```

SENTENCE PRACTICE *(2 copies)*

Space twice after each sentence.

```
I like Ilka.  I like Ida.  I like Jack.
I like Jim.  I like Fred.  I like music
as a critic likes it.  I like the lake.
I like ice cream; I like cake.  I guess
that I like all that Mr. MacAfee likes.
```

JOB 15

Radio script
Words: 274

WMAQ & NET   ONE-MINUTE COMMERCIAL   #17

(STATION BREAK)

INTERNATIONAL SUPPLY COMPANY, INC.

SATURDAY, DECEMBER 4, 19--, 10:29-10:30 CST

(DEAD AIR)

SOUND   (CLATTER OF DISHES BEING WASHED)

HUSBAND   (HUMMING...STOPS HUMMING AND SPEAKS SOLICITOUSLY) Darling,
           you take care of those hands of yours! The old boy doesn't
           mind doing up these dishes. Matter of fact, might show you
           a thing or two!

MUSIC   (SPRIGHTLY VERSION OF "PRISONER'S SONG"...STAB...UP...UNDER)

ANNCR   Good old Jonesy. It's Saturday, and this businessman is at
           home. Doesn't mind doing the dishes. Not at ALL!

MUSIC   (SWEEP IN, SLIGHTLY SLOWER "PRISONER'S SONG"...FADE)

HUSBAND   Hands still bad, Trudie? Well, I'll do up the dishes.

SOUND   (CLATTER OF DISHES BEING WASHED)

ANNCR   Good old Jonesy! He's a trooper! He doesn't mind doing the
           dishes...once in a while. But DAY after DAY?

MUSIC   (SWEEP IN HEAVY, SLOW "PRISONER'S SONG"...FADE)

HUSBAND   Honest to goodness, Trudie, the boys in the office are accus-
           ing me of having dishpan hands!

WIFE   You know, Dear, they ARE starting to look like mine.

HUSBAND   Didn't anyone ever invent a machine for this job?

ANNCR   (BREAKING IN) You BET someone did, Mr. Jones! It's the fam-
           ous INTERNATIONAL dishwasher--INTERNATIONAL. Mr. Jones, you
           ought to see your International dealer today!

MUSIC   (SWELLS IN WITH SWING VERSION OF "PRISONER'S SONG"...FADE)

#

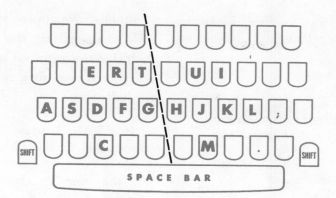

WARMUP REVIEW *(Each line 2 times)*

a ; s l d k f j g h f j d k s l a ; s l d k f j g
ded kik frf juj fgf jhj ftf jmj dcd l.l F J D K S
fir sir; jet get; kid lid; cut hut; mad sad; Mrs.

STROKE-REVIEW WORDS *(Each line 2 times)*

ee see ee set ee jet ee let ee led ee lea ee lead
ii fit ii hit ii kit ii kid ii aid ii air ii fair
aa sat aa mat aa mar aa far aa fad aa lad aa glad
uu rug uu jug uu jut uu cut uu hut uu hug uu huge
cc ice cc ace cc act cc cud cc cut cc cue cc duck

STROKE-REVIEW SENTENCES *(Each line 2 times)*

He fed us eggs. She sells seeds. He seeks deeds.
I said I like this light lime juice if it is iced.
Alec has a fast car. Ella ate a salad I had made.
Julie cut a rug; she cut a fur cuff; she sued Gus.
Clark cut the cakes as Clara cut ice cream slices.

TIMED WRITINGS . . .

It is helpful to time some of your practice efforts. Doing so lets you know how fast and how accurately you are typing. If you record your scores, you can compare your work and note your progress.

In measuring typing speed, every 5 strokes (letters or spaces) counts as 1 word. Typing speed is expressed in terms of *words a minute*—the number of 5-stroke words typed in a minute. To figure the *wam* (words a minute) on a timed writing—

1. Determine how many words (groups of 5 strokes) you typed.

2. Divide the total by the number of minutes for which you typed.

Examples: 30 words in 3 minutes gives 10 wam; in 2 minutes, 15 wam; in 1 minute, 30 wam; in ½ minute, 60 wam.

Your employer is A. T. Lawrence, advertising manager. He uses half-page letterheads, full-blocked style, and this closing:

```
Cordially yours,


A. T. Lawrence, Advertising Manager
International Supply Company, Inc.
```

 **JOB 14** Dictated telegram
Words: 66

December 3

richard k. young, pratt & wilson, inc.,   8
418 s. dearborn street, chicago: cancel   16
script on washing machine for saturday,   24
december 4. new script on dishwasher to   32
be delivered to you today.—a. t. lawrence,   41
international supply company, inc.   48

 **JOB 15** Radio script
Words: 274

"This is rush," says Mr. Lawrence, giving you the script shown on the next page.

"Mr. Gibson has okayed this new script. Now we need 10 copies—carbon or duplicated. Mark in colored pencil the clue lines on the copies for music, sound, and speakers."

Note how *Husband* clue lines were marked.

 **JOBS 16-20** 5 form letters
Total words: 611

"Several publications," says Mr. Lawrence, "have repeated one of our ads without our authorization and have calmly sent us a bill for the space, hoping we might pay it. Take this letter, please—"

gentlemen: your statement of december   8
1 is returned to you for correction.   15

if you will refer to my letter of . . . . . (I'll   26
give you the dates in a moment) . . . , you   27
will find that you were authorized to run   35
our advertisements only according to the   44
exact schedule included in that letter.   52

although we appreciate the value of ad-   59
ditional advertising, it is manifestly not our   69
fault that the error was made; and we must   77
ask you to send us a corrected statement.   86
cordially yours,   89

"Here," Mr. Lawrence continues, "are the addressees and the dates of my letters—"

the danville sentinel, 216 west main street, danville, illinois, october 20
the country monthly, 394 north hays street, kansas city, kansas, july 18
homemakers' household journal, 417 first avenue, sioux city 3, iowa, september 22 ("dear ladies" on this one)
the farmers' digest, continental building, 3615 olive street, st. louis 8, missouri, august 19
farmside fireside, 1510 hanna building, cleveland 15, ohio, september 9

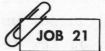 **JOB 21** Dictated letter
Words: 158

mrs. hettie b. lawson, business manager,   8
the evanston suburbanite, 1046 davis street,   17
evanston 2, illinois   21

dear mrs. lawson: we find it rather diffi-   30
cult to refuse to expand our advertising   38
space in your newspaper, especially in view   47
of the information you sent showing the   55
tremendous increase in your circulation.   63
our advertising budget was drawn up after   72
very careful study, however, and it will not   81
be possible to alter it this quarter.   88

if it appears that we can rearrange our   96
plans, you may depend on hearing from me   105
in plenty of time to catch your holiday is-   113
sues. cordially yours,   118

ps—please give my personal regards to   126
bob elliott and assure him i will do the best   135
i can in this matter.   139

In this book, the best selections for timed practice are accompanied by counts and scales that will make it easy for you to count the 5-stroke words and compute your speed. Note these aids in the Complete-Review Sentences below:

1. *The numbers at the ends of the lines* tell how many 5-stroke words there are from the start of the exercise to the end of each line, cumulatively.

2. *The scale above the copy* marks off the 5-stroke "zones" that count as words. It shows that there are 10 words in these sentences. The zones are useful in determining how many words you may count for an incomplete line. If you finish *red* in line 1, for example, you end up in zone 7 and so may count 7 words. If you finish all of line 1 and through *Dick* in line 2, you may count 15 words.

THE "REVIEW" SELECTIONS . . .

recommended for timed practice are very special in two regards:

1. *To help your accuracy* by systematic review of all reaches, each review contains all the letters of the alphabet that have been introduced.

2. *To help your speed,* the difficulty of each review has been controlled. You will not feel the difference at first, but later on you will be quite sensitive to the ease or difficulty of material. The length of the material is one factor of control. The length of the timings is another. A third control is the "si" score (average number of syllables per word, given after the exercise title), which enables you to com-

pare and classify the relative ease or difficulty of the different reviews, like this:

Very, very easy . . . . si 1.00 − 1.20
Very easy . . . . si 1.20 − 1.30
Easy . . . . si 1.30 − 1.40

By way of comparison: business letters range si 1.35 − 1.45, average at 1.40.

YOUR INSTRUCTOR WILL TELL YOU . . .

when you are to take timed writings on reviews instead of copying them the assigned number of times. If you wish to time your own work, so that you may estimate your speed, note closely how many seconds it takes you to type a line or group of lines, and then use this table for computing your rate of typing the material:

5-Stroke Words Typed	SECONDS							
	60	50	40	30	20	15	12	10
	WORDS A MINUTE							
10	10	12	15	20	30	40	50	60
12	12	14	18	24	36	48	60	
15	15	18	22	30	45	60		
18	18	22	27	36	54			
20	20	24	30	40	60			
25	25	30	37	50				
30	30	36	45	60				
35	35	42	52					
38	38	46	57					
40	40	48	60					
45	45	54						
50	50	60						
60	60							

Example: If 18 words are typed in 40 seconds, the speed is 27 words a minute.

This signal tells you (1) to insert a clean side or new sheet of paper; and (2) to use the indicated length of line. ◢ ◁**50**▷

COMPLETE-REVIEW SENTENCES *(3 copies, or one or more 1-minute writings on each sentence / si 1.06)*

1-Min. Writings   1 | 2 | 3 | 4 | 5 | 6 | 7 | 8 | 9 | 10

The girls had trimmed their red fur jackets alike.   10

I feel sure that Dick hid three red jugs; ask him.   20

Jack Drugg has a jet; it seems as fast as a flash.   30

JOB 9

Revised letter
Words: 295

December 1, year

Mr. E. R. Peebles
Rural Route No. 2
Hoxie, Arkansas

Your letter of November 28, concerning the shipment we made to you on Nov. 25 by railway Express, was recieved this morning.

We should have explained, when we filled your order, why we substituted X-L Spark Plugs #35P7261 for #35P7260. After our catalogue was issued, you see, the company manufactring this spark plugs discontinued the type you ordered because, while that type was somewhat chaeper than the standardized type, it did not stand up under constant use. The type we send you is guaranteed by the manufacturer for 10,000 miles and costs only six cents more than the discontinued plug.

We are very glad that you tested the nitrogen headlights and tail lights immediately upon recieving them. We take precaution to securely pack electric blubs, but occasionally they recieve exceptionally rough handlin g in transit. Since you no doubt

Since you doubtlessly need some of them now, we are are sending you by pre-paid express, six tested blubs--#35P6593---as replacements. Please rap the deflective bulbs carefully and return them to us by parcel postal. We enclose fifteen cents in stamps to cover the postage. We are retruning #J240613 invoice, as you requested, together with invoice #K197631 covering the replacements, which will be cancelled when the defective bulbs reach us. Yours very truly,

INTERNATIONAL SUPPLY COMPANY, inc.

Assistant Manager
Receiving & Shipping Department

MM:URS
2 enclsoures

298 PROJECT 2

◁50▷

WARMUP REVIEW *(Each line 2 times)*

```
a;sldkfjghfjdksla; a;sldkfjghfjdksla; a;sldkfjghfj
aa ;; ss ll dd ee cc kk ii ff rr jj uu tt mm gg hh
due hue cue; rag tag sag; meg leg keg; Mr. Jr. Fr.
```

CAPITAL-SHIFT REVIEW *(Each line 2 times)*

```
aA lL sS kK dD jJ fF hH gG iI eE uU rR .. tT mM cC
Ada Ada Ada; Jim Jim Jim; Fae Fae Fae; Lum Lum Lum
Gus Gus Gus; Ida Ida Ida; Tim Tim Tim; Mac Mac Mac
```

STROKE-REVIEW WORDS *(Each line 2 times)*

```
ff far ff fur ff fir ff fit ff fig ff fed ff fame.
jj jag jj jig jj jug jj jet jj jar jj jam jj jade.
tt the tt tie tt tug tt tag tt sit tt set tt that.
mm mit mm mut mm mum mm mad mm aim mm dim mm dime.
rr are rr art rr arc rr arm rr red rr rue rr rail.
```

STROKE-REVIEW SENTENCES *(Each line 2 times)*

```
Cliff fed them figs.  Freda fluffed the fur cuffs.
Judge Jesse judged the jets.  Jeff jarred the jug.
Little Tim tied all the cut trees that Ted tagged.
Mac made Jimmie Hammer skim much milk last summer.
Rita read her letter.  Her red dress has fur trim.
```

COMPLETE-REVIEW SENTENCES *(Each line 3 times / si 1.10)*

◁50▷

1-Min.
Writings

```
   1 |  2 |  3 |  4 |  5 |  6 |  7 |  8 |  9 | 10 |
I hear that Jack might sell us a light deer rifle.   10
Jed makes the dress cuffs that all the girls like.   20
Fred Ames liked that delightful fresh fruit juice.   30
```

Part 1
LESSON **6**
Unit 1

Your employer is Montgomery Moeller, assistant manager of the Receiving and Shipping Department. He prefers semiblocked form and this letter-closing arrangement:

```
        Very truly yours,

        INTERNATIONAL SUPPLY COMPANY, INC.


        Assistant Manager
        Receiving & Shipping Department
```

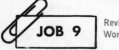 **JOB 9** Revised letter Words: 295

December 2

"Please retype this letter," Mr. Moeller says, giving you the letter shown on the next page, "which I typed myself!"

It should, of course, be single spaced.

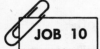 **JOB 10** Invoice Words: 53

"Prepare the invoice for Mr. Peebles' replacement bulbs, too," Mr. Moeller adds.

The invoice number is K197631. The   7
shipment will go Railway Express, prepaid.   16
One item: 6 #35P6593 nitrogen bulbs, at   24
35 cents each; total, $2.10. Add this note in   34
the Descriptions column, near the bottom   42
of the invoice: 45

Replacement shipment; charges to be   52
canceled upon receipt of 6 defective bulbs,   61
by parcel post.—M.M. (R&S)   67

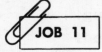 **JOB 11** Dictated letter Words: 177

mr. robert l. armstrong, general freight   8
agent, rock island lines, 821 south LaSalle   17
station, chicago 2, dear sir: 23

we are greatly indebted to you for your   31
promptness in investigating the shipment   39
of kitchen equipment that we forwarded   47
via your lines on november 16 to mr. don-   55
ald cantwell, of des moines, iowa.   62

we note from your letter of november   70
28 that the authorities at moline were suc-   78
cessful in apprehending the thieves and in   87
recovery our property. This is certainly a   96
fortunate outcome.   100

mr. cantwell has been put to some in-   107
convenience; so, we are writing him that a   116
substitute shipment is being sent him today   124
via your lines. you may return the recov-   133
ered goods to us at your convenience. we   141
will then bill you for any missing items.   150
very truly yours,   153

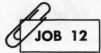 **JOB 12** Dictated letter Words: 151

mr. donald cantwell, 1786 grand avenue,   8
des moines 7, dear mr. cantwell: 15

we have carefully checked the shipment   23
of kitchen fixtures that left our warehouse   32
on november 16 via the rock island railroad   41
and find that everything was in order at the   50
time of shipment.   54

the rock island reports that the car in   62
which the shipment was carried was broken   71
into at moline, illinois. they report also that   80
the police have caught the criminals and   89
recovered the goods.   93

to hasten arrival of your order, we are   101
sending you a duplicate shipment today.   109
we greatly regret the delay and any incon-   118
venience to which you may have been put.   126
very truly yours,   129

 **JOB 13** Telegram Words: 53

the harper agency, 833 carter street, des   8
moines, iowa: drop investigation of cant-   17
well shipment. car was pilfered in moline.   26
police have guilty parties.—M. Moeller, in-   34
ternational supply.   38

WARMUP REVIEW *(Each line 2 times)*

◁**40**▷

omit

```
a;sldkfjghfjdksla;sldkfjghfjdksla;sldkfj
fret jet get set rug hug mid lid kid aid
Della Irma Gail Tess Hugh Mike Jack Fred
```

NEW STROKES *(Each line 2 times)*

LEFT HAND
S-finger reaches
up, to W.
F-finger reaches
down, to V.

RIGHT HAND
J-finger reaches
up, over, to Y.
K-finger reaches
down, to comma.

*each line
I time*

```
sss sws www sws wed wed wet wet sew sew
ww well ww will ww were ww wise ww Walt

jjj jyj yyy jyj yes yes say say eye eye
yy year yy away yy they yy city yy Yes.

fff fvf vvv fvf vet vet vim vim vie vie
vv veer vv five vv have vv rave vv Vera
```

double space

Space once
after comma.

```
kkk k,k ,,, k,k we, we, ye, ye, me, me,
very wet, very dry, very wry, every way
```

proof read

STROKE-REVIEW SENTENCES *(Each line 2 times)*

◁**50**▷

each one

```
Will said Wally was wide awake while we were away.
Yes, they say they really fly every truly dry day.
Five vets have five views, every view very varied.
Dick Drake asked Kim why they skated at Lake Keys.
Dave said Dee did it.  Dee said Dave did it first.
```

COMPLETE-REVIEW SENTENCES *(Each line 3 times / si 1.17)*

1-Min.
Writings

```
   1  |  2  |  3  |  4  |  5  |  6  |  7  |  8  |  9  |  10
The girls heard Mack gravely say Freddie was just.    10
Meg liked all the fresh juice we wisely saved her.    20
Jack Hummell drives his swift jet car mighty fast.    30
```

JOB 1

Revised table
Words: 224

OVERDUE ACCOUNTS--COOPERATIVE ASSOCIATIONS

~~October 31,~~ 19--
November 30

Account	30 Days Overdue	60 Days Overdue	Total Overdue
Mr. Harry Pepper, Treasurer Consumers' Co-operative Assn. 3123 Washington Avenue Racine, Wisconsin	$ 215.48 (circled) ~~$1,210.45~~	$--------	$ 1,425.93 ~~$1,210.45~~
Mr. R. N. ~~Maxwell, Manager~~ ~~Central Wabash Association~~ ~~322 Arcade Building~~ ~~Terre Haute, Indiana~~	--------	~~Paid~~ ~~68.75~~	~~68.75~~
Mrs. Mark E. Smythe, Manager The Danville Farmers League 616 North Jackson Street Danville, Illinois	294.75 (circled)	--------	294.75
~~Grover B. Magruder, Secretary~~ ~~Society of Quaker Employees~~ ~~Quaker Oats Plant~~ ~~Cedar Rapids, Iowa~~	~~127.85~~ Paid nov. 15		~~127.85~~
Mr. M. M. Zimmerman, Manager Consumer's Exchange, Inc. 217 United Farmers Building East Lansing, Michigan	563.91 ~~1,430.50~~	--------	563.91 ~~1,430.50~~
Miss Evangeline C. Springer Manager, Elkhart Association Elkhart, Indiana	811.38 (circled)	~~438.44~~	811.38 ~~1,249.82~~
Miss Ella Q. Wilcox, Manager Michigan Co-operative Assn. 314 Phoenix Building Bay City, Michigan	51.75 ~~149.68~~	49.68 --------	101.43 ~~149.68~~
TOTALS	~~$4,024.61~~ ?	~~$ 507.19~~ ?	~~$4,531.80~~ ?
James T. Beckman, Manager Kalamazoo Citizens' League 623 Second Avenue Kalamazoo, Michigan	193.82	------	193.82

WARMUP REVIEW *(Each line 2 times)*

◁ **40** ▷

```
a;sldkfjghfjdksla;sldkfjghfjdksla;sldkfj
try dry wry fry cry, give jive live hive
sew dew mew few hew, make cake lake take
```

NEW STROKES *(Each line 2 times)*

LEFT HAND
S-finger reaches
down, to X.

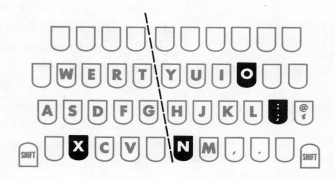

RIGHT HAND
L-finger reaches
up, to O.
J-finger reaches
down, to N.
Colon is shift
of semicolon.

```
lll lol ooo lol old old low low too too
oo cool oo look oo took oo wool oo Lola

sss sxs xxx sxs six six fix fix mix mix
xx tax xx text xx sixes xx affix xx Max

jjj jnj nnn jnj sun sun sin sin son son
nn noon nn soon nn none nn nine nn Nina
```

Space twice
after colon.

```
;;; ;:; ;:; ;:; one:  two:  four:  six:
Short words:  of, or, is, it, and, for.
```

STROKE-REVIEW SENTENCES *(Each line 2 times)*

◁ **50** ▷

```
To do our work or not to do it is no worry to Joe.
Max fixed six, Alex fixed six, and Ajax fixed six.
Lillian will like lilacs:  All lilacs look lovely.
She sells seeds; she sings songs; she makes cakes.
No one can run on and on and on as Nancy Dunn can.
```

COMPLETE-REVIEW SENTENCES *(Each line 3 times / si 1.25)*

1-Min.
Writings

```
    1 | 2 | 3 | 4 | 5 | 6 | 7 | 8 | 9 | 10
Judge Faye said that Alexander Vick won the games.   10
For just sixty days, the sick men have full wages.   20
Next time you can, judge the five slowest workers.   30
```

16   NEW KEYS: O X N :

Part 1
LESSON 8
Unit 2

Your employer is Lincoln Collyer, assistant manager of the Accounting and Billing Department. He prefers blocked letter style, with his signature arranged like this:

Yours very truly,

INTERNATIONAL SUPPLY COMPANY, INC.

Assistant Manager
Accounting & Billing Department

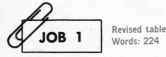

JOB 1   Revised table
Words: 224

December 1

Giving you the revised table shown on the next page, Mr. Collyer says, "I have brought up to date our list of overdue accounts. Please type this list, with two carbons."

Note that he did not compute the new totals figures; you are to do this.

JOB 2   Interoffice memo
Words: 140

"Then," Mr. Collyer continues, "send the original copy to Mr. Busk—that is William P. Busk, on the eighth floor—along with the following memorandum." He dictates as follows:

i have attached the december 1 listing	8
of overdue accounts. you will be interested	17
to know that consumer's exchange paid up	25
its $1,430.50 account and then proceeded to	34
fall in arrears again, this time for $563.91.	43
you will be pleased to learn, too, that the	52
long-overdue account that bob maxwell has	60
been holding out on has finally been paid.	69
there is only one new account on the	77
overdue list. It is that of the kalamazoo	85
citizens' league. i was surprised to see this,	95
for they have always paid up their bills	103
promptly heretofore.	107
we shall dispatch the usual notices to all	116
the current overdue accounts.	122

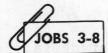

JOBS 3-8   6 form letters
Total words: 1,296

"Next," says Mr. Collyer, "as soon as that memo is on its way to Mr. Busk, please write the following letter to each of the overdue accounts on the list." He dictates:

dear . . . . your account shows a bal-	10
ance of [insert the correct amount], now	14
[insert correct number of days, written in	15
figures] days overdue.	19
doubtless you are aware that, with the	27
exception of such organizations as the one	35
you represent, our terms are strictly cash.	44
our splendid service and low prices are	52
based on our ability to dispense with an	60
expensive credit and accounting organiza-	68
tion.	70
we appreciate that many co-operative as-	77
sociations find it necessary to extend credit	87
to their members; but, since our position	95
and policies are so well known, we feel that	104
you should have made some arrangement	112
to liquidate this account within the usual	120
30-day period.	123

[Insert the next paragraph only in the "60 days overdue" letters.]

since your account is now more than 60	131
days overdue, we are compelled to call your	140
attention to our policy of shipping C. O. D.	149
any goods you may order in the future until	158
you remit the [insert balance due] that is	164
now due.	166
we hope you will find some way to clear	174
up this matter shortly. in the meantime, we	183
shall continue to serve you promptly and	192
well. yours very truly,	196

[Note: To conserve your workbook supplies, type only the first 30-day letter and the first 60-day letter on the workbook letterheads; type the other four letters on plain paper, allowing for a similar letterhead.]

WARMUP REVIEW *(Each line 2 times)*

◁40▷

1. a;sldkfjghfjdksla;sldkfjghfjdksla;sldkfj
2. saw sat sag sad sax, axis axes axel exit
3. now not nor nod non, woke coke joke yoke
4. fan can van ran man, huge hunt hulk hurt

NEW STROKES *(Each line 2 times)*

LEFT HAND
F-finger reaches
down, right, to B.
A-finger reaches
down, to Z.

RIGHT HAND
;-finger reaches
up, to P.

5. fff fbf bbb fbf bad bad bid bid big big
6. bb buff bb ball bb bass bb boom bb Bill

7. ;;; ;p; ppp ;p; pep pep pen pen pan pan
8. pp purr pp putt pp pull pp pill pp Paul

9. aaa aza zzz aza zoo zoo zig zig zag zag
10. zz size zz fizz zz fuzz zz lazy zz Zora

STROKE-REVIEW SENTENCES *(Each line 2 times)*

◁50▷

11. Bill builds big buildings, but Bobby builds boats.
12. Pop picks apples; Pal rips up papers; Pat pays up.
13. Zora is lazy; the zebra is crazy; the sky is hazy.
14. Hal has high hopes: He hopes the haze helps them.
15. George got Gary to go along. Gary got Gail to go.

COMPLETE-REVIEW SENTENCES *(Each line 3 times / si 1.33)*

1-Min.
Writings

double spacing

| 1 | 2 | 3 | 4 | 5 | 6 | 7 | 8 | 9 | 10 |

Jeffrey moved six dozen last night by power truck. 10
Rex proved lucky in my fights with the jazz bands. 20
Six pony jets zoomed by, fought wickedly overhead. 30

UNITS 34-35
SIX PROJECTS IN OFFICE-STYLE TYPING

In Units 30, 31, and 32, you tried to build sustained working power while typing *one kind* of production work—letters, manuscripts, or tables. Now you must practice for sustained working power while typing *different kinds* of production work in rapid succession.

Units 34 and 35 are therefore combined into a series of six projects in office-style typing. Each project is alloted the time of two lessons. An experienced office worker would be able to complete each project in an hour. Each will probably take you a little longer since you are not familiar with the work, as an office typist would be; but *try* to finish each project in an hour.

Your production will be boosted if you keep the Workbook record (page 302) of your work. Clock yourself. Find how much time elapses from the moment you insert paper into your machine until you take it out. Since the word count for each job is given, you can divide the words by the minutes to ascertain your production speed in each kind of work.

Your production score will also be boosted if you study each project before beginning to type it, if you lay out all your working materials before you start, and if you get yourself as ready as you possibly can.

If you wish to compute your "worth" as a typist, estimate your "earnings" on a scale like this: form letters, 25 cents; other letters, 35 cents; envelopes, 5 cents; tables, 35 cents; business forms, 15 cents; manuscript page, 35 cents; display pages, 50 cents. How much can you "earn" per hour?

◁ **60** ▷

Start each period by copying this material:

CONTROL SENTENCES:

	1 2 3 4 5 6 7 8 9 10 11 12	
½- Min. Writings	My work axiom evolved from analyzing typing job techniques.	12
	The blazing jamb quivered as ax points struck flying blows.	24
si 1.55	Five or six dozen clubs may sign up with Karl for jonquils.	36
	We acquire jerky habits from having typed exercises lazily.	48

SPEED PARAGRAPHS:

	1 2 3 4 5 6 7 8 9 10 11 12	
1-Min. Writings	If we are to get the order that all of us have been waiting	12
	for since the first of the year, we shall have to find some	24
si 1.10	way to make the deal a lot more worth while to them. Their	36
	margin of profit is much too small, they tell us. They say	48
	that the margin is so small that the risk of their money is	60
	hard to defend. We may have to cut our own profit to help.	72

	You may have noted that most of us are a lot more likely to	12	84
	pay our big bills when they come due than we are to pay our	24	96
si 1.15	small ones. When you stop to think about it, you see there	36	108
	are many reasons why this is true. For one thing, we worry	48	120
	about the big ones; and no one hesitates to remind you when	60	132
	you owe him a big sum of money. We get ready for big ones.	72	144

WARMUP REVIEW *(Each line 2 times)*

◁ **40** ▷

```
a;sldkfjghfjdksla;sldkfjghfjdksla;sldkfj
2 as ad ah am an ax aw at, is it if pi in,
3 so do go ho no to of or ok on ox, by my,
4 he me be we ye, us up; co. jr. viz. bbl.
```

NEW STROKES *(Each line 2 times)*

LEFT HAND
A-finger reaches
up, to Q.

RIGHT HAND
;-finger reaches
down, to / (the
diagonal mark).
? is shift of /.

```
;; ;/ // /; /; and/or, his/her, they/we
W/B is waybill; C/A is capital account.

aa aq qq qa qa quit quit quiz quiz quip
qq qui qq quite qq quo qq quote qq Quen

;; ;/ ;? ?? ?; Who?  Why?  When?  What?
Can he?  Did they?  Who, me?  Shall he?
```

STROKE-REVIEW SENTENCES *(Each line 2 times)*

◁ **50** ▷

```
For each child, send us his/her I. Q. and/or A. Q.
Quoting my quip, he quietly took the quaint quilt.
He quickly quizzed the queen; she was quite quiet.
Who will?  Is that it?  Was it Mark?  Is it Ralph?
Was it Mark and/or Ralph?  Can I get his/her name?
```

ALPHABET-REVIEW SENTENCES *(Each line 3 times / si 1.36)*

1-Min.
Writings

```
        1 | 2 | 3 | 4 | 5 | 6 | 7 | 8 | 9 | 10 |
Pack my box with five dozen jugs of liquid veneer.   10
Jack Powers was quite vexed by their lazy farming.   20
Jim quietly picked six zippers from the woven bag.   30
```

Part 1
LESSON **10**
Unit 2

WARMUP *(Each line 3 times)* ◁ 52 ▷

12-Sec.
Writings

```
a b c d e f g h i j k l m n o p q r s t u v w x y z
2 for 4 and 6 but 8 did 10 or 12 got 14 had 16 then
1 not 3 the 5 all 7 now 9 its 11 but 13 and 15 more
```

12-Sec. 5| 10| 15| 20| 25| 30| 35| 40| 45| 50|

SYMBOL DRILL *(Each line 3 times)*

```
Use the apostrophe:   A's B's C's D's E's F's 10's
Use quotation mark:   "A" "B" "C" "D" "E" "F" "10"
Use the hyphen key:   -A- -B- -C- -D- -E- -F- -10-
Use some per cents:   10% 20% 30% 40% 50% 60% 100%
Use a dollars sign:   $10 $20 $30 $40 $50 $60 $100
```

SYMBOL SENTENCES *(Each line 3 times)*

1 | 2 | 3 | 4 | 5 | 6 | 7 | 8 | 9 | 10

½-Min.
Writings

```
Total receipts were:  $238, $190, $145, and $167.    10
My box is 2' 6" wide, 4' 3" long, and 3' 6" high.    20
Smith's house cost $12,000; Miller's was $15,000.    30
Highest scores are:  98%, 95%, 94%, 92%, and 91%.    40
I spent $125 for the 8-, 10-, and 12-foot boards.    50
```

NUMBER-SYMBOL DRILL: Concentration *(3 copies)* ◁ 50 ▷

1-Min. Writings   1 | 2 | 3 | 4 | 5 | 6 | 7 | 8 | 9 | 10

**Double all
quantities,
but not the
other numbers.**

```
Gentlemen:  Please ship us 14 sets of #28 cartons    10
and 28 sets of #47.  Send us also 1,000 big boxes    20
(#12 size) and 150 small ones (#18 size).  Please    30
ship these in 100 crates, by May 1.  Yours truly,    40
```

NUMBER-TABULATION DRILL *(1 copy)*

Set tab every
9th space from
the left margin.

1-Min.
Writings

```
2801    3902    4703    5604    1005    6506     6
7407    8208    9309    1010    2311    4512    12
6713    8914    9015    2216    9917    3318    18
4419    7720    8821    5522    6623    1224    24
1025    1326    1927    1428    1829    1530    30
```

CENTURY DRIVE *(1 complete copy, up to 100)*

2-Min.
Writings

```
Got 1 got 2 got 3 got 4 got 5 got 6 got 7 got 8 got
9 got 10 got 11 got 12 got 13
```
[Continue on up to 100. Ultimate goal is to reach 100 in 2 minutes.]

ACTURER OF AIDS TO HAIR BEAUTY

QWERTYUIOPLKJHGFDSAZXCVB..

QAZXSWEDCVFRTGBNHYUJ.,K

> **SPEED SPURTS**
> To boost speed, take frequent 12-second writings on easy sentences. Each stroke counts as 1 word a minute. The color scales show the words a minute for 12-second writings.

WARMUP REVIEW *(Each line 2 times)*

```
a;sldkfjghfjdksla;sldkfjghfjdksla;sldkfjghfjdksla;s
a b c d e f g h i j k l m n o p q r s t u v w x y z
Bob Earl Flo Guy Joe Ken Max Pat Quen Susan Vic Zoe
```

2-LETTER SPEED-UP DRILL *(Each line 2 times)*

```
to to it it or or if if us us go go is is do do do
if it, it is, is to, to do, do so, so we, if we do
If it is to be, do we go on as we do or do we not?
```
12-Sec. 5| 10| 15| 20| 25| 30| 35| 40| 45| 50|

3-LETTER SPEED-UP DRILL *(Each line 2 times)*

```
the the man man and and for for she she her her her
for the, the man, man and, and for, and for the man
The man and the boy got the day off but got the ad.
```
12-Sec. 5| 10| 15| 20| 25| 30| 35| 40| 45| 50|

4-LETTER SPEED-UP DRILL *(Each line 2 times)*

```
than than make make they they paid paid duty duty
than they, they make, make that, than they found.
They know that this plan will save her much time.
```
12-Sec. 5| 10| 15| 20| 25| 30| 35| 40| 45| 50|

PUNCTUATION AND SPACING REVIEW *(2 copies)*

Space once after a comma, a semicolon, or a period that follows an abbreviation. Space twice after a colon and after the end of any sentence.

```
Dear Mr.¹ Ames:² We want to thank you,¹ in behalf of
the club,¹ for two favors:² first,¹ for the cash you
loaned us;¹ second,¹ for the hints you gave to us at
our last meeting.² Need we say more?² Yours truly,
```

TURN
PAGE

WARMUP: Number-Reach Review *(Each line 3 times)* ◁50▷

```
aqa ;0; s2s 191 d3d k8k f4f j7j f5f j6j 234567890
1 and 2 and 3 and 4 and 5 and 6 and 7 and 8 and 9
and 10 and 11 and 12 and 13 and 14 and 15 and 16.
```

NUMBER DRILL: Pair Pattern *(Each line 3 times)*

```
39 39 39 : We had 39 hats, 39 shoes, and 39 caps.
28 28 28 : We saw 28 men, 28 women, and 28 girls.
47 47 47 : We got 47 hams, 47 eggs, and 47 rolls.
56 56 56 : Our team won 56, lost 56, and tied 56.
10 10 10 : Put 10 boxes in 10 stores in 10 towns.
```

Flash the numbers.

NUMBER DRILL: We 23's *(Each line 3 times)*

12-Sec. Writings

```
we 23 eye 363 ere 343 ewe 323 ewer 3234 eery 3346
ye 63 you 697 yet 635 yew 632 your 6974 yore 6943
up 70 put 075 rue 473 our 974 pure 0743 true 5473
```

12-Sec. 5| 10| 15| 20| 25| 30| 35| 40| 45| 50|

NUMBER SENTENCES: Mixed Numbers *(Each line 3 times)* ◁50▷

½-Min. Writings

1 | 2 | 3 | 4 | 5 | 6 | 7 | 8 | 9 | 10

```
The team is here June 7-14, 19-28, and July 6-10.    10
You should read pages:  28, 39, 47, 105, and 156.    20
Scores were:  97, 96, 95, 94, 93, 92, 91, and 80.   30
She may be at 1560 East 47 Street, phone PL 3928.    40
```

NUMBER DRILL: Cumulative Count *(3 copies)*

1-Min. Writings

1 | 2 | 3 | 4 | 5 | 6 | 7 | 8 | 9 | 10

```
2801 3902 4703 5604 1005 6506 7407 8208 9309 1010    10

9811 7912 1613 9014 2515 1716 2017 9818 2619 1420    20

8021 3622 3523 3924 7925 1526 3627 6028 7929 8830    30

9931 4632 9733 8934 7035 4536 9337 8238 7439 6540    40
```

NUMBER-REVIEW PARAGRAPH *(3 copies / si 1.48)* ◁50▷ DS

2-Min. Writings   1 | 2 | 3 | 4 | 5 | 6 | 7 | 8 | 9 | 10

0	40	A Federal Reserve Act for December 23, 1913,	9
5	44	designed a more efficient monetary system. There	19
10	49	are 12 Reserve banks and 24 branches to serve the	29
15	54	member banks in this country. By 1953, the total	39
20	59	of member banks was 6,765. Of this amount, 4,784	49
25	64	were national banks and 1,891 state banks. These	59
30	69	banks handled checks totaling over 1,026 billions	69
35	74	of dollars during 1953, which was quite a record.	79

Plus ➡ 1 | 2 | 3 | 4 | 5

```
Dear Mr. Hale:               Dear Mr. Hale:               Dear Mr. Hale:

     I do appreciate very much        I do appreciate very much    I do appreciate very much your
your help in tracking down the   your help in tracking down the   help in tracking down the list
                                 list of customers in Iowa.       of customers in Iowa.
list of customers in Iowa.
                                     If there is ever a chance     If there is ever a chance that
     If there is ever a chance   that I can repay the favor, do    I can repay the favor, do give
                                 give me a chance to do so.        me a chance to do so.
that I can repay the favor, do
                                     I think that your company     I think that your company will
give a chance to do so.          will be rather pleased to know    be rather pleased to know that
                                 that your bid got our order.      your bid got our order.
```
Double spaced, indented   **Single spaced, indented**   **Single spaced, blocked**

TO INDICATE THE START OF A NEW PARAGRAPH . . .

1. If it is double spaced, indent the first word 5 spaces, using the tabulator.

2. If it is single spaced, precede it with a blank line. The first word may be either (a) indented or (b) blocked, depending on the nature of the work.

TO INDENT A PARAGRAPH . . .

1. Check that margin stops are set.

2. Clear any tab stops that may already be set: On a Smith-Corona or Allen, press the *Total Clear* (top right end of carriage); on other machines, move the carriage to the end of the line and then return the carriage while holding down the key marked *Clear*.

3. Set a tab stop: Space in 5 strokes from the left margin stop, and then press the key marked *Set*, to set a tab stop there.

4. Indent from the left margin: Press the *Tab* bar or key; the carriage will hop to the tab stop you have set. On a manual machine, the tab key or bar must be held down firmly until the carriage stops moving.

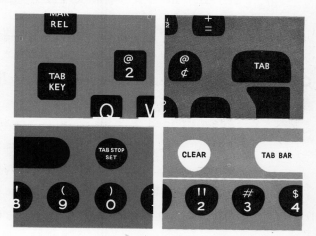

Find the Tab key or bar, Set key, and Clear key on your machine. Location of these parts varies, but each is in plain sight and labeled.

ALPHABET-REVIEW PARAGRAPHS (*Each, 2 times/si 1.37*)

Watch for signals like these:
New paper; length of line: ◁**50**▷
Use double spacing: **DS**

For these paragraphs, use double spacing and a 5-space paragraph indention. Practice each paragraph separately:

1. Type it all the way through (or for 1 minute) without stopping.

2. Without removing the paper, proofread what you typed. Circle all errors.

3. Practice the circled words and any other hard ones until they are easy.

4. Now, retype the paragraph (or take another 1-minute writing), making an effort to improve your speed and accuracy.

1-Min.
Writings

```
          1  |  2  |  3  |  4  |  5  |  6  |  7  |  8  |  9  |  10
 5 ▶     The plane crews quickly move from the flight        9
        deck just before the sizzling fuses will explode.   19
 5 ▶     The best typists know that the accurate jobs       28
       required zest for relaxed arms and even stroking.    38
```

The 5 spaces in the paragraph indention do not count as a word.

WARMUP: Capital Control *(Each line 3 times)* ◁**60**▷

```
a B c D e F g H i J k L m N o P q R s T u V w X y Z / ? ; :
Al and Bob and Cal and Dan and Ed and Frank and Gus and Hal
and Ike and Joe and Ken and Len and Max and Nat and William
```

CONTROL DRILL: Rock Sequences *(Each line 3 times)*

Type very
evenly.

```
mo mo mob more most moan moth month model money moist moral
mo mo mow mount smoke smote lemon humor among almost remote

ad ad add adult adept adapt admit adobe adorn adjust advice
ad ad dad lads glad fads lead sadly plead grade blade ready

in in inn into index incur infer inlay indent income induce
in in ink line thin find coin bring train point drain hinge

ar ar arm army arch avid arms arena argue arise arbor array
ar ar are vary dear hard near early clear heard spear large
```

CONTROL SENTENCES: Rock Sequences *(Each line 3 times)* ◁**60**▷

½-Min.
Writings

1	2	3	4	5	6	7	8	9	10	11	12		

```
Adam spaded his yard and installed a fine motor on a mower.    12
A large area near the army camp was made ready for archery.    24
Windy made almost enough money to invest in a modern motel.    36
Mother made her famous lemonade for the cadets in training.    48
Harold arranged for them to read part of the printed story.    60
```

CONTROL DRILL: Concentration Paragraph *(3 copies / si 1.25)*

½- and 1-Min.
Writings

Fill in the
missing copy
as you type.

1	2	3	4	5	6	7	8	9	10	11	12

```
Dear --- Williams:  I shall -- very pleased -- help you ---    12
your staff set -- a new filing sys---.  As you ----, I have    24
been doing much -- this kind -- work recently.  -- you will    36
notify -- when to begin, I shall be -----.  Cor------ yours    48
```

CONTROL SENTENCES: Troublesome Words *(Each line 3 times)* ◁**60**▷

1- and 3-Min.
Writings

		1	2	3	4	5	6	7	8	9	10	11	12		

```
 0 | 36   Our school received extra money for researches in business.   12
 4 | 40   Experience is quite relevant in business and related areas.    24
 8 | 44   The month of February was especially rugged this past year.    36

12 | 48   Judgment placement is necessary while addressing envelopes.   12 |  48
16 | 52   I expect to travel in Arizona and Colorado relatively soon.   24 |  60
20 | 56   Employers always prefer steady habits from their employees.   36 |  72

24 | 60   Their boat capsized before the ocean journey was completed.   12 |  84
28 | 64   That highway bridge was completed a couple of months early.   24 |  96
32 | 68   Practice is often necessary before improvement is possible.   36 | 108
```

Plus ➧   1 | 2 | 3 | 4

WARMUP REVIEW *(Each line 2 times)*

```
a;sldkfjghfjdksla;sldkfjghfjdksla;sldkfjghfjdksla;s
z y x w v u t s r q p o n m l k j i h g f e d c b a
Alex Babs Fred Hugh Joan Moby Pats Quin Vicky Whiz.
```

ONE-HAND WORD DRILL *(Each line 2 times)*

Goal:
rhythm

```
wade join free milk fact look face hull dare hill
fare hump stew link wave pull vase loin rate pink
best mill east pony raft hulk sags puny fast lump
date only test pump afar oily fads upon draw poll
```

OPPOSITE-HAND WORD DRILL *(Each line 2 times)*

Goal:
speed-up

```
chapel bushel endow angle they lend for the it is
profit formal bugle right work duty vow rib or if
height dismay their gland than this owl pan do so
handle mangle handy giant coal mend lay cut ox of
```

SPEED-UP SENTENCES *(Each line 3 times)*

Goal:
smooth
stroking

```
If we are to go to it, is he not to go to it, too?
Can you see that the boys and man get the day off?
They have four more days that they will work here.
```
12-Sec. 5| 10| 15| 20| 25| 30| 35| 40| 45| 50|

ALPHABET-REVIEW PARAGRAPHS *(Each, 2 times / si 1.35)*

1-Min.   1 | 2 | 3 | 4 | 5 | 6 | 7 | 8 | 9 | 10
Writings

5 ▶   The six jets took off with a wail of engines   9

and, like queenly comets, zoomed up far above us.   19

5 ▶   The quiet dockman judges that any five boxes   28

of a larger size will be enough for our purposes.   38

CONTROL PREVIEW *(Each line 3 times)*

```
to say size wood nylon fibers exactly whatever chemicals manufactured
if can each thin worth supply treated thickness expensive combination
is way it's pick cloth grade, ribbons qualities stationery summarized
```

ALPHABET-REVIEW PARAGRAPHS *(1 copy / si 1.32)*

7-Min. Writings	1	2	3	4	5	6	7	8	9	10	11	12	13	14		

```
 0        The subject of paper is a broad one; yet, while paper is made in      13
 2   many sizes and many grades, each suited for some special purpose, the      27
 4   general qualities of paper can be briefly summarized.  Paper is manu-      41
 6   factured from both wood and rag fibers, treated with chemicals.  Wood      55
 8   and rag may be mixed; and many of the things that affect the cost and      69
10   the life of paper depend on the ratio of rag to wood:  the more wood,      83
12   the less strength.  If strength and life are important, then you look      97
14   for more rag and less wood.  Papers vary also in thickness and in the     111
16   finish--two more factors that affect the quality of the paper.  It is     125
18   wise, as you guess, to have a good friend in the stationery business!     139
```

si 1.36 (line 8)

```
20        The matter of carbon paper is just as broad a subject as that of  13 | 152
22   regular stationery.  Carbon can be purchased in an equally wide range  27 | 166
24   of price and quality; you may be sure that there is some carbon paper  41 | 180
26   made exactly for whatever kind of typing task lies before you.  There  55 | 194
28   are thick carbons and thin ones, big size and small size--every kind.  69 | 208
30   When you go exploring into carbons, you will find that they vary con-  83 | 222
32   cerning their weight, their finish, and their inking; and you have to  97 | 236
34   find the combination that is right for your touch and your typewriter 111 | 250
36   and the number of copies you want.  All this takes some looking into. 125 | 264
```

si 1.30 (line 28)

```
38        Another major supply item with which every typist is required to  13 | 277
40   be expert is the ribbon.  Taking care to pick out the proper kind can  27 | 291
42   make a great difference in the appearance of your work.  Most typists  41 | 305
44   use cloth ribbons whose threads are made of cotton, silk, or nylon; a  55 | 319
46   few have special machines that use reels of plastic or carbon tapes--  69 | 333
48   they are used just "one time through."  The cloth ribbons, if you buy  83 | 347
50   a good grade, will last a long time.  One way to summarize ribbons is  97 | 361
52   simply to say, "Buy the most expensive you can; it's worth the cost." 111 | 375
```

si 1.30 (line 44)

Plus ▶   1   2

WARMUP REVIEW (*Each line 2 times*)

◁40▷

```
aa;;ssllddkkffjjgghhffjjddkkssllaa;;ssll
aB cD eF gH iJ kL . mN oP qR sT uV wX yZ
to the, to you; to her, to him, to do so
```

NEW STROKES (*Each line 2 times*)

LEFT HAND
D-finger reaches up, to 3.
To type only capitals, depress shift lock (by A or ;). To unlock, touch opposite shift.

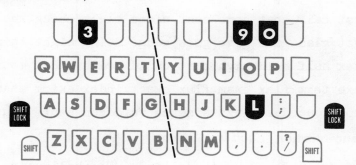

RIGHT HAND
L-finger reaches up, to 9.
;-finger reaches up, to 0.
1 is small L.

```
lo lo9 191 999 1 day 9 days 1 19 91 1919
11 and 19 and 119 and 191 and 91 and 99.

de de3 d3d 333 3 days 3 hours 13 39 1913
13 and 33 and 133 and 139 and 39 and 33.

;p ;p0 ;0; 000 0 days 10 hours 100 1,000
10 and 30 and 90 and 101 and 130 and 90.

We MUST sign up AT LEAST 1,390 more men.
THE PLACE:  Troy.  THE DATE:  May, 1930.
```

STROKE-REVIEW SENTENCES (*Each line 2 times*)

```
She worked 11 hours a day for 11.1 days.
The 19 men WORKED until 9 p.m. on May 9.
Did the 3 men catch 333 fish in 33 days?
The 10 men in Squad 10 counted 100 jets.
```

ALPHABET-REVIEW PARAGRAPHS (*Each, 2 times / si 1.33*)

◁50▷
DS

1-Min.
Writings

```
   1 |  2 |  3 |  4 |  5 |  6 |  7 |  8 |  9 | 10
     If Mr. Quigley can have sixteen crews out by      9
the middle of June, you can take the first prize.     19
     This prize is worth taking, too; it provides     28
a January excursion up to Quimby for all winners.     38
```

WARMUP: Alphabet Review *(Each line 3 times)*   ◁ **60** ▷

```
q r s t u qrstu v w x y z vwxyz abcdefghijklmnopqrstuvwxyz.
ago boy copy does done each early favor going having inches
joy kid kind left many most never offer prove quoted report
say toy used very void when where young zones axioms extent
```

CONTROL DRILL: C, G, M, X, Z *(Each line 3 times)*

```
cc co cot calf coat come cent close elect check knock price
gg go got glad game give goes gauge doing eight thing might
hh he hex half held high hurt child beach other month short
xx ax axe text flax exam flux exact index axiom annex sixth
zz zo zoo zone daze jazz size zebra dozen azure gauze razor
```

CONTROL DRILL: Concentration *(Each line 3 times)*

Note, but do not mark, the word transpositions; correct them as you type.

```
We are sorry order your is delayed.  We shall ship soon it.
We are doing best our, but we realize that must we improve.
Please us call when come you into town; we to want see you.
We shall give better you service; that a is sincere pledge.
```

CONTROL SENTENCES: Alphabet Review *(Each line 3 times)*   ◁ **60** ▷

½-Min. Writings

```
 1 | 2 | 3 | 4 | 5 | 6 | 7 | 8 | 9 | 10 | 11 | 12
Luvicy Mix was quite dazed from the big knock upon the jaw.      12
Bess Major won five or six prizes with equally good checks.      24
Hazel expects Jack to give May five quaint bowls for candy.      36
Queen Zolan examined every subject--but kept fighting wars.      48
Elizabeth gladly indexed Pam's quota of Java working cards.      60
```

CONTROL PARAGRAPHS: Alphabet Review *(2 copies / si 1.40)*

1-Minute Writings on each paragraph and on both paragraphs

```
     1 | 2 | 3 | 4 | 5 | 6 | 7 | 8 | 9 | 10 | 11 | 12
     Each typist must have more than mere dexterity or high     11
skill at the typewriter.  In addition to being a true whizz     23
at the machine, he is frequently expected to know all about     35
his supplies.  He must know what quality is, so that he can     47
buy supplies just as confidently as he buys a shirt or hat.     59
```

```
     1 | 2 | 3 | 4 | 5 | 6 | 7 | 8 | 9 | 10 | 11 | 12
     The typist is exposed more to stationery than to other     11 |  70
supply items, and he will have to realize that he must know     23 |  82
what quality means when he buys paper.  Unless he does know     35 |  94
such things, his training cannot justly be called complete;     47 | 106
for there are as many kinds of paper as there are purposes.     59 | 118
```

WARMUP REVIEW *(Each line 2 times)*   ◁ **40** ▷

aa;;ssllddkkffjjgghhffjjddkkssllaa;;ssll
Ab Cd Ef Gh Ij Kl . Mn Op Qr St Uv Wx Yz
1 and 3 and 9 and 1 and 0 and 10 and 39.

NEW STROKES *(Each line 2 times)*

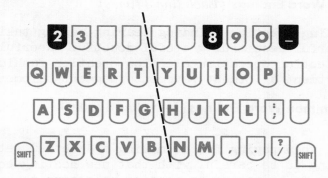

LEFT HAND
S-finger reaches
up, to 2.

RIGHT HAND
K-finger reaches
up, to 8.
;-finger reaches
up, to hyphen.

ki ki8 k8k 888 8 days 8 hours 18 89 1918
18 and 88 and 188 and 189 and 80 and 138

sw sw2 s2s 222 2 weeks 2 years 2 12 1912
12 and 22 and 23 and 28 and 29 and 1,200

Dash is 2 hyphens
with no spaces.

;p ;p- ;-; ;-; one-half one-third in-law
He asked--begged--for his father-in-law.

A "we 23" drill:
words and numbers
typed alike.

we 23 we 23 ow 92 ow 92 owe 923 owe 923.
pi 08 pi 08 pie 083 pie 083 we 23 we 23.

STROKE-REVIEW SENTENCES *(Each line 2 times)*

Did 88 men pack 1,818 boxes in 818 bags?
The 22 men and 22 boys ate up 222 cakes.
His in-laws asked--SUED--for his estate.
We need 39 bikes, 28 cars, or 10 trucks.

ALPHABET-REVIEW PARAGRAPH *(2 copies / si 1.29)*   ◁ **50** ▷
DS

1-Min.
Writings

| 1 | 2 | 3 | 4 | 5 | 6 | 7 | 8 | 9 | 10 |

    The hyphen is most frequently used in divid-   9
ing words of six--or more--strokes; it is used in   19
compounds and in dashes, also. Any full-page job   29
will call for the use of a dozen or more hyphens.   39

WARMUP: "TO" Drill *(Each line 3 times)*   ◁ **60** ▷

```
a;qpa;z/ slwoslx. dkeidkc, fjrufjvm ghtyghbn a;sldkfjghfjdk
told tort tore tour toil tomb torn tone tong tope toot tops
retort intone stole stove stout story stone stock stow stop
contralto ghetto grotto motto octo auto veto unto alto into
```

SPEED DRILL: Common Word Endings *(Each line 3 times)*

Flash the
endings.

```
-ing trusting greeting blinding bearing asking taking doing
-ful wonderful deceitful grateful doubtful cheerful hopeful
-tion protection operation election creation fashion motion
-ment apartment allotment pavement judgment shipment cement
```

SPEED SENTENCES: Common Word Endings *(Each line 3 times)*

12-Sec. and
30-Sec.
Writings

| 1 | 2 | 3 | 4 | 5 | 6 | 7 | 8 | 9 | 10 | 11 | 12 |

```
Be careful when paying for or making a doubtful settlement.    12
Is he trying to be careful with that new heating equipment?    24
He is going to be making an amazing selection this evening.    36
He was grateful to us for passing the cheerful motion then.    48
I am hopeful that a shipment of cement will be coming soon.    60
```

12-Sec. 5| 10| 15| 20| 25| 30| 35| 40| 45| 50| 55| 60|

SPEED DRILL: Concentration Paragraph *(3 copies)*   ◁ **60** ▷

Type only
the correct
word in
each group.

```
I have for four friends who wood would like to buy bye by up
sum some nice, old pitchers pictures to hang in there their
homes.  I tolled told the men about you're your store, but I
could knot naught not tell them on witch which sighed side of
the block ewe you yew had putt put up you're your knew new
place.  Aye eye I hope yew ewe you get there their order.      48
```

SUSTAINED-SPEED SENTENCES *(Each line 3 times / si 1.09)*   ◁ **60** ▷

1- and 3-Min.
Writings

| 1 | 2 | 3 | 4 | 5 | 6 | 7 | 8 | 9 | 10 | 11 | 12 |

0	40	The form they sent you is the usual one and needs no study.	12
4	44	They think it is his duty to spend more time with his sons.	24
8	48	Both of them paid more than they should for the new chapel.	36
12	52	The time from six to nine is the right one for such a plan.	48
16	56	They are not the kind of firm with whom it is easy to work.	60
20	60	It is a shame that you did not buy some of the stock today.	12	72
24	64	The group came into the bay just as the sun was going down.	24	84
28	68	We do not wish to have as much stock as you ask us to take.	36	96
32	72	It is just about time for them to be rolling down the road.	48	108
36	76	For that reason, it would be a shame to turn the chap down.	60	120

Plus ▶   1   2   3   4

Part 9
LESSON
Unit 33
202

WARMUP REVIEW *(Each line 2 times)*

◁ **40** ▷

```
aa;;ssllddkkffjjgghhffjjddkkssllaa;;ssll
aB cD eF gH iJ kL . mN oP qR sT uV wX yZ
39 28 10 39 28 10; we 23 woe 293 pie 083
and the, for the, to the, in the, at the
```

NEW STROKES *(Each line 2 times)*

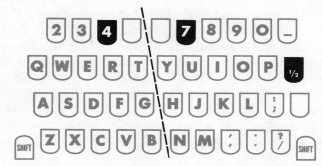

LEFT HAND
F-finger reaches up, to 4.

RIGHT HAND
J-finger reaches up, to 7.
;-finger reaches up, right, to ½.

```
ju ju7 j7j 777 7 days 7 hours 17 77 1917
17 to 27; 37 to 77; 87 to 97; 700 to 770

fr fr4 f4f 444 4 weeks 4 years 4 47 1944
14 to 24; 34 to 44; 47 to 84; 400 to 940

;; ;½; ;½; ½½½ ½ day ½ hour ½ week ½ day
1½ to 2½; 3½ to 4½; 7½ to 8½; 9½ to 10½.

we 23 err 344 were 2343 ore 943 ire 843.
up 70 pup 070 pour 0974 our 974 pie 083.
```

STROKE-REVIEW SENTENCES *(Each line 2 times)*

```
Look for numbers 70, 71, 72, 73, and 77.
The 4 men lost 4 of their 44 golf games.
Is it 17½ inches to A but only 14½ to B?
We now have sizes 47½, 39½, 28½, and 10.
```

ALPHABET-REVIEW PARAGRAPHS *(Each, 2 times / si 1.26)*

◁ **50** ▷
DS

1-Min. Writings

```
      1  |  2  |  3  |  4  |  5  |  6  |  7  |  8  |  9  |  10
        Pat now realizes that Gus was able to fix my        9
machine by his quick jabs with two screw drivers.          19
        I must be ready for quick work when the crew        28
arrives for the six big grazing projects in Lane.          38
```

SPEED PREVIEW (*Each line 3 times*)

consistently cliques concede tidbit can't for the
impression probably wasteful answer blame one for
effective becoming criticize others can't win the

SUSTAINED-SPEED PARAGRAPHS (*1 copy / si 1.25*)

5-Min.
Writings

1 | 2 | 3 | 4 | 5 | 6 | 7 | 8 | 9 | 10

0	The first and quickest step to take, for the	9
2	person who wants to win the title of The Pest, is	19
4	to become the ear of the head of the office. Run	29
6	to him with every tidbit of news you can. He may	39
si 1.23 8	not seem grateful, and it is hardly surprising to	49
10	learn that your fellow workers will be unhappy to	59
12	have you do this; but there is no doubt that they	69
14	will know who you are. This is a sure method for	79
16	becoming well known, even if not very well liked.	89
18	Another effective step, and it is not a very	9	98
20	hard one for most of us, is to become the one who	19	108
22	knows all the answers--right or wrong. If you do	29	118
24	not know an answer, invent one. Don't hold back;	39	128
26	speak up. When a group in the office is talking,	49	138
si 1.26 28	barge in and have your say. There is probably no	59	148
30	better way to break up office cliques and prevent	69	158
32	wasteful use of office time. It also keeps other	79	168
34	folks from talking about you, something that they	89	178
36	will be prone to do if you really take this step.	99	188
38	A third step that you can take if you desire	9	197
39	more direct action in winning the title is to ask	19	207
41	everyone for help. Give the impression that your	29	217
43	work load is tougher than that of the others (and	39	227
45	much more important, too) and that the least they	49	237
si 1.30 47	can do is lend a hand. Now, you can't make head-	59	247
49	way in this step unless you take it consistently;	69	257
51	grab at least two helpers every day. Watch them,	79	267
53	too, and make sure that you criticize whatever is	89	277
55	done for you. They will soon concede your title.	99	287
57	There are, of course, many other tricks that	9	296
59	you can do to become The Pest. You can always be	19	306
61	late, you can make mistakes and pass the blame on	29	316
63	to others, you can wear strange clothing and talk	39	326
si 1.20 65	about it a lot, you can tell others to take phone	49	336
67	calls for you, and so on; but the truly effective	59	346
69	steps are the three outlined above. And when you	69	356
71	have won the title, cherish it; for, you will not	79	366
73	be there long enough to make very much use of it.	89	376

Plus ▶   1   2

WARMUP REVIEW *(Each line 2 times)*

◁ **40** ▷

```
aa;;ssllddkkffjjgghhffjjddkkssllaa;;ssll
aBc dEf gHi jKl mNo pQr sTu vWx yZ /? ;:
39 39 39½ 28 28 28½ 47 47 47½ 10 10 10½.
to the, to her, to him, to his, to them.
```

NEW STROKES *(Each line 2 times)*

LEFT HAND
F-finger reaches up, to 5.

When reaching for 5 and 6, keep the A- and ;-fingers close to home keys.

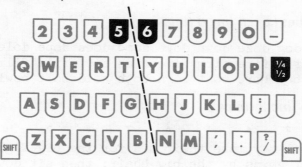

RIGHT HAND
J-finger reaches far up, to 6.
¼ is shift of ½.

Note spacings in "mixed" fractions: 1¼ but 1 1/4.

```
;: ;½¼ ;¼; ¼¼¼ ¼ day ¼ hour ¼ week ¼ day
Type one and one-quarter as 1¼ or 1 1/4.

jy jy6 j6j 666 61 days 61 hours 61¼ 1946
1/6 and 2/6 and 3/6 and 4/6 total 1 2/3.

ff f5f f5f 555 5 days 5 hours 5 51¼ 1955
1/5 and 3/5 and 4/5 and 5/5 total 2 3/5.

we 23 wet 235 were 2343 our 974 out 975.
it 85 wit 285 you 697 your 6974 wry 246.
```

STROKE-REVIEW SENTENCES *(Each line 2 times)*

```
The 6 men drove 66 miles in 66½ minutes.
Were the 55 sheets 5 feet wide, 15 long?
It is 15¼ miles to E but 16¼ to Point F.
Send him No. 39¼, 28¼, 47¼, 56¼, or 10¼.
```

ALPHABET-REVIEW PARAGRAPHS *(Each, 2 times / si 1.21)*

◁ **50** ▷
DS

1-Min. Writings

```
   1 | 2 | 3 | 4 | 5 | 6 | 7 | 8 | 9 | 10
  With a quick jerk of his wrist, Dave got all      9
six matches blazing; but the light was very poor.  19
  I took a jet Viscount flight to Quebec; then      28
a Northern Star zipped me out to Halifax by dawn.   38
```

PART 9

◁ 60 ▷

WARMUP: Phrase Drill (*Each line 3 times*)

```
aqaz ;p;/ swsx lol. dedc kik, frfv jujm gtgb hyhn asdf ;lkj
and they, and make, and then, and wish, for them, and such,
but they, but then, with the, than the, when the, wish for,
```

SPEED DRILL: Word Families (*Each line 3 times*)

```
DO dot doe dog doze down dove dome does dope dole dolt doom
FI fit fir fin fire firm five fish fist file film find fife
BO bog bow boy bore boat born both bold bolt bowl bond bone
```

SPEED SENTENCES (*Each line 3 times*)

12-Sec. Writings

| 1 | 2 | 3 | 4 | 5 | 6 | 7 | 8 | 9 | 10 | 11 | 12 |

```
The eight men may make their bid for the big fight by then.    12
Hang the fur gowns by the big chair; then sit down with us.    24
The men paid us for six pans; but did they pay us for soap?    36
```

12-Sec. 5| 10| 15| 20| 25| 30| 35| 40| 45| 50| 55| 60|

SPEED PARAGRAPH (*3 copies / si 1.13*)

1-Min. Writings

| 1 | 2 | 3 | 4 | 5 | 6 | 7 | 8 | 9 | 10 | 11 | 12 |

```
Those who forge ahead in any field of work get there not by    12
luck alone.  More times than not, they will have had an aim    24
or set of aims that kept them on the proper path.  When one    36
starts any task, no matter how small, he should study it to    48
see what is involved and then work out a goal for that job.    60
```

SPEED DRILL: Concentration Paragraph (*3 copies*)

◁ 60 ▷

Write all words out correctly.

```
Dear Joe:  I hope that U R not going 2 B L8 4 our              12
luncheon D8 next week.  I have 2 B at a meeting an hour        24
L8R.  It will B EZ 4 me 2 make it if U can arrive             36
on time.  I am looking 4ward 2 Bing with U 4 lunch.           48
```

SUSTAINED-SPEED PARAGRAPHS (*1 copy / si 1.27*)

3-Min. Writings

| 1 | 2 | 3 | 4 | 5 | 6 | 7 | 8 | 9 | 10 | 11 | 12 |

0	39	You, too, can become the one person in your office who	11
4	43	is the best known. There are two ways by which you can win	23
8	47	this distinction. The first is the hard method: You might	35
12	51	do more work and better work than anyone else; if you adopt	47
16	55	this method, you may end up in a lonely office of your own.	59
20	59	The second method is much easier and is therefore used	11	70
23	63	by more persons. It consists of becoming known as The Pest	23	82
27	67	in your office. You would be surprised at how many persons	35	94
31	71	vie for this title; in some offices, you might even have to	47	106
35	75	share it. The essay on the next page is a Guide for Pests.	59	118

Plus ➡   1   2   3   4

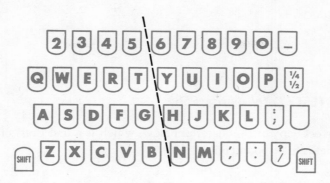

WARMUP
(Each line 2 times)

◁ **50** ▷

```
a;sldkfjghfjdksla;sldkfjghfjdksla;sldkfjghfjdksla;
cab feed jig hulk lazy men part quip sued vox stow
Cal Fred Joe Hugh May Pard Quin Sue Vick Stan Zita
```

FINGER-REACHES REVIEW *(Each line 2 times)*

Fore-fingers
```
ffrf jjuj fftf jjyj ffgf jjhj ffbf jjnj ffvf jjmj
turf jury tuft hymn grub hung ruby rung hunt numb
```

Second fingers
```
dded kkik ddcd kk,k dded kkik ddcd kk,k decd ki,k
deed kick dice eke, deck dike cede kick died deck
```

Third fingers
```
ssws llol ssxs ll.l ssws llol ssxs ll.l swxs lo.l
slow solo sox. low. oxen loss wax. lox. lax. sows
```

Little fingers
```
;;p; aaqa ;;/; aaza ;;P; aaQa ;;?; aaZa ;;:; ;;-;
papa aqua a/p; faze quip quay zip? quiz A::Z A-Z;
```

Numbers
```
jj7j ff4f jj6j ff5f kk8k dd3d ll9l ss2s ;;0; ;;½;
we 23 up 70 or 94 it 85 ye 63 pi 08 re 43 ire 843
```

ALPHABET-REVIEW PARAGRAPH *(2 copies / si 1.11)*

◁ **50** ▷
DS

2-Min. Writings*

```
        1  |  2  |  3  |  4  |  5  |  6  |  7  |  8  |  9  |  10
```

2-Min. Writings*		
0 | 19	There must have been sixty, or more, cars in	9
5 | 24	the freight train on which the two men jumped; it	19
10 | 29	slowly worked its way through the maze of the old	29
15 | 34	freight yards and then quickly boosted its speed.	39

```
Plus ▶   1       2       3       4       5
```

* To figure your speed on a 2-minute writing, use either of these methods:

   1. *Using the black figures and scale:* Find the total words typed and divide by 2. Fractions count as whole words. If you type 29 words, your speed is 14½ (call it 15) wam.

   2. *Using the color figures and scale:* Note the number in front of the line you were typing when you stopped (the first number, if you did not finish the paragraph; the second number, if you finished it and started over). To that number, add the color figure under the part of the line where you stopped. *Then*, in line 4, would be $15 + 3 = 18$, or $34 + 3 = 37$ wam.

PART D: MANUSCRIPT TEST *(Total words, 256)*

Make a correct copy of the material below, which is a first draft of page 2 of a manuscript that is to be bound on the left.

SECRETARIAL INFLUENCE   Page 2

(Use horizontal rules, please)

Table 2

HOW ~~THEY~~ *SECRETARIES* INFLUENCE OTHER PURCHASES   *(6 spaces here)*

Item	Per Cent	Rank
Adding machines	24%	10
Calculating machines	17%	11
Copyholders	39%	5
Desk pen sets	38%	6
Desk staplers	45%	4
Dictation machines	31%	8
Duplicating machines	27%	9
Electric typewriters	48%	1
Manual typewriters	47%	2
Office desks	32%	~~2~~ 7
Posture chairs	46%	3
Photocopy equipment	16%	12
AVERAGE	34$%	--

(Eliminate all these leaders — just put 6 spaces between columns)

(Center these columns under their headings)

(more space →) The secretarial influence in purchases of desk and office equipment is less but is still considerable. As shown by ~~all~~ the figures in Table 2, above, a third of the secretaries influence ~~the~~ purchase of office equipment, *accessories, etc.* ~~and office machines~~.

The editor of the magazine made an interesting comment in her editorial ~~comments~~ *remarks* about the findings *of the* survey: "...apparent that employers trust their secretaries' judgment more in the things that secretaries themselves will use (45.5 per cent) than in the things that will have to be shared with others (21.0 per cent)."[1]

(display the quote)

1. Sally Browne, "The Survey Told Us So," *Modern Secretary*, Vol. 59, No. 11 (July, 1956), page 9.

TO CENTER HORIZONTALLY . . .

set the carriage at the center of the paper and then backspace once for every two spaces that the centered material will occupy. Say the letters and spaces in pairs, accenting the second stroke of each pair and backspacing once as you say it. Special notes:

Backspace key is located beside the 2 key— or beside the hyphen key.

1. If a letter is left over after calling the pairs, ignore it. Do not backspace for the left-over letter.

2. To backspace a few strokes, use the little finger; for many strokes, use the thumb, which is surer and firmer.

3. The center is at 50 if the paper guide is placed correctly (page 3).

4. If several lines are to be centered, set a tab stop at the center and tabulate to it each time you center the carriage.

TO GET ASSIGNED TOP MARGIN . . .

when you are directed to start typing on a particular line of typing (as in the exercise below, where you start on line 28), take the three numbered steps given in the next column.

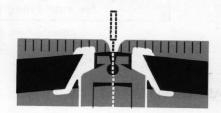

Aligning scale is on each side of the point where type bars strike the paper.

1. Insert and straighten paper as usual.

2. Instead of rolling the paper back to the paper bail, roll it back until it is even with the aligning scale (above). If it does not come perfectly even, pull out or press in (depending on the make of the typewriter) the variable spacer in the left cylinder knob while you turn the cylinder until the paper *is* even with the aligning scale. Then, return the variable spacer to its normal position.

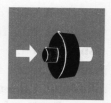

Some variable spacers must be pulled out; some must be pressed in.

3. Space up the required number of lines. You may use the cylinder knob, counting the clicks as you turn it; or, you may use the carriage return. If you use the latter, check the setting for the spacing. To start on line 28, for example, you may use 28 single or 14 double carriage returns.

Watch for signals like these —
New paper; length of line: ◁**50**▷
Use double spacing: **DS**
Start typing on line: **28**
▽

TECHNIQUE PRACTICE: Centering *(1 copy)*

Use a clean side or sheet of paper for this practice, and begin on line 28. Center each line horizontally, double spaced. Set a tab stop at the center, to expedite recentering the carriage for each line. Use the shift lock for the first line. Center your full name, as indicated, for line 5.

```
THE MERCHANT OF VENICE
          by
   William Shakespeare
       Reviewed by
      [Your Name]
```

TAKE OFF:	—3 for each major error (top margin, line length, linespacing, general form, etc.) —2 for each minor error (blocking, aligning, indenting, etc., of each part of a job) —1 for each typographical error	TOTAL TAKEN OFF	10-9	8-5	4-3	2-0
		GRADE	D	C	B	A

Grade Parts B, C, and D (each separately) on this grading scale.

PART B: LETTER TEST *(Total words, 281 / si 1.36)*

Capitalize, paragraph, and type the following letter in blocked style.

mr. james e. flaherty, 392 howard street, albany 1, new york. dear jim: 15

i am delighted to learn of your speedy 23 recovery from the accident. it does not seem 32 possible that you are ready to come back 40 to work already; but, of course, i am ex- 48 tremely happy that you are. i hope that you 57 will not overdo things at the start. take it 66 easy for a while, jim. please do not try to 75 step back into full harness right away. i 84 suspect that the deal at harding-hill com- 92 pany will be the first thing you will wish to 101 follow up. i found mr. thompson, the con- 109 tact at harding-hill, to be a very congenial 118 man who really knows what the score is. 127 he was promoted up from the ranks. he has 135 been an operator of most kinds of office 143 machines and is now in charge of the mail- 152 room production work for the firm. he 159 knows exactly what he wants and how he 167 will use whatever equipment he buys. if 175 you can, jim, write him two or three days 184 before you call to see him; and when you 192 do, tell him that you will be bringing the 201 special folding machine that he has asked 209 us to prepare. mr. thompson is almost cer- 217 tain to order a battery of eight or nine of 226 our model 19's; but he also wants a folder 235 that will handle a special paper stock. the 244 factory is now completing this special ma- 252 chine and will have it in your hands within 261 a week. 263

cordially yours, portland products com- 270 pany, theodore wilson, sales manager 277

PART C: TABULATION TEST *(Total words, 98)*

From the following news item, prepare and type *Table 1—How Secretaries Influence Supply Purchases*, with three columns: *Items, Per Cent,* and *Rank.* Use horizontal rules and double spacing. Put 6 spaces between the columns.

NEW YORK, Dec. 20—Fifty per cent of secretaries get the kind of office supplies 16 they want, according to a recent national survey. 26

They are most influential in buying carbon paper; 60% have the say in this regard. 43 Typewriter ribbons are second (59%), and erasers are third (55%). Other items: type- 60 writer cleaners (50%), typing paper (49%), writing ink (43%), filing supplies (53%), and 78 duplicating supplies (33%). 83

WARMUP REVIEW *(Each line 2 times)*

◁ **50** ▷

a;sldkfjghfjdksla;sldkfjghfjdksla;sldkfjghfjdksla;

back dent high joke melt hope quiz rust vows foxy.

Jack Dave Ruth John Mell Hope Quen Russ Vera Maxie

FINGER-REACHES REVIEW *(Each line 2 times)*

Fore-
fingers

jjuj ffrf jjyj fftf jjhj ffgf jjnj ffbf jjmj ffvf
The jury was in a hurry to get the truth about it.

Second
fingers

kkik dded kk,k ddcd kkik dded kk,k ddcd ki,k decd
Dick kicked the ice, then skidded on the icy deck.

Third
fingers

llol ssws ll.l ssxs llol ssws ll.l ssxs lo.l swxs
Miss Lois sews so slowly. Mr. Wollo lolls in sox.

Little
fingers

;;p; aaqa ;;/; aaza ;;:; aaqa ;;?; aaza ;;p; ;;/;
Was the zoo paid for and equipped by Pappy Quazzo?

Numbers

jj7j ff4f jj6j ff5f kk8k dd3d 1191 ss2s ;;0; ;;½;
Send 39 of No. 28 or 47 of No. 56 by September 10.

ALPHABET-REVIEW PARAGRAPH *(2 copies / si 1.15)*

DS

2-Min. Writings		1	2	3	4	5	6	7	8	9	10	
0	29	When you wish to leave two blank lines after										9
5	34	a title, turn the paper up three lines--two lines										19
10	39	for the blank space, and one for the next line of										29
15	44	typing. You realize, of course, that you must be										39
20	49	quite sure to turn up just one line at a time--by										49
25	54	hand, if the linespace is set for double spacing.										59
Plus ↓		1		2		3		4		5		

TECHNIQUE REVIEW *(1 exact copy)*

◁ **50** ▷
DS
24
▽

Titles should be
centered in all
caps and followed
by 2 blank lines.

WORD DIVISION ₃ ←

5 ↓ 1. Divide as few words as possible.

2. Do not divide a word with fewer than six
strokes. The sixth may be a punctuation mark.

3. Do not divide a word of one syllable.

4. Do not divide a proper noun.

5. Do not divide a contraction.

[Additional rules
for word division
appear on page 30.]

You will need 2 sheets of plain paper or Workbook pages 295-298. Type Parts A and B on opposite sides of one sheet and Parts C and D on opposite sides of the second.

PART A: STRAIGHT-COPY TEST *(si 1.50)*

Take a 7-minute test on the copy below; or, type it once and grade your work as though it were typed at 62 words a minute.

◁ **70** ▷
SS

GRADING SCALE FOR PART A

Step 1: Compute words a minute.	Step 2: Deduct for errors—		Step 3: Grade the remaining words a min-ute this way:	60 or higher: A
	1 error: —2	5 errors: —11		55 to 59 wam: B
	2 errors: —4	6 errors: —14		50 to 54 wam: C
	3 errors: —6	7 errors: —17		45 to 49 wam: D
	4 errors: —8	8 errors: —20		

7-Min. Writings

1 | 2 | 3 | 4 | 5 | 6 | 7 | 8 | 9 | 10 | 11 | 12 | 13 | 14

0	48	The day is not far off when the person looking for a position as		13
2	49	secretary in a large firm will find that his employment test includes		27
4	51	a section on office supplies and equipment. There have been a number		41
6	53	of surveys on the role of the secretary in selecting such materials--		55
8	55	and every survey shows a higher and higher level of responsibility is		69
10	57	being placed upon him. This is particularly true in regard to supply		83
12	59	items that he will himself use: his paper and carbons and eraser and		97
14	61	typewriter ribbons, and the like. What are you going to do about it?		111
16	63	There ought to be a rule that says that every would-be secretary	13	124
18	65	has to work in a modern stationery store for five or six months. Oh,	27	138
20	67	that is not a practical suggestion, of course; but, were it possible,	41	152
22	69	the trainee would come out of it with a much clearer knowledge of the	55	166
24	71	ins and outs of office supplies and equipment than he is bringing his	69	180
26	73	employer today. The number of different items with which a secretary	83	194
28	75	should be familiar, ranging from posture chairs to erasers, runs into	97	208
30	77	the scores, perhaps hundreds; and when you realize that many of these	111	222
32	79	things are manufactured by scores of firms, the problem grows on you.	125	236
34	81	If the suggestions of secretaries concerning the kind or quality	13	249
36	83	of office supplies are followed in half the cases, and the polls show	27	263
38	85	that this is so, then the secretaries have a grave responsibility for	41	277
40	87	knowing what they are talking about. Too many millions of dollars in	55	291
42	89	supplies are at stake. How many of these millions are wasted? Visit	69	305
44	91	any office, and you will be shocked at the amount of waste that faces	83	319
46	93	you. You know, that idea of working in a stationery store isn't bad!	97	333

Plus ▶   1   2

WARMUP REVIEW (*Each line 2 times*)

```
a;sldkfjghfjdksla;sldkfjghfjdksla;sldkfj
Abc Def Ghi Jkl Mno Pqr Stu Vwx Yz ?/ :;
39, 28, 47, 56, 100; 39½ 28½ 47½ 56½ 10½
Did the boy and the man get the day off?
```
12-Sec. 5| 10| 15| 20| 25| 30| 35| 40|

NEW STROKES (*Each line 2 times*)

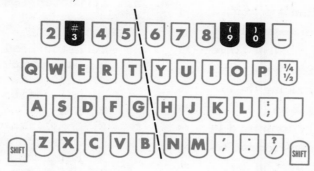

LEFT HAND
D-finger controls # (sign for number and pounds), which is shift of 3.

RIGHT HAND
L-finger controls (, shift of 9.
;-finger controls), shift of 0.

```
lo lo9 lo9(1 1(1 1(1 (39 (28 (47 (56 (10
;p ;p0 ;p0); ;); ;); 39) 28) 47) 56) 10)
(39) (28) (47) (56) (10) (a) (b) (c) (d)

de de3 de3#d d#d d#d #39 #28 #47 #56 #10
I needed 3# (3 pounds) of #9 (number 9).
```

after a numeral is "pounds"; # before a numeral is "number."

ALPHABET-REVIEW PARAGRAPHS (*Each, 2 times / si 1.25*)

2-Min. Writings   1 | 2 | 3 | 4 | 5 | 6 | 7 | 8 | 9 | 10

```
 0 | 24        As quickly as you can, ship us sixty sets of     9
 5 | 29    Judge rubber shoes, as advertised.  All should be    19
10 | 34    in size 11.  We do want them as soon as possible.    29
15 | 39        If we get that right size by air express, we     38
19 | 43    could enjoy a quicker turnover in our mail sales.    48
```

Plus ➧   1 | 2 | 3 | 4 | 5

TO CENTER VERTICALLY:

1. Count the number of typed and blank lines in the material to be centered.

2. Subtract that number from the number of lines that can be typed on the paper. There are 6 lines to an inch; so, there are 66 lines on standard (11-inch) typing paper and 33 lines on a half sheet.

3. Divide the difference by 2; the answer (drop any fraction) is the number of the line on which to start typing.

Example 1. To center 45 lines, start on line 10. Calculations: 66 — 45 = 21, and 21 ÷ 2 = 10½, or 10.

Example 2. The next exercise, on page 30, requires 20 lines (10 typed, 10 blank). Calculations: 66 — 20 = 46, and 46 ÷ 2 = 23.

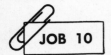

JOB 10

Manuscript
Page 10
Unarranged
Words: 261

The material below comprises the final page of the Correspondence Manual, page 10. Use the same arrangement you used in typing the preceding pages.

Part 3. Letter Punctuation Styles 7

No variation in punctuation is permitted 15
in the body of a letter; the demands of cor- 24
rect English style must be fulfilled. There 33
are, however, three different styles of punc- 42
tuation that are used for treating the dis- 50
played heading and closing lines. 56

Standard Punctuation, the form used in 64
the great majority of business letters, re- 72
quires a colon after the salutation and a 81
comma after the complimentary closing. 89
No other punctuation (except the period 97
that follows any abbreviation) is used to 105
end or "close" any of the displayed heading 114
and closing lines. 118

Open Punctuation eliminates all end-of- 126
line punctuation marks (except the period 134
that follows any abbreviation) for the dis- 143
played heading and closing lines. Not even 151
the colon and comma found in the Stand- 158
ard style are used. 162

Full Punctuation, no longer commonly 170
used, requires that every display heading 178
and closing line end with a punctuation 186
mark. Periods are required after the date, 195
after the last line of the inside address, after 205
the last line of the signatures, and after all 214
the final notations (reference initials, en- 223
closures, etc.). A colon is used after the 231
salutation. All other lines must end with a 240
comma. No line ends without punctuation. 249

JOB 11

Contents page
Words: 234

Center this contents page on a full sheet. Use a 50-space line, open leaders, and any suitable vertical spacing.

T A B L E   O F   C O N T E N T S

LIST OF TABLES

JOB 12

Cover page
Words: 27

Display lines 1-3 in the top half of a full sheet; display lines 4-7 in the lower half. Use any suitable spacing.

CORRESPONDENCE MANUAL
Prepared by
Type Your Name Here

Name of the Course
Name of Your Instructor
Name of the School
Date

TECHNIQUE PRACTICE
(Center 1 copy)

WORD DIVISION ₂ ➡

(Continued) ₃ ➡

Subtitles should
be preceded by 1
blank line and
followed by 2.

◁ **50** ▷
DS

⁵ ◆ 6. Do not divide an abbreviation.

7. Do not divide a number.

8. Do not separate a one-letter syllable from the beginning or ending of a word.

9. If you must divide a word, divide between whole syllables.

⁴ ◆ 10. If you must divide a word, leave at least two letters, followed by a hyphen, on the top line.

OPTIONAL* PRACTICE
(Center 1 copy)

◁ **50** ▷
DS

WORD DIVISION ₂ ➡

(Continued) ₃ ➡

⁴ ◆ 11. Carry at least three strokes to the second line. The third stroke may be a punctuation mark.

12. If there is a prefix (such as con-, com-, anti-, extra-, intro-, etc.), divide after it.

13. If there is a suffix (such as -tive, -ing, -tion, -able, -ment, etc.), divide before it.

14. If there are two strong vowels together, divide between them (as, radi-ator).

15. If there is a one-letter syllable within a word, divide after that letter (as, sepa-rate).

*Optional exercises should always be
studied; they need not be typed,
however, unless your instructor
specifically directs you to do them.

JOB 9

Manuscript
Page 9
In pica
Words: 306

Note that the text discussion of Table 5 is on the preceding page. It is desirable to have text and table together; but when there is not enough room for both on the same page (as is the case here), the discussion must come first, with the table held over for the top of the following page.

CORRESPONDENCE MANUAL   Page 9

Table 5

SOME CORRECT FORMS OF ENCLOSURE NOTATIONS

One Enclosure	More than One	Enumerated
Enclosure	2 Enclosures	Enclosures:
Enc.	2 Encs.	Check
Encl.	2 Enc.	Invoice
1 Enc.	Enc. 2	
1 Enclosure	Enclosures (2)	Enclosures--
Check Enclosed	Enclosures: 3	1. Check
Bill Enclosed	Enclosures--4	2. Invoice

<u>N. A Postscript</u> is an extra paragraph added at the very bottom of the letter and is treated as such: It is indented or blocked as are the other paragraphs. The initials <u>PS.</u>, <u>PS:</u>, <u>P. S.</u>, or <u>PS--</u> are typed at the start of the paragraph.

O. A "CC" Notation is typed under the enclosure notation to indicate to the addressee that carbon copies (hence "CC") are being sent to the persons indicated. Examples of styles:

   CC **Mr.** Stone   c.c. JJS   CC--Stone   cc: Stone
      Miss Bond   MEB   Bond   Bond

<u>P. A "BCC" Notation</u> indicates to whom copies of the letter are being sent without the addressee's knowing about it.

   To type a "blind carbon copy" (hence "BCC") note, a typist removes the letter pack, peels off the original letter and top sheet of carbon, reinserts the carbon pack, and then types the BCC note (in any of the CC styles, but with BCC used instead of CC) about an inch from the top of the paper at the left margin.

WARMUP REVIEW *(Each line 2 times)*

◁ **40** ▷

```
a;sldkfjghfjdksla;sldkfjghfjdksla;sldkfj
AbC DeF GhI JkL MnO PqR StU VwX Yz ?/ :;
(39) (28) (47) (56) (10) #39 #28 #47 #10
The two old men did not get the day off.
```
12-Sec. 5| 10| 15| 20| 25| 30| 35| 40|

NEW STROKES *(Each line 2 times)*

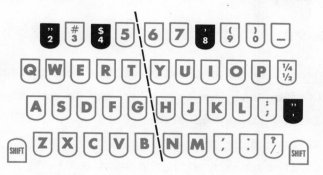

LEFT HAND
S-finger controls ",
  shift of 2.
F-finger controls $,
  shift of 4.

RIGHT HAND
K-finger controls ',
  shift of 8.
On some electrics, the
  ' and " are on the
  key beside ; and are
  typed by the ;-finger.

Type these 3 lines
only if " is on 2
and ' is on 8.

```
ki ki8 ki8'k k'k k'k 39' 28' 47' 56' 10'
sw sw2 sw2"s s"s s"s 39" 28" 47" 56" 10"
He ran it in 3' 56".  He is 5' 11" tall.
```

Type these 3 lines
only if both ' and
" are on the key
beside the ;-key.

```
;; ;'; ;';'; ;'; ;'; 39' 28' 47' 56' 10'
;; ;'; ;'"'; ;"; ;"; 39" 28" 47" 56" 10"
He ran it in 3' 56".  He is 5' 11" tall.
```

```
fr fr4 fr4$f f$f f$f $39 $28 $47 $56 $10
Send me $39 or $28 or $47 or $56 or $10.
```

Exclamation mark:
1. Type period.
2. Backspace once.
3. Type apos-
   trophe.

```
"Look!" Al shouted.  "Here's Tom's cap!"
The crowd shouted, "Watch that man run!"
My hat cost $10; Joe's cap cost only $2!
```

ALPHABET-REVIEW PARAGRAPHS *(Each, 2 times / si 1.29)*

◁ **50** ▷
DS

2-Min.
Writings
      1 | 2 | 3 | 4 | 5 | 6 | 7 | 8 | 9 | 10

```
 0 24      It's rumored that five or six squadrons from      9
 5 29   this wing will sortie to La Paz and back in July.    19
10 34      Our skipper plans one exercise to be a joint      28
14 38   operation with surface ships equipped with radar;    38
19 43   so we must fly to La Paz, even if there is a fog.     48
```

Plus ➧   1 | 2 | 3 | 4 | 5

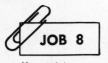

JOB 8

Manuscript
Page 8
In elite
Words: 342

THINGS TO NOTE:

1. A displayed quotation is blocked unless it begins a new paragraph in the original source (as was the case on page 276)
2. That the writer may insert a remark or explanation in a quotation by enclosing his words in brackets
3. That *Ibid.* in a footnote means "the same book as the one in the preceding footnote, but a *different* page" (whereas, *Loc. cit.* means "the same book and the *same* page")

CORRESPONDENCE MANUAL   Page 8

K. The Subject Line is a preview of the message and so is typed between the salutation and the body. It may be centered; it may be blocked at the left. It may be arranged in many different styles, as shown in Table 4, preceding page.

Most subject lines begin with the word Subject, followed by a colon or a dash. The Latin expressions Re and In re both mean subject and may be used instead of the English word.[7]

L. The Company Signature is typed in all-capital letters a double space below the complimentary closing. Illustrations of its use are shown in Table 3, page 6. It is often omitted, but Hutchinson points out that it may sometimes be required:

...on formal or contractual letters, in which the writer acts as a representative of his company /and not in his own behalf7, the company's name should always be typed...exactly as it is printed on the letterhead.[8]

M. Enclosure Notations are signals, like the ones shown in Table 5, next page, to remind both the sender and receiver of a letter that something is enclosed in the same envelope. The notation is typed one or two lines below the reference initials.

The notation is always helpful. It is essential when more than one item is enclosed or when the writer has reason to believe that "a third person is to mail the letter.../or7 to aid the receiver in checking the enclosures"[9] of the letter.

---

[7] John L. Rowe and Alan C. Lloyd, Gregg Typing, New Series (New York: Gregg, 1953), page 199.

[8] Hutchinson, op. cit., page 296.

[9] Ibid., page 298.

TECHNIQUE PRACTICE *(Center 1 copy)*

QUOTATION MARKS

The closing quotation mark goes—

1. After a period ....
2. After a comma ....
3. Before a semicolon ....
4. Before a colon ....
5. After a question mark if the quotation asks a question ....
6. Before a question mark if the question is not in the quotation ....
7. After an exclamation mark if the quotation makes an exclamation ....
8. Before an exclamation mark if the exclamation is not in the quotation ....

1. I said, "Please give that to us now."
2. "It was good to see Bill," said John.
3. He said, "Hand those over"; so I did.
4. Our "pledge": always to do our best.
5. She wrote, "When will it be shipped?"
6. Did she really say, "Oh, never mind"?
7. They shouted, "Yes, we won the game!"
8. How silly it is for him to "quibble"!

Lesson 21 : % ¢ @

WARMUP REVIEW *(Each line 2 times)*

```
a;sldkfjghfjdksla;sldkfjghfjdksla;sldkfj
Zyx Wvu Tsr Qpo Nml Kji Hgf Edc Ba ?/ :;
39' 28' 47' 56' 10'; 39" 28" 47" 56" 10"
Why did the new boy not get his day off?
```

12-Sec. 5| 10| 15| 20| 25| 30| 35| 40|

NEW STROKES *(Each line 2 times)*

LEFT HAND
F-finger controls
%, shift of 5.

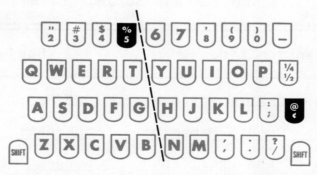

RIGHT HAND
;-finger reaches
right, to ¢.
;-finger controls
@, shift of ¢.

```
f5f  f5%f  f5%  f%f  f%f  39% 28% 47% 56% 10%
A 5% raise, a 10% dividend, a 15% bonus.
```

Type these 3 lines only if ¢ and @ are on the key beside the ;-key.

```
;¢;  ;¢¢;  ;¢;  ;¢;  ;¢;  39¢ 28¢ 47¢ 56¢ 10¢
;¢;  ;¢@;  ;@;  ;@;  39 @ 28 @ 47 @ 56 @ 10¢
Send me 10 @ 39¢ or 47 @ 28¢ if you can.
```

JOB 7

Manuscript
Page 7
In pica
Words: 326

CORRESPONDENCE MANUAL   Page 7

    I. The Reference Line is used in businesses where records
are kept in numerical files or where transactions are handled
by a very large staff. It is a line, When Replying, Refer to,
printed in the letterhead. The typist of the outgoing letter
types the correct file number alongside that reference guide.

    When replying to a letter with such a notation, a typist
includes a subject line (in which he refers to the same reference file number) in his letter of response.

    J. An Attention Line is an extension of the inside address
and is typed between the inside address and the salutation.
It is always preceded and followed by one blank line. It is
usually centered but may begin at the left margin. It may be
arranged in many different styles, as shown in Table 4, below.

Table 4

ATTENTION AND SUBJECT LINES

Attention Lines	Subject Lines
ATTENTION: CREDIT MANAGER	SUBJECT: SPECIAL SALE
Attention: Credit Manager	Subject: Special Sale
Attention of the President	Subject--Special Order
Attention of the President	Subject--Special Order
Attention Legal Department	Refer to File 158-6599
ATTENTION Legal Department	RE: The Lewiston Case
Attention--Mr. Jack Dennis	In re Shaw vs. Shipley

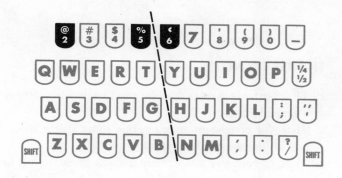

LEFT HAND
On some electrics, the @ sign is the shift of 2, typed by the S-finger.

RIGHT HAND
On some electrics, the ¢ sign is the shift of 6, typed by the J-finger.

Type these 3 lines only if @ is on 2 and ¢ is on 6.

```
j6j j6¢j j¢j j¢j j¢j 39¢ 28¢ 47¢ 56¢ 10¢
s2s s2@s s@s s@s 39 @ 28 @ 47 @ 56 @ 10¢
Send me 10 @ 39¢ or 47 @ 28¢ if you can.

He made 100% profit by selling 39 @ 10¢.
He bought 5% @ 28¢, 5% @ 39¢, 90% @ 47¢.
```

ALPHABET-REVIEW PARAGRAPHS *(Each, 2 times / si 1.35)*

◁ **60** ▷
DS

2-Min. Writings

| 1 | 2 | 3 | 4 | 5 | 6 | 7 | 8 | 9 | 10 | 11 | 12 |

0	35	Mr. Barque, we are very grateful for your assisting us	11
6	41	at our sixth company conference; we do realize how busy you	23
12	47	are. We found your talks to be both helpful and enjoyable.	35
18	53	Our executives have told me how much your zestful pre-	46
23	58	sentation pleased them, Mr. Barque. They feel that our men	58
29	64	will like their jobs more, thanks to the helps you gave us.	70

Plus ➡

| 1 | 2 | 3 | 4 | 5 | 6 |

THE TYPEWRITER BELL . . .

rings a few spaces before the carriage reaches the right margin stop, as a warning. Machines vary; count the number of warning spaces on your typewriter. Within that many spaces or strokes:

1. If possible, finish the word you are typing and then return the carriage; or,

2. Divide the word you are typing (if it is too long to be finished in the space left) and return the carriage; or,

3. Finish the word you are typing; if the line ends short, fill it by typing all or part of the next word. Return the carriage.

TECHNIQUE PRACTICE *(1 copy)*

◁ **40** ▷

Using a 40-space line and double spacing, and starting on line 23, type another copy of the Alphabet-Review Paragraphs (above). See whether you can type both paragraphs without looking up once. Here is how the first two lines will appear:

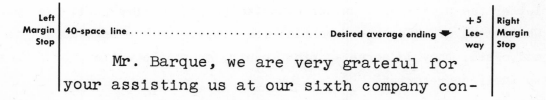

Left Margin Stop

40-space line . . . . Desired average ending ➡

+5 Lee-way

Right Margin Stop

```
    Mr. Barque, we are very grateful for
your assisting us at our sixth company con-
```

JOB 6

Manuscript
Page 6
In elite
Words: 253

THINGS TO NOTE:

1. That horizontal rules may be used to divide sections of a long table or, as here, a special display
2. That, for consistent spacing, one must single space before typing a ruled line and double space after typing it
3. That, to conserve space, only 2 blank lines are left here in each signature space, instead of the usual 3 blank lines

CORRESPONDENCE MANUAL   Page 6 ₂ ➡

Table 3

SOME CORRECT FORMS OF SIGNATURE ARRANGEMENTS ₁ ➡

                                                                             ₂ ➡

| Cordially yours, | Yours very truly, ₃ ➡ |
| President | President ₁ ➡ |

                                                                             ₂ ➡

| Very sincerely yours, | Respectfully submitted, ₃ ➡ |
| John Kerr, President | Tom Evans, Secretary |

Very truly yours,	Yours sincerely,
THE DOWN CORPORATION	HALE CONSTRUCTION COMPANY
Harrison Meyers	Richard F. Hughes
President	Vice-President

Yours truly,	Very cordially yours,
THE INTERNATIONAL COMPANY	S T Y L E , I N C .
Alexander Parke	Miss Ruth Osborne
Chairman of the Board	Advertising Department

                                                                             ₄ ➡

SUPPLEMENTAL LETTER PARTS

In the course of many years of business communication, the business letter has picked up a number of extra parts to serve particular purposes. While none of these are essential for getting the message across to the addressee, they do serve as aids to him, or to the writer, or to both, or to their secretaries.

Table 2, page 3, lists eight supplemental letter parts.

WARMUP REVIEW (Each line 2 times)

◁ **40** ▷

```
a;sldkfjghfjdksla;sldkfjghfjdksla;sldkfj
ZyX WvU TsR QpO NmL KjI HgF EdC Ba ?/ :;
39% 28% 47% 56% 10%; 39¢ 28¢ 47¢ 56¢ 10¢
The boy did not yet ask for his day off.
```
12-Sec. 5| 10| 15| 20| 25| 30| 35| 40|

NEW STROKES (Each line 2 times)

On some electrics, the asterisk (*) is shift of 8, and underscore is shift of hyphen.

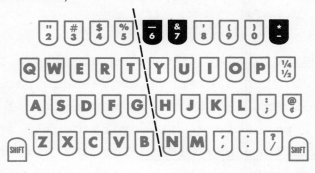

RIGHT HAND
J-finger controls under-score, shift of 6.
J-finger controls &, shift of 7.
;-finger controls *, shift of hyphen.

Type these 3 lines only if underscore is on 6 and asterisk is on hyphen.

```
j6j j6_j j6_j j_j j_j 39 28 47 56 and 10
;-; ;-*; ;*; ;*; ;*; 39* 28* 47* 56* 10*
Hale* said it in Chapter II of Your Age.
```

Type these 3 lines only if underscore is on hyphen and asterisk is on 8.

```
;-; ;-_; ;-_; ;_; ;_; 39 28 47 56 and 10
k8k k8*k k*k k*k k*k 39* 28* 47* 56* 10*
Hale* said it in Chapter II of Your Age.
```

```
j7j j7&j j7&j j&j 39 & 28 & 47 & 56 & 10
Jones & Co., Smith & Co., Wilson & Bros.
*Adam Hale, of Martin & Sons, I believe.
```

ALPHABET-REVIEW PARAGRAPHS (Each, 2 times / si 1.29)

◁ **50** ▷ *
DS

2-Min. Writings

  1 | 2 | 3 | 4 | 5 | 6 | 7 | 8 | 9 | 10 | 11 | 12

0	34
6	40
11	45
17	51
23	57
29	63

```
     To underline a word or line, first type what must be        11
underscored.  Next, quickly move the carriage back to the        22
first stroke to be underlined--by pushing the carriage or,       34
if you have just five or fewer spaces, by backspacing.  With     46
a zipping, light touch, tap the underscore key once for each     58
space or stroke that you are to put a line under.                68
```

Plus ▶   1 | 2 | 3 | 4 | 5 | 6

* The copy is on a 60-space line, but you are to use a 50-space line—and listen for the bell.

JOB 5

Manuscript
Page 5
In pica
Words: 326

THINGS TO NOTE:

1. That omissions in a quotation are shown by an "ellipsis": four periods when it comes at the end of a sentence or when the omission includes the end of a sentence; otherwise, three periods
2. That *op. cit.* in footnotes means "the book already mentioned, by this same author or authors"
3. That two footnotes, if short enough, can be typed on one line

CORRESPONDENCE MANUAL   Page 5

  E. The Body contains the message. It is most likely to be single spaced with a blank line between paragraphs. If a letter is very short (50 or fewer words) or if it is a report that is several pages long, it may be double spaced.

  F. The Complimentary Closing is the signing-off phrase. It begins at the left margin in some letter arrangements; but most commonly it begins at, or near, the center. It almost always ends with a comma. Only the first word is capitalized.

  G. The Signer's Identification, which is typed under the space left for the handwritten signature, may be the name, or the title (or department), or both, of the writer. Illustrations of various arrangements and various combinations of the signer's identifications are included in Table 3, next page.

  Ordinarily, 3 blank lines are left for the penwritten signature; but some leeway is allowed: "...you may leave as few as 2 or as many as 6 lines...."[5]

  H. The Reference Initials include (1) the initials of the person who dictated the letter, (2) then some kind of separation mark or a space, and (3) then the typist's own initials.

  The two most common forms are DIC:TYP and DIC/typ; but d-t, DCp, and other combinations are equally acceptable when those concerned know what they mean. Reference initials are normally typed at the left margin, a double space below the signer's identification; but they can be higher or lower.[6]

_____

 [5] Lloyd, op. cit., page 153.   [6] Smith, op. cit., page 201.

TECHNIQUE PRACTICE

◁ **40** ▷
DS

(Center 1 copy on a half sheet)

DISPLAY TECHNIQUES ₃ ➡

Indenting
Underscoring
Using All Caps
Vertical Centering
Horizontal Centering
Using Double Spacing

```
                 DISPLAY TECHNIQUES

                     Indenting
                    Underscoring
                   Using All Caps
                 Vertical Centering
               Horizontal Centering
               Using Double Spacing
```

There are 33 lines (½ of 66) on a half sheet; 33 − 14 = 19, and 19 ÷ 2 = 9½, or 9. So the adjacent Technique Practice should begin on line 9.

Lesson 23 : Review

WARMUP REVIEW *(Each line 2 times)*

◁ **40** ▷

```
a;sldkfjghfjdksla;sldkfjghfjdksla;sldkfj
zyxwvutsrqponmlkjihgfedcba : ½1234567890
The two old men and the boy got the pay.
```
12-Sec. 5| 10| 15| 20| 25| 30| 35| 40|

SPEED-UP PREVIEW *(Each line 2 times)*

```
important emphasize expert strokes judge
quick never know what item most type one
the how may say big is us to up we or in
```

ALPHABET-REVIEW PARAGRAPHS *(Each, 1 time / si 1.26)*

◁ **60** ▷ *
DS

2-Min. Writings		1 | 2 | 3 | 4 | 5 | 6 | 7 | 8 | 9 | 10	
0	35	It is very hard to know what one item is the	9
5	40	important thing to emphasize in learning how to	19
10	45	type. One expert may say that using quick strokes	29
15	50	is half the job, half the art.	35
18	53	Another judge will claim that a big thing to	44
22	57	emphasize is posture. All experts tell us that it	54
27	62	is quite important for us never to look up; we must	65
32	67	keep our eyes on our work.	70

1 | 2 | 3 | 4 | 5

Plus ➡

* The copy is on a 50-space line, but you are to use a 60-space line—and listen for the bell.

JOB

Manuscript
Page 4
In elite
Words: 299

THINGS TO NOTE:

1. That a quotation that will fill less than 3 full lines, as in paragraph 1, is quoted in the running text and not displayed
2. That a quotation that will fill 3 or more lines is single spaced and indented 5 spaces from each margin
3. That *Loc. cit.* in the footnote means "in exactly the same place indicated in the preceding footnote"

CORRESPONDENCE MANUAL   Page 4 ₃ ➡

    C. The Inside Address includes the identification and the mailing address of the addressee. It is normally typed above the body of the letter; but, as one expert, Smith, observes, "...in personal letters, in Government correspondence, and in formal letters it may be placed below the body."[3]

    When the business title of an addressee is used in addition to his name, the title may be placed after the name, or on a line by itself, or at the start of the next line--

> Mr. Harry Loft, Manager
> Florida Fashion Company
>
> Dr. Lawrence Coulter
> Secretary-Treasurer
>
> Miss Rowena G. Thompson
> Manager, Seabeach Hotel

In a display like this, center longest line and align the other lines with it.

--depending on the lengths of the name and title. A principle for placing titles and using abbreviations is stated by Smith:

> The typist should attempt always to keep the lines of the inside address about even in length, but should avoid the use of abbreviations unless the full word would be <u>much</u> too long.[4]

    D. The Salutation is placed between the inside address and body. It is typed at the left margin, always preceded and followed by a blank line. It is almost always followed by the colon. One should capitalize only the first word, any title, and any noun; thus, <u>Dear Doctor Jones</u> and <u>My dear Doctor Jones</u>. ₁ ➡

─────────────────────── 2 ➡

[3] Harold H. Smith, <u>College Typewriting Technique</u> (New York: Gregg, 1952), page 198.

[4] <u>Loc. cit.</u>

COMPLETE NUMBER-SYMBOL REVIEW (*Each line 1 time*)

◁ **50** ▷
DS

Copy these 7 lines.

3 *and* #	ddd d3d#d Do we need 3313 of #333 or 333 of #3313?
4 *and* $	fff f4f$f He gave $4 to Joe, $4 to Bill, $4 to me.
5 *and* %	fff f5f%f We should get 5% interest on 5% bonuses.
7 *and* &	jjj j7j&j Hale & Sons got 7 or 77 from Smith & Co.
9 *and* (	lll l9l(l ;;; ;0;); The 90 men (90th Regiment) may
0 *and*)	destroy (a) 900 rounds and (b) 90 shells (9 inch).
½ *and* ¼	;;; ;½;¼; 3 minus ½ is 2½, the same as 1¼ plus 1¼.

Copy these 5 lines if your machine has THESE combinations of numbers and symbols; or . . .

2 *and* "	sss s2s"s "Send 22 knives, 22 forks," said "Duke."
6 *and* _	jjj j6j_j Try for 666, but get at least 66 extras.
8 *and* '	kkk k8k'k The class of '88 drew 88's on Bob's cap.
– *and* *	;;; ;-;*; My son-in-law* has dyed-in-the-wool sox.
¢ *and* @	;;; ;¢;@; Yes, 11 @ 1¢ is 11¢; and 1 @ 11¢ is 11¢.

Copy these 5 lines if your machine has THESE combinations of numbers and symbols.

2 *and* @	sss s2s@s We bought 22 @ 12; 222 @ 21; and 2 @ 22.
6 *and* ¢	jjj j6j¢j Ten cost 6¢, six cost 16¢, two cost 61¢.
8 *and* *	kkk k8k*k The 1888 report* said Arnold* had 8 men.
' *and* "	;;; ;';"; "What is Mary's 'pet peeve'?" she asked.
– *and* _	;;; ;-;_; The son-in-law did have a two-tone Ford.

. . . and these if you have these keys.

| = *and* + | ;;; ;½=; ;½+; ;=;+; 11 + 11 = 22 and 22 + 11 = 33. |
| 1 *and* ! | aaa aqla aq!a a1a!a I want 1! I want 11! No, 12! |

Part 1
LESSON
Unit 4
23

JOB 3

Manuscript
Page 3
In pica
Words: 280

THINGS TO NOTE:

1. That *Table 2* begins only 2 lines under the running head, instead of the usual 3, because the heading is such a short line
2. That 2 lines precede the separation line above the footnote instead of the usual 1, to give *29 June 1958* more display
3. That *et al.* in the footnote means "and others," an abbreviation used when a book has three or more coauthors

CORRESPONDENCE MANUAL   Page 3 ₂➤

Table 2

PARTS OF THE BUSINESS LETTER ₁➤

Essential Parts	Supplemental Parts
A. Letterhead	I. Reference Line
B. Date Line	J. Attention Line
C. Inside Address	K. Subject Line
D. Salutation	L. Company Signature
E. Body	M. Enclosure Notation
F. Complimentary Closing	N. Postscript
G. Signer's Identification	O. CC Notation
H. Reference Initials	P. BCC Notation

    A. The Letterhead contains the name and address of the
company, in print. Most letterheads are 1 3/4 inches wide, but
they may be as narrow as 1 inch and as deep as 3 inches. When
a letterhead is more than 1 3/4 inches wide, the date should be
positioned at least 2 lines below the bottom of the printing.[2]

    B. The Date Line contains the month, day, and year. In
business letters it always appears in this form:

                         June 29, 1958
In special display letters, the date may be shown like this:

                              J u n e
                           Twenty-Nine
                             1 9 5 8
In military correspondence, date lines appear in this form:

                         29 June 1958 ₂➤

_____

    [2] Alan C. Lloyd, et al., Gregg Typewriting for Colleges
(New York: Gregg, 1957), page 49.

WARMUP REVIEW *(Each line 2 times)* ◁**50**▷

```
aa ;; ss ll dd kk ff jj gg hh ff jj dd kk ss ll aa
and big fix how ink job men que sic try vel you zip
"39" "28" "47" "56" "10"; (39) (28) (47) (56) (10).
They said that they find that they must wait there.
```
12-Sec. 5| 10| 15| 20| 25| 30| 35| 40| 45| 50|

NUMBER REVIEW *(Each line 2 times)*

```
we 23 wet 235 were 2343 weep 2330 pep 030 pet 035
up 70 pup 070 pure 0743 pore 0943 ore 943 ire 843
yo 69 you 697 your 6974 pour 0974 our 974 out 975
```

WORD-DIVISION REVIEW *(Each line 2 times)*

Line 1: Divide after the one-letter syllable that occurs within a word. *Line 2:* Do not separate a one-letter syllable from the beginning or ending of a word. *Line 3:* Do not break up the syllable *ment* at the end of a word. *Line 4:* Many common words divide easily between double letters.

```
domi-nate posi-tive resi-dence heri-tage mani-fest
around enough about aboard aware ideal hearty many
judg-ment frag-ment ship-ment pay-ment compli-ment
sum-mary com-ments let-tered run-ning intel-ligent
```

RHYTHM PREVIEW *(Each line 2 times)*

```
very kind long list very much this same long time
have done for all our men and are did you the job
and the was aid for you may the to be it of up we
```

ALPHABET-REVIEW PARAGRAPHS *(Each, 1 time / si 1.20)* ◁**50**▷ *
DS

2-Min. Writings | 1 | 2 | 3 | 4 | 5 | 6 | 7 | 8 | 9 | 10 | 11 | 12

```
 0      Dear Miss Queen:  It was very kind of you to correct    11
 6  our long list of jobbers.  We have needed to have it fixed   22
11  up for a long time.  All our men realize what a big task     34
17  you did and are grateful.                                    39
20      Would it be possible for you to do this same task        49
25  every week, Miss Queen?  It would be exactly the job you     61
31  have done--the same size and arrangement.  We should very    72
36  much like to have your aid.                                  78
```
Plus ▶   1 | 2 | 3 | 4 | 5 | 6

* The copy is on a 60-space line, but you are to use a 50-space line—and listen for the bell.

JOB 2

Manuscript
Page 2
In elite
Words: 304

THINGS TO NOTE:
1. That an extra blank line precedes a centered subheading
2. That an extra blank line precedes an all-cap sideheading
3. That a 2-inch typed line separates text and footnote
4. That "ff" in the footnote means "and following pages"
5. That when a table is mentioned, its location is given

CORRESPONDENCE MANUAL   Page 2   7/3

and 200 words. He uses his judgment in perfecting a placement arrangement that will, for his letterhead, fit letters in the 100-200 span
"well enough." He spreads shorter letters by--

> Indent listings the same as a paragraph or center longest line and align the other lines with it.

    1. Allowing more space after the date
    2. Dividing the letter into more paragraphs
    3. Allowing more space for the signature
    4. Lowering the reference symbols

--to make them average in length, so that he can use his basic placement
plan for them, too. When he has longer letters, he reverses the procedure: He condenses the longer letters by--

    1. Allowing less space after the date
    2. Dividing the letter into fewer paragraphs
    3. Edging the lines a little farther to the right
    4. Allowing less space for the signature
    5. Raising the reference symbols.

--to make them, too, fit his basic plan. Only for extremely long or short
letters does he make a margin adjustment. His basic plan: Make all letters fit the space of an average one.

Part 2. Parts of a Letter

    A business letter may have as many as 16 different parts,[1] as listed
in Table 2, next page, although it is rare that any one letter would ever
contain them all.

ESSENTIAL LETTER PARTS

    Every business letter has eight parts that are so basic that the let-
ter would be incomplete if any one of them were omitted. These parts are
listed in Table 2, next page.

---

[1] Lois I. Hutchinson, <u>Standard Handbook for Secretaries</u>, Seventh
Edition (New York: McGraw-Hill, 1956), page 290 ff.

TECHNIQUE PRACTICE *(Center 1 copy)*

Read these rules before typing the examples:

DO NOT SPACE . . .

PUNCTUATION SPACING

a. Between quotation marks and the words enclosed . . . . Mr. Black said, "Come along, son."

b. Between parentheses and the material enclosed . . . . Fred Hale (our president) replied.

c. Before or after a hyphen . . . . My brother-in-law joined the Army.

d. Before or after a dash *(two hyphens)* . . . . I tried hard--but not hard enough.

e. Between numbers and a decimal point . . . . My 3.9% Federal bond costs $28.47.

f. Before or after a comma used in numbers . . . . He sold us 3,928 grams for $1,000.

g. Between number sign and numbers used with it . . . . Order #372-928 weighed about 746#.

h. Before per cent sign . . . . Their 5% bonds will be sold @ 5½%.

i. Before apostrophe and quotation marks used for feet, inches . . . . . . This is 39' 10" long and 10' wide.

j. Before apostrophe and quotation marks used for minutes, seconds . The sloop made the mile in 4' 26".

k. After period following an uncapitalized abbreviation . . . . It may cost $1,000 f.o.b. Detroit.

l. Before or after a colon used to indicate time . . . . On an 11:45 a.m. or 1:15 p.m. bus?

OPTIONAL TECHNIQUE PRACTICE *(Center 1 copy)*

Rarely must a typist use special symbols not on his typewriter; but when occasion demands, he should be able to construct or apply these characters.

	NAME	EXAMPLE	CONSTRUCTION
a.	Times	What is 2 x 2?	expressed by small letter *x*.
b.	Equals	12 x 12 = 144.	two hyphens, one below the other *(turn roll by hand)*.
c.	Minus	106 - 14 = 92.	a single hyphen.
d.	Divided by	144 ÷ 12 = 12.	hyphen intersected by colon.
e.	Plus	92 + 14 = 106.	hyphen intersected by apostrophe *(turn roll by hand)*.
f.	Degrees	Freeze at 32°.	small letter *o*, raised slightly *(turn roll by hand)*.
g.	Superiors	$4^3 - 5^2 = 39^a$.	type number or letter above line *(turn roll by hand)*.
h.	Inferiors	H_2O is--water!	type number below line *(turn roll by hand)*.
i.	Star	✭ ✭ ✭ ✭ ✭	capital *A* typed over small letter *v*.
j.	Bracket	He ⟋Williams⟍	diagonals, with underscores facing inside.
k.	Caret	We tried/hard.	underscore, diagonal; center inserted word.
l.	Pounds	£5 is English.	capital *L* typed over small letter *f*.
m.	Romans	Chapter XXXVI.	capitals of *I, V, X, L, C,* and *M*.
n.	Cents	He charged 2¢.	small *c*, intersected by diagonal.
o.	Military zero	Start at 18ØØ.	*o*, intersected by diagonal.

CORRESPONDENCE MANUAL ₃ ➡

Part 1. Letter Placement

A letter should be so arranged that the margins serve as a white frame around the letter. In general, the arrangement should be in the same proportion as the paper (longer than wide) and be approximately centered in the writing area. The bottom margin should be slightly wider than the side margins.

Many letter-placement plans have been developed; but none are completely satisfactory, because the length of letters and the width of letterheads vary widely. Table 1, below, shows one plan that is widely used by learners; even it, however, is just a general guide and has to be adapted for many letters.

The veteran office typist does not use a guide. He knows that a great majority of business letters contain between 100₄ ➡

Manuscript tables go at top or bottom of page, separated from running text by ½-inch space.

Table 1

LETTER-PLACEMENT PLAN

(With date on line 14, but at least 2 lines below letterhead) ₁ ➡

Letter Factor	Short	Average	Long
Words in the body	Under 100	100-200	Over 200
Length of Line	4 inches	5 inches	6 inches
Date to address	8 lines	6 lines	4 lines

For this test you will need 1 sheet of plain paper or Workbook page 19-20. Type Parts A and B on one side and Parts C and D on the other. Using the grading scales provided, correct and grade each part of the test.

PART A: STRAIGHT-COPY ALPHABET-REVIEW TEST *(si 1.15)*

◁ **50** ▷
DS
10
▽

Take two 2-minute writings on the paragraph; grade the better paper of the two. Or, type 1 complete copy and grade it as though you had typed it at 32 words a minute.

Step 1: Compute words a minute.	Step 2: Deduct for errors—		Step 3: Grade the remaining words a minute this way:	30 or higher: A 25 to 29 wam: B 20 to 24 wam: C 15 to 19 wam: D
	1 error: —2 2 errors: —4 3 errors: —6	4 errors: — 9 5 errors: —12 6 errors: —15		

2-Min. Writings

    1 | 2 | 3 | 4 | 5 | 6 | 7 | 8 | 9 | 10

0 The group of us stood by the small twig fire   9

5 and wished we could be dry, even if just for five   19

10 minutes. Max pushed a wet stick into the flames.   29

15 It squeaked and sizzled in the blaze, and then it   39

20 burst into long tongues of smoke. We jumped back   49

25 quickly and yelled at Max. He was quietly laugh-   59

30 ing at us for jumping back from the bit of smoke.   69

Plus ▶   1 | 2 | 3 | 4 | 5

PART B: STRAIGHT-COPY NUMBER-REVIEW TEST *(si 1.00)*

Begin 6 lines below Part A.
▽

Take two 1-minute writings on the lines of numbers below; grade the better of the two. Or, type 1 complete copy and grade your work on the "15 to 17" part of this grading scale.

Examples: 15 with 3 errors is C; 12 with 1 error is B.	SPEED	11 to 14			15 to 17				18 or more			
	ERRORS	3	2	1-0	4	3	2	1-0	5	4	3	2-0
	GRADE	D	C	B	D	C	B	A	D	C	B	A

    1 | 2 | 3 | 4 | 5 | 6 | 7 | 8 | 9 | 10

1101 2202 3303 4404 5505 6606 7707 8808 9909 1010   10

1111 1212 1313 1414 1515 1616 1717 1818 1919 2020   20

2121 2222 2323 2424 2525 2626 2727 2828 2929 3030   30

3131 3232 3333 3434 3535 3636 3737 3838 3939 4040   40

Part 1
LESSON
Test 1
25

UNIT 32
SUSTAINED MANUSCRIPTS

This unit will help you build sustained *go* power in typing manuscripts. The unit is a 10-page manuscript. It reviews what you should remember about letters. It gives you practice in typing tables in running context. It illustrates the arrangement of a formal report, complete with footnotes and quotations.

The unit will be easiest if, before starting the jobs, you (*a*) review pages 101-104 and 126; (*b*) study pages 272-283 of this unit carefully; and (*c*) answer the study questions on Workbook pages 289-290.

The pages are shown in facsimile, as they should be arranged (except that some have been telescoped somewhat to make room for the helpful notations at the tops of the pages). You will be able to copy half the pages exactly, line for line; for, half the pages are in pica type, and half are in elite.

Type the manuscript in *sidebound* form with one carbon copy that you can keep for future reference. You may use the visual guide in your workbook—or make your own:

Visual guide should show:

A. **Top margins of 2 inches on first page, 1 inch on other pages.**

B. **Side margins of 1 inch at right, 1½ at left.**

C. **Bottom margin, 1 to 1½ inches wide.**

D. **Warning signal, 1 inch above bottom margin.**

E. **Centering line midway between side margins.**

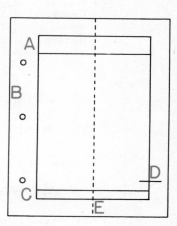

While on this unit, start each period by copying this material:

CONTROL SENTENCES:

◁ **60** ▷

½-Min. Writings

si 1.26

	1	2	3	4	5	6	7	8	9	10	11	12	

Kay reviewed the subject before giving Max and Paul a quiz.   12
My fine black ax just zipped through the wood quite evenly.   24
Jacqueline was very glad the day her film took a prize box.   36
Jack found the gravel camp six below zero quite a few days.   48

SPEED PARAGRAPHS:

1-Min. Writings

si 1.11

	1	2	3	4	5	6	7	8	9	10	11	12	

If you put a lot of little stones and one or two big stones   12
in a bottle and shake it, the big ones will quickly rise to   24
the top. Turn the bottle upside down and shake it, and the   36
big stones are back at the top in no time flat. There is a   48
moral in that story, and it has to do with life. When life   60
is dull, no one rises; it takes a shake to find the leader.   72

si 1.17

The men ran down the dock to catch the light lines spouting   12 | 84
from the deck of the big ship. Hauling in these lines, the   24 | 96
men on the dock pulled the big cables from the sides of the   36 | 108
ship and soon had the ends looped over the mooring posts on   48 | 120
the dock. The deck engines whirred into action, taking the   60 | 132
dips from the cables and inching the ship against the dock.   72 | 144

PART C: CENTERING TEST

Center the following list of names in the top half of the page (assume that you are using only a half sheet), centering the group of lines vertically and each line horizontally. If you center horizontally as you should, the letter *I* in every line will line up vertically. Correct your work and grade it on this grading scale:

◁ **40** ▷
SS
?
▽

TAKE OFF:	—3 if top margin is incorrect* —2 for each line not centered horizontally —1 for each typographic or other error	TOTAL PENALTY	8-7	6-5	4-3	2-0
		GRADE	D	C	B	A

*To check top margin: Fold top of paper down to bottom of last name; then crease paper. The crease should run through or slightly below the second name on the list.

```
Richard I. Edwards
Alvin Dwight Smith
Quintin Dark
Aloysius Witt
Henry Ira Brown
Griffith Dunn
Dominic Wirt
J. Gilbert
Emil Lisle Park
Demetrius Kinn
Paul Patrick Everett
Philip Hall
George I. Martin
```

PART D: SYMBOLS AND PROOFREADING TEST

Begin 6 lines below Part C.
▽

Each of the following pairs of sentences shows a right and a wrong way to use symbols and numbers. Select and copy the sentences that are typed correctly. Your finished paper should contain only the 10 correct sentences, one below another, numbered from 1 to 10. If you do this correctly, all lines will end evenly. Correct your work and grade it on this grading scale.

TAKE OFF:	—3 for typing the wrong sentence —2 for each error in typing a symbol or number —1 for each error of any other kind	TOTAL PENALTY	8-7	6-5	4-3	2-0
		GRADE	D	C	B	A

```
1.  Send us 28# of #10 nails.    or   1.  Send him #28 of 10# nails.
2.  Rush them to Mills & Co.!    or   2.  Rush it out to Mills & Co!
3.  They prefer a %15 discount.  or   3.  We prefer a 15% discount.
4.  Ask them for 1,200 @ 16¢.    or   4.  John asked for 1,200@16¢.
5.  Can we take 1/4 or 1/2 off?  or   5.  Do they need ¼ or ½ more?
6.  Where are his "favorites?"   or   6.  Where are my "favorites"?
7.  Deliver the 10 1/3 boxes.    or   7.  Send over the 10-1/3 boxes.
8.  Could we have $114,please?   or   8.  May we have $114, please?
9.  He may - or may not - help.  or   9.  He may--or may not--help.
10. Joe (senior) is not here.    or   10. Joe (senior) is not there.
```

Table 16

WHERE OUR EMPLOYEES WENT ON VACATION, IF THEY WENT ANYWHERE

Place	Men	Women	Both
Metropolitan City	18%	34%	25%
Seaside Resort	20%	26%	22%
Mountain Resort	19%	16%	18%
Motor Trip	16%	13%	14%
Lake Resort	12%	6%	9%
Skiing Resort	6%	4%	5%
Fishing Resort	8%	1%	5%
Camping	8%	1%	5%
Cruise	1%	6%	4%
Miscellaneous	5%	8%	6%
TOTALS*	113%	115%	113%

Sequence of items should have some pattern. Here, they are listed by their importance, indicated by "Both" scores in last column. Sequence could be alphabetic.

"Miscellaneous" or "others" item is always at the bottom of a list.

"Totals" may be blocked or may be indented 1 space for each column in the table.

Per cent sign must be repeated every time. It cannot be dropped like a $ sign.

When columns get narrower, shift the tab stops.

* Totals exceed 100% because some employees went to more than one place on their vacations.

Center a 1-line footnote, but arrange a longer one as shown here.

JOB 9 Dictated unarranged table
Words: 77

JOB 10 Dictated unarranged table
Words: 126

Mr. Hildreth continues his dictation.

"Now for Table 2," he says. "It is to be entitled *Do Our Supervisors Recommend That* on the first line, and *A Coffee Break Be Authorized?* on a second line.

"Table 2 has five columns. They are to be headed *Dept., Yes, Indifferent, No,* and, of course, *Total.*

"Department A has 2 yes, 1 indifferent, 1 no, for a total of 4. Department B has 4 yes, 1 indifferent, and 0 no, for a total of 5. Department C has 4 yes, 0 indifferent, 0 no, and a total of 4. Department D has 3 yes, 0 indifferent, 0 no, for a total of 3. Department E has 3 yes, 0 indifferent, 1 no, for a total of 4. Department F has 3 yes, 1 indifferent, 1 no, for a total of 5. The bottom totals are 19 yes, 3 indifferent, 3 no, for a 25 total."

"Table 3," says Mr. Hildreth, "also has a 2-line title; you'll have to experiment to see how to arrange it best. It is *What 382 Large Firms Have Found Upon Introducing Coffee Breaks, Serviced by a Caterer.*

"There are four columns. Head them *Question, Yes, Perhaps,* and *No.*

"Question *Has it been popular?* got 95% yes, 3% perhaps, 2% no. Question *Has it improved morale?* got 80% yes, 15% perhaps, 5% no. Question *Has it reduced tardiness?* got 72% yes, 18% perhaps, 10% no. Question *Has it saved time?* got 60% yes, 30% perhaps, 10% no. Question *Has it been convenient?* got 60% yes, 25% perhaps, 15% no. Question *Has it been inexpensive?* got 50% yes, 0% perhaps, 50% no. Question *Has it reduced absenteeism?* got 40% yes, 36% perhaps, 35% no. Question *Would you recommend it?* got 80% yes, 12% perhaps, 8% no. There are no total figures."

ORGANIZATION . . .

1. The remaining lessons in this book are in 25-lesson *parts*. Each part includes four 6-lesson *units* and a test, like this:

> **A 6-lesson unit on skill building**
> **A 6-lesson unit on correspondence**
> **A 6-lesson unit on tables or forms**
> **A 6-lesson unit on manuscripts**
> **A final (25th) lesson that is a Test**

2. The first of the four units is always a drive for more skill. The other three units are *production units* in which you learn how to apply your skill to the production of practical business papers.

THE SKILL-DRIVE UNITS . . .

1. Each skill-drive unit consists of 2 lessons on speed, 2 on control (accuracy), and 2 on numbers and symbols.

2. A full practice period should be devoted to each lesson in a skill drive.

3. The skill-drive lessons are so helpful that you can profitably return to them and retype them many times. Any time you feel your speed is slipping, retype any speed-building lesson. If your accuracy weakens, retype any control-building lesson.

THE PRODUCTION UNITS . . .

1. The 6 lessons in each production unit are divided into 3 pairs of lessons.

2. The first pair introduces and gives practice in a new production technique.

3. The second pair introduces and gives practice in another technique—like, but somewhat different from, the first one.

4. The third pair is a review of both techniques and of all other production techniques introduced in that same part.

5. Each pair of production lessons includes skill-drill material, to sustain or even add to the power developed in the preceding skill-drive unit. Skill-drill material may be used in either, or both, of the production lessons. Alternate plans for using any pair of production lessons:

Activity	Plan No. 1		Plan No. 2	
	Period 1	Period 2	Period 1	Period 2
Skill drill	1/3	1/3	2/3	. . .
Production	2/3	2/3	1/3	3/3

DIRECTIONAL SIGNALS . . .

The following signals, some of which are familiar and some of which are new to you, will be used from this point on:

◁40▷ ◁5 in.▷	New paper; margins for line (in spaces or inches) indicated.
5 ◗	Indent number spaces indicated.
4 ➡	Drop down number lines indicated.
DS	Use double spacing.
SS	Use single spacing.
Words: 92	Number 5-stroke words in exercise.
Words: 105 Body: 87	Number 5-stroke words in a letter, with number in the body only.
26 ▽	Line on which to start typing.
12-Sec. 10| 15| 20| 25| 30|	This scale counts words-a-minute speed on 12-second writings on speed sentences. See page 19.
1 | 2 | 3 | 4 | 5 | 6 | 7 |	Word-count scale. See pages 12-13.
2-Minute Writings 0 28 5 33	This material particularly fine for timed practice of the length indicated. See page 26 for use of numbers in determining your speed.

PRODUCTION PRACTICE (*Jobs 1-4*)

There are 4 exercises (jobs) for you to do in this pair of lessons.

Job 1
Pica

This production exercise is shown in pica type. You can copy it exactly if your machine is pica (but you cannot if it is elite).

(Each line 2 times)

Minimum number of copies to type.

LOOKING AHEAD

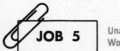

JOB 5 Unarranged table
Words: 65

"The next job is easier, but it does require your making another tally," says Mr. Hildreth. "Mr. Dorsey wants the score on the number of women vs. the number of men who were employed, January through May, in each office. Let's see: You'll have four columns in the table: *Branch, Men, Women,* and *Total.*"

"Original and two carbons?" you ask.

"Yes," he replies. "Centered, full page."

JOB 6 Unarranged table
Words: 63

"While you were typing that job," says Mr. Hildreth, "I got the next one ready. This is the same as the one you just did except that it shows the percentages instead of the actual figures. Please center this on the page. Yes, with two carbons. Thanks."

New Employees--All Branches

Branch	Men	Women
Chicago	66.7%	33.3%
New York	66.7%	33.3%
San Francisco	40.0%	60.0%
TOTAL	60.0%	40.0%

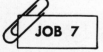

JOB 7 Unarranged table
Words: 131

"Next," says Mr. Hildreth, "please make a tally *by departments*. Mr. Dorsey wants to know which departments in each branch are taking on the new employees."

Your tally sheet will have five columns on it: *Department, Chicago, New York, San Francisco,* and *Total.* You make your tally and check the totals: Chicago 18, New York 12, San Francisco 10. Then, looking in the files, you see [top, right] how your predecessor in this job arranged similar material.

NEW EMPLOYEES--ALL BRANCHES			
(By Departments)			
January 1 - June 30, 1955			
Department	Chicago	New York	San Francisco	Total
Accounting	2	1	-	3
Advertising	1	2	1	4
Boys' Wear	-	1	-	1
Building	1	-	2	3

Subtitles of a table tell a lot.

JOB 8 Dictated unarranged table
Words: 89

"Well," says Mr. Hildreth, as you finish Job 7, "we are ready to start a new project—an investigation that I have been making for Mr. Dorsey. My report consists of three tables, and I think they are interesting."

Mr. Hildreth hands you the table that is shown at the top of the *next* page.

"This is the *form* I want you to use," he says. "Center each table on a full page. Use horizontal rules, as shown here. Use double spacing. Put the columns 6 spaces apart. One of the titles will go on one line; but two of them will take two lines, as shown in this model table."

You make a note to study the sample table *very* closely. You are not to type *it.*

"I must leave on a short trip," says Mr. Hildreth, "and I know that you could not understand my scribbled notes. So, let me dictate the tables. Here is the first one:

"Table 1 is entitled *Do Our Employees Take A Coffee Break?* There are five columns, to be headed *Dept., Often, Sometimes, Never,* and *Total.* Department A has 12 often, 18 sometimes, 3 never, for a total of 33. Department B has 18 often, 21 sometimes, 11 never, for a total of 50. Department C has 16 often, 6 sometimes, 3 never, for a total of 25. Department D has 19 often, 10 sometimes, 4 never, for a total of 33. Department E has 13 often, 9 sometimes, 3 never, for a total of 25. Department F has 20 often, 4 sometimes, and 10 never, for a total of 34. The bottom totals are 98 often, 70 sometimes, 34 never, for a total of 200."

PART 2

WARMUP: Alphabet Review *(Each line 2 times)*

```
a; sl a;sl dk a;sldk fj a;sldkfj gh a;sldkfjgh a;
work wish they lazy quit cove oak six jam pay own
and the in so do to is it if ox or go do by an am
```

SPEED DRILL: Word Families *(Each line 2 times)*

```
than thus them thou then thud they thug that thin
fort fowl form fore fork ford folk fold foes foul
bush busy burn bunk bury bulk buff bulb bull burr
```

SPEED SENTENCES *(Each line 2 times)*

```
       1 | 2 | 3 | 4 | 5 | 6 | 7 | 8 | 9 | 10
```

12-Sec.
Writings

```
It is their duty to pay us for the six fuel signs.   10
She is busy with the big social but may come down.   20
The forms she got for them may also work for this.   30
```

12-Sec. 5| 10| 15| 20| 25| 30| 35| 40| 45| 50|

SPEED PARAGRAPH *(2 copies / si 1.05)*

```
       1 | 2 | 3 | 4 | 5 | 6 | 7 | 8 | 9 | 10
```

1-Min.
Writings

```
There is just one sure way that we can get from a   10
job what we should like to get, and that seems to   20
be to build a keen liking for it.  The person who   30
likes his work is the one who moves up out of it.   40
```

SPEED PREVIEW *(Each line 2 times)*

```
lesson longer smooth times pace even best try set
fingers flying least speed part help type you way
```

SUSTAINED-SPEED PARAGRAPH *(2 copies / si 1.10)*

2-Min.
Writings

```
       1 | 2 | 3 | 4 | 5 | 6 | 7 | 8 | 9 | 10
```

| 0 | This is the first speed lesson in this book. You | 10 |

[For use of scales, review page 26.]

5	can add to your speed if you make the most of the	20
10	work on this page, which is set up to help you to	30
15	type at a smooth and fast pace. First you type a	40
20	lot of easy words that will get your fingers fly-	50
25	ing, and then you try to keep them flying at your	60
30	best speed for a longer and longer time. Be sure	70
35	that you try to keep the pace very even while you	80
40	type and that you type each part of the lesson at	90
45	least two times; such is the way to higher speed.	100

Plus ➧   1 | 2 | 3 | 4 | 5

```
From:     John Hildreth, Statistics        June 8, 1956

To:       Janet McKinley
          President, Women's Club
          Shipping Department

Subject:  Names of New Women Employees

A few days ago, Miss McKinley, you asked for a list of the women
who had joined the Company since the first of the year.  Here are
the names that you requested:

                    NEW WOMEN EMPLOYEES

                  January Through May, 1955


          Name              Branch           Department
       Allerton, Marian   San Francisco    Accounting
       Foster, Priscilla  Chicago          Shipping
       Homs, June         Chicago          Executive
       Leslie, Betty      New York         Drugs

       Lewis, Dorothy     San Francisco    Advertising
       McNaughton, Anna   Chicago          Furniture
       Parker, Marynelle  New York         Boys' Wear
       Reuters, Lois      Chicago          Mail Sales

This list does not, of course, include the persons who joined the
company but left before May 31.

                                               J. H.

JH/pnw
```

Interoffice memo with table, in blocked form, on plain paper

JOB 2

Unarranged table in memo
Words: 215

"Now for the Women's Club request," says Mr. Hildreth. "Please take off, from the list of new employees, all the *names* of women, along with their *branches* and their *positions*. We must send this information to the president of the Women's Club, who is Evangeline Prescott—she's in the Billing Department. Put the table in the body of this memo—"

Last week, Miss Prescott, you requested   8
the names of the women who have joined   16
the Company during the months of January   24
through May. Here are the names: [Table]   31

This list includes only the women who   39
have remained in our employ, as of this   47
date.   48

Wanting to see what form Mr. Hildreth was accustomed to using for such reports, you look in the files. You find the report shown above and use it as a guide.

JOB 3

Unarranged table in memo
Words: 239

"Let's make the same kind of report for the Men's Club," says Mr. Hildreth, "even though the request has not yet come. The name of the president is George Montgomery. He is in the Accounting Department. We'll need to change the memo. Let's make it—"

Someone in the Men's Club always asks   8
for a list of the spring crop of new men em-   16
ployees along about this time, George; so,   25
I am jumping the gun. Here's the list: 33

JOB 4

Unarranged table in memo
Words: 128

"Fred Dorsey [president of the firm] wants a report that shows the monthly employment record of each branch," says Mr. Hildreth.

"I tried to get it tallied for you, but I made a mistake somewhere. I get a total of 19 for Chicago, which ought to be 18; and 11 for New York, which ought to be 12. You will need to recheck my tally and then type the report—two carbons. Send the original to Mr. Dorsey, along with this memo—"

Here is the first of the employment rec-   8
ords that you asked us to prepare for you,   16
Mr. Dorsey. [Table]   19

We shall have the others very soon; we   27
have all the data and just need a little more   36
time to analyze them and then to prepare   44
the reports.   47

Month	Chi	N.Y.	S.F.	Totals
Jan	III	II	IIII	7
Feb	III	III	I	7
Mar	HTT III	I	I	10
Apr	I	III	IIII	8
May	IIII	IIII	II	8
Totals	19 (X)	11 (X)	10	40

Tally sheet for planning a table

WARMUP: "AN" Drill *(Each line 2 times)*

◁ **50** ▷

```
a;sldkfjghfjdksl a;sldkfjghfjdksl a;sldkfjghfjdksl
anchors angry ankle angel want sand many land bank
began clan plan mean than bran pan man fan ran ban
```

SPEED DRILL: Doubled Letters *(Each line 2 times)*

```
sleep speed meet keep feel need flee been fee see
shall skill sell full bill call tell well ill all
essay gloss issue guess cross loss boss less miss
broom stood floor crook proof book soon good look
```

SPEED SENTENCES: Doubled Letters *(Each line 2 times)*

½-Min.
Writings

```
1 | 2 | 3 | 4 | 5 | 6 | 7 | 8 | 9 | 10
Dee will see that all the new book fees are paid.   10
Ross needs good brooms to give the floor a gloss.   20
Bill took three weeks to sell all his old assets.   30
Bess will miss her book and will need to call us.   40
```

SPEED DRILL: Alternate-Hand Words *(Each line 2 times)*

1-Min.
Writings

```
1 | 2 | 3 | 4 | 5 | 6 | 7 | 8 | 9 | 10
such they hand half soap held mane naps dusk amen   10
clan diem when firm pair girl with down roam curl   20

rich hang clay wish paid lake land fork make fuel   30
duty coal clam disk fish cork dock flap duel cozy   40

urns alto worn dial bowl goal furl then city maps   50
gown corn wish hack auto them name than turn town   60
```

SUSTAINED-SPEED SENTENCES *(2 copies / si 1.02)*

◁ **50** ▷
DS

2-Min.
Writings

```
      1 | 2 | 3 | 4 | 5 | 6 | 7 | 8 | 9 | 10
 0  When can we two men find time to visit the house?   10
 5  I do seem to have left my work at the old school.   20
10  He may call him and ask him to work with us soon.   30
15  The man we met on the street came here to see us.   40
20  He may ask him to visit the club for a good time.   50
25  The old man said he will come down here if I can.   60
30  It is time for you and the man to leave for town.   70
35  I can make the class if I can get there by eight.   80
40  Both of you like to roam by the side of the lake.   90
45  I can be here by one and may see it at that time.  100
 Plus ▶      1  |    2   |    3   |    4   |    5
```

JOB 1

Rough draft

New Employees -- All Branches
January 1 - May 30

Name	Branch	Department	Position	Date	
Adams, Yvonne	San Fran	Music	Clerk	Jan 20	26
Allison, Allan	Chicago	Advertising	Layouts	Mar 10	36
Baker, Alexander	Chicago	Drugs	Buyer	Mar 12	45
Boer, Willard	New York	Drugs	Clerk	Apr 2	53
Brown, Jerome	Chicago	Boys' Wear	Buyer	Jan 18	63
Burton, Frederick	San Fran	Executive	Asst Mgr	Jan 2	73
Chinnock, Susan	New York	Executive	Secy	Apr 19	82
Counts, Edward	Chicago	Advertising	Photog	May 27	92
Doyle, Richard	New York	Off Eqt	Salesman	May 15	102
Drury, Caroline	Chicago	Jewelry	Clerk	Feb 8	111
Edwards, John	Chicago	Off Eqt	Salesman	Mar 10	120
Everett, Polly	New York	Shipping	Steno	Jan 18	129
Farmer, Paul S.	New York	Furniture	Buyer	Jan 25	139
Farmer, Ralph	New York	Furniture	Clerk	Feb 8	148
Esuark, Ruthetta	Chicago	Personnel	Director	Mar 18	158
Fein, Henrietta	Chicago	Boys' Wear	Asst Buyer	May 16	168
French, Mary	Chicago	Jewlry	Buyer	May 23	177
Gordon, Howard	New York	*Advertising*	Writer	Apr 19	186
Graham, Ruppert	Chicago	Drugs	Clerk	Mar 25	195
Hamilton, Wilma	San Fran	Boys' Wear	Buyer	Feb 1	205
Harper, Jerry	Chicago	Off Eqt	Asst Mgr	Mar 17	214
Harrison, Joe	Chicago	Building	Porter	Feb 15	223
Jones, Jeremiah	New York	Executive	~~Steno~~ *Secy*	Apr 12	232
Kenwood, Martin	Chicago	Shipping	Wrapper	Apr 19	242
Kliptok, Virgilia	New York	Mail Sales	Supervisor	May 18	253
Llewelyn, Inez	San Fran	Mail Sales	Asst Mgr	Apr 25	263
Morrison, Joanne	New York	Building	Elev Op	Feb 8	273
Norton, Willard	San Fran	Shipping	Supervisor	Mar 19	283
Olivia, Sarah	San Fran	Personnel	Recep	May 15	293
Parker, Josephine	Chicago	Accounting	Clerk	Jan 2	302
Potter, Alice	San Fran	Drugs	Clerk	May 29	311
Quincy, Jason	San Fran	Mail Sales	Clerk	Apr 2	320
Rawlson, Robert	New York	Building	Porter	Feb 8	330
Reilly, Patrick	New York	Executive	Vice-Pres	Mar 15	340
Rowe, Howard	San Fran	Accounting	Asst Mgr	Apr 12	350
Sullivan, Anne	Chicago	Furniture	Asst Buyer	Feb 3	360
Stone, Freeman	Chicago	Accounting	Clerk	Jan 2	369
T Rarranti, Angelo	Chicago	Personnel	Interviews	Mar 11	379
Tomlinson, Bertha	San Fran	Shipping	Steno	May 18	389
Wilhelms, Francis	Chicago	Music	*Buyer*	Mar 25	398

WARMUP: Balanced-Hand Words (*Each line 2 times*)   ◁**50**▷

```
ab abc abcd abcde abcdef abcdef abcde abcd abc ab
and but cot dog eye for got hem icy jam keys land
men nap own pan qua row sod tub ugh vow with yams
fix zig apt but cog dot eke fit gob hen idle also
```

CONTROL DRILL: Concentration (*Each line 2 times*)

½-Min.
Writings   1 | 2 | 3 | 4 | 5 | 6 | 7 | 8 | 9 | 10

```
Joe quietly picked six razors from the woven bag.
.gab nevow eht morf srozar xis dekcip ylteiuq eoJ
```

CONTROL DRILL: P, Q (*Each line 2 times*)

```
pay pad pal pan pen peg pet pie pig pot page paid
peep pulp pipe help paper pumps piped happy piper

quad quit quiz quip quart quite quiet quick quote
equals equate equine liquid equity opaque marquis
```

CONTROL SENTENCES: Alphabet Review (*Each line 2 times*)   ◁**60**▷

1-Min.
Writings   1 | 2 | 3 | 4 | 5 | 6 | 7 | 8 | 9 | 10 | 11 | 12

```
Jack fixed my five poor bridges quite easily and with zeal.   12
Alex was quizzed by Kay on the seven major points of cages.   24
Many given jobs require extra zeal and perfect work habits.   36
Zoe was given pay for that queer black box of jade markers.   48
Kay reviewed the subject before giving Max and Paul a quiz.   60
```

CONTROL PREVIEW (*Each line 2 times*)

```
must next type packed control practice important techniques.
when help just master purpose accurate emphasize understood
```

ALPHABET-REVIEW PARAGRAPH (*2 copies / si 1.27*)   **DS**

2-Min.
Writings   1 | 2 | 3 | 4 | 5 | 6 | 7 | 8 | 9 | 10 | 11 | 12

```
 0   If you wish to type with a high degree of sure control, you   12
 6   must find out what kind of practice to emphasize.  The work   24
12   on this and the next page is packed with the kinds of drill   36
18   that help you master the techniques most important in accu-   48
24   rate typing.  Just remember to study the purpose of a drill   60
30   before you type it.  A drill does more for you when its aim   72
36   is understood.  There is some, but not much, value in copy-   84
42   ing a drill without knowing what kind of practice it gives.   96
```

Plus ▮   1 | 2 | 3 | 4 | 5 | 6

One more guide worth[1] mentioning here as an aid[2] for designing new tables[3] concerns headings. There are[4] three kinds of them:[5] titles and subtitles and[6] column headings. Every[7] tabulation has to have a[8] title, of course, but not[9] all tables justify both[10] the others. Use the other[11] two as expedients to trim[12] down the size of a table[13] or make it clearer for[14] your reader. The subtitle[15] is used most frequently[16] as a date line for a table.[17] It is also used, with[18] parentheses, to explain[19] where the data came[20] from or what units of measure[21] are used, like: "All[22] figures are hundreds of[23] bushels" or "All figures are[24] in millions of dollars."[25]

     15
     32
     50
     67
     84
    101
    118
    125

Column headings are, of[26] course, the most useful[27] expedients; they are[28] frequently the main heart of[29] the table. They must be[30] kept brief, concise, and[31] clear. A group of such[32] headings should be, if[33] possible, phrased in similar[34] terms—don't use nouns for[35] some and adjectives for[36] others unless there is[37] no other way out of the[38] problem. If feasible, keep[39] equal headings to the same[40] number of lines; but if[41] some are long and some[42] are short, at least make[43] sure that all end on the[44] same line. What about rules?[45] The majority of firms[46] like horizontal rules,[47] which make any table look[48] better, but are indifferent[49] about vertical lines.[50]

    141
    158
    175
    192
    208
    225
    241
(START OVER) 250

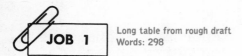

JOB 1 Long table from rough draft
Words: 298

"At this time of the year, we get many requests for information about new employees," says Mr. Hildreth. "The girl who just left compiled this information." He gives you the rough draft shown on the next page.

"Please type this up for us. Between us, we shall need several copies—better make half a dozen carbons, or else duplicate the table."

"Why so many copies?" you ask.

"Well," he replies, "we have to prepare a number of reports that consist of portions of this table. It will be a lot easier for us if we have copies that we can use as our work sheets. For example, the next job for you will be to pick out the names, branches, and departments of all the women on the list. If we have spare copies, you can simply cross out everything else, then copy what is left on the work sheet."

You study the job, noting particularly:

1. The page looks crowded. You decide to put just 4 spaces between the columns.

2. The lines are grouped in five's, with a blank line after each 5-line group. (That's a good idea; it helps in reading the table. Five's are used because there are 40 names in the list. If there were 18 names, you might group in three's. If there were 24, you might group in either three's or four's.)

3. The year was overlooked. You decide to add it, right after *May 30.*

4. Unpunctuated abbreviations are shown. They are satisfactory on a work sheet, but they would not be satisfactory on a report to be sent outside your own office.

WARMUP: Left-Hand Security *(Each line 2 times)*

```
abcdef abcdef abcdef abcdef abcdef abcdef abcdef
aaba aaca aada aaea aafa aaba aaca aada aaea aafa
Ann Ben Cal Don Eve Flo Ada Bog Con Dan Ella Fred
```

CONTROL DRILL: Concentration *(Each line 2 times)*

```
  1   |   2   |   3   |   4   |   5   |   6   |   7   |   8   |   9   |  10
Pack my box with five dozen jugs of liquid veneer.
.reenev diuqil fo sguj nezod evif htiw xob ym kcaP
```

CONTROL DRILL: Rocking Sequences *(Each line 2 times)*

```
at ate hat atom date flat atone plate great abate
out you oust four pour ought pounds amount ounces
avow save avid rave pave aver leave brave average
on one son once pond upon onto prone rayon onward
```

CONTROL SENTENCES: Rocking Sequences *(Each line 2 times)*

◁**60**▷

½-Min.
Writings

```
  1   |  2  |  3  |  4  |  5  |  6  |  7  |  8  |  9  | 10  | 11  | 12
Our son won the debate and found it was a great experience.    12
You ought to save your hats and have them for show at Avon.    24
Once you pave that path, you should have no ponds to drain.    36
What lone avenue might be available for paving on Saturday?    48
```

CONTROL DRILL: Alphabet Review *(Each line 2 times)*

1-Min.
Writings

```
  1   |  2  |  3  |  4  |  5  |  6  |  7  |  8  |  9  | 10  | 11  | 12
am us he no win can fit gum job key lax pay adz quo vie are    12
do it an my but car vex for gay jar ask apt lad why zoo qua    24
age boy use cut had men few jig put six like quit very lazy    36
who box act vie fly jog you ram son lot part zeal kind quad    48
```

ALPHABET-REVIEW PARAGRAPH *(2 copies / si 1.28)*

2-Min.
Writings

```
        1   |  2  |  3  |  4  |  5  |  6  |  7  |  8  |  9  | 10  | 11  | 12    DS
 0   Control in typing comes not so much from what we do as from    12
 6   what we do not do that might jeopardize accuracy.  If we do    24
12   not push so hard for speed that we wreck our control, we do    36
18   not get the habit of making and excusing a lot of mistakes.   48
24   If we do not slump down or squirm, we give our fingers what   60
30   they need most:  the chance to keep following the same path   72
36   for each stroke.  If we do not raise our eyes from the copy   84
42   in the book, then we do not skip letters or lose our place.   96
Plus ▶    1    |    2    |    3    |    4    |    5    |    6
```

UNIT 31
SUSTAINED TABULATION

This unit, like the preceding one, will help you develop sustained working power. In Unit 30, you worked with correspondence; in this unit, with tabulations. You will also set up tables from unorganized information.

This unit will be easiest if, before starting the jobs, you (*a*) review the tabulation instructions on pages 57-64 and 125-132; (*b*) read through this unit; and (*c*) answer the study questions on Workbook pages 285-286.

Your employer is John Hildreth, a statistician who gathers data and prepares reports for his firm. He has no outgoing letters; but he does dictate memos, which you type on plain paper in blocked form (see page 92) to accompany the reports that he prepares.

Most of your work consists of tabulations. Some you center on full sheets of paper; some are made part of a dictated memo. Mr. Hildreth suggests that you always make two carbon copies — one for filing and one for possible use as a first draft in another problem.

To keep your skill up while you work on the tables, type an alphabetic paragraph (below and on the next page) on the back of each job as soon as you finish it.

Type 1 paragraph on the back of each job in this unit:

5-Min. Writings
si 1.35

◁ **70** ▷
DS

For a long time there has[1] been an air of mystery[2] surrounding the most[3] interest- 16
ing aspect of typing:[4] designing a table from[5] unarranged information. I[6] do not know 33
why this[7] should be considered hard.[8] Yes, this kind of work[9] takes time; but I should[10] 50
like to emphasize the fact[11] that planning is not hard.[12] It takes a little[13] experience, 67
that's all. Nine[14] times out of ten, the[15] grouping of the data is quite[16] obvious when 83
you read[17] over the information; for[18] the tenth instance, the[19] files will probably have[20] 100
a precise model that you[21] can follow. I have often[22] felt that planning a[23] table is not 117
as hard as[24] adjusting the machine for it.[25] 125

There are several guides[26] that could be kept in[27] mind when you are planning[28] a 141
table. The first guide:[29] If the table is one of[30] a series, then it should[31] be made to look 159
and read[32] exactly like the others;[33] this applies not only[34] to tables in a report or[35] 175
thesis but equally to those[36] that you type in business,[37] where most tabulations[38] are 191
just the newest version[39] of the tables you typed[40] last month. The second[41] guide: 207
Where you can,[42] make a table longer than[43] it is wide; try to make[44] its general size 223
in the[45] same shape as the sheet of[46] paper. Another guide:[47] If you can, get the totals[48] 240
figures typed down at the[49] bottoms of the columns.[50] (START OVER) 250

WARMUP: Reach Review (*Each line 2 times*)   ◁ **50** ▷

```
aqa ;p; sws lol ded kik frf juj ftf jyj fgf jhj
fbf jnj fvf jmj dcd k,k sxs l.l aza ;/; ;0; s2s
l9l d3d k8k f4f j7j f5f j6j 39, 28, 47, 56, 10.
```

NUMBER DRILL: 1, 2, 8 (*Each line 2 times*)

```
s 2 s2 12 21 122 221 1221 2212 1212 122 221 12 21
k 8 k8 18 81 188 881 1881 8818 1818 188 881 18 81
1 1 12 18 28 128 821 1281 1821 1228 812 821 88 22
```

NUMBER DRILL: We 23's (*Each line 2 times*)

```
we 23 you 697 two 529 rip 480 wore 2943 pipe 0803
it 85 yet 635 put 075 rut 475 pity 0856 wiry 2846
or 94 wet 235 our 974 eye 363 your 6974 type 5603
```

NUMBER SENTENCES: Pair Pattern (*Each line 2 times*)

½-Min.
Writings

| 1 | 2 | 3 | 4 | 5 | 6 | 7 | 8 | 9 | 10 |

```
The sum of 39 and 28 and 47 and 56 and 10 is 180.   10
I need 39 or 28 blue, 47 or 56 white, and 10 red.   20
Add up 10 and 28 and 39 and 47 and 56 to get 180.   30
Ship it May 28 to 4756 West 39 Street, Newark 10.   40
```

NUMBER DRILL: Cumulative Count (*Each line 2 times*)   ◁ **50** ▷

1-Min.
Writings

| 1 | 2 | 3 | 4 | 5 | 6 | 7 | 8 | 9 | 10 |

```
1201 1802 8803 1104 2805 2206 1807 2108 2809 1810   10
2211 2112 1213 2814 8115 1816 2817 8118 8819 1120   20
8121 1122 1223 2124 2225 2826 2827 8128 2829 1830   30
1231 2132 1833 8834 8235 8136 1137 2138 8139 2240   40
```

NUMBER-REVIEW PARAGRAPH (*2 copies / si 1.11*)   DS

2-Min.
Writings

| 1 | 2 | 3 | 4 | 5 | 6 | 7 | 8 | 9 | 10 |

```
 0│25  They are making plans for a fine group of from 60   10
 5│30  to 75 for the meeting on June 13.  Of this group,   20
10│35  14 should come from the East, 12 from the West, 8   30
15│40  or 9 from the North, and either 17 or 18 from the   40
20│45  South.  There may be as many as 20 local members.   50
```

Plus ▶ | 1 | | 2 | | 3 | | 4 | | 5 |

JOB 11

Telegram
Workbook form

mr. marvin j. thompson 5
harding-hill company 9
1067 s. clinton street 13
syracuse 4, new york 18

james flaherty, our representative, was 26
injured in auto accident while en route to 34
see you. he will be held up at least a month. 44
will come myself if you feel trip justified. 53
general sales manager, portland products 61
company 63

JOB 12

Letter
(3 paragraphs)

mr. james e. flaherty 4
392 howard street 8
albany 1, new york 12
dear jim: 14

i don't know whether i was more shocked 22
at hearing of your accident or relieved at 31
learning that you will recover fully. appar- 39
ently it was a bad smashup, and we are all 48
lucky that your injuries did not turn out 56
worse than they did. as soon as i heard what 66
had happened and made sure that there 73
was nothing more that we could do for you, 82
i wired mr. thompson, up in syracuse, and 90
offered to come to see him myself; he en- 98
couraged me to come. if i am as persuasive 107
as you are, jim, you'll be able to enjoy that 116
hospital bed on the commissions i hope to 125
earn for you with your customer. cordially 134
yours, 135

JOB 13

Memo
(5 paragraphs)

to mr. elroy, president 5
subject: advanced plan- 9
ning for the next general 15
meeting of the sales staff. 20

at the last meeting of the district sales 29
managers, here in new york city, we agreed 37
that the program for the forthcoming semi- 46
annual meeting of the sales staff might prof- 54
itably include the following: 1. a demonstra- 64
tion of each operation that the new folding 72
machine will perform. 2. a sales demonstra- 81
tion on "how to present the features" of the 90
new machine. 3. a panel discussion on 98
methods for broadening sales by getting 106
more of our customers to use the whole 114
portland line. it is now time to confirm the 123
details of the program. have you any sug- 131
gestion to offer? would you like to partici- 140
pate personally in any part of the program? 149
i am sure that all the men would enjoy 157
another of those spirited talks for which you 166
are so well known. ted 171

JOB 14

Letter
(3 paragraphs)

office supplies journal 5
375 sixth avenue 8
newark 7, new jersey 12
attention news editor 17
gentlemen: 19

i have been watching closely the column 27
in your publication in which you review 35
and announce new products of interest to 43
office executives. i hoped to see in it some 53
mention of the new Portland Folding Ma- 60
chine. when the new issue came to my desk 69
today, i realized that we might have over- 77
looked sending you the material that you 84
would need; so, i am taking the liberty of 93
sending you the following aids with this 101
letter: 103

1. a glossy photo of the new machine 110
2. a descriptive brochure 116
3. clippings of other reviews 122
4. photo series showing how the new 129
   machine is used 133

if there is additional information—even a 141
personal demonstration!—that would be of 150
help to you, i should be happy to provide it. 159
cordially yours, 162

WARMUP: Reach Review *(Each line 2 times)* ◁ **50** ▷

```
;p; aqa ;0; sws lol s2s 191 ded kik d3d k8k frf
juj f4f j7j ftf jyj f5f j6j fgf jhj fbf jnj fvf
jmj dcd k,k sxs 1.1 aza ;/; .39 .28 .47 .56 .10
```

NUMBER DRILL: 2, 3, 8, 9 *(Each line 2 times)*

```
2 8 12 18 28 128 1281 2839 8382 1821 82 81 21 8 2
3 9 13 19 39 139 1391 3939 9393 1931 93 91 31 9 3
28 39 2839 28 39 2839 28 39 2839 28 39 2839 28 39
```

NUMBER DRILL: We 23's *(Each line 2 times)*

```
we 23 yew 632 try 546 pop 090 writ 2485 riot 4895
to 59 wry 246 ewe 323 pup 070 tire 5843 rout 4975
up 70 yip 680 out 975 ire 843 tout 5975 yore 6943
```

SYMBOL DRILL: " & *(Each line 2 times)* ◁ **50** ▷

If " on 2
If " on '
```
s2s s"s s"s s"s j7j j&j j&j j&j s"s j&j " & " & "
;'; ;"; ;"; ;"; j7j j&j j&j j&j ;"; j&j " & " & "
1 & 2 & 3 & 4 & 5 & 6 & 7 & 8 & 9 & 10 & 11 or 12
1" 2" 3" 4" 5" 6" 7" 8" 9" 10" 11" 12" 13" or 14"
```

SYMBOL SENTENCES: " & *(Each line 2 times)*

```
        1 |  2 |  3 |  4 |  5 |  6 |  7 |  8 |  9 | 10
```

½-Min.
Writings
```
The names are Black, Blue & Sons; and White & Co.   10
"Please order it from Foster & Riley," she wrote.   20
"John," said Mary, "when will the car be washed?"   30
```

1-Min.
Writings
```
"I am proud," he wrote, "to buy from Frank & Co."   10
"Order 22 from Rogers & Smith," the man wrote us.   20
You do not get a "bargain" from Harpers & Saints.   30
```

NUMBER DRILL: Century Drive *(1 copy)* **DS**

2-Min.
Writings
```
And 1 and 2 and 3 and 4 and 5 and 6 and 7 and 8
and 9 and 10 and 11 and 12 and 13 and 14 and 15
and 16 and 17 and 18 and 19 and 20 and 21 and 22
and 23 and 24 and  [Continue on up to 100. Ultimate
                    goal is to reach 100 in 2 minutes.]
```

Part 2 **LESSON 31** Unit 5

JOB 8

Letter

mr. eugene r. gordon | 4
818 rhodes-haverty build- | 9
ing | 10
atlanta 3, georgia | 14
dear gene: | 16

we seem to be having another tussle with | 24
your friend Simmons at martin miller & | 32
sons, as you can tell from the enclosed copy | 41
of my current letter to him. I don't know | 50
why we have had so much trouble with the | 58
installation in his department. | 64

i am beginning to wonder whether there | 72
might be someone in that office who, for | 80
reasons of his own, is deliberately fouling | 89
up the equipment. the last two times you | 98
visited mm&s, remember, you noted that | 105
the motor governors on the duplicators and | 114
postal meter had been tampered with and | 122
"cleaned." i simply cannot believe that the | 131
same thing could go wrong with each of | 139
the five pieces of equipment that we have | 147
installed there. | 151

in any case, gene, if you cannot find the | 159
answer when you visit them again, please | 167
yank out the whole installation. i'd rather | 176
take a loss on this matter than jeopardize | 185
our very considerable volume with the rest | 194
of the mm&s organization. cordially yours, | 202

JOB 9

Letter

mr. thomas j. simmons | 4
martin miller & sons | 9
58 broad street | 12
atlanta 1, georgia | 16
dear mr. simmons: | 19

thank you for your patient letter about | 27
the unsatisfactory service that you are get- | 36
ting from your Portland Duplicator. I am | 44
deeply concerned about the situation and | 53
am asking our atlanta dealer, eugene gor- | 61
don, to stop in to see you about it. | 68

this newest breakdown is the fifth you | 76

have had with as many machines, isn't it? | 85
how annoying it must be to you! we are, | 93
naturally, disturbed about this record; for, | 102
while we have had a few machines get out | 110
of order before, we have never had so many | 119
collapse in one installation. most of our cus- | 128
tomers have never had even one service | 136
call, let alone any need for the replacement | 145
of our equipment. and, no other installation | 154
has ever had the drum of the duplicator | 162
"run backwards," as you have described it. | 171

i am writing to mr. gordon, giving him | 178
complete authority to settle the matter. | 187
your friends in this company appreciate | 195
your patience. yours truly, | 200

JOB 10

Letter

mr. kenneth w. kling | 4
business manager | 8
dallas business show | 12
national bank building | 16
dallas 1, texas | 20
dear mr. kling: | 23

we appreciate very much your invitation | 31
to exhibit in the business show that your | 39
organization will sponsor next spring. we | 48
have read your prospectus with interest; | 56
but, for the following reasons, we have de- | 65
cided not to reserve space: | 70

1. your space rates are much higher than | 79
for shows drawing bigger crowds. | 86

2. your conference activities are to be | 94
held away from the exhibit hall, thus draw- | 102
ing away prospective customers. | 109

3. the innumerable extra fees for labor | 117
and facilities that are normally a part of the | 126
flat exhibit charge has priced your space | 135
beyond reason, we believe. | 140

if there occurs a basic change in the ad- | 148
ministration of these three items, we may | 157
be interested. cordially yours, | 163

This is the first of the "production units" described on page 41. To profit most from this or any production unit:

1. Leaf through the pages of the unit. See what they cover.

2. Go through the unit again, reading the Alphabet-Review Paragraphs, all explanations, and all model illustrations.

3. Answer the study-guide questions for the unit on Workbook pages 41-42. Use your book to find or verify your answers.

4. With the basic information in mind, type skill drills and production-practice jobs as directed. If you grade your jobs, use the appropriate grading scales on pages 73 and 74.

UNIT 6
CORRESPONDENCE

WARMUP (*Each line 2 times*) ◁ **52** ▷

```
g H i J k L m N o P q R s T u V w X Y Z a B c D e F
39 28 47 56 10 we 23 or 94 tip 580 you 697 rue 473.
The old man did not get pay for the day he had off.
```
12-Sec. 5| 10| 15| 20| 25| 30| 35| 40| 45| 50|

ACCELERATION PREVIEW (*Each line 2 times*)

```
AA approve machine manager arrange agency save tax
BB tabulate blocked begins about both bill but job
CC accountant conference course office common cost
-- and far but can say ask any all tab are art had
```

ALPHABET-REVIEW PARAGRAPH (*2 copies / si 1.20*) ◁ **60** ▷
DS

3-Min. Writings   1 | 2 | 3 | 4 | 5 | 6 | 7 | 8 | 9 | 10 | 11 | 12

```
 0      As you work this unit on letters, you must be able for      11
 4   the first time to find the answer to this question:  Do you    23
 8   type on a pica or on an elite machine?  The words here were    35
12   printed in pica type.  If your printing is the same size as    47
16   this, your machine is pica; but if your printing is smaller    59
20   and if your line takes about half an inch less space across    71
24   your page, your machine is elite.  When you use the letter-    83
28   placement chart on the next page, or when you type all jobs    95
32   in this unit, you have to know which size of type you have.   107
```
Plus ▶   1 | 2 | 3 | 4

PRODUCTION PRACTICE (*Jobs 1-3*) ◁ **4 in.** ▷
SS

Study pages 49 and 50; then type Jobs 1, 2, and 3 on the workbook letterheads. If you do not have a workbook, rule or crease a line about 2 inches from the top of your paper, to represent the depth of a letterhead. Use a 4-inch line on all three letters.

JOB 4

Memo

To: Alexander Ferguson   5
Advertising Department   9
Subject: Promotion Pieces   15
for the Portland Folder   20

With this memo, Alex, I am sending you 27
first drafts of two pieces for promotion mail- 36
ings. I am sure that you will be able to im- 45
prove on both of them; indeed, I am count- 53
ing on your doing so. 58

The first piece is a display letter; the 66
other is a simple postal-card message. In- 75
asmuch as we are a duplicator manufac- 82
turer, I think it is advisable to prepare both 91
pieces on the duplicator or, at least, to ar- 100
range them so that they give the appear- 108
ance of being duplicated. 113

I think, also, that both pieces ought to 122
be tested by sample mailings before we go 130
all out on the whole mailing list. We shall, 139
of course, need complete cost estimates be- 148
fore we can release these pieces. Budgets, 156
you know!   Ted 159

JOB 5

Display letter

To All Office Managers   5
Who Worry About Costs   9
In Handling Mailings   13
Gentlemen: 16

This letter was printed on a duplicator, 24
folded by a folding machine, placed in its 32
envelope by an inserting machine, and 40
then sealed and stamped by a mailing ma- 48
chine. Each of the machines did its part in 57
preparing this mailing, which is of 7,500 65
pieces, in an hour or less. A real accomplish- 74
ment, that! Can you do as well with your 83
staff and equipment? 87

If your answer is "No, I cannot," then 95
it is time to take a look at the line of 103
Portland machines. 107

The newest member of the Portland line 115
of mailing machinery is the Portland Fold- 123
er, which will fold any paper that can be 132
run through a duplicating machine. It can 140
give you 1, 2, 3, or 4 folds on any sheet of 149
paper from 4 to 9 inches wide and from 4 157
to 14 inches long. You ought to see how fast 167
it works! 169

There's an idea: See how fast the Port- 177
land Folder works! Write us to arrange 185
a demonstration for you. 190

And when your friendly Portland Man is 198
there for the demonstration, ask him for 206
more details about the whole line of Port- 214
land machines. Cordially yours, 221

JOB 6

First-draft
postal card

Rule on a sheet of paper a box,
5½ by 3¼ inches, to represent the
postal card. Type within this box.

Dear Mr. Stationer: 4

Three weeks ago, the new Portland Fold- 12
ing Machine was unveiled at the NOMA 19
Business Show in New Orleans. It was an 27
instant success; some said "It was the hit of 37
the show." If you would like one or more of 46
these machines on consignment, let us know 55
now. Production is moving so smoothly that 64
we should be able to deliver your machines 73
within three weeks after receiving your 81
order. Don't wait—act now! 87

Portland Products Company, 3 Park Ave- 94
nue, New York 16, New York 99

JOB 7

Telegram
Workbook form

General Manager   3
The Portland Factory   7
5720 Touhy Avenue   11
Chicago 31, Illinois   15

Can you deliver 500 Model 19 Folders to 23
Washington within two weeks? Ted Wilson 31

THE BASIC ELEMENTS OF A BUSINESS LETTER . . .

Letterhead ▶

Date Line ▶

Inside Address ▶

Salutation ▶

Body ▶

Complimentary Closing ▶

Signer's Identification ▶
Reference Initials ▶

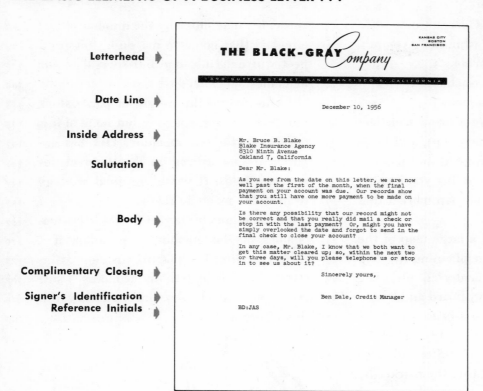

Separate the parts of a letter by 1 blank line, except—

◀ **1. Put extra space between the date and the inside address**—see the table below.

◀ **2. Put extra space above the signer's identification, to provide room for his signature**—leave 3 blank lines for it.

HOW TO PLACE A LETTER ON THE PAGE . . .

STEP **1**: Drop to date-line position (line 14, or 2 lines below letterhead, whichever is lower).

STEP **2**: Estimate number of words in body of the letter . . . .

STEP **3**: Set margin stops for corresponding line length* . . . .

STEP **4**: Type date; then drop this many lines to address . . . .

    *Reminder: There are 10 pica spaces to an inch,
    12 elite spaces to an inch.

SHORT	AVERAGE	LONG
Under 100	100 to 200	Over 200
4 inches	5 inches	6 inches
8 lines	6 lines	4 lines

PLACEMENT GUIDE

HOW TO USE THE MODEL LETTERS IN THIS BOOK . . .

The various styles in which letters may be arranged are presented in the correspondence units. Each style is illustrated by a model. Before typing any model, study it carefully. Things to note in each model and each job:

1. *The name and pattern* of the style.

2. *The job directions.* They tell you—

—whether the model is in pica or elite.

—whether to use a workbook letterhead.

—how many tab stops to set, and where.

—the number of words in the job.

3. *Marginal notes* and explanations.

4. *Marginal signals.* They remind you—

—what length of typing line to use.

—on what line to start the heading.

—how far to drop to the inside address.

—what spacing you should use.

5. *The arrows* for vertical spacing.

6. *The date.* Change it: Use the current day's date, and type the year in full.

7. *The reference initials.* Substitute your initials for the "URS" that is shown.

JOB 1
Letter

G. B. George Company 4
54 Washburne Avenue 8
Cambridge 4, 11
    Massachusetts 14
Gentlemen: 16

I have learned that your firm specializes 24
in making signal markers, clips, and tacks 33
for use with filing equipment and maps. I 42
am writing to find out whether you include 50
in your line some kind of map marker that 59
may be used over glass. 64

I recently purchased a large map of the 72
United States to use in planning my trip 80
itineraries, our sales territories, etc. The 89
map is mounted on heavy board and is cov- 97
ered with glass. The map is fastened on the 106
wall of my office. What I need is some kind 115
of marker with a suction-cup or adhesive 123
base, for it is important that the marker be 132
removable. 135

If you have a product that fits my need 143
or if you have any suggestion concerning a 151
solution to my problem, I should be happy 160
to hear from you. 164

Cordially yours, 167
PORTLAND PRODUCTS COMPANY

Sales Manager
TW:URS

JOB 2
Letter

Mr. James E. Flaherty 4
392 Harvard Street 8
Albany 1, New York 12
Dear Jim: 14

As you will see from the letter I am en- 22
closing, we have a strong prospect in the 30
Harding-Hill Corporation, in Syracuse. 38
Your itinerary indicates that you will be in 47
Syracuse about the end of next week. 55
Could you get there a day or two ahead of 63
schedule and give the firm some time? I am 72
particularly anxious to land this deal be- 80

cause, if I may judge by the number of HH 89
circulars that come to my desk, this pros- 97
pect will need not one but several of the 105
machines. 108

I checked on the weight of paper stock 115
that HH is using; it varies, but none of it is 125
too heavy for our machine. HH has ap- 132
parently standardized on No. 10 envelopes 141
and two folds. It would be good strategy 149
to have the machine ready. 155

I should not bother to go into the me- 162
chanics of the machine's operation, if I 170
were you, Jim; I think this customer is in- 179
terested in only one thing: economy. I sus- 187
pect that that is the line to follow this 196
time. Cordially yours, 200

JOB 3
Letter

Mr. Marvin J. Thompson 5
Harding-Hill Company 9
1067 S. Clinton Street 13
Syracuse 4, New York 18
Dear Mr. Thompson: 22

We appreciate very much your inquiry 29
about our new folding machine. I assure 37
you that it will fold all the standard sizes 46
of paper used in duplicating machines. As 55
a matter of fact, it will fold papers as small 64
as 4 inches square and as large as 9 by 14 73
inches. 75

Our representative for upper New York, 82
Mr. James Flaherty, to whom I am sending 91
a copy of this letter, will be in your city in 100
about 10 days. I am certain he will be able 109
to stop in to see you when he arrives in 117
Syracuse. He has a model of the folding ma- 126
chine and can let you see for yourself how 134
efficient it is. 138

I am enclosing literature about the new 146
machine. If there is any other help that I 155
can give, Mr. Thompson, please let me 162
know. Cordially yours, 167

Blocked Letter Style

Date and Closing Lines Blocked at Center • All Other Lines Blocked at Left Margin

Some Persons Call This the "Modified Block Style"

JOB 1

Blocked letter
Shown in pica
Use letterhead
Center tab
Words: 98
Body: 71

◁4 in.▷
SS
14/8
▽

October 15, 19-- ₈ ➡

Mr. Henry L. Hale
3928 Dumont Avenue
Brooklyn 8, New York ₂ ➡

Standard
punctuation:
colon after
salutation.

Dear Mr. Hale: ₂ ➡

This letter is in blocked style, one of
the most common letter forms. All lines
begin at the left margin except the date
line and the closing lines, which begin
at the center of the paper. ₂ ➡

When you use this letter form, set a tab
stop at the center of the paper so that
you can tabulate to it whenever you wish
to type the date line or a closing line. ₂ ➡

Standard
punctuation:
comma after
closing line.

Yours very truly, ₄ ➡

Training Director ₂ ➡

Reference initials:
the dictator's and
typist's (use yours),
separated by colon.

JLW:URS

If your machine is pica, copy this letter exactly, line for line—but listen for the bell as
you type Job 2, next page. If your machine is elite, listen for the bell as you type this
letter—but copy Job 2 line for line. Use a 4-inch line (40 pica, 50 elite) for both letters.

UNIT 30
SUSTAINED CORRESPONDENCE

This unit is different from the preceding correspondence units. It is designed to help you develop the ability to keep going — to type one letter after another — as typists do in an office. This unit introduces no new techniques. It consists of a series of 14 messages, which you are to type as expertly, rapidly, and attractively as you can.

Like an office typist, you must plan your letter placement. Be on guard for enclosure notations, subject lines, and the like. Make enough carbons for the files and enclosures.

The letters are to be typed in blocked style, with the date (use the current date) at the right and the closing lines blocked at the center. Use a company signature. Use standard punctuation — colon after the salutation and comma after the complimentary closing. Your employer is Theodore Wilson, who is Sales Manager of the Portland Products Company.

To conserve your workbook supplies, type the letters on plain paper. Draw or crease a line about 1½ inches from the top, to represent the depth of a letterhead.

To keep your skill from slipping, type a copy of the exercises below on the back of each letter as soon as you finish typing it.

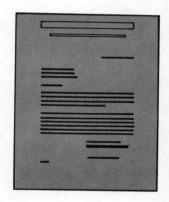

Mr. Wilson prefers you to use blocked form for his letters and memos, like the form shown on pages 83 and 92. The placement table is on page 119.

Type 1 copy on the back of each job in this unit:

1 | 2 | 3 | 4 | 5 | 6 | 7 | 8 | 9 | 10 | 11 | 12

PARAGRAPH PREVIEW:　　　　　　　　　　　　　　　　　　◁ **60** ▷

```
aa maintain bb about cc cards dd hundred ee require ff file    12
gg long hh that ii despite jj just kk quick ll long mm more    24
nn many oo open pp type qq require rr words ss side tt that    36
uu quite vv have ww what xx expensive yy easy zz dozen size    48
```

ALPHABET-REVIEW PARAGRAPH:

```
         You will find that more and more postal cards are used    11
in business.  They are quick and easy to prepare.  They are    23
not expensive; you can type two dozen for what might be the    35
cost of just one long letter.  A card does not require that    47
you make a file copy.  It is quite easy to type on the card    59
if you remember to maintain margins of about a half inch on    71
all sides.  Despite its modest size, you can get as many as    83
a hundred words on the open side of a standard postal card.    95
```
si
1.25

JOB 2

Blocked letter
Shown in elite
Use letterhead
Center tab
Words: 104
Body: 73

October 16, 19-- ₈

◁ **4 in.** ▷
SS
14/8
▽

Mr. Paul J. Thorne
The Thorne Agency
220 North Canal Street
Chicago 6, Illinois ₂

Dear Paul: ₂

We are glad to approve the layouts and the artwork for the two-page ad. We believe that you and Bill have done a fine job. ₂

We shall need to check the wording of the copy very carefully, of course. I should like to suggest that you plan to come for a conference on Friday. Could you come at noon and have lunch with me? Doing so would save time for both of us. ₂

Cordially yours, ₄

Benjamin I. Foster ₂

BIF:URS

JOB 3

Blocked letter
Shown in pica
Use letterhead
Center tab
Words: 107
Body: 76

October 16, 19-- ₈

◁ **4 in.** ▷
SS
14/8
▽

Miss Lee Anne Smith
56 Willis Street
Elgin, Illinois ₂

Dear Miss Smith: ₂

We were pleased to receive your letter, in which you asked whether we have an opening in our office for which you might apply. ₂

In about two weeks, we shall have open a position for an accountant who is familiar with cost and tax work. If you would like to be considered for this position, please call Miss Wells, at this office; she will then arrange a time for an interview. ₂

Yours very truly, ₄

David L. Colfax
Personnel Director ₂

DLC:URS

If a name and a title are both used but are too long to fit on one line, type the name first and put the title under it.

WARMUP *(Each line 3 times)*   ◁ 50 ▷

12-Sec.
Writings

```
abc def ghi jkl mno pqr stu vwx yz. 123 456 789 0
1 and 2 but 3 can 4 did 5 for 6 got 7 had 8 its 9
jay 10 kid 11 let 13 may 14 nor 15 oar 16 pray 17
```
12-Sec. 5| 10| 15| 20| 25| 30| 35| 40| 45| 50|

SYMBOL-REVIEW SENTENCES *(Each line 3 times)*

½-Min.
Writings

   1 | 2 | 3 | 4 | 5 | 6 | 7 | 8 | 9 | 10

```
" " : "Oh," he said, "thank you."  He paused 10".      10
# # : Ship it on Truck #11.  It weighs just 128#.      20
$ $ : I owe him $11.10.  Al owes him $11.10, too.      30
% % : I get 5% discount.  Savings now pay 2 3/8%.      40
_ _ : We took third, second, but not first place.     50
& & : Jones & Dodd Company took over Hale & Sons.     60
' ' : Here's Bill's best race:  a mile in 4' 10"!     70
( ) : The star (Jack) got the best plane (a jet).     80
* * : Use the asterisk (*) to refer to footnotes.     90
¢ ¢ : One cent is 1¢, too cents is 2¢, and so on.    100
@ @ : Ship us 100 gross @ 96¢ or 150 gross @ 88¢.    110
```

NUMBER-SYMBOL PARAGRAPH *(2 copies)*   ◁ 50 ▷

1-Min.
Writings

   1 | 2 | 3 | 4 | 5 | 6 | 7 | 8 | 9 | 10

```
We left the city on Route #7 on April 28 for a 2-     10
week trip.  We stayed at 14 different motels, for     20
an average cost of $8 per night.  Most meals cost     30
us about 60¢ for breakfast, 75¢ for lunch and (as    40
I recall) about $2 for dinners, for a daily total    50
of $3.35 for food, or $11.35 for living expenses.    60
```

NUMBER-TABULATION DRILL *(1 copy)*   Set tab every 9th space from the left margin.

1-Min.
Writings

2801	3902	4703	5604	1005	8206	6
9307	7408	6509	2310	9011	3412	12
9813	4514	8715	5616	2217	9918	18
3319	8820	4421	7722	5523	6624	24
8225	9326	7427	6528	1029	5630	30
2831	3932	4733	5634	1035	1336	36

CENTURY DRIVE *(1 complete copy, up to 100)*

2-Min.
Writings

```
Big 1 big 2 big 3 big 4 big 5 big 6 big 7 big 8 big
9 big 10 big 11 big 12 big 13
```
⌈Continue on up to 100. Ultimate⌉
⌊goal is to reach 100 in 2 minutes.⌋

WARMUP *(Each line 2 times)*   ◁52▷

```
j K l M n O p Q r S t U v W x Y z A b C d E f G h I
"39" "28" "47" "56" "100" '39' '28' '47' '56' '100'
When did the two men go to get the pay for the day?
```
12-Sec. 5| 10| 15| 20| 25| 30| 35| 40| 45| 50|

ACCELERATION PREVIEW *(Each line 2 times)*

```
DD including ordinary dictator spending allowed and
EE references schedules pleased streets letters end
FF information flights offices France firm from fly
not you too are for the but all and our how use let
```

ALPHABET-REVIEW PARAGRAPH *(2 copies / si 1.20)*   ◁60▷
                                                              DS

3-Min.
Writings   1 | 2 | 3 | 4 | 5 | 6 | 7 | 8 | 9 | 10 | 11 | 12

```
 0      It will not make you too pleased to find that rules do      11
 4   vary in typing, just as the rules vary in any other kind of    23
 8   work.  For example, the first initials down at the end of a    35
12   letter are those of the dictator of the letter, followed by    47
16   a colon and then those of the typist; but you may see, too,    59
20   the initials in small letters, not in capitals at all, with    71
24   the slant mark used instead of a colon.  This is all a mat-    83
28   ter of taste--and taste varies quite a bit, as you know.  I    95
32   feel that the use of hard rules might help us to learn some   107
36   one way to work, but such rules may kill our zeal for work.   119
```
Plus ➡   1 | 2 | 3 | 4

PRODUCTION PRACTICE *(Jobs 4-6)*

Study page 53; then type Jobs 4, 5, and 6 on plain paper. So that the date will
be on line 14, start the return address on line 12 in each job. Use a 4-inch line.

WARMUP: Reach Recall *(Each line 3 times)*   ◁**50**▷

```
aqqa ;pp; swws lool deed kiik frrf juuj fttf jyyj
fggf jhhj fbbf jnnj fvvf jmmj dccd k,,k sxxs l..l
azza ;//; ;00; s22s 1991 d33d k88k f44f j77j f55f
j66j f55f j77j f44f k88k d33d 1991 s22s 1991 ;00;
```

NUMBER DRILL: 39, 28 *(Each line 3 times)*

Keep eyes on copy!

```
22 88 28 28 82 2828 8282 1281 1821 1218 1818 2882
33 99 39 39 93 3939 9393 1391 1931 1319 1919 3993
22 88 33 99 29 2839 8282 9393 8293 2882 3993 2983
```

NUMBER DRILL: We 23's *(Each line 3 times)*

12-Sec. Writings

```
we 23 wet 235 wow 292 wry 246 writ 2485 weep 2330
wore 2943 wiry 2846 wire 2843 were 2343 wept 2305
pipe 0803 prop 0490 pure 0743 pout 0975 pity 0856
```

12-Sec. 5| 10| 15| 20| 25| 30| 35| 40| 45| 50|

NUMBER SENTENCES: Mixed Numbers *(Each line 3 times)*

½-Min. Writings

```
  1  |  2  |  3  |  4  |  5  |  6  |  7  |  8  |  9  |  10
Their scores totaled 123, 145, 167, 189, and 190.      10
The number for 12 North 56th Avenue is PO 8-3947.      20
They used 1,234 jeeps, 896 trucks, and 756 tanks.      30
Order #14590, for 678 units, might arrive May 23.      40
```

NUMBER DRILL: Cumulative Count *(3 copies)*   ◁**50**▷ DS

1-Min. Writings

```
  1  |  2  |  3  |  4  |  5  |  6  |  7  |  8  |  9  |  10
2801 3902 4703 5604 1005 6506 7407 8208 9309 1010      10
9911 5512 3313 4414 5515 6616 7717 8818 9919 2820      20
3921 4722 5623 1024 8925 9826 2827 3928 4729 5630      30
1031 9632 8233 7434 6535 1036 6837 1938 8939 7840      40
```

NUMBER-REVIEW PARAGRAPH *(3 copies / si 1.22)*   ◁**50**▷ DS

2-Min. Writings

```
        1  |  2  |  3  |  4  |  5  |  6  |  7  |  8  |  9  |  10
0  40       Orville Wright had his first airplane flight    9
5  44   on December 17, 1903.  This flight lasted only 12   19
10 49   seconds and covered about 120 feet.  Planes first   29
15 54   carried the mail in 1920; and by using trains for   39
20 59   night travel, flight time from coast to coast was   49
25 64   down to 78 hours.  By 1937, the time has been cut   59
30 69   to less than 16 hours; and since 1945, total time   69
35 74   for the flights (nonstop) has been under 8 hours.   79
```

Plus ▶   1 | 2 | 3 | 4 | 5

JOB 4

Blocked letter
 Shown in pica
 Use plain paper
 Return address
 Center tab
Words: 134
 Body: 96

3928 Dumont Avenue
Brooklyn 8, New York
October 17, 19-- ₈ ➤

◁ **4 in.** ▷
SS
12/8
▽

Mr. Edward Whitman
Letter Typing Service
1047 Fifth Avenue
New York 28, New York ₂ ➤

Dear Mr. Whitman: ₂ ➤

This letter shows how to use the blocked
style for typing your personal business
letters on ordinary, plain paper.

So that the person to whom you write will
know your address, type it, in two lines,
above the date line. Type the number and
street on the first line and the city and
state on the second. Like the date, the
two lines begin at the center.

At the end of the letter, type your name
under the space where you will sign your
letter. Do not type reference initials.

Yours very truly, ₄ ➤

Henry L. Hale

Use no reference
initials in letters
that you type for
yourself.

If your machine is pica, copy this letter exactly, line for line—but listen for the bell as
you type Job 5, next page. If your machine is elite, listen for the bell as you type this
letter—but copy Job 5 line for line. Use a 4-inch line (40 pica, 50 elite) for both letters.

WARMUP: Capital Control *(Each line 3 times)* ◁ **60** ▷

```
abcdefghijklmnopqrstuvwxyz : - : zyxwvutsrqponmlkjihgfedcba
Anne Bill Carl Dick Edna Fred Gwen Hale Inez Joan Kane Lois
Mary Nate Orie Paul Quen Ruth Saul Tina Vera Will Alex Zora
```

CONTROL DRILL: Row Reaches *(Each line 3 times)*

DE
```
de de den deed deal debt deny debit delay depth dense defer
de de dew idea ride index abide model decide folded outside
```

KI
```
ki ki kit kick kind kiss king kilt kinky kitty skiff asking
ki ki kid skill skirt making liking taking milking thinking
```

MU
```
mu mu mud much mule must mute mural music mulch musty muddy
mu mu mug amuse humus immune tumult bemuse commute formulas
```

CE
```
ce ce ace cede cent cease cedar celery censor center cereal
ce ce ice iced nice faced force accept advice decent chance
```

CONTROL SENTENCES: Row Reaches *(Each line 3 times)* ◁ **60** ▷

½-Min.
Writings

1	2	3	4	5	6	7	8	9	10	11	12	
Kim decided that too much working inside must concern them.												12
The censor must kid the skipper about this musty old music.												24
The mutt was not much, but these kids took a liking to him.												36
Cecile delighted the community audiences with choice music.												48

CONTROL DRILL: Concentration Paragraph *(3 copies / si 1.25)*

½- and 1-Min.
Writings

Fill in the
missing e's
as you type.

1	2	3	4	5	6	7	8	9	10	11	12	
D-ar Mr. Williams: I shall b- v-ry pl-as-d to h-lp you and												12
your staff s-t up a n-w filing syst-m. As you know, I hav-												24
b--n doing much of this kind of work r-c-ntly. If you will												36
notify m- wh-n to b-gin, I shall b- th-r-. Cordially yours												48

CONTROL SENTENCES: R through Z *(Each line 3 times)* ◁ **60** ▷

3-Min.
Writings

		1	2	3	4	5	6	7	8	9	10	11	12	
0	36	Red agreed to read every real report regarding our acreage.													12
4	40	Sam says Sara should stay in class and pass the state test.													24
8	44	Ted took three guests to tea after the team left the track.													36
12	48	Unless you unite your units under the union, you must quit.													48
16	52	Vick visited the caves and loved the view above the valley.													60
20	56	We walked with Wade while his wife watched the water shows.													72
24	60	Alex expects to examine his text next and extract examples.													84
28	64	Your yard stays pretty all year, and we envy it every year.													96
32	68	Buzz and Zeke gazed at my waltz magazine with amazing zest.													108

Plus ➡ 1 | 2 | 3 | 4

JOB 5

Blocked letter
  Shown in elite
  Use plain paper
  Return address
  Center tab
Words: 105
  Body: 72

3928 Dumont Avenue
Brooklyn 1, New York
October 18, 19-- ₈➡

◁ 4 in. ▷
SS
12/8
▽

First National Bank
1000 Eighth Avenue
New York 19, New York ₂➡

Gentlemen: ₂➡

I should like to obtain full information about your
new plan for issuing letters of credit to your customers who wish to take a trip to those countries
in which your firm has branch offices. ₂➡

I shall leave in about three weeks for a long trip
through France and England. I shall probably be
gone for nine weeks or so, spending most of my time
in Paris and London. ₂➡

                    Yours very truly, ₄➡

                    Henry L. Hale

JOB 6

Blocked letter
  Shown in pica
  Use plain paper
  Return address
  Center tab
Words: 117
  Body: 86

3928 Dumont Avenue
Brooklyn 1, New York
October 18, 19-- ₈➡

◁ 4 in. ▷
SS
12/8
▽

International Air Ways
156 West 33 Street
New York 1, New York ₂➡

Gentlemen: ₂➡

I wish to fly to Paris, then to London,
then back to New York. Do you have any
direct flights for such a trip? ₂➡

If you do, please let me have complete
information, including flight schedules,
the cost of the fare, the luggage weight
allowed, and the steps I should take in
order to get the passport that I need. ₂➡

If you do not have flights to these two
cities, please let me know which airline
does provide direct service to them. ₂➡

                    Yours very truly, ₄➡

                    Henry L. Hale

CONTROL PREVIEW (*Each line 3 times*) ◁ **60** ▷

are done point wrists realize expended impressed acquainted
tap care relax zenith machine response equipment operations
has been equip manual amazing required electrics difference

ALPHABET-REVIEW PARAGRAPHS (*1 copy / si 1.42*)

5-Min. Writings		1 | 2 | 3 | 4 | 5 | 6 | 7 | 8 | 9 | 10 | 11 | 12		

0.0	Most employers are apt to be quite impressed with some		11
2.2	piece of equipment that will realize more value for them on		23
4.6	cash expended. Studies of electric machines throughout the		35
7.0	country show it to be true that results are boosted to high		47
9.4	levels if the tasks being done are typical day-by-day jobs.		59
11.8	In addition, it has been found that fatigue becomes less of		71
14.2	a problem when electrics are used. Too, employers discover		83
16.6	a boost in office morale resulting from using the machines.		95
19.0	You will enjoy using these electrics in the classroom,	11	106
21.2	too. However, in order to become skilled on them, you will	23	118
23.6	be required to spend some time just getting acquainted with	35	130
26.0	the machines. The fact that your machine has a motor to do	47	142
28.4	most of the operations does not assure you of success. The	59	154
30.8	exact number of hours required to reach the zenith of skill	71	166
33.2	differs for each one, but ten to twelve hours is desirable.	83	178
35.6	A student who is typing in this part of the text is no	11	189
37.8	beginner. You will be anxious to see how much the electric	23	201
40.2	may affect your present skill. First of all, you will find	35	213
42.6	that your stroking habits will change greatly; and you will	47	225
45.0	be amazed by the ease with which the keys can be activated.	59	237
47.4	Remember just to tap the keys; the two wrists should remain	71	249
49.8	quite still. For a short while, you will probably discover	83	261
52.2	some unwanted letters, caused by your low-dangling fingers.	95	273
54.6	You might also be surprised by the ease with which the	11	284
56.8	special keys can be operated. The return key, most of all,	23	296
59.2	is a pleasure. It makes an amazing difference in your ease	35	308
61.6	of typing; you are able to relax as the carriage returns to	47	320
64.0	its starting point--you have no worry about the left hand's	59	332
66.4	getting back into position. You might also enjoy the quick	71	344
68.8	response of the other keys and get better speeds with them.	83	356
71.2	You may not realize that electrics equip one to become	11	367
73.4	a more expert manual typist: Skills gained on the electric	23	379
75.8	carry over and result in a general improvement. Just a few	35	391
78.2	hours of practice on an electric can improve manual typing.	37	403
Plus ▶	.2 | .4 | .6 | .8 | 1.0 | 1.2 | 1.4 | 1.6 | 1.8 | 2.0 | 2.2 | 2.4		

WARMUP *(Each line 2 times)*

N o P q R s T u V w X y Z a B c D e F g h i J k L m
(39) (28) (47) (56) (100) --39 --28 --47 --56 --100
Did the old man and the boy get the pay of one day?

12-Sec. 5| 10| 15| 20| 25| 30| 35| 40| 45| 50|

ACCELERATION PREVIEW *(Each line 2 times)*

GG suggestion bargain getting college enough giving
HH sympathy honored thanks should happy whole which
II initials official receiving position inside this
all you can end did not use got our job how get two

PRODUCTION PRACTICE *(Jobs 7-9)*

Study the letter below; then type it and Job 8 on plain paper, with the inside address below the letter instead of above it. Type Job 9 on a workbook letterhead.

JOB 7

Blocked letter
  Shown in pica
  Use plain paper
  Return address
  Address below
  Center tab
Words: 121
  Body: 89

This arrangement, with both a return address and an inverted address, is called "the personal style" by many typists.

◁ **4 in.** ▷
SS
12/8
▽

2856 Monroe Street
Eugene, Oregon
October 19, 19-- 8 �ža

Dear Miss Falk: 2 �ža

You can remove the "commercial" touch and   8
tone from any letter style by moving the   17
inside address to the end of the letter.   25

You should make this change in a personal   33
letter, in any formal or respectful letter   42
to a public official or other honored per-   50
son, and in any letter of appreciation or   59
sympathy or congratulation.   64

Do not use reference initials in any such   73
letter. If the person receiving the let-   81
ter knows you, do not even type your name.   89

                  Cordially yours, 4 �ža

                    Valerie Young 2 ➚

Miss Dorothy Falk
1047 North Dekum Street
Portland 3, Oregon

WARMUP: Alphabet Review (*Each line 3 times*)   ◁ **60** ▷

```
i j k l m n o p ijklmnop i j k l m n o p ijklmnop ijklmnop
zeal your yawn word view vast usual truly study reply quite
play open over note much most leave knows joint items heard
gone gain four ever done dark could bring about annex exile
```

CONTROL DRILL: N, B, T (*Each line 3 times*)

```
nn nip not name near none neck next noise night never nasty
nn nor nab kind turn many sign long human doing given thing

bb but bye back beam bias blow base begin birth blend board
bb big bud baby numb debt barb crib plumb debit sahib doubt

tt tow ton type twin town time tame tense throw tight tweed
tt tap ten item sent into left stet debit vital exist sixth
```

CONTROL SENTENCES: Concentration (*3 copies*)

```
.tsez htiw stseuqer dexim sevig dna ojnab tsrif syalp kcuhC     12
Chuck plays first banjo and gives mixed requests with zest.  12 | 24
```
12-Sec. 5| 10| 15| 20| 25| 30| 35| 40| 45| 50| 55| 60|

CONTROL SENTENCES: Alphabet Review (*Each line 3 times*)   ◁ **60** ▷

½-Min.
Writings

  1 | 2 | 3 | 4 | 5 | 6 | 7 | 8 | 9 | 10 | 11 | 12
```
Tex may give quite a few jacket prizes on the model barges.    12
Buzz rejected every required exam with all kinds of gripes.    24
Judge Black was very puzzled from Alex's queerest thinking.    36
Cap was amazed as requests gave his textbook first in July.    48
```

CONTROL PARAGRAPHS: Alphabet Review (*2 copies / si 1.40*)

  1 | 2 | 3 | 4 | 5 | 6 | 7 | 8 | 9 | 10 | 11 | 12

1-Minute
Writings on
each paragraph
and on both
paragraphs

```
        The electric typewriter has now arrived in many of our    11
schools.  Even though some may not have any, or just one or       23
two, they are probably requesting some for the next year or       35
two.  Did you realize that the electrics were so well liked       47
in most schools?  Their popularity is mounting, day by day.       59
```

  1 | 2 | 3 | 4 | 5 | 6 | 7 | 8 | 9 | 10 | 11 | 12

```
        Business has been buying more and more electrics, too.  11 | 70
We do not have the exact figures, but it has been estimated     23 | 82
that one out of every five or six office typewriters is now     35 | 94
an electric, which is an amazing jump in recent years.  The     47 | 106
modern typist has come to think quite well of the electric.     59 | 118
```

Blocked letter
  Shown in elite
  Use plain paper
  Return address
  Address below
  Center tab
Words: 129
  Body: 90

3910 Franklin Avenue
Des Moines 10, Iowa
October 20, 19-- 8 ➡

◁ **4 in.** ▷
SS
12/8
▽

Dear Doctor Brown: 2 ➡

Thank you very, very much for giving me so much of   10
your time yesterday morning. I did follow up your   20
suggestion; and, I am happy to report, I got the   30
position for which you recommended me. I begin my   40
work this coming Saturday, at noon. 2 ➡   48

Getting this weekend job means that I shall be able   58
to continue my education and, at the same time, get   69
experience that should actually help my classwork   79
and my career. I do not know how I can thank you   89
enough. 2 ➡   90

Respectfully yours, 4 ➡

Albert C. Mills 2 ➡

Dr. Foster Brown
Institute of Commerce
1000 Fleming Building
Des Moines 8, Iowa

JOB 9

Blocked letter
  Shown in elite
  Letterhead
  Center tab
Words: 122
  Body: 93

October 20, 19-- 8 ➡

◁ **4 in.** ▷
SS
14/8
▽

Miss Ruth W. Green
1028 Florence Avenue
Evanston, Illinois 2 ➡

My dear Miss Green: 2 ➡

We shall soon announce our annual sale of fine suits   11
and coats. It will begin the first of next month.   21
It will be quite an affair, featuring our whole line   32
of Mac Moore suits and coats--all colors, all sizes. 2 ➡ 42

As a courtesy to you and our other regular customers,   53
this sale will really begin two days prior to the   63
first of the month. We hope that it will be conven-   73
ient for you to stop in during these two preview days   84
and to pick up a fine bargain for yourself. 2 ➡   93

Very truly yours, 4 ➡

Manager, College Shop 2 ➡

RPG:URS

WARMUP: "NE" Drill *(Each line 3 times)* ◁ **60** ▷

```
aa;;zz//ssllxx..ddkkcc,,ffjjvvmmgghhbbnn a;sldkfjghfjdksla;
near neat nest neck neon nets next news need nebs neap Neal
general finest dined enemy money inert knelt knew ones knee
done fine gone line cane bone mane tone wane cone pane sane
```

SPEED DRILL: Doubled Letters *(Each line 3 times)*

```
dd addition address middle fiddle daddy caddy toddy odd add
tt pattern letters attends attach little bottom pretty putt
oo poodle snooze smooth bloom drool look pool ooze food too
pp scrapple flipper puppets supper moppet apple upper puppy
```

Keep rhythm very steady.

SPEED SENTENCES: Double Letters *(Each line 3 times)*

12-Sec. Writings

```
Address the letter and attach it to the bottom of the form.   12
The poodle puppy is happy to be snoozing soon after supper.   24
The pool in Seattle is getting an addition near the middle.   36
It looks like Mr. Potts is getting better with his putting.
```

12-Sec.5| 10| 15| 20| 25| 30| 35| 40| 45| 50| 55| 60|

SPEED DRILL: Alternate-Hand Words *(Each line 3 times)* ◁ **60** ▷

1-Min. Writings

1	2	3	4	5	6	7	8	9	10	11	12	

```
chairman auditor element island social usurp right dial men   12
neighbor visitor chaotic orient lament world their held key   24
quantity rituals ancient jangle theory handy usual down icy   36
sorority bushels ambient dismay formal audit theme they the   48
```

SPEED DRILL: Keeping Hands Low *(Each line 3 times)*

```
flasks salads shall flash halls slash flags flask gala glad
glass jags half fads asks dads gaff slag fall sash flag add
hall dash lads gags sass lash sags lass ask dad all gag has
```

Keep wrists very still.

SUSTAINED-SPEED SENTENCES *(Each line 3 times / si 1.12)* ◁ **60** ▷

3-Min. Writings

1	2	3	4	5	6	7	8	9	10	11	12	

```
 0 | 40   When the six boys throw rocks and sod, they vow to pelt us.   12
 4 | 44   Did they sign their name to the form when they got to town?   24
 8 | 48   The chairman of the problems panel did form a theme for it.   36
12 | 52   If they do make a profit, they may hand it to the sorority.   48
16 | 56   She may endow the chapel and pay for the big pane for them.   60

20 | 60   Hale may go to work for them and pay for fuel with the pay.   72
24 | 64   They may pay a visit to the city to bid for the high chair.   84
28 | 68   Bob kept both handy men busy with sod work by the big pens.   96
32 | 72   Now is the time for the girls to take their pals to chapel.  108
36 | 76   They own eight big oaks, down by the end of the key island.  120
```

Plus ➧   1   2   3   4

UNIT 7
TABULATION

In this unit, you will learn to type columns and to set up tables. There are many tables, but all are short ones, so that you will get enough practice in setting them up quickly. This unit will be easiest if you will read through pages 57-64 carefully and answer the study questions on Workbook pages 35-36 before beginning jobs.

WARMUP (*Each line 2 times*)   ◁**52**▷

```
U v W x Y z A b c D E f G h I J K l M n O p Q r S t
39 28 47 56 10 we 23 put 075 you 697 up 70 too 599.
I know she will want this plan done over once more.
12-Sec.  5|    10|    15|    20|    25|    30|    35|    40|    45|    50|
```

ACCELERATION PREVIEW (*Each line 2 times*)

```
JJ jewelry jiffy Jones just jump John join Jean job
KK backspace backhaul quickly kinds clock work take
LL pleasant longest listing problem simply list all
one the job can set you and all are zip out get six
```

ALPHABET-REVIEW PARAGRAPH (*2 copies / si 1.30*)   ◁**60**▷
                                                                  DS

```
3-Min.
Writings   1 | 2 | 3 | 4 | 5 | 6 | 7 | 8 | 9 | 10 | 11 | 12
 0      One of the pleasantest duties that many typists get to    11
 4   do on the job is to arrange information in column form.  If   23
 8   there is just one column, it is called a listing.  The typ-   35
12   ist can set up a listing in a jiffy; it is quite easy.  You   47
16   simply center the longest item in the list and then line up   59
20   all the items with that one item.  Here are the exact steps   71
24   you take:  You center the carriage; you backspace enough to   83
28   center the longest line; you move in the margin stop to the   95
32   point to which you backspaced; then, you zip down the list.  107
Plus ▶      1   |      2    |      3    |      4
```

PRODUCTION PRACTICE (*Jobs 1-4*)

Study pages 58 and 59; then type Jobs 1-4, centering each (both horizontally and vertically) on half sheets of plain paper. Be sure the paper guide is set correctly (page 3).

SPEED PREVIEW (*Each line 3 times*)

typewriter surprised alphabet systems versed sharp next use
instantly, preceding increase Federal charge staff huge and
important difficult agencies accuracy money; third most new

SUSTAINED-SPEED PARAGRAPHS (*1 copy / si 1.28*)

5-Min. Writings	1	2	3	4	5	6	7	8	9	10	11	12		
0.0				Before one can hope to become adept in the whole field										11
2.2			of filing, he has to be versed on all parts of the alphabet											23
4.6			and able to use the rules that are basic in filing systems.											35
7.0			You would be surprised how many persons cannot tell you in-											47
9.4			stantly, if you call out a letter, what the next letter is;											59
11.8			and even more hesitate to say what the preceding letter is.											71
14.2			In an office, time is money; and it is quite important										11	82
16.4			to make use of some plan that gives speed in filing without										23	94
18.8			too much error. Records ought to be filed so that they can										35	106
21.2			be found in a short time. Accuracy is vital to good filing										47	118
23.6			because so much depends upon the skill the clerk uses while										59	130
26.0			she is putting the papers in the files. Lack of care might										71	142
28.4			cost a firm money and lead to some very confusing problems.										83	154
30.8			The advent of the typewriter in an office has been the										11	165
33.0			cause of many changes. One of the most common of these has										23	177
35.4			been the large increase in the quantity of papers that have										35	189
37.8			to be filed. The big increase in the number of typists, as										47	201
40.2			well as their use of carbon paper for more copies, has made										59	213
42.6			paper control a real task. Figures show that about a third										71	225
45.0			of most records should be kept in the files, a third stored										83	237
47.4			for a while, and the final third thrown out from the start.										95	249
49.8			The large increase in the number of papers sent out of										11	260
52.0			a normal office has had much to do with the sharp growth of										23	272
54.4			filing. The need for more records to meet the needs of the										35	284
56.8			Federal agencies has been a big factor in this growth, too.										47	296
59.2			In fact, files have become so huge in some large firms that										59	308
61.6			they have to study new papers and get rid of those that are										71	320
64.0			of little value. This can be a difficult chore to perform.										83	332
66.4			There is a lot of challenge in filing. It takes a lot										11	343
68.6			more skill than the humorists realize. So, when you under-										23	355
71.0			take a new job and are asked to start by helping the office										35	367
73.4			staff to catch up with its backlog of filing, do not be un-										47	379
75.8			happy about it. Instead, grasp the chance to master at the										59	391
78.2			outset one of the main duties involved in an office career.										71	403

Plus ▶	.2	.4	.6	.8	1.0	1.2	1.4	1.6	1.8	2.0	2.2	2.4

HOW TO CENTER 1 COLUMN . . .

1. Clear the machine: Move the margin stops to the ends of the line, and clear out any tab stops that may be set.

2. Compute the top margin, to center the copy vertically (review page 29).

3. Insert paper. Straighten it. Drop to the line determined by Step 2.

4. Center the title, in all capitals.

5. Drop down 3 lines, to the body of the table, and center the carriage.

6. Select the key item (longest item) in the column.

7. Backspace to center that key item.

8. Set the left margin stop at the point to which you have backspaced.

9. Type the column, beginning each line at the margin stop.

HOW TO CENTER 2 COLUMNS . . .

1. Clear the machine.

2. Compute the top margin.

3. Insert the paper.

4. Center the title.

5. Drop 3 lines. Center the carriage.

6. Select the key item (longest item) in *each* column. The key items in Job 2, for example, are *sentence* and *though*.

7. From the center of the paper, backspace enough to center the key items 6 spaces apart, like this:

sentence......though

The easiest way to do this: backspace (*a*) 3 times, to allow for centering the 6 spaces, and (*b*) 1 time for each pair of strokes in the combined key items.

8. Set the left margin stop at the point to which you have backspaced.

9. Space over to Column 2 (tap the space bar once for each stroke in the key item of Column 1 and once for each of the 6 strokes in the blank area between the columns). Set a tab stop at this point.

10. Pull the carriage back to the margin. Type the first item in Column 1; tabulate to the stop and type the first item in Column 2. Return the carriage and begin the second line. Type the whole table in this same way, line by line.

JOB 1

1-column table
Center
Half sheet
Words: 35

TRANSPORTATION TERMS

airline
automobile
backhaul
baggage
boxcar
carload
carrier
coastwise
collision
commutation
compartment
consignee
consignor
demurrage
destination
drayage

Key: commutation

← **Margin stop**

JOB 2

2-column table
Center
Half sheet
1 tab stop
Words: 19

TABULATING ₃ ←

Always	Tab ▶	type
tables		line
by		line
as		though
you		were
typing		a
sentence		like
this		one.

Key: sentence......though

← **Margin stop**   ← **Tab stop**

PART 8

WARMUP: Alternate-Hand Words *(Each line 3 times)* ◁ **60** ▷

```
aa;; zz// ssll xx.. ddkk cc,, ffjj vvmm gghh bbnn aa;; ssll
ritual chapel angle giant sprig fight bugle amble lake gown
bushel mangle throw chant gland world endow handy make fuel
profit formal slept lapel audit amend cycle cubic rich town
```

SPEED DRILL: Word Families *(Each line 3 times)*

```
HA hat had has halt half hang hand have hale haul hair hawk
TI tie tip tin tidy tile tilt time tint tick tire tide tier
CO cot coy cog cosy cork corn come cold comb code coal cord
```

SPEED SENTENCES *(Each line 3 times)*

12-Sec.
Writings
```
I kept the keys to the chapel and may form the panel in it.
I burn oak for fuel but also for a blend of flame and odor.
Is it right for us to rob the rich of their own social tie?
```

12-Sec.5| 10| 15| 20| 25| 30| 35| 40| 45| 50| 55| 60|

SPEED PARAGRAPHS *(3 copies / si 1.00)*

1-Min.
Writings

   1 | 2 | 3 | 4 | 5 | 6 | 7 | 8 | 9 | 10 | 11 | 12

```
Pride in your work is one thing that will make you like the    12
job you now have.  To work so well that you can be proud of    24
what you do and what you turn out, you have to have all the    36
skill that you can use in the job.  If you do not have what    48
it takes, you will not do work in which you can take pride.    60
```

SPEED DRILL: Space-bar Speed-up *(Each line 3 times)* ◁ **60** ▷

```
hand duck kept torn name ends slow wish held disk keys soft
tool look keen nook keep peer room mood deer roll loop pool
let two one end dry yet the elf for rim may yes sit tug gem
```

SUSTAINED-SPEED PARAGRAPHS *(1 copy / si 1.40)* **DS**

2-Min.
Writings
        1 | 2 | 3 | 4 | 5 | 6 | 7 | 8 | 9 | 10 | 11 | 12

```
 0      Filing is now one of the really essential functions in    11
 6   the modern office.  At one time, one would feel it to be an    23
12   insult to be asked to work with the files; but almost every    35
18   person who works in an office today has to be familiar with    47
24   the rules and procedures of filing.  It is truly essential.    59

30      No one topic has ever taken the brunt of so many jokes    11 | 70
35   and jibes as filing has; it is certainly a favorite subject   23 | 82
41   of cartoons, too.  Not all the tales are without truth, nor   35 | 94
47   has the humor been a total waste; it has made many aware of   47 | 106
53   the vital need for accurate application of rules in filing.   59 | 118
```

Plus ▶   1 | 2 | 3 | 4 | 5 | 6

HOW TO CENTER TABLES WITH SEVERAL COLUMNS . . .

The basic steps are the same as those for a 2-column table. The difference is simply that there are more columns with which to work—more "longest items" to pick out, more 6-space blank areas between columns to allow for, and more tab stops to set. Job 3, for example, requires that you set the left margin stop and *two* tab stops; Job 4 requires the margin and *three* tab stops. Tables with many columns take more time but are not *harder* to do.

> **STANDARD RULE:** Always put 6 spaces between columns unless you are specifically told to put more or fewer than 6.

JOB 3

3-column table
Center
Half sheet
2 tab stops
Words: 49

DS 7/3

TRANSPORTATION TERMS ₃ ➧

airline	Tab ➧	collision	Tab ➧	dunnage
automobile		commutation		embargo
backhaul		compartments		excursion
baggage		consignee		f.o.b.
boxcar		consignor		freightage
carload		demurrage		gondola
carrier		destination		hangars
coastwise		drayage		helicopter

Key: automobile......compartments......freightage

⬅ Margin stop   ⬅ Tab stop   ⬅ Tab stop

JOB 4

4-column table
Center
Half sheet
3 tab stops
Words: 49

DS 9/3

TRANSPORTATION TERMS ₃ ➧

airline	Tab ➧	carrier	Tab ➧	consignor	Tab ➧	excursion
automobile		coastwise		demurrage		f.o.b.
backhaul		collision		destination		freightage
baggage		commutation		drayage		gondola
boxcar		compartments		dunnage		hangars
carload		consignee		embargo		helicopter

Key: automobile......compartments......destination......helicopter

⬅ Margin stop   ⬅ Tab stop   ⬅ Tab stop   ⬅ Tab stop

CARD 2. Harriet B. Stewart, of 1778 Harper Street, Terre Haute, Indiana, applied yesterday for a stenographic job. She wanted only $60 a week, but there was no vacancy. Miss Stewart was born July 12, 1935, and attended high school in Indianapolis, graduating in 1954. She worked as receptionist ($40 a week) at the Jackson-Lord Company from 1954 through 1956; since then she has worked as a stenographer in the same company at $55 a week. Note: Miss Stewart should be contacted for the next stenographic vacancy.

NAME: Wilcox, Marjory			JOB WANTED: Secretary
ADDRESS: 1644 South Park Lane			PAY ASKED: $80 Week
Terre Haute, Indiana			WHY WE DID: Failed
			NOT EMPLOY: Test
BIRTH: November 17, 1932			DATE: 10/22/57

EDUCATION (Last first)			
Years	School	Place	Grad
50-52	Metropolitan B. C.	New York, New York	1952
46-50	High School	Newark, New Jersey	1950

EXPERIENCE (Last first)			
Years	Company	Position	Salary
55---	Aetna Life	Stenographer	$70
52-54	Paramount Corp.	Stenographer	$60

Comments: Will take evening-school work, then try test again. Almost made the grade on first attempt.

Duplicated personnel card, 6 by 4 inches

PART D: LETTER TEST (254 total words / si 1.50)

Type this 220-word "dictated" letter in blocked form, the date at the right margin. Be sure to capitalize correctly. The letter should be divided into four paragraphs. Grade your work on the scale on page 251.

today's date. mr. robert f. buckner, 889 west bend street, terre haute, 15
indiana. dear mr. buckner: 21

i am very sorry to tell you that we are not able to meet your salary 35
request for the accounting vacancy that we have open. We are disap- 48
pointed, for your qualifications are almost exactly what we had hoped 62
for when we advertised the vacancy. we should be happy to accept 75
your application if you would be willing to start at $6,600 a year instead 90
of the $7,200 that you requested. i personally believe that you would 104
be well advised to consider the lower figure. to conform to our salary 119
schedule, the position must begin at $6,600; but over a period of a few 133
years, the salary potential for the position will range up to $9,600. 147

if you wish to reconsider your decision, we should be pleased to hear 161
from you. we shall advertise the position again in next sunday's papers; 176
if you contact us before we commit ourselves to another applicant, we 190
should most surely give you priority at the advertised figure. it was a 205
pleasure to meet you, mr. buckner; i enjoyed our interview. mr. young 219
has told me that he, too, enjoyed interviewing you and that he would 233
be delighted to have you on his staff. 241

cordially yours, stephen j. kellock, personnel manager 252

WARMUP *(Each line 2 times)*   ◁ **52** ▷

```
B c D e F g H i J k L m N o P q R s T u V w X y Z a
39 and 28 and 47 and 56 and 10 or 39 or 28 or more.
Why should they have this plan done over once more?
```
12-Sec. 5| 10| 15| 20| 25| 30| 35| 40| 45| 50|

ACCELERATION PREVIEW *(Each line 2 times)*

```
MM something somehow morning minute moving amaze me
NN suspended window hands seven kinds fine been and
OO located corner clocks before front for now or to
study where there eight clock quite sizes oval that
more than year been each fine that have set all you
for now has the get bus and six due big of to it is
```

ALPHABET-REVIEW PARAGRAPH *(2 copies / si 1.35)*   ◁ **60** ▷
DS

3-Min. Writings   1 | 2 | 3 | 4 | 5 | 6 | 7 | 8 | 9 | 10 | 11 | 12

```
 0      For more than a year now, it has been my pleasure each    11
 4   morning to study the window of a fine jewelry store that is   23
 8   located at the corner where I get my bus.  I arrive there a   35
12   little before eight each morning and have six or seven min-   47
16   utes to wait before the bus is due.  While I wait for it, I   59
20   study the big display of clocks in the window; it is really   71
24   quite something to see, with clocks of all sizes and kinds.   83
28   There are several timepieces that always amaze me.  You see   95
32   no moving parts whatsoever--just the oval faces and pointed  107
36   hands, somehow suspended in the front corner of the window.  119
```
Plus ▶   1   2   3   4

PRODUCTION PRACTICE *(Jobs 5-8)*

Study page 61; then type Jobs 5-8. Note that Jobs 5, 6, and 7 are to be centered on full sheets of plain paper; but Job 8 is to be centered on a half sheet.

TAKE OFF:	−3 for each major error (top margin, line length, linespacing, general form, etc.) −2 for each minor error (blocking, aligning, indenting, etc., of each part of a job) −1 for each typographical error	TOTAL TAKEN OFF	10-9	8-5	4-3	2-0
		GRADE	D	C	B	A

Grade Parts B, C, and D separately, using this scale for all the work in each Part.

PART B: MANUSCRIPT-DISPLAY TEST *(135 total words)*

Center the following display on a full sheet of paper, being sure to justify all lines. Note that the copy is shown in first draft, ready for you to retype.

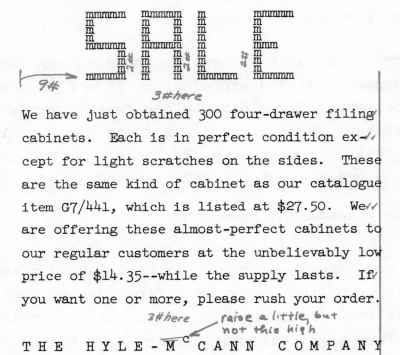

We have just obtained 300 four-drawer filing cabinets. Each is in perfect condition except for light scratches on the sides. These are the same kind of cabinet as our catalogue item G7/441, which is listed at $27.50. We are offering these almost-perfect cabinets to our regular customers at the unbelievably low price of $14.35--while the supply lasts. If you want one or more, please rush your order.

THE HYLE-M^cCANN COMPANY

PART C: BUSINESS-FORMS TEST *(119 total words)*

Arrange the following information on the two personnel forms, 6 by 4 inches, on Workbook page 275. If you lack forms, make your own, arranged like the illustration at the top of the next page, using slips of paper 6 by 4 inches. Grade your work on the scale above; do not grade each form separately, but rather grade both forms as one job.

CARD 1. Robert F. Buckner lives at 889 West Bend Street, Terre Haute, Indiana. When he applied to your firm for a job as accountant yesterday, he was turned down because your company does not pay as much as he wanted—$7,200. Mr. Buckner was born on May 1, 1922. He attended the high school in Muncie for 4 years, graduating in 1940; and In- diana University, graduating in 1944. He was in the Navy from 1944 to 1946, earning an annual salary of $4,200 as a supply officer. Then he worked as an accountant for the Laughlin Steel Company, at $5,400, from 1947-1953. Since then he has been an accountant for the Corning Glass Company, receiving $6,300 a year. (TURN PAGE)

HOW TO DISPLAY A COLUMN HEADING . . .

1. The heading is underscored. If it consists of two or more words, underscore them solidly.

2. Each important word in the column heading begins with a capital letter.

3. Separate the column heading from the column by *1* blank space; separate the heading from the title of the table by *2* blank spaces.

4. Each heading is centered above the column it identifies.

5. When columns have headings, set the margin and tab stops for the columns before typing the column headings.

HOW TO CENTER A COLUMN HEADING . . .

1. Note the difference between the length of the heading and the length of the longest item.

Juniors ¹²³⁴⁵⁶⁷⁸⁹

Ruth Anne Fisher

Divide the difference by 2 (ignore fractions) to find out how much to indent the shorter line from the start of the longer line. Thus:

1234 Juniors 56789

Ruth Anne Fisher

2. When the column heading is longer than any other item in its column (as in Columns 1 and 3 of Job 8), the heading itself is used as the longest line when positioning the table. After the heading has been typed, the margin or tab stop is then moved in so as to center the column under the heading.

JOB 5

2-column table
Center
Full sheet
1 tab stop
Words: 69

HONOR ROLL ₃ �;

SS
25/3

Juniors	Seniors ₂ ➤
Beverly Barton Tab ➤	Elizabeth Allen
Ruth Ann Fisher	Georgette Cox
Marian Fosdick	David Davis
Nathan Friedman	Edward Eyster
Alice Graham	Richard Falkner
Henry Howell	Dorothy Friedman
Pauline Lewis	Lucretia Jones
Howard Norwin	Anna June Miller
Yvonne Treaux	Emily Porter
Albert Watson	Susan Strong
Martin Williams	Jack Winters

Key: Ruth Ann Fisher......Dorothy Friedman
         ▲ **Margin stop**   ◄ **Tab stop**

You will need 2 sheets of plain paper or Workbook pages 273-276. Type Parts A and B on opposite sides of one sheet, and Parts C and D on opposite sides of the second sheet.

PART A: STRAIGHT-COPY TEST *(si 1.30)*

Take a 5-minute writing on the copy below; or, type the copy once and grade your work as though you had typed it at the rate of 58 words a minute. Grading scale:

Step 1: Compute words a minute.	Step 2: Deduct for errors—		Step 3: Grade the remaining words a minute this way:	
	1 error: —2	4 errors: —10		55 or higher: A
	2 errors: —4	5 errors: —14		50 to 54 wam: B
	3 errors: —7	6 errors: —18		45 to 49 wam: C
				40 to 44 wam: D

◁ **70** ▷
DS

5-Min. Writings

Of all the skills that[1] people wish they had, the[2] skill of typing ranks first.[3] Just about   18

every person[4] who knows that you can[5] type has said to you that[6] he wishes that he,   34

too,[7] knew how to type; the[8] person who is a skilled[9] typist is the envy of all[10] his friends.   52

One evidence[11] that typing is so popular[12] is shown by the fact that[13] more persons   68

take courses[14] in typing than in anything[15] else — except English,[16] that is; but then,[17]   84

English is a required course.[18] Today, it is not just[19] the office trainee who[20] learns to   101

type, although he[21] must, of course; but everyone[22] else seems to be taking[23] the course,   118

too. I visited[24] a college a short[25] time ago and found that[26] the school had just taken[27]   134

a poll to find what purpose[28] the students had in mind[29] when they signed up for[30] typ-   150

ing. You would be[31] amazed at the findings of[32] the poll. Enrolled for[33] the typing   166

course was at[34] least one person from every[35] major field in the college.[36]   180

It is natural to[37] marvel and to wonder why so[38] many persons desire this[39] skill. The   197

answer is[40] that almost all careers in[41] modern life now involve[42] the use of much paper   214

and[43] require that you be able[44] to express yourself—whether[45] what you wish to report[46]   230

is a new plan for packaging[47] snow, a new scheme[48] for a sales campaign, a[49] history   246

of jazz, a formula[50] for splitting the atom,[51] or a news account of life[52] in Quebec. And   263

the simple[53] truth is that what you[54] write has to be typed.[55] No editor worth his salt[56]   279

would look at a penned[57] manuscript these days. So[58] it is that anyone who wants[59] to   295

write or wants to[60] get a job that involves[61] writing finds that he jolly[62] well better learn   313

to type[63] — and to do so expertly.[64]   319

JOB 6

2-column table
Center
Full sheet
1 tab stop
Words: 52

NATIONAL BOX COMPANY ₃ ➡

Branch	Manager ₂ ➡
Albuquerque	Richard Miller, Jr.
Atlanta	Earl Lane Simpson
Dallas	Irwin F. Massey
Detroit	Gertrude Slattery
Los Angeles	Robert Wellerton
Miami	Harold H. Webb
Mobile	John R. Dubinsky
New Orleans	Jean F. Bordeaux

Key: Albuquerque......Richard Miller, Jr.
      ⬅ **Margin stop**   ⬅ **Tab stop**

JOB 7

3-column table
Center
Full sheet
2 tab stops
Words: 72

TEN RECORDS FOR RUNNING A MILE ₃ ➡

Record	Runner	Country ₂ ➡
3:58.0	John Landy	Australia
3:58.8	Roger Bannister	England
3:59.0	Laszlo Tabori	Hungary
3:59.4	Roger Bannister	England
3:59.6	John Landy	Australia
3:59.8	Chris Chataway	England
3:59.8	Brian Hewson	England
4:00.5	Wes Santee	U. S. A.
4:00.6	Wes Santee	U. S. A.
4:00.7	Wes Santee	U. S. A.

Key: Record......Roger Bannister......Australia
      ⬅ **Margin stop**   ⬅ **Tab stop**   ⬅ **Tab stop**

JOB 8

4-column table
Center
Half sheet
3 tab stops
Words: 80

DUTY ROSTER, OCTOBER 24 ₃ ➡   DS

Watch	Officer of the Deck	Junior Officer of the Deck	Quarter-master ₁ ➡ ₂ ➡
0000	Lt. Martin	Ens. Hughes	QM3 Williams
0400	LCdr. Greene	Ens. Shaw	QM1 Parker
0800	Lt. Foster	Ltjg. Carews	QM3 Virgil
1200	Ltjg. Young	Ens. Krell	QM2 Shannon
1600	Lt. Martin	Ens. Hughes	QM3 Williams
2000	LCdr. Greene	Ens. Shaw	QM1 Parker

Key: Watch......LCdr. Greene......Junior Officer......QM3 Williams
      ⬅ **Margin stop** ⬅ **Tab stop**   ⬅ **Tab stop**   ⬅ **Tab stop**

JOB 9

Fill-in form
Workbook
Words: 109

PERSONNEL DEPARTMENT

Record of Interviews on _____

TIME	PERSON, ADDRESS	POSITION	ACTION
9:15	Marianne Irwin 3161 West Elm Street	Stenographer	To be interviewed 1:30 tomorrow by J. E.
9:30	Elizabeth White 273 Park Road	Secretary	Good, but out of our price range
11:15	Roger Trytten Box 138 Dumont Pike	Machinist	To be interviewed at 9:30 tomorrow by L. B.
2:30	Marianne Irwin (see 9:15 above)		Withdrew application; has other job
2:45	Robert K. Plumber 573 Ninth Avenue	Lathe operator	To be interviewed at 10:15 tomorrow by L. B.
3:00	Mrs Susan Williams 2291 Hopkins Street	Switchboard operator	Took name only; no vacancy

◁ **68** ▷

JOB 10

Manuscript display
Plain paper
First draft
3 carbons
Words: 228

HELP ← 6 → WANTED
#

Center > (<u>YOUR</u> HELP, THAT IS!)

For publication in the picture page of our new magazine, HI MAC, we need many good photographs--the kind you show your friends at the ✓ next desk or the next bench. Have any you can let us use? We should like pictur(e)s of your new offspring, of your children's graduation ✓✓✓ from high school or college, of you and the family on vacation, of ✓✓✓ you with fellow Hyle-McCann workers . . . pictures and more pictures!

The photographs should be glossy ones--the bigger, the better. ✓✓ They should be clear, with lots of sharp contrast. By and large, we ✓ think outdoor shots may be better than inside ones. We will be sure ✓ to see that your photographs are returned to you. Help us, please?

⌐ --Nick Edelsen, Editor, HI MAC →

WARMUP *(Each line 2 times)*

◁52▷

```
r S t U v W x Y z A b C d E f G h I J K l M n O p Q
$39 $28 $47 $56 $10 $39 $28 $47 $56 $10 $39 $28 $47
Must they have that same plan done over once again?
```
12-Sec. 5| 10| 15| 20| 25| 30| 35| 40| 45| 50|

ACCELERATION PREVIEW *(Each line 2 times)*

```
PP products policies company deposit happy play pay
RR necessary December reserve curtain dollar recent
SS executives enclosed tickets please seats wish us
   you for the and how pay one are top any our can see
```

PRODUCTION PRACTICE *(Jobs 9-11)*

Review the form for blocked letters (page 50) and the procedure for typing tables with column headings (page 61); then type Jobs 9, 10, and 11, noting carefully the directions printed under the job numbers. Type Jobs 9 and 11 on workbook letterheads; center Job 10 on a half sheet of plain paper. You may use the body of the letter below for timed practice.

1 | 2 | 3 | 4 | 5 | 6 | 7 | 8 | 9 | 10

October 28, 19-- 8 ➡

◁ **4 in.** ▷
SS
14/8
▽

JOB 9

Blocked letter
  Shown in elite
  Letterhead
  Center tab
Words: 128
  Body: 98

Miss Florence Stahl
3928 Lakeview Avenue
Detroit 15, Michigan

Dear Miss Stahl:

Thank you for your recent letter in which you asked   10
about the plays for which you might still be able   20
to obtain tickets for the first week of December.   31
Enclosed you will find a list of such plays.   40

If you wish us to reserve tickets for you, please   50
let us know within the next week. Tell us which   60
play you wish to see and how much you wish to pay   70
for the seats. It is necessary for you to deposit   80
one dollar on each ticket; then we will hold the   90
tickets until 24 hours before curtain time.   98

Cordially yours, 4 ➡

John Wilkes, Agent 2 ➡

When something
is to be mailed
with a letter,
type "Enclosure"
beneath the
initials, as a re-
minder.

JW:URS
Enclosure

Part 2
LESSONS
Unit 7
42/43

WARMUP *(Each line 3 times)*

```
a;qpa;z/a; slwoslx.sl dkeidkc,dk fjrufjvmfj tyghbnghfj fjrufjvmfj dke
Abner Chuck Davis Floyd Gregg Henry Hazel Jed Maxie Percy Quent Wilma
pi 08 rot 495 rote 4953 pour 0974; 39 28 47 56 10 39" 28" 47" 56" 10"
The game had hardly begun before the folks began to stamp their feet.
12-Sec.5|   10|   15|   20|   25|   30|   35|   40|   45|   50|   55|   60|   65|   70|
```

RHYTHM PREVIEW *(Each line 3 times)*

```
wishes report please office letter Doctor Powers agency scores Borden
Dear Miss know that work will call this soon make your most when have
used test let you the was and add his for can has our own new any use
```

PRODUCTION PRACTICE *(Jobs 7-10)*

7-8. Miss Trotter dictates the letters below; each contains two paragraphs. Use half-page stationery and blocked form (page 190).

9. Type the record of her interviews (on page 249). Date the record for yesterday.

10. Someone has typed (page 249) a first draft of a bulletin-board display. Working from the draft, center a copy on a full page.

JOB 7

Blocked letter
Dictated form
Letterhead
(½-page size)
2 carbons
Words: 90
Body: 72

Today's date. Miss Roslyn Carpenter, 3161 Pennsylvania Avenue, Baltimore 17, Maryland.

```
    1 | 2 | 3 | 4 | 5 | 6 | 7 | 8 | 9 | 10 | 11 | 12
dear miss carpenter:  i am pleased to let you know that the          12
interview with mr. elston was successful and that he wishes          24
to add you to his staff as soon as you can report for work.          36
will you please, therefore, call our office, as soon as you          48
can after receiving this letter, to make an appointment for          60
your physical examination and to complete your arrangements          72
for starting work.   cordially yours, miss priscilla trotter         84
```

JOB 8

Blocked letter
Dictated form
Letterhead
(½-page size)
2 carbons
Words: 95
Body: 73

Today's date. Dr. Harold R. Powers, Scientific Test Bureau, 756 North Front Street, Baltimore 2, Maryland.

```
    1 | 2 | 3 | 4 | 5 | 6 | 7 | 8 | 9 | 10 | 11 | 12
dear doctor powers:  in most of the cases when we have used     12 |  96
the tests supplied us by your agency, your analysis of test     24 | 108
scores has very closely paralleled our own evaluation of an     36 | 120
applicant.  in the case of miss marguerite borden, however,     48 | 132
your report is so contradictory to our observations that we     60 | 144
are wondering whether her scores could have been mixed with     72 | 156
those of someone else.  yours truly, miss priscilla trotter     84 | 168
```

JOB 10

3-column table
Center
Half sheet
2 tab stops
Words: 70

THEATER TICKETS AVAILABLE ₂ ➡

For Week of December 3 ₃ ➡

Subtitles should
be preceded by 1
blank line and
followed by 2.

Play	Star	Price Range ₂ ➡
Shadowed Rainbow	Nancy Reeves	$1.20 - $3.30
Seventh Daughter	Gloria Langley	2.20 - 7.50
Inherit the Rain	Paul Montrose	2.20 - 8.80
Holly Ann	Ross Willard	4.40 - 8.80
Comedy of Errors	Victor Bennett	1.75 - 4.40
Smiling Sympathy	Janis Prell	2.20 - 5.50

Key: Shadowed Rainbow......Gloria Langley......$1.20 - $3.30

⬆ **Margin stop**   ⬆ **Tab stop**   ⬆ **Tab stop**

Note: After typing the $ sign,
move the tab stop in 1 space.

JOB 11

Blocked letter
  Shown in pica
Letterhead
2 tab stops
  (for table)
Words: 104
  Body: 75
  Table: 26

October 28, 19-- ₈ ➡

◁ **4 in.** ▷
SS
14/8
▽

Mr. Ralph F. Lemon
4710 West Fourth Street
San Diego 11, California

Dear Mr. Lemon:

We are happy to tell you the names of the
top executives of this company. They are
as follows: ₂ ➡

A table in a letter
is set up like any
other table: Center
it by backspacing
after clearing the
machine. Allow
the usual 6 spaces
between columns.

President	Edward Smither
Manager	Richard Rosser
Treasurer	Willard Holman
Comptroller	Jackson Grissom
Secretary	Virgil Harris ₂ ➡

If there is any other information about
our company that I can tell you--size or
products or policies--I shall be happy to
do so, at your request.

Yours very truly, ₄ ➡

Virgil Harris ₂ ➡

VH:URS

JOB 5

Manuscript
display

WELCOME TO HYLE-McCANN! We are very pleased that you have joined our staff. Our company is young, but it is growing and ~~is full of~~ offers many opportunity ies for every newcomer. We sincerely hope that you will like your position on our staff, that you will enjoy your work, and that you will contribute to the growth ~~and spirit~~ of the company.

The purpose of this booklet is to tell you in detail about the policies and products of Hyle-McCann. We hope that you will find ~~it~~ this booklet interesting ~~to read.~~ It ~~will~~ should answer most of your questions about pay days, vacations, ~~special~~ benefits, holidays, absences, and so on. If ~~there is any~~ you have a question that is not answered in this booklet, please do not hesitate to stop in the Personnel Office and present your question to any member of the personnel staff.

PERSONNEL DEPARTMENT

JOB 6

Manuscript
display

UNIT 8
MANUSCRIPTS

In this unit you learn to arrange and type short manuscript displays in which the tabulator helps you produce work efficiently. This unit will be easiest if you first read through pages 65-72, noting what is said in each job and how each job is arranged; and then answer the study questions on Workbook pages 43-44.

WARMUP (*Each line 2 times*) ◁ 52 ▷

```
I j k L m n O p q R s t U v w X y z A b c D e f G h
39 XXXIX 28 XXVIII 47 XLVII 56 LVI 10 X 100 C 500 D
He can make the long trip there in less than a day.
```
12-Sec. 5| 10| 15| 20| 25| 30| 35| 40| 45| 50|

ACCELERATION PREVIEW (*Each line 2 times*)

```
TT different separate little letter other step that
UU enumeration manuscripts sequence unique count up
VV Government Seventeenth however divide above give
all out put for the and are job you use two set any
```

ALPHABET-REVIEW PARAGRAPH (*2 copies / si 1.30*) ◁ 60 ▷
DS

3-Min. Writings

	1	2	3	4	5	6	7	8	9	10	11	12	

```
 0      All of us like to classify things, to put them in neat    11
 4    little pigeon holes, to sort them out.  In typewriting, for    23
 8    example, we like to classify the different kinds of jobs as    35
12    letters or tables or manuscripts, and so on, as though each    47
16    were done in separate steps that are unique to that kind of    59
20    job.  It is good to realize, however, that most of the jobs    71
24    are much more like than unlike each other.  A poem is typed    83
28    in the same way as a one-column table; indeed, you will use    95
32    the tab stops almost as much in typing a poem or an outline   107
36    or a list of books as you do when you type up a tabulation.   119
Plus ➡        1          2          3          4
```

PRODUCTION PRACTICE (*Jobs 1-4*)

Study pages 66 and 67; read carefully the information contained in Jobs 1, 2, and 3. Then, using the procedure described in Job 1, center the four jobs on separate full sheets of paper. Copy all the material line for line, exactly as it is shown.

HOW TO "JUSTIFY" THE RIGHT-HAND MARGIN . . .

There are three ways to make lines end evenly at the right margin (that is, to "justify" the lines):

1. You may sometimes change a word or a sentence so that all your lines will come out even; this is what the authors of this book did in order to make all the timed-writing lines end evenly at the right margin.

2. You may put some extra spaces between the words, to spread them out so that they fill lines evenly, as in this paragraph. When you do this, try to avoid putting the extra spaces of one line directly under those of the preceding line.

3. You may spread or squeeze some words, if you prefer, thus stretching or condensing a line to make it fit.

In all cases, you must type a line first, then see how much space is to be saved or added, and then type it over with all the lines "justified."

-oOOo-

HOW TO "HALF SPACE" VERTICALLY . . .

STEP 1. Type the material that will appear on the regular single-spaced lines.

STEP 2. Using the variable line spacer in the left cylinder knob, turn the paper down half a line (until the top of a small letter like *w* or *m* disappears under the aligning scale). Check the position by typing lightly one or two of the strokes that you wish to type between the single-spaced lines.

STEP 3. Having adjusted the paper for in-between writing, complete the fill-ins.

1.   2.   3.

HOW TO PREPARE DISPLAY LETTERING . . .

Made with small "m's" and half-spacing

Made with pairs of parentheses, the underscore, and some diagonals

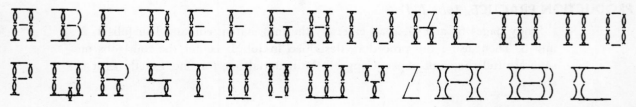

JOB 1

Manuscript
(enumeration)
Exact copy
Full sheet
1 tab stop
Words: 124

TYPING AN EXACT COPY ₃ →

Tab → When you are asked to type an exact copy, use the same steps that you take to center a column:

Step 1: To find out on what line to start the typing, count the typed and blank lines in the copy, subtract the total from the number of line spaces on a page, and divide the difference by two.

Step 2: Pick out the longest line in the copy,

Key: backspace enough to center it, and set the left margin stop at the point to which you backspaced.

This easy process may be used in making a quick and exact copy of almost any typed work--including all the jobs that you will type in this unit.

← Tab stop

JOB 2

Manuscript
(enumeration)
Exact copy
Full sheet
1 tab stop
Words: 153

TYPING AN ENUMERATION ₃ →

1. An enumeration is any series of numbered steps,
Tab → items, or paragraphs.

2. The numbers make clear the sequence of thought or action; so, they should be displayed.

3. One way to display the numbers is to underscore them, as in the job above.

4. Another way to display the numbers is to let them "hang" in the margin, as in this job.

Key: 5. To hang the numbers, indent all lines except the ones that begin with a number.

6. After you set the margin stops, set a tab stop to which you can indent without looking up.

7. The period after the number may be followed by either one or two spaces. Two is normal.

8. Letters may be used instead of numbers.

9. It is normal to use single spacing, with a blank line left before each new item.

← Tab stop

WARMUP *(Each line 3 times)* ◁**70**▷

```
a;qpa;z/a;  slwoslx.sl  dkeidkc,dk fjrufjvmfj tyghbnghfj fjrufjvmfj dke
Bill Ches Dave Ezra Fred Gwen Hank Jack Marx Myra Nora Pete Quen Ruth
or 94 rye 463 poor 0994 were 2343; 39 28 47 56 10 39% 28% 47% 56% 10%
We came back from the race with a layer of dust all over our clothes.
```
12-Sec.5| 10| 15| 20| 25| 30| 35| 40| 45| 50| 55| 60| 65| 70|

RHYTHM PREVIEW *(Each line 3 times)*

```
enough making evenly others design skills demand typist master parts.
once task that take look when line with jump over they easy them true
wish make has for him up, who can use see big and fun you are not its
```

ALPHABET-REVIEW PARAGRAPHS *(2 copies / si 1.32)* ◁**70**▷
DS

5-Min.
Writings

Once in a while a typist[1] has a task that is important[2] enough for him to take[3] extraor- 17

dinary pains in[4] making it look professional.[5] When that occasion[6] comes up, the typist 34

who[7] can make every line end[8] evenly with the others and[9] can design big display[10] 50

letters to use in headings[11] will see that he has a big[12] jump over other typists.[13] Such 67

specialized skills[14] require a bit of practice,[15] but they are easy and[16] fun after you have 84

got[17] the knack of them. They are[18] not skills for a beginner;[19] they demand that the[20] 100

typist be a true master[21] of the machine and its[22] parts. 111

When you wish to[23] justify a group of lines (that[24] is, make all the lines[25] end at the 128

same point),[26] you start by typing a first[27] draft. You set the[28] margins for the length 144

of[29] line you want to fill; and[30] then you type the material,[31] making every line come[32] 161

as close as you can to[33] your desired point of line[34] ending. In general, it[35] is better to 178

have lines[36] too short than to have[37] them too long. Scrutinize[38] the draft carefully and[39] 195

note exactly how many spaces[40] have to be saved or[41] inserted to make the lines[42] end 211

evenly. With a pencil,[43] indicate where you will[44] squeeze or spread the[45] words. Finally, 228

retype your[46] good copy, being sure[47] that you observe your[48] markings. If you forget 244

one,[49] you will soon know it![50] 250

PRODUCTION PRACTICE *(Jobs 5-6)*

"Two special jobs for you!" says Miss Trotter, giving you the two jobs on page 247.

5. "First, retype this revision of the preface for our employees' booklet. Center it on the page. Make the lines end evenly." The first two lines will be exactly as shown.

6. "Then, make a clean copy of the *Employee Notices* display, to put on the bulletin board outside our office," she says.

Read page 246 before starting Jobs 5 and 6. If you have time, make a copy of the alphabets displayed on page 246, too.

TYPING A BIBLIOGRAPHY ₃ ➡

JOB 3

Manuscript
(enumeration)
Exact copy
Full sheet
1 tab stop
Words: 125

1. Tab ➡ The next job shows the most common (but not the only) form for typing a list of writings.

2. The general form is that of an enumeration.

3. The sequence of the list is alphabetic by names of the authors; so, numbers are not needed.

4. So that the names of the writers will stand out clearly, all indentions are for 10 spaces.

Key: 5. When both books and articles are in the list, it is normal to group them separately.

6. The titles of books and magazines are indicated by a solid underscore.

7. The titles of magazine articles are quoted.

8. The last name of each writer is given first.

9. The next job shows the correct sequence of data for each of several different kinds of listings.

⬆ Tab stop

JOB 4

Manuscript
(bibliography)
Exact copy
Full sheet
1 tab stop
Words: 142

BIBLIOGRAPHY ₃ ➡

A. Books ₂ ➡

Adams, Richard G. The American Rebels. Boston: Book by
Tab ➡ Coe-Hart Press, 1955.   1 author

Burton, Ruth L.; and Farley, John H. Backgrounds   Book by
of a Free America. Chicago: The Scott   2 authors
Company, 1954.

Key: U. S. Bureau of the Census. Seventeenth Census of   Government
the United States, 1950. Washington: publication
Government Printing Office, 1951. ₃ ➡

B. Magazine Articles ₂ ➡

Hanson, Dora I. "Paul Revere, Man on a Horse,"   Article by
Nation's History, Vol. XIX (February,   1 author
1955), pages 36-38.

Lauren, Thomas J.; and Willis, Ann R. "Democracy   Article by
from the Start," American Historian's   2 authors
Monthly, Vol. VIII (January, 1956),
pages 216-232.

⬆ Tab stop

JOB 4

Manuscript
display
  Plain paper
  First draft
  3 carbons
Words: 385

Use single spacing

SPECIAL NOTICE TO EMPLOYEES →] *Center*
Insert Friday's date ← 1#
← 2#

The Hyle-McCann Company is pleased to announce that it will
soon begin publication of a magazine for employees and ~~for~~ their
families. ~~The publication~~ *It* will ~~feature~~ *contain* news items, pictures, and
special features of interest to members of the (H-M) staff. ~~It~~ *The magazine* is
being launched at the suggestion of the Employee-Relations Committee, headed by Shop Steward Nick Edelsen.

~~Our~~ *The* first step, of course, is to develop ~~a~~ *an editorial* staff. So, each
Department is asked to appoint a reporter whose ~~task it~~ will ~~be~~
~~to report~~ *send* to the editor all news ~~that will be~~ of interest to fellow employees. ~~Miss Priscilla Trotter, of the Personnel Depart-~~
Mr. Edelsen
~~ment,~~ will serve as editor until we find ~~someone on the staff~~ *a volunteer* who
has had experience in getting out a magazine. The first meeting
the Personnel Department
of the staff will be in ~~Miss Trotter's~~ office, in the Administra-
tion Building, at 2:30 on Thursday, (*Insert date of Thursday of next week*).

The staff will appreciate suggestions concerning the kind of
material that H-M employees would like to ~~see~~ *read* in their magazine.
shall
We ~~will~~ want news of new employees (who they are, what their jobs
are, where they went to school, etc.), of engagements and marriages,
of retirements, of promotions, and other personnel news of that
of
kind. We shall also want pictures ~~from~~ departmental social affairs,
(pictures of families,) pictures of employees who are now in *military* uniform,
and many others ~~of that nature.~~ ← (*pictures that show H-M staffers.*)
the magazine will need a clever name.
~~And,~~ of course, we ~~will want a good name for our magazine.~~
mr. Richard McCann, executive vice-president, ~~has~~ *is* offer~~ed~~*ing* a check
to
for $25 ~~for~~ the person who ~~is~~ first ~~to~~ submit the magazine name
that the staff ~~finally~~ selects. ~~We hope to pick the name~~ at ~~the~~ *its*
~~staff~~ meeting on (*same date as above*) *Put* Send your suggestions
a
for ~~the~~ name in any of the employee-suggestion boxes; these boxes
will be checked twice each morning and twice each afternoon from
now until noon (*same date as above*) *Suggest as many names as you*
wish, being sure to give your name and
department with each suggestion.   PERSONNEL DEPARTMENT

WARMUP *(Each line 2 times)*

◁ **52** ▷

```
d E f g H i J K l m N o p Q r s T u v W x y Z a b C
(39) (28) (47) (56) (10) II.  A.  1.  2.  B.  1.  2.
Can she make the long trip here in less than a day?
```
12-Sec. 5| 10| 15| 20| 25| 30| 35| 40| 45| 50|

SPECIAL RHYTHM PREVIEW *(Each line 2 times)*

```
clocks shapes spires church doubt shelf small quite
wrist there store wound seems built would have been
that like some slim when sign days must all are the
one and you see two job for key put big it of as is
```

ACCELERATION PREVIEW *(Each line 2 times)*

```
WW weather winding jewelry window wound allow twice
YY vertically display hyphen prayer very may you by
ZX Zinsser exactly stanzas experts extra sizes lazy
```

ALPHABET-REVIEW PARAGRAPHS *(Each, 2 times / si 1.35)*

◁ **60** ▷
DS

3-Min.
Writings   1 | 2 | 3 | 4 | 5 | 6 | 7 | 8 | 9 | 10 | 11 | 12

```
 0    I have never seen so many clocks in different sizes or     11
 4   shapes as appear there in the display at the jewelry store.  23
 8   You see shelves of small, squatty alarm clocks and two rows  35
12   of small, slim china clocks shaped exactly like spires of a  47
16   church.  There is a very big display of wrist watches, too.  59
20       One particular clock, a sign explains, is wound by the   70
24   changes in the weather.  That one dumfounds me, and I admit  82
27   to considerable doubt about it.  Deep inside, I cherish the  94
31   quiet little prayer that the experts who built that job for 106
35   us lazy folks must, surely, have put a winding key in some- 118
39   where as insurance on days when the weather stays the same. 130
```
Plus ▶   1 | 2 | 3 | 4

PRODUCTION PRACTICE *(Jobs 5-9)*

Study page 69; read carefully the information contained in Jobs 5 and 6. Then, using the exact-copying technique (described in Job 1, page 66), type Jobs 5, 6, 7, 8, and 9 in accordance with the directions printed under the job numbers.

HOW TO CENTER PARAGRAPH COPY . . .

STEP 1. Count or estimate the words in the body of the copy. To estimate, count the words in 3 or 4 lines, find the average, and multiply it by the number of lines (count a short line as a full one when you multiply).

STEP 2. Set margins: Use a 4-inch line (40 spaces pica, 50 elite) if there are fewer than 100 words in the body; a 5-inch line (50 pica, 60 elite) for 100 to 200; a 6-inch line (60 pica, 70 elite) for more than 200 words.

STEP 3. Divide the line length by 5, to find how many words you will get on a line.

STEP 4. Divide the total words by the words-per-line figure (Step 3) to find how many lines of typing the body will fill. Count a fractional line as a whole line.

STEP 5. Adjust the Step 4 line count to include any blank lines: If single spacing, add 1 for each between-paragraph blank line; if double spacing, double the Step 4 line count.

STEP 6. Add to the Step 5 line count the lines needed for a heading, date line, signature, and any other special lines and for the spaces that separate them from the body.

STEP 7. Find on what line to start typing: Subtract the Step 6 line count from 66 (or 33, if using half sheets), and then divide the remainder by 2.

PRODUCTION PRACTICE (Jobs 1-4)

Your employer is Priscilla Trotter, personnel director of the Hyle-McCann Company.

1-3. Dictating the two notices on page 242 and giving you the one shown below, Miss Trotter says, "Please center each of these notices on *half* pages. We'll need copies for four bulletin boards and for our files."

4. Miss Trotter gives you the notice shown on the next page and adds, "Then type up this one, too."

Looking in your files, you note (1) that it is apparently company policy to single space all notices; (2) that all notices have at least two paragraphs; (3) that all notices are headed *Notice to Employees*, with the date a double space below; and (4) that the words *Personnel Department* always appear a double space below the notice, even with the right margin.

JOB 3

Manuscript
display

If we may judge from recent inquiries, there have been a number of misunderstandings about the deductions that are made in pay checks. There are two kinds of deductions:

First, there are the deductions required by law. These include income taxes that must be withheld and your contribution to your Social Security benefits.

Second, there are the special deductions you have authorized the Company to make. These include your payment of your share of the retirement plan, the group-insurance plan, your medical insurance, and so on. They also include your purchase of Government Bonds via the payroll-savings plan.

The Payroll Department will be pleased to review with you the details of all deductions from your check.

Personnel Department

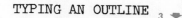

JOB 5

Manuscript
(outline)
  Exact copy
  Full sheet
  2 tab stops
  Words: 142

I. MARGINS ₂

Tab ▶ A. Set margin stops to center the longest line,
Tab ▶ Tab ▶ being sure to allow for the roman numerals.
     B. Center the outline vertically on the paper.₃

II. INDENTIONS ₂

    A. Steps should be indented 4 spaces each.
       1. Set several tab stops 4 spaces apart.
       2. Indent similar parts in similar steps.
    B. Guide letters or numbers precede the steps.
       1. Follow the guide with a period.
       2. Space twice after the period.
    C. For roman numerals that take more than one
       space, use the margin release and backspace
       from the left margin stop.₃

III. SPACING ₂

    A. Put 2 blank lines before a roman numeral.
    B. Put 1 blank line after a roman numeral.
    C. Single space all the other lines.

▲   ▲
Tab stops

JOB 6

Manuscript
(outline)
  Exact copy
  Full sheet
  2 tab stops
  Words: 141

TYPING A POEM ₃   SS

I. MARGINS

    A. Set margin stops to center the longest line.
    B. Center the poem vertically on the paper.₃

II. SPACING

    A. Either single or double spacing may be used.
    B. Use extra blank lines to display the poem.
       1. Separate the verses or stanzas.
       2. Keep couplets together.
    C. Use indentions to display the rhymes.
       1. If alternate lines rhyme, indent them.
       2. If couplets rhyme, do not indent them.
    D. Be consistent in the spacing plan used.₃

III. NAME OF AUTHOR

    A. It may be centered under the title.
    B. It may be typed at the end of the poem.
       1. Precede it by a dash (two hyphens).
       2. Start the dash at the center.
    C. The word "by" may be used or omitted.

▲   ▲
Tab stops

UNIT 28
MANUSCRIPTS

In this unit: special manuscript display: (1) centering paragraph copy both vertically and horizontally; (2) "justifying" lines, to make them end evenly; (3) preparing display lettering; and (4) creating displays for bulletin boards.

Read pages 242-249 and answer the study-guide questions on Workbook pages 265-266 before you begin typing the jobs in this unit.

Read pages 242-249 and answer the study-guide questions on Workbook pages 265-266 before you begin typing the jobs in this unit.

WARMUP *(Each line 3 times)*   ◁**70**▷

```
a;qpa;z/a; slwoslx.sl dkeidkc,dk fjrufjvmfj tyghbnghfj fjrufjvmfj dke
cry eve fix got hat ink job lad pay quiz sly who zoo : 39 28 47 56 10
If you will prop your book up, the light will not glare in your eyes.
```
12-Sec.5| 10| 15| 20| 25| 30| 35| 40| 45| 50| 55| 60| 65| 70|

RHYTHM PREVIEW *(Each line 3 times)*

```
enroll winter office invest course policy salary review always assure
wish next this know have form kind time will more past size from date
once year all who let are for use job any ten not new on, per one and
```

ALPHABET-REVIEW PARAGRAPHS *(Each 2 times / si 1.37)*   ◁**60**▷
                                                                      DS

3-Min.
Writings

| 1 | 2 | 3 | 4 | 5 | 6 | 7 | 8 | 9 | 10 | 11 | 12

JOB 1

si
1.33

```
 0      all members of the staff who wish to enroll for train-       11
 4   ing classes next winter are invited to let this office know      23
 8   by the first of next month.  all supervisors have a request      35
12   form for your use; on it you check the kind of job training      47
16   you wish and the time you would be willing to invest in it.      59
20   this department will undertake to offer courses of any kind      71
24   for which ten or more express an interest; we have found in      83
28   the past that classes of any smaller size are not feasible.      95
```

JOB 2

si
1.41

```
32      you will be pleased to learn that, starting on june 1,    11  106
35   the Company will begin a new policy of salary review.  from   23  118
39   that date on, all salaries will be reviewed at least once a   35  130
43   year; and all salaries under four hundred dollars per month   47  142
47   will be reviewed at least twice a year.  we know that staff   59  154
51   members will realize that a review of a salary does not al-   71  166
55   ways mean an increase; but the new program will assure that   83  178
59   no one is overlooked and will prevent inequities in differ-   95  190
63   ent departments.  we hope to issue more details next month.  107  202
```
Plus ➡   1 | 2 | 3 | 4

JOB 7

Manuscript
(poem)
  Exact copy
  Half sheet
  No tab stops
Words: 61

STREET CORNER ₃➡

Read Job 6 before
typing Jobs 7-8.

We met as unknown strangers may
When one would ask the hour of day.

We met and spoke, we shared a smile
And lingered on a little while.

We met, and then the signal changed
As though this all were prearranged.

We went our ways. I wonder when,
And if, we'll ever meet again. ₂➡

         --Chester Allen

JOB 8

Manuscript
(poem)
  Exact copy
  Half sheet
  1 tab stop
Words: 51

N O V E M B E R ₂➡

By Michael C. Trent ₃➡

When the dark sky is scowling
    With a snow-clouded face,
And the wild wind is howling
    In a leaf-chasing race; ₂➡

When the frost is out prowling
    And there's mist in the glen,
There's no use in growling--
    It's November again!

When a title is "spread,"
put 1 space between the
letters, 3 between words.
  Quick method: From the
center, backspace once
for each letter (except
the last) and each space
the title would occupy
if it were not spread.

Special*

JOB 9

Manuscript
(cover page)
  2 copies*
  Center lines
    horizontally
  Full sheets
  1 tab stop
  (at center)
Words: 50 each

Barton & Bruce Company

PROPOSED ADVERTISING SCHEDULE

For the Quarter
Beginning January 1, 19--

Submitted and Recommended by

Richard H. Wells, Sales Promotion Manager
Edward Hess, Advertising Manager
Jean Zinsser, Advertising Director

November 1, 19--

*Cover page, Job 9: On first copy, use double spacing and center the group of lines on a full sheet of paper. On the second copy, use single and double spacing as shown; center the first 4 lines in the top half of a full sheet of paper (begin on line 13) and the last 5 lines in the bottom half of the sheet (begin on line 46).

JOB 10

Display letter
Exact line-
for-line copy
Stencil
Words: 315

◁ **60** ▷
6
▽

NATIONAL FEDERATION OF VETERANS
190 University Drive
Iowa City 11, Iowa

Dear Fellow Member   September 25, 19--
of the National
Federation of Veterans:

       Do you feel that our organization of more than 25,000 men
can build a National Headquarters Building without having to
borrow money from a bank and to pay interest on the money?

                    OF COURSE WE CAN!

       Our new building is going to cost us about $100,000. Of
this amount, more than $65,000 has already been paid to the
architect and builders. This money was drawn from the special
building fund into which a share of members' dues was deposited
every year for the past eight years. We have $10,000 that we
can draw from our national treasury. That leaves us with just
$25,000 that we must raise. Can we do it?

                    OF COURSE WE CAN!

       Our Constitution forbids our raising dues; but it doesn't
forbid our going straight to every member of the Federation
and asking him, "How about anteing up for the building fund?"
That's the purpose of this letter. How about it? How about
anteing up for the building fund? All you do is fill in the
form below and mail it back with your check for a dollar or
more. Can we count on you?

                    OF COURSE WE CAN!

                    Roger Wilkins, Executive Secretary

- -

National Federation of Veterans
190 University Drive, Iowa City 11

Sure, you can count on ME! Here's my check for $_____ for the
NFV Building Fund.

                         Name _____

                       Street _____

        City, Zone, State _____

WARMUP *(Each line 2 times)*

S t u V w x Y z a B c d E f g H i J K l m N o p Q r

39:00 & 28:00 & 47:00 & 56:00 & 10:00 (THEME) case!

Can we make the trip there and back in a day or so?

12-Sec. 5| 10| 15| 20| 25| 30| 35| 40| 45| 50|

NAME PREVIEW *(Each line 2 times)*

Pittsburgh Greensboro Hartford Trenton Edward Ralph

Providence Baltimore Richmond Buffalo Albany & Vane

Charleston Savannah Syracuse Monarch Atlanta Please

PRODUCTION PRACTICE *(Jobs 10-12)*

Review the form for blocked letters (page 50); then type Job 10 on a workbook letterhead. Review the procedure for typing tables with column headings (page 61); then center Job 11 on a full sheet of paper. Study the arrangement of the script in Job 12 (it is much like an enumeration or bibliography); then center it on a full sheet of paper.

1 | 2 | 3 | 4 | 5 | 6 | 7 | 8 | 9 | 10 |

November 5, 19-- ? ◄

JOB 10

Blocked letter
Shown in elite
Letterhead
Center tab
Enumeration tab
Words: 130
Body: 95

Mr. Edward T. Potter
Potter & Vane, Inc.
2856 Madison Avenue
New York 28, New York

Dear Mr. Potter:

We are happy to approve your campaign for the next   10
radio series, except for these two changes: 19

1. We do want to alter the tenth script; a revision   30
   is enclosed for you to look over. What do you   39
   think of it?   42

2. We wish to drop the two Ohio stations from the   52
   plan, since we have no dealers in that state.   61
   The revised list of stations is also enclosed.   72

Please let me know that you have received this note.   83
I shall be interested to learn what you think of the   92
new script.   95

Very sincerely yours, ? ◄

Paul N. Trenton ? ◄

For more than one enclosure, use the plural "Enclosures." The actual number of enclosures may precede the word.

PNT:URS
2 Enclosures

WARMUP *(Each line 3 times)*

◁ **70** ▷

```
a;qpa;slwosldkeidkfjrufjghtyghfj ... a;z/a;slx.sldkc,dkfjvmfjghbnghfj
Alice Betty David Eliza Frank Homer Jewel Maxil Oscar Peggy Quinn Ray
to 59 put 075 ripe 4803 rope 4903; 39 28 47 56 10 -39 -28 -47 -56 -10
They stood on the top of the hill and let the wind clear their minds.
```

12-Sec.5| 10| 15| 20| 25| 30| 35| 40| 45| 50| 55| 60| 65| 70|

RHYTHM PREVIEW *(Each line 3 times)*

```
25,000 having borrow amount COURSE forbid member asking that's dollar
feel that more than from bank this cost been paid into year past draw
just dues our has can and the new was but him how you can for all it?
```

PRODUCTION PRACTICE *(Jobs 8-9)*

8. "Please prepare form postal cards to acknowledge today's contributions to the building fund," says Mr. Wilkins, giving you the list shown below.

9. "Then, fill in today's report on them."

10. He adds, "We may need more copies of the solicitation letter [next page]. Please get another stencil or master ready to run."

Forms for Jobs 8 and 9 are in the Workbook. If you lack them, use slips of paper, 5½ by 3¼, for postal cards for Job 8; and use plain paper for Jobs 9 and 10.

JOB 8

6 postal cards
Workbook
Words: 130

JOB 9

Report on ruled form
Workbook
Words: 78

BUILDING FUND RECEIPTS	Today's date		AMOUNT $41.00	
Name	Address			Amt
Jason F. Faucett	35-21 85th Street	Jackson Heights 72, N.Y.		$5—
Ruben L. Edwards	138 Duquesne Road	Homestead, Pa.		5—
Evan I. Marshall	560 So. Park Avenue	Decatur 2, Illinois		1—
Harrison Lasser	476 Imperial Avenue	Lemon Grove, Calif.		2—
Edmund Stuart	10 South Lee Street	Jacksonville 3, Florida		25—
Christopher Blaidler	391 Hamilton Lane	Corpus Christi, Texas		3—
				$41—

```
┌────────────────────────────────────────┐
│                            ┌────────┐   │
│                            │        │   │
│                            │        │   │
│  ┌──────────────────────┐  └────────┘   │
│  │ THIS SIDE OF CARD IS FOR ADDRESS │   │
│  └──────────────────────┘              │
│                                         │
│        Mr. Jason F. Faucett             │
│        35-21 85th Street                │
│        Jackson Heights 72, New York     │
│                                         │
└────────────────────────────────────────┘
```

Postal card address begins 3 lines under "of" in printed line. Use single spacing only where there are 4 or more lines in address.

```
NATIONAL FEDERATION OF VETERANS
190 UNIVERSITY DRIVE          IOWA CITY 11, IOWA
                              September 24, 19--

Dear Mr. Faucett:

    We should like to acknowledge receipt of your check for

        $5.00

    as a contribution to the National Headquarters Building
    Fund of the National Federation of Veterans. Your con-
    tribution is gratefully accepted by the national officers
    of the Federation.

                    ROGER WILKINS, Executive Secretary

    URS
```

Fill-in card requires only insertions, such as (in this illustration) a date, a salutation, amount of money, and initials.

JOB 11

3-column table
Exact copy
Full sheet
2 tab stops
Words: 59

THE MONARCH CAMPAIGN ₂
First Quarter, 19-- ₃

Station	City	Time ₂
WOK	Albany	6:30
WGS	Atlanta	6:30
WCA	Baltimore	6:00
WKB	Buffalo	7:15
WCS	Charleston	6:00
WGI	Greensboro	6:15
WDR	Hartford	5:30
KQV	Pittsburgh	6:00
WPR	Providence	6:15
WRV	Richmond	6:30
WTO	Savannah	6:00
WFB	Syracuse	6:15

Inserting a blank
line after every
three lines makes
a long table much
easier to read.

Key: Station......Charleston......Time

◄ Margin stop   ◄ Tab stop   ◄ Tab stop

JOB 12

Manuscript
(radio script.)
Exact copy
Full sheet
1 tab stop
Words: 171

Script No. 10 (Revised) ₃

◄ 60 ►
SS
16/3

MUSIC: (THEME)

ANNCR: Your typing tip for today--

MUSIC: (UP AND FADE ON THEME)

ANNCR: --from Monarch, the portable typewriter for today!

MUSIC: (UP AND FADE INTO . . .)

MARY: Ralph, I've put off writing to the folks much too
           long. Get out the Monarch for me, will you?

RALPH: Sure enough. (SOUND) There's the table . . . and
           here is Monnie, good ol' Monnie. (SOUND)

MARY: Hey, don't take the machine out of the case! Just
           unhook the cover!

RALPH: Hey yourself, Mary! You SHOULD take any portable
           out of its case when you want to type.

Key:

ANNCR: Ralph is right, Mary. Don't leave your portable in
           its carrying case. Lift it out. Get it out so the
           nonskid rubber feet can grip the table. Remember:

               To keep a portable from starting to skid,
               Take it out of the case and out of the lid!

MUSIC: (THEME)

Set tab 10 spaces from left margin.

JOB 6

5-column table
Handwritten
Center
Plain paper
4 carbons
Words: 55

Please alphabetize

National Federation of Veterans
MISSOURI DEPARTMENT
Analysis of Membership, date

Post	Members Paid up Jan. 1	Members Paid up July 1	6-Month Gain or Loss	Per Cent of Change
Kansas City	153	168	+15	+9.8%
Jefferson City	95	79	−16	−16.8%
Springfield	60	66	+6	+10.0%
Joplin	86	97	+11	+12.8%
St. Joseph	115	109	−6	−5.2%
Kirksville	52	54	+2	+3.8%
Hannibal	75	80	+5	+6.7%
St. Louis	210	225	+15	+7.1%
TOTALS	846	878	+32	+3.8%

JOB 7

8 fill-in cards
Like model here
Workbook forms
Data from Job 6
Words, total: 58

Use variable spacer
as aid in positioning
typing midway between
the horizontal rules.

Pennsylvania, Harrisburg				Post Membership Card, Form 20a	
Calendar Year	Members Paid Up Jan. 1	Members Paid Up July 1	Gains	Losses	Per Cent of Change
1956	324	335	11	--	∤ 3.4

Fill-in printed index card

For this test, you will need 2 sheets of plain paper or Workbook pages 49-52. Type Parts A and B (below) on opposite sides of one sheet, and Parts C and D (next page) on opposite sides of the second sheet. Use the grading scales indicated for grading your work.

PART A: STRAIGHT-COPY TEST (*si 1.17*)

◁ **60** ▷

Take two 3-minute writings on the *body* of the letter below; grade the better of the two. Or, copy the body once and grade it as though you had typed it at 35 words a minute.

Step 1: Compute words a minute.	Step 2: Deduct for errors—		Step 3: Grade the remaining words a minute this way:	35 or higher: A 30 to 34 wam: B 25 to 29 wam: C 20 to 24 wam: D
	1 error: —2 2 errors: —4 3 errors: —6	4 errors: — 9 5 errors: —12 6 errors: —15		

PART B: LETTER TEST (*si 1.28*)

Type this 86-word letter in blocked form, placing it correctly on the page and using the correct line of writing. When finished, grade your work on this scale:

TAKE OFF:	—3 Each placement error (margin, line length, etc.) —2 Each arrangement error (blocking, spacing, etc.) —1 Each typographical error	TOTAL PENALTY	8-7	6-4	3-2	1-0
		GRADE	D	C	B	A

```
  1  |  2  |  3  |  4  |  5  |  6  |  7  |  8  |  9  |  10  |  11  |  12
                                              November 24, 19--

The Norman Press
3956 South Third Street
Louisville 1, Kentucky

Gentlemen:

Please let us know your charge for printing the two display    12
jobs that we have enclosed.  We shall need 10,000 copies of    24
each display, printed on a Government postal card.             34

Let us know, also, what you would charge to print both jobs    46
in blue ink instead of in black and whether you have a bold    58
type of large size you can use for the headings.               68

We want to mail these cards early next month; so we hope we    80
may have your bid quite soon.                                  86

                         Yours very truly,


                         Sales Manager

LSG:URS
2 Enclosures
```

JOB 4

Semiblocked
memorandum
Like model
Workbook
1 carbon
Enclosure
Words: 151

si
1.46

Today's date. Martin F. Quill, Post Commandant, Joplin, Missouri (for envelope: 893 Main Street, Joplin 3)

| 1 | 2 | 3 | 4 | 5 | 6 | 7 | 8 | 9 | 10 |

40	Please let me be among the first, Mr. Quill,	9	207
41	to congratulate you and your staff for your great	19	217
43	success in building the enrollment of your Joplin	29	227
45	post. As the figures on the enclosed table show,	39	237
47	your per cent of gain is higher than those of the	49	247
49	seven other posts in Missouri. This is certainly	59	257
51	an excellent record, showing that Joplin veterans	69	267
53	recognize the leadership that you and the Federa-	79	277
55	tion are giving them. Once more I should like to	89	287
57	congratulate you. I shall certainly look forward	99	297
59	to meeting you when I next visit the Joplin post.	109	307

JOB 5

Semiblocked
memorandum
Like model
Workbook
1 carbon
Enclosure
Words: 156

si
1.42

Today's date. Kenneth Barnes, Post Commandant, Jefferson City, Missouri (for envelope: 6617 West Fourth Street, Jefferson City 8)

61	I am deeply concerned, Mr. Barnes, about the	9	316
63	loss of active members in the Jefferson City post	19	326
65	during the past six months. Is there anything we	29	336
67	at national headquarters can do to help you? The	39	346
69	figures on the enclosed table show that your loss	49	356
71	has been the most of any post in Missouri. More-	59	366
73	over, our records indicate this is the third con-	69	376
75	secutive year that you have had sizable decreases	79	386
77	in membership. I am sure that you are planning a	89	396
79	vigorous program to recruit more men, Mr. Barnes;	99	406
81	and I am confident that you can lick the problem.	109	416

Plus ➧ 1 | 2

PRODUCTION PRACTICE (*Jobs 4-7*)

4-5. Mr. Wilkins dictates the two memos shown above, to be set up in semiblocked form. He prefers a military-style date (day before the month) and room for his signature. Note that he did not indicate the paragraphs; there are three paragraphs in each of the two memos.

6. He asks you to type the table, page 239, that he has prepared in handwriting. You need an original for his file of such data, carbons to send as enclosures to the memos, and more carbons to file with the carbons of the memos.

Need to review tabulation? See pages 59, 61, and particularly 126-127.

7. Finally, he asks you to fill in a membership statistics card (workbook) for each of the eight posts listed in the handwritten table.

NATIONAL FEDERATION OF VETERANS
290 UNIVERSITY DRIVE   IOWA CITY 11, IOWA

DATE: 20 September 1956

FROM: Roger Wilkins, National Headquarters

TO: Wilbur F. Harmony, Post Commandant
     Boise, Idaho

ABOUT: News for the NFV News Bulletin

      I want to thank you, Mr. Harmony, for
sending us so complete a picture story about

expect to use the entire story in the October
issue of the News Bulletin.

                  Executive Secretary
RW/jlk
Enclosure

Semiblocked memo form

PART C: TABULATION TEST

Center this table on a full sheet of paper. Grade your finished work on this scale:

TAKE OFF:	—3 Each placement error (margins, column spaces) —2 Each arrangement error (headings, spacing) —1 Each typographical error	TOTAL PENALTY	8-7	6-4	3-2	1-0
		GRADE	D	C	B	A

COST OF A BUSINESS LETTER

Item of Cost	Cents
Time of the dictator	33.33
Time of the typist	33.33
Overhead, rent, etc.	16.67
Postal, mail service	03.57
Stationery	02.20
Filing expenses	01.62
Use of a typewriter	00.56
Use of a desk	00.28
Typewriter ribbon	00.17
Carbon paper	00.10
Use of a chair	00.08
TOTAL COST	91.91

WORDS: 67

PART D: MANUSCRIPT-DISPLAY TEST *(si 1.33)*

Center this enumeration on a full sheet. Grade your finished work on this scale:

TAKE OFF:	—3 Each placement error (each margin) —2 Each arrangement error (indenting, etc.) —1 Each typographical error	TOTAL PENALTY	8-7	6-4	3-2	1-0
		GRADE	D	C	B	A

CARE OF THE MACHINE

1. Daily: Clean the type faces by brushing them with a stiff brush or by using some commercial product made for the purpose.

2. Daily: Dust the machine carefully, using a long-handled brush to whisk out the inside and a soft cloth to wipe off the outside.

3. Daily: Wipe off the desk, being sure to wipe under the machine as well as around it.

4. Daily: Keep machine covered when not in use.

5. Weekly: Wipe the carriage rails with a soft cloth that has been dampened in oil. Never put oil directly on any part of the machine.

6. Monthly: Wipe the cylinder with a soft cloth that has been dampened in alcohol.

WORDS: 129

WARMUP (*Each line 3 times*) ◁**70**▷

```
a;qpa;slwosldkeidkfjrufjghtyghfj ... a;z/a;slx.sldkc,dkfjvmfjghbnghfj
Anne Drew Fawn Hugh Inez Jock Mary Paul Rocq Ruby Sara Tony Vera Xeno
it 85 pie 083 wire 2843 pyre 0643; 39 28 47 56 10 '39 '28 '47 '56 '10
The key to both speed and accuracy is a smooth pace of steady rhythm.
```
12-Sec.5| 10| 15| 20| 25| 30| 35| 40| 45| 50| 55| 60| 65| 70|

RHYTHM PREVIEW (*Each line 3 times*)

```
Joplin Quill, devote lines; having divide third, answer higher active
must have will find that keep down open with each item tell what sign
turn left and set off the for few try one six and for may let you out
```

ALPHABET-REVIEW PARAGRAPHS (*1 copy / si 1.40*) ◁**50**▷ **DS**

5-Min. Writings		1 | 2 | 3 | 4 | 5 | 6 | 7 | 8 | 9 | 10		
	0	One of the skills that a typist must have is		9
	2	the ability to find and set off the paragraphs in		19
	4	a letter without someone doing it for him. There		29
	6	are just a few rules to keep in mind. First, try		39
si 1.39	8	to devote a separate paragraph to each subject in		49
	10	the letter. Next, try to keep paragraphs down to		59
	12	six or seven lines; avoid having one with a dozen		69
	14	lines--divide it into two with six lines. Third,		79
	16	keep an eye open for enumerations; each item in a		89
	18	numbered sequence should be a separate paragraph.		99
	20	You will find that a majority of letters are	9	108
	22	split into three paragraphs: one to explain what	19	118
	24	the letter is about, one to tell what is inquired	29	128
si 1.34	26	for or what has been decided, and one to sign off	39	138
	28	on a cordial note. It is the middle one of these	49	148
	30	that may turn out long and need to be subdivided.	59	158
	32	If a subject line is used or if the letter is one	69	168
	34	in quick answer to another, the opening paragraph	79	178
	36	might be left out. Always try to squeeze out two	89	188
	38	paragraphs at least, even in a very short letter.	99	198
Plus ➧		1 | | 2		(CONTINUE ON NEXT PAGE.)

PART 3

WARMUP (*Each line 2 times*)

◁ **50** ▷

```
qpa; wosl eidk rufj tyfj ghfj bnfj vmfj c,dk x.sl
paid firm born hand pair land burn busy form half
girl held soap turn them body then down also sigh
```

Leave a blank line (return carriage twice) before you start a new line of drills.

SPEED DRILL: Word Families (*Each line 2 times*)

```
helm heal heir help hero here hey hew hen hem her
tore toil tone tort town torn tot tow top ton toe
lack land lair lake lane lame law lag lap lax lab
```

SPEED SENTENCES (*Each line 2 times*)

12-Sec.
Writings

```
They paid a firm to make an audit for their town.
The men may go to town if he pays for their work.
They may make us pay if he did sign for the work.
```
```
12-Sec.  5|    10|    15|    20|    25|    30|    35|    40|    45|    50|
```

SPEED PARAGRAPH (*2 copies / si 1.02*)

1-Min.
Writings

```
     1  |  2  |  3  |  4  |  5  |  6  |  7  |  8  |  9  |  10
The chap we all envy is the man who has more time        10
than he knows what to do with.  Most of us are so        20
short of time that we have to make a plan for the        30
work we do each hour, lest we do not get it done.        40
```

SPEED PREVIEW (*Each line 2 times*)

```
spelling steady group flash trot fast job all out
strokes letters times slows note many you ups has
```

SUSTAINED-SPEED PARAGRAPH (*2 copies / si 1.09*)

◁ **50** ▷
DS

2-Min.
Writings

[For use
of scales,
review
page 26.]

```
        1  |  2  |  3  |  4  |  5  |  6  |  7  |  8  |  9  |  10
 0  If you were to hear a fast typist at work, one of    10
 5  the things that you would note would be the sound     20
10  of his work.  It has a steady flow, with many ups     30
15  and downs; it is not an even jog trot.  Each time     40
20  he comes to a short word or a group of strokes he     50
25  has typed many times, his fingers flash the group     60
30  of letters in a spurt, with no spelling.  When he     70
35  comes to a long word or a hard one, he slows down     80
40  and spells out the letters.  If you would like to     90
45  build speed, learn to flash all the common words.   100
Plus ▶     1    |    2    |    3    |    4    |    5
```

JOB 2

6 invoice forms
Like model here
Workbook forms
Words, total: 94

Fill in the
dues (50 cents a
month, starting the
first of next month),
and total dues.

NATIONAL FEDERATION OF VETERANS

190 UNIVERSITY DRIVE   **IOWA CITY 11, IOWA**

Mr. Kenneth J. Powell   June 14, 1956
Apartment J-8
948 Edwards Avenue
San Antonio 4, Texas

Initiation Fee $15.00
Membership Emblem 5.00
Dues until next December 31 .... 3.00

Total Amount Due 23.00

(Please return this statment with your remittance)

Fill-in printed invoice form

JOB 3

6 fill-in cards
Like model here
Workbook forms
Words, total: 168

Align inserts
squarely beside
guide words.
Use chainfeeding
technique (page 230).

Powell, Kenneth J.
LAST NAME   FIRST NAME   MIDDLE NAME OR INITIAL

Post .... San Antonio, Texas
Initiation ... June 4, 1956
Address .... Apartment J-8
948 Edwards Avenue
San Antonio 4, Texas

Service .... Air Corps
Rank ...... 2d Lieut.
Years Service 2½
Occupation . Tax accountant

Fill-in printed index card

WARMUP: "OR" Drill *(Each line 2 times)*   ◁**50**▷

```
a;qpa; slwosl dkeidk fjrufj ghtygh rufjeidkwosla;
orange ordain organ order orate orgy oral orb ore
torn born corn worn morn form horn more fore tory
anchor motor labor honor favor color odor nor for
```

SPEED DRILL: Finger Reaches *(Each line 2 times)*

```
funny numb burn runt bunt rub nut rum buy tub but
ceded dice kick cede deck kit irk cud die cue ice
lowly solo lost rows slow sox sol low lot old owl
aqua lazy hazy quiz zeal quip quad daze zany gaze
```

SPEED DRILL: One-Hand Words *(Each line 2 times)*

½-Min.
Writings

| 1 | 2 | 3 | 4 | 5 | 6 | 7 | 8 | 9 | 10 |

```
zest fear gab wed saw get few eat dew car bad are   10
fact ease draw date card case beat best area acre   20

hip joy oil pin you mum ply ink him pup join lump   10
holy polo puny punk kink lily milk only yolk upon   20
```

SPEED SENTENCES: One-Hand Words *(Each line 2 times)*   ◁**50**▷

1-Min.
Writings

| 1 | 2 | 3 | 4 | 5 | 6 | 7 | 8 | 9 | 10 |

```
After you agreed on wages, we feared bad effects.   10
You were as safe in my car as you were in a pool.   20
Were you after extra gate fees in fast car races?   30
In my opinion, you were in bad after you acceded.   40
We agreed on fees after you created a union wage.   50
```

SUSTAINED-SPEED SENTENCES: Fours *(2 copies / si 1.00)*   **DS**

2-Min.
Writings

| 1 | 2 | 3 | 4 | 5 | 6 | 7 | 8 | 9 | 10 |

```
 0  They were free from hard work four days last week.   10
 5  That last cold wave fell when they came from town.   20
10  They will need help when they take that boat home.   30
15  Both boys were well when they came from that trip.   40
20  Will they have that plan that they said they made?   50
25  Tell them they must make time when they work late.   60
30  That firm will have much more work than they want.   70
35  They must have been back when your good news came.   80
40  Some boys were seen near that lake just last week.   90
45  This town must have some firm that will make them.  100
```

Plus ➡   1 | 2 | 3 | 4 | 5

PRODUCTION PRACTICE (Jobs 1-3)

Your employer is Roger Wilkins, executive secretary of the National Federation of Veterans. "I have three tasks for you," he says, giving you the list shown below.

1. "First, retype the list on one of our office forms. Arrange the names alphabetically, please, typing the last name first, each time.

2. "Then, address a dues bill for each member. Dues are 50 cents a month, starting the first of next month.

3. "Finally, fill in a membership card for each new member, for our index file."

The forms are on Workbook pages 247-254. If you do not have a workbook, prepare forms similar to the typed one shown below and the two printed forms on page 236.

```
Dep't store buyer
Dep't store buyer
Dep't store buyer
Dep't store buyer
Dep't store buyer
```

Squeezing:
If you lack enough space for an insertion, squeeze letters together by pushing against the left end of the carriage or by partially depressing the backspace key, to keep the carriage from spacing normally.

JOB 1 — Fill-in form / Workbook / Words: 108

National Federation of Veterans

Chapter **NASHVILLE, TENNESSEE**   Initiation Date **JUNE 16**

REPORT OF NEW MEMBERS

Name	ROBERT E. PORTER	Service	NAVY
Address	1222 WINDING WAY	Highest Rank	ENSIGN
	NASHVILLE 6	Years in Service	6
		Present Work	DEP'T STORE BUYER
Name	EUGENE L. CARR	Service	AIR CORPS
Address	719 CUMBERLAND CIRCLE	Highest Rank	STAFF SERGEANT
	NASHVILLE 14	Years in Service	4
		Present Work	LAWYER
Name	PAUL N. PERKINS	Service	NAVY
Address	103 TRINITY LANE	Highest Rank	YEOMAN 1/c
	NASHVILLE 7	Years in Service	5
		Present Work	H.S. TEACHER
Name	RUDOLPH G. GORDON	Service	ARMY
Address	5602 VINERIDGE AVENUE	Highest Rank	1ST LIEUT.
	NASHVILLE 9	Years in Service	3 1/2
		Present Work	OWNS MEN'S STORE
Name	OSCAR T. MOELLER	Service	AIR CORPS
Address	2311 HIGHLAND AVENUE	Highest Rank	LT. COLONEL
	NASHVILLE 5	Years in Service	4
		Present Work	MINISTER
Name	HENRY V. JOHNSTON	Service	ARMY
Address	1704 BLAIR BOULEVARD	Highest Rank	CORPORAL
	NASHVILLE 4	Years in Service	3 1/2
		Present Work	BAKER

WARMUP: Balanced-Hand Words *(Each line 2 times)*

◁**50**▷

```
gh ghij ghijk ghijkl ghijkl ghijk ghij ghi gh
alto born cork duel envy form gown hang irks jamb
kept lamb melt name odor pale quay rich soap town
urns vial work yams zygo also bowl cowl disk fish
```

CONTROL DRILL: L, O, S *(Each line 2 times)*

```
like list late last lose life lead lady long loss
held sale olds plan deal jail fail talk else sail

open once only oaks omit over oars oath obey oboe
work oleo some also come alto down solo whom memo

send said same sake says safe sash sour site spot
last does also days busy this lost ways best news
```

CONTROL DRILL: Alphabet Review *(Each line 2 times)*

◁**60**▷

1-Min.
Writings

```
  |  1  |  2  |  3  |  4  |  5  |  6  |  7  |  8  |  9  |  10  |  11  |  12
quiz week such play over taxi been fine good jump also them   12
away does give quay joke came best four hope long zest exam   24
along black first homey jewel paper dozen quite extra brave   36

Inez says Jack plays a very quaint game of bridge with Rex.   12
Five or six dozen clubs may sign up with Karl for jonquils.   24
```

CONTROL PREVIEW *(Each line 2 times)*

```
to can lead tired errors fatigue amazing exactly directions
so sag long slump squirm typists wrists important shoulders
```

ALPHABET-REVIEW PARAGRAPH *(2 copies / si 1.32)*

DS

2-Min.
Writings

```
  |  1  |  2  |  3  |  4  |  5  |  6  |  7  |  8  |  9  |  10  |  11  |  12
 0  If you are making many errors in your typing, look first at   12
 6  your posture.  It is amazing how important posture is.  You   24
12  get control so long as the fingers move in exactly the same   36
18  directions to jab the same keys; anything that changes your   48
24  finger paths can lead to errors.  For most typists, fatigue   60
30  is the great cause of error.  It is when you are tired that   72
36  you let your wrists sag, squirm in your chair, change posi-   84
42  tion, slump your shoulders, and so change the finger paths.   96
```

Plus ▶ | 1 | 2 | 3 | 4 | 5 | 6

UNIT 27
BUSINESS FORMS

In this unit: typing on (1) ruled report forms, (2) invoices, (3) a variety of printed fill-in index cards, (4) memo letterheads, and (5) printed fill-in postal cards. You will also type a display letter with a coupon. Before starting the jobs in this unit, read pages 234-241 and answer the study-guide questions on Workbook pages 243-244.

WARMUP (*Each line 3 times*)   ◁ **70** ▷

```
a;qpa;slwosldkeidkfjrufjghtyghfj ... a;z/a;slx.sldkc,dkfjvmfjghbnghfj
but cap dye fox his joy irk lot men quip vie wag zip : 39 28 47 56 10
Nothing will help you quite so much as being and staying on the ball.
```
12-Sec.5| 10| 15| 20| 25| 30| 35| 40| 45| 50| 55| 60| 65| 70|

RHYTHM PREVIEW (*Each line 3 times*)

```
errors letter manage moving spread detail enough cannot simply method
high cent left case find ways half vary plan keep push long next part
down this per was out way are for the one and how you and can key or,
```

ALPHABET-REVIEW PARAGRAPHS (*2 copies / si 1.30*)   ◁ **60** ▷
                                                                    DS

3-Min. Writings			

1 | 2 | 3 | 4 | 5 | 6 | 7 | 8 | 9 | 10 | 11 | 12

0	A high per cent of typing errors involve a space prob-	11
4	lem (that is, a letter was left out, in which case you must	23
8	squeeze it in; or an extra letter or space was inserted, in	35
12	which case you must find a way to conceal the extra space).	47
16	There are several different ways to manage the spreading or	59
si 20	squeezing. All methods require your erasing the whole word	71
1.30 24	that is to be corrected and then your making the correction	83
28	half a space to the left, for a squeeze; or half a space to	95
32	the right, for a spread. In just one detail do the methods	107
36	vary: how you go about moving the correction half a space.	119

40	One plan is to brace your hand against the left end of	11	130
43	the carriage to keep it from spacing in the usual way. You	23	142
47	push the carriage half a space and hold it at that position	35	154
51	long enough to hit the next letter; you do this pushing and	47	166
55	holding for each space in the correction. Or, you can hold	59	178
si 59	the carriage in half position by pressing the backspace key	71	190
1.30 63	part way down--but you cannot do this on an electric. When	83	202
67	you must reinsert the paper to type a correction, you might	95	214
71	simply shift the paper a half space. On some machines, you	107	226
75	move the carriage a half space by holding down on the space	119	238
79	bar. Whatever spreading or squeezing method is used, prac-	131	250
83	tice is required for getting skill in judging half a space.	143	262

Plus ▶   1 | 2 | 3 | 4

The paragraphs above tell how to squeeze or spread a word when you make a correction.

```
A squeze and an spread are
A squeeze and a  spread are
```

WARMUP: Right-Hand Security *(Each line 2 times)*

◁**50**▷

```
ghijkl ghijkl ghijkl ghijkl ghijkl ghijkl ghijkl
;;h; ;;j; ;;k; ;;l; ;;u; ;;n; ;;i; ;;m; ;;,; ;;o;
Mary Hugh Inez Jane Karl Lola Opal Hans Irma Jack
```

CONTROL DRILL: Concentration *(Each line 2 times)*

```
Ce sont de grandes constructions en pierre avec
des poutres de bois apparentes sur la facade.
```

CONTROL DRILL: Rocking Sequences *(Each line 2 times)*

```
stable static steady staple past lost first twist
none nose known piano cannot enough casino notify
ear each earn east year leave ideal creamy bleach
hob how hold horns whole those short shown anchor
```

CONTROL SENTENCES: Rocking Sequences *(Each line 2 times)*

◁**60**▷

½-Min. Writings

| 1 | 2 | 3 | 4 | 5 | 6 | 7 | 8 | 9 | 10 | 11 | 12 |

```
Who knows how early the staff shows up each day for school?   12
Stuart cannot stay in Reno; he hopes to start east at noon.   24
We heard that those who leave early will not eat any meals.   36
Stella earns money by playing piano in Noel's beach casino.  48
```

CONTROL DRILL: Alphabet Review *(Each line 2 times)*

1-Min. Writings

| 1 | 2 | 3 | 4 | 5 | 6 | 7 | 8 | 9 | 10 | 11 | 12 |

```
would today vexes since equip bring froze joint knife might   12
write prize party major eight vexed brisk close equal front   24

Chuck joined Zeb's party to give a quorum for an extra law.   12
Jack found the gravel camp six below zero quite a few days.   24
```

ALPHABET-REVIEW PARAGRAPH *(2 copies / si 1.35)*

DS

2-Min. Writings

| 1 | 2 | 3 | 4 | 5 | 6 | 7 | 8 | 9 | 10 | 11 | 12 |

```
 0  The person who types everything at his top speed finds many   12
 6  an error in his work.  If you do anything at top speed very   24
12  long, whether it is playing or dancing or washing dishes or   36
18  anything else, you strain your endurance; then fatigue sets   48
24  in and errors result.  The trick of true efficiency lies in   60
30  working at a pace just under the edge of your top speed.  A   72
36  true expert keeps a speed reserve on which he can draw when   84
42  he realizes that his typing technique is beginning to slip.  96
```

Plus

| 1 | 2 | 3 | 4 | 5 | 6 |

JOB 9

Display letter
Rough draft
Plain paper
2 carbons
Words: 230

An order-reply letter is one kind of display letter. When the typist is given the information for such a letter, he (1) makes a first draft; (2) retypes it with improved appearance and placement; (3) gets his superior to approve or further revise the letter; and finally (4) retypes the letter in final form. The final retyping (which is what you do in Job 9) is simply a matter of centering the copy both vertically and horizontally.

Judd-Kane, Inc.
1410 Glenarm Street
Denver 2, Colorado

~~Spring~~ *Fall*, ~~1955~~ →⌉

Gentlemen:

Pleas, send me, ~~postage~~ *express* prepaid, the indicated quantities of *the*
~~the~~ following advertising aids for Judd-Kane Products:

Quantity   Item No.   (Description)   *center* →⌉

	WC8R	Large window cards in which a J-K radio may be ~~inset~~ *placed*. **Approx.** 4x4 feet. *← /# here*
	WC8T	Large window cards that may be used to frame a J-K television set. 5x6 feet.
	SC3R	Set cards to place beside a J-K radio. Hand points to dials. 18x8 inches.
	SC3T	Set cards to place ~~atop~~ *on* a J-K television set. Hand points to dials. 18x8 inches.
	Ne5R	News mat, for use in advertising any J-K radio in newspaper. ~~4x4~~ *3x3* inches.
	Ne5T	News mat, for use in advertising any J-K television *set* in newspaper. ~~6x4~~ *5x3* inches.

I understand that these aids come to me without charge and may be used or not used, as I may prefer.

Send to:
Person or Dep't
Company Name _____

Street Address _____   *OK as corrected T.G.H*

City, Zone, State _____

WARMUP: Reach Review *(Each line 2 times)* ◁50▷

```
aqqa ;pp; swws ;00; s22s lool deed 1991 d33d kiik
frrf k88k f44f juuj fttf j77j f55f jyyj fggf j66j
fbbf jnnj fvvf jmmj dccd k,,k sxxs l..l azza ;//;
```

NUMBER DRILL: 1, 3, 9 *(Each line 2 times)*

```
d 3 d3 13 31 133 331 1331 3313 1313 133 331 13 31
1 9 19 19 91 199 991 1991 9919 1919 199 991 19 91
13 19 39 139 193 319 1933 1399 9913 391 931 91 31
```

NUMBER DRILL: We 23's *(Each line 2 times)*

```
wee 233 too 599 tee 533 yee 633 woo 299 root 4995
purr 0744 poor 0994 putt 0755 weep 2330 tree 5433
peep 0330 error 34494 putty 07556 trotter 5495534
```

NUMBER SENTENCES: Pair Pattern *(Each line 2 times)*

½-Min. Writings

| 1 | 2 | 3 | 4 | 5 | 6 | 7 | 8 | 9 | 10 |

```
How much is 39 plus 28 plus 47 plus 56 plus 1000?   10
How could all 10 orders be numbered 3928 or 4756?   20
How could 47 men and 56 women use up 139 tickets?   30
Check on all orders numbered 3928, 4756, or 1039.   40
```

NUMBER DRILL: Cumulative Count *(Each line 2 times)* ◁50▷

1-Min. Writings

| 1 | 2 | 3 | 4 | 5 | 6 | 7 | 8 | 9 | 10 |

```
1101 3302 9903 1304 1905 3106 9107 3908 9309 3110   10
3911 2812 4713 5614 1015 9316 8217 7418 6519 0120   20
2121 2222 3323 9924 9825 9726 7727 6628 5529 4430   30
4931 7032 5933 2834 3935 2736 8437 5238 1739 1340   40
```

NUMBER-REVIEW PARAGRAPH *(2 copies / si 1.15)* DS

2-Min. Writings

| 1 | 2 | 3 | 4 | 5 | 6 | 7 | 8 | 9 | 10 |

```
 0│25  Some 44 boys showed up on September 3.  The coach   10
 5│30  split them into 4 teams of 11 each and held a few   20
10│35  scrimmage plays.  The Blues scored 15 points; the   30
15│40  Reds, 7; the Greens, 26; and the Browns, 19.  The   40
20│45  outstanding player was Trout, who made 18 points.   50
```

Plus ▶ | 1 | 2 | 3 | 4 | 5 |

WARMUP *(Each line 3 times)* ◁**70**▷

```
a;sldkfjghfjdksla;sldkfjghfjdksla; a;sldkfjghfjdksla;sldkfjghfjdksla;
Alvin Bruce Daisy Edith Fritz Gwynn Jaxon Kathy Morse Parks Queen Tom
up 70 pew 032 tour 5974 wipe 2803; 39 28 47 56 10 $39 $28 $47 $56 $10
He saluted smartly and then handed the three dispatches to the major.
```
12-Sec.5| 10| 15| 20| 25| 30| 35| 40| 45| 50| 55| 60| 65| 70|

RHYTHM PREVIEW *(Each line 3 times)*·

```
recent course mailed dealer return marked window beside placed charge
make fall when came desk held copy mail list send back next sale wait
fill this for the new our me, was you use may set say mat any not few
```

PRODUCTION PRACTICE *(Jobs 7-9)*

Mr. Harris says to you, "I have corrected the order-reply letter [page 233]. Please retype it with enough carbons to have one for each of the two letters I shall dictate to you." He dictates the two letters below.

Both letters are short. The first has an inside address that takes 4 lines; the second inside address takes 5 lines. You must supply the capitals in both letters—can you do so without marking your book?

JOB 7

Blocked letter
Dictated form
Letterhead
1 carbon
Words: 128
Body: 98

Today's date. Mr. Harry Meyers, Manager, Graham Electric Company, 1229 East 152 Street, Cleveland 10, Ohio

| 1 | 2 | 3 | 4 | 5 | 6 | 7 | 8 | 9 | 10 | 11 | 12 |

```
    dear mr. meyers:  i am sorry for the delay in replying      11
to your recent letter in which you asked whether we planned      23
to make new advertising aids available to our dealers.  our     35
fall announcement was being prepared when your inquiry came     47
to my desk.  i held up my reply until i had a copy for you.     59

    you will, of course, receive another copy when we mail      70
the announcement to our entire list of dealers.  you do not     82
need to wait for the mailing, however; you may fill in this     94
advance copy and send it back to us.  very sincerely yours,    106
```

JOB 8

Blocked letter
Dictated form
Letterhead
1 carbon
Words: 121
Body: 87

Today's date. Mr. Edward Preston, Advertising Manager, Morgan and Hyle, Inc., 345 Boylston Street, Boston 16, Massachusetts

| 1 | 2 | 3 | 4 | 5 | 6 | 7 | 8 | 9 | 10 | 11 | 12 |

```
    dear ed:  as i promised you at the convention in south      11 | 117
hampton, i am sending to you an advance copy of the general     23 | 129
announcement about our new fall advertising aids.  it won't     35 | 141
be mailed to our dealer list until the first of next month.    47 | 153

    if you will fill out your order and rush it back to me      58 | 164
by return mail, marked for my personal attention, i will do     70 | 176
everything possible to see that your package gets to boston     82 | 188
in time for you to use in your sale.  very sincerely yours,     94 | 200
```

WARMUP: Reach Review *(Each line 2 times)*   ◁ **50** ▷

```
aqza ;p/; swxs lo.l decd ki,k frvf jumj ftgh jyhj
;00; s22s 1991 d33d k88k f44f j77j f55f j66j ;--;
;)); s""s l((l d##d k''k f$$f j&&j f%%f j__j ;**;
```

NUMBER DRILL: 4, 5, 6, 7 *(Each line 2 times)*

```
f4f f4f 444 44 41 j7j j7j 777 77 71 144 177 47 47
f5f f5f 555 55 51 j6j j6j 666 66 61 155 166 56 56
144 155 166 177 441 551 661 771 44 55 66 77 47 56
```

NUMBER DRILL: We 23's *(Each line 2 times)*

```
we 23 ure 743 our 974 toe 593 your 6974 pour 0974
rue 473 rut 475 rupe 4703 rutty 47556 rupee 47033
wit 285 wiry 2846 wire 2843 wipe 2803 witty 28556
```

SYMBOL DRILL: # ( ) *(Each line 2 times)*

```
d3d d#d d#d d#d # #3 #33 #333 #39 #29 #47 #56 #10
#1 #2 #3 #4 #5 #6 #7 #8 # 8# 7# 6# 5# 4# 3# 2# 1#
191 l(l l(l l(l ;0; ;); ;); ;); () () (a) (b) (c)
(1) (2) (3) (4) (5) (--) (39) (28) (47) (56) (10)
```

SYMBOL SENTENCES: # ( ) *(Each line 2 times)*   ◁ **50** ▷

½-Min.
Writings

```
     1 | 2 | 3 | 4 | 5 | 6 | 7 | 8 | 9 | 10
She filled orders #28, #39, #47, and #56 by noon.   10
I ordered the following:  #65, #74, #82, and #93.   20
We found #9382 but did not locate #7465 anywhere.   30

The comma (,) and period (.) are used very often.   10
A new model (#10) is better than an old one (#9).   20
They weighed (1) 3900#, (2) 4700#, and (3) 5600#.   30
```

NUMBER DRILL: Century Drive *(1 copy)*   DS

2-Min.
Writings

```
The 1 and 2 the 3 the 4 the 5 the 6 the 7 the 8
the 9 the 10 the 11 the 12 the 13 the 14 the 15
the 16 the 17 the 18 the 19 the 20 the 21 the 22
the 23 the 24 the
```
⎡Continue on up to 100. Ultimate⎤
⎣goal is to reach 100 in 2 minutes.⎦

PRODUCTION PRACTICE (Jobs 4-6)

4. Mr. Harris says, "Address a small envelope for each name on this prospect list.

5. "Then, prepare an index card for each person, for our *alphabetic* name file.

6. "Finally, prepare another card for each person, for our *geographic* name file."

You will need 25 envelopes (or slips of paper, 6½ by 3⅝ inches) and 50 index cards (slips of paper, 5 by 3 inches).

Study the illustrations on page 230 before you start. Be sure to use the chain-feeding technique on all three jobs.

JOBS 4-6
Envelopes and
Index cards

Mrs. Alan A. Ackerman	319 Alabama Road	Martindale Arkansas	12
Miss Barbara B. Babbitt	937 Burbank Boulevard	Boston 2 Massachusetts	26
Mrs. Charles C. Cochran	162 Chewick Street	Chicago 24 Illinois	38
Dr. Donald D. Dedman	389 Dowd Street	Durham North Carolina	50
Miss Edith E. Everett	321 Edgar Avenue	Effingham Illinois	62
Prof. Frank F. Flauffer	561 Fulton Street	Fresno 1 California	74
Mr. George Guggenhuggard	47 Greenville Street	La Grange Georgia	87
Mr. Harold H. Hotham	285 Highland Avenue	Hampton Beach New Hampshire	101
Miss Inez I. Libirtin	Illinois State Library	Springfield Illinois	114
Dr. John J. Johnson	476 Jewett Avenue	Jersey City 4 New Jersey	126
Mrs. Kenneth K. Kinkman	Kurtz & Kurtz 10 Oak Lane	Frankfort Kentucky	140
Mr. Lloyd L. Llewellyn	2803 Dillon Street	Baltimore 24 Maryland	153
Miss Miriam M. Montmart	3956 Blooming Avenue	Minneapolis 7 Minnesota	167
Prof. Paul P. Pepper	Park College 87 Pine Place	Gulfport Mississippi	180
Mr. Quenton Q. Quest	Queen Department Store 2 Quincy Road	Dubuque Iowa	195
Rev. Robbin R. Ruben	7 North Franklin Street	Greensboro North Carolina	209
Sr. St. Sophia	975 Dorchester Avenue	South Boston 27 Massachusetts	222
Mr. Theodore T. Totterstadt	545 Stuart Street	Chattanooga 6 Tennessee	236
Dr. Ulysses U. Underwood	787 Hulburt Avenue	Naugatuck Connecticut	249
Rev. Vivian V. Vivers	455 Victoria Avenue	Danville Virginia	261
Miss Wilma W. Woodward	232 West Wisconsin Avenue	Milwaukee 3 Wisconsin	276
Mr. Xerxes Praxiteles	Texas City Tax Bureau	Texas City Texas	288
Mrs. Yvonne Y. Zinnsser	567 Goodyear Plaza	Yuma Arizona	299

UNIT 10
CORRESPONDENCE

In this unit you will learn to address envelopes, to fold letters, to arrange letters in semiblocked style, and to use company-name signatures. Your work will be easiest if, before beginning the jobs, you first read pages 81-89 and answer the questions on Workbook pages 55-56.

WARMUP *(Each line 2 times)*   ◁ **60** ▷

Joe saw six big packs of cards and very quietly seized them.
39 28 47 56 10 we 23 yet 635 owe 923 ire 843 pip 080 pup 070
I did not try to tell them that they could or could not win.
12-Sec. 5| 10| 15| 20| 25| 30| 35| 40| 45| 50| 55| 60|

CONTROL PREVIEW *(Each line 2 times)*

aa answer bb blocked cc catch dd date ee prefer ff influence
gg give hh what ii like jj judge kk pick ll letter mm matter
nn one's oo others pp purpose qq unique rr better ss persons
tt that uu use vv have ww would xx extreme yy yes zz bizarre

ALPHABET-REVIEW PARAGRAPHS *(Each, 2 times / si 1.35)*   ◁ **60** ▷
                                                                        DS

3-Min. Writings															

3-Min. Writings
   1 | 2 | 3 | 4 | 5 | 6 | 7 | 8 | 9 | 10 | 11 | 12

0   What is the best letter style? That question does not   11
4   have an answer, for preference in letter styles is a matter   23
8   of your own taste. For example, some persons like a letter   35
12 to be blocked; others may prefer it indented. Some like to   47
16 use a company name. Some prefer the date centered horizon-   59
20 tally. There is no way to judge what one form is the best.   71

24   The purpose of a letter might influence your choice of   82
27 style, too. For example, you might pick for an advertising   94
31 letter a bizarre form that would catch one's eye because it   106
35 is unique; but you would reject the same form for, say, any   118
39 letter of sympathy. Yes, these are extreme cases; but they   130
43 do show that the purpose of the letter can affect its form.   142

Plus ▶   1   2   3   4

PRODUCTION PRACTICE *(Jobs 1-4)*

JOB 1   Study page 82; then address in blocked style a No. 6¾ envelope for each letter in Jobs 2-4. Use real envelopes, or the ones printed on Workbook pages 57-58, or slips of paper cut to 6½ by 3¾ inches.

HOW TO ADDRESS ENVELOPES . . .

[Review pages 82, 119]

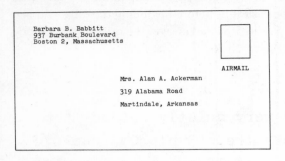

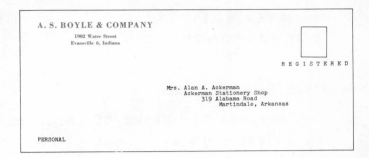

1. Begin address about ½ inch to left of the center, on line 12 of a small envelope (6½ by 3⅝ inches) and on line 14 of a large envelope (9½ by 4⅛ inches). Double space a 3-line address; single space one of 4 or more lines. Use either indented (in 5-space steps) or blocked form.

2. If return address is typed, use blocked form. Begin ½ inch from edge, on line 3.

3. Type any handling directions (such as *Airmail, Special Delivery,* etc.) under the stamp. Type other notations (*Care of, Please Forward,* etc.) in lower left-hand corner.

HOW TO TYPE ON INDEX CARDS . . .

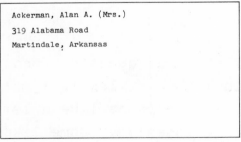

Name file

Geographic file

1. Start on third space from edge, on line 2.

2. Arrange first line in filing sequence. Do not indicate *Mr.* or *Miss,* but do indicate (parenthetically) all other personal titles.

3. Leave 1 blank line under the first line. Other lines may be blocked or indented 3 spaces, using either single or double spacing. Indicate parenthetically all titles other than *Mr.* and *Miss.*

HOW TO CHAINFEED ENVELOPES (OR CARDS) . . .

After typing first envelope, roll it back until only ½ inch or so is showing. Insert next envelope from the front, placing its bottom edge between the first envelope and the cylinder. Turn cylinder to back out the first envelope and to draw the second into position. Continue "feeding" the envelopes in this manner (from the front) until all are done. The completed envelopes stack up on the paper table in the same sequence in which typed.

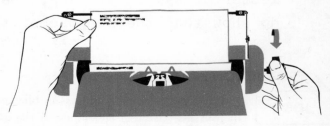

Chainfeeding

HOW TO FOLD LETTERS...

For small envelopes ...3 folds

  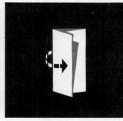 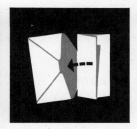

| Bring bottom up to ½ inch from the top. | Fold right-hand third toward left. | Fold left-hand third toward right. | Last crease goes in envelope first. |

For large envelopes ...2 folds

   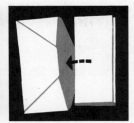

| Fold up the bottom third of the paper. | Fold the top third over bottom third. | Swing paper so last fold is at left. | Last crease goes in envelope first. |

HOW TO ADDRESS ENVELOPES IN BLOCKED STYLE...

THE RETURN ADDRESS ...

is usually printed. If it must be typed, use single spacing and start ½ inch from the left edge of the envelope, on line 3.

USE DOUBLE SPACING ...

when address has 3 lines, but single spacing when address has more than 3 lines.

SPECIAL NOTATIONS ...

such as "Please Forward" and "Personal" are typed at bottom left, a double space below address, ½ inch from the left side edge.

THE LARGE ENVELOPE ...

used in business is the "No. 10" (9½ by 4⅛ inches). Begin address on line 14, about ½ inch to the left of the center.

THE SMALL ENVELOPE ...

used in business is the "No. 6¾" (6½ by 3⅝ inches). Begin address on line 12, about ½ inch to the left of the center.

MARTIN MILLER & SONS
58 BROAD STREET   ATLANTA 1, GEORGIA

```
Mr. Ben Dale, Credit Manager
The Black-Gray Company
1398 Sutter Street
San Francisco 6, California
```

WARMUP *(Each line 3 times)*   ◁**70**▷

```
a;sldkfjghfjdksla;sldkfjghfjdksla; a;sldkfjghfjdksla;sldkfjghfjdksla;
Alex Beth Cora Dick Fran Gary John Miss Paul Quen Tess Vera Will Zeke
we 23 tie 583 pout 0975 type 5603; 39 28 47 56 10 #39 #28 #47 #56 #10
The big flight took off with a mutter of engines and a whine of jets.
```
12-Sec.5| 10| 15| 20| 25| 30| 35| 40| 45| 50| 55| 60| 65| 70|

RHYTHM PREVIEW *(Each line 3 times)*

```
modern office expert agency junior pencil staffs stream drafts zigzag
done from copy that type with bill work very much many adds able make
good bell lot far may his own and the now all how fix get jot but use
```

ALPHABET-REVIEW PARAGRAPHS *(2 copies / si 1.34)*   ◁**70**▷
DS

*5-Min. Writings

A lot of the typing that[1] is done in a modern office[2] is from copy that is[3] far from   16
perfect. A copy[4] expert in an advertising[5] agency may type from his[6] own sketchy notes.   34
A junior[7] accountant may prepare[8] his quarterly reports[9] from his own pencil work,[10]   50
complete with corrections[11] and erasures. The bill[12] clerk types from handwritten[13] copy,   67
too; while editors[14] and their staff work[15] with a stream of rough drafts.[16] And most   83
secretaries[17] spend many hours transcribing[18] those zigzag marks[19] that are called short-   99
hand.[20] We do not work very much[21] with perfect copy matter.[22]   111

Now all this adds up[23] to the simple fact that[24] a typist must learn how to[25] think   127
while he is typing.[26] He must be able to make[27] grammatical corrections;[28] he must be   143
able to manage[29] capitalization and[30] quotations, read rough drafts,[31] catch and fix wrong   160
dates[32] and names, think through[33] problems of word[34] division at the ends of[35] lines—   176
and all this thinking[36] must be done in a quick[37] flash of good judgment.[38] These skills   192
require practice;[39] the place to get it is[40] not on the job but in[41] the classroom. Asked   209
to[42] select which one of these[43] skills is most worth[44] concentrating upon, I should[45] pick   226
on the use of the[46] warning bell. The other[47] skills are worthless if you[48] must look up   243
at the end[49] of every line of typing.[50]   (START OVER)   250

*The tiny number nearest where you stop is your speed on a 5-minute writ-
ing. For writings of other lengths: (1) Note number at the end of the last
full printed line you copied; (2) add 1 for each additional 5 strokes (letters
or spaces) you typed; (3) divide by number of minutes for which you typed.

Blocked Letter Style

Date Backspaced from Right Margin • Closing Lines Blocked at Center • Other Lines Blocked Left

With Date at Right and with a Company Signature

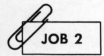

JOB 2

Blocked letter
    Shown in pica
    Use letterhead
    Date, right
    Center tab
Words: 151
    Body: 121

December 1, 19-- 6 ◁ **5 in.** ▷
SS
14/6
▽

Mr. Henry L. Hale
3928 Dumont Avenue
Brooklyn 8, New York 2

Dear Mr. Hale: 2

This letter is in blocked form similar to the style
of the last letter I wrote to you, but this letter
has two points of style that are worth noting.

First, note that the date is placed so that it ends
even with the right margin. To place the date line
in this way, backspace from the margin once for each
space that the date line will occupy. This is, by
far, the most popular position for the date line.

Second, note that this letter includes the name of
our company in the closing lines. If the company
name is used, it is always typed in capital letters
two lines below the complimentary closing.

See letter
on page 50.

Yours very truly, 2

Use shift lock
when typing the
company name.

MARTIN MILLER & SONS 4

Training Director 2

Remember: Type
your initials,
not "URS."

JLW:URS

JOB 3

Semiblocked letter
Exact copy
Plain paper
3 carbons
Words: 207
Body: 148

UNITED APPLIANCES COMPANY

1851 Diversey Parkway

Chicago 14, Illinois

Center essential data
of incoming letterhead
on lines 6, 8, and 10.

C
  O
    P
      Y

August 18, 1956

Make it clear
that letter
is a copy.

Mr. Frank G. Harris
Sales Manager
Judd-Kane, Inc.
1410 Glenarm Street
Denver 2, Colorado

Copy an incoming
letter exactly
(including errors),
line for line,
and display the
word "copy."

Dear Mr. Harris:

    This is not the usual kind of letter in which
a dealer writes to protest about something. To the
contrary, it is a letter of appreciation.

    We have now been handling Judd-Kane television
and radio sets for almost exactly one year. In that
time we have sold more than a thousand J-K units.
At no time have we had to wait for deliveries. At
no time have we suffered either loss or inconvenience
from shipping damages. At all times your firm has
moved promptly and effectively to serve us.

    So, this is just a quiet note to let you know
that at least one of your dealers truly appreciates
the service that your company gives its dealers. It
is a real privilege, we feel, to carry the J-K sign
on our door and to represent you in Chicago.

            Yours very sincerely,

            UNITED APPLIANCES COMPANY

                (Signed)

            E. L. Houston, Manager

After typing
original set
of initials,
add your own
in a contrast-
ing style.

ELH:FTT/urs

JOB 3

Blocked letter
Shown in elite
Letterhead
Date, right
Center tab
Words: 161
Body: 128

| 1 | 2 | 3 | 4 | 5 | 6 | 7 | 8 | 9 | 10 | 11 | 12 |

◁ **5 in.** ▷
SS
14/6
▽

Mr. Frederick Williams
1039 Statler Building
Boston 3, Massachusetts

Dear Fred:

I am writing to you in the hope that between us we can find   12
a way to speed up the plans for our new building in Boston.   24
I know that your best men are working on the Hall project,   36
but the question of whether or not we shall be able to go on   48
with the building at all is being held up by your delay.   60

Costs are going up at a rapid rate, as you know; and credit   72
is getting very tight. The first budget that you and I had   84
planned is already quite out of date.   92

Is there any chance of your getting the plans ready within a   104
month or two? Please tell me frankly. I know that members   116
of our board will soon be pressing me for a progress report.   128

Yours sincerely,

MARTIN MILLER & SONS

Initials?

Roland I. Miller

JOB 4

Blocked letter
Unarranged
Letterhead
Date, right
Center tab
Words: 168
Body: 136

| 1 | 2 | 3 | 4 | 5 | 6 | 7 | 8 | 9 | 10 | 11 |

◁ **5 in.** ▷
SS
14/6
▽

December 2, 19--   Dr. James Kendall   Lake Stone
College   Savannah, Georgia   Dear Doctor Kendall:

We are glad to learn that it will be possible for   10
you to speak to our staff at our next meeting. It will   21
be easy for us to set the meeting for either of the two   32
dates that you suggested; please tell us which would be   44
the more convenient for you.   50

We should like to know the title that you plan to   60
give your talk. We have a staff news journal that car-   70
ries notes on such events as your visit, and we feel   81
that having the title of your talk will make our news   92
story better and stir up more interest.   100

If you will let us know when you will arrive here   110
in Atlanta, I shall see that your train is met by some-   121
one on the staff who will drive you to your hotel and   132
then to the meeting.   136

Yours very truly,   MARTIN MILLER & SONS   Roland
I. Miller   Initials?

PRODUCTION PRACTICE (Jobs 1-3)

Your employer is Frank G. Harris, sales manager of Judd-Kane, Inc. He prefers the blocked letter form, with his name and his title typed below his signature (as on page 191).

1-2. "Please type these letters," says Mr. Harris, giving you the letters below. Make 2 carbons of the first and 1 of the second.

3. "And," he adds, as he gives you the letter shown on the next page, "enclose or attach a copy of this letter with each of the letters and each of the file-copy carbons." You will need 4 copies of the letter on the next page — an original and 3 carbons.

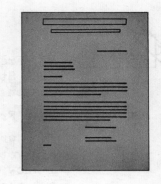

JOB 1

Blocked letter
Unarranged
Letterhead
2 carbons
Words: 127
Body: 87

◁ **4 in.** ▷
SS
14/8
▽

Today's date. Mr. E. L. Houston, Manager, United Appliances Company, 1851 Diversey Parkway, Chicago 14, Illinois

| 1 | 2 | 3 | 4 | 5 | 6 | 7 | 8 | 9 | 10 | 11 | 12 |

Dear Mr. Houston: Some while ago you were kind enough · 11
to send us a fine letter concerning the services that we in · 23
Judd-Kane extended to you during your first year as a Judd- · 35
Kane representative. I am enclosing a copy of your letter. · 47

If you still feel as enthusiastic about our service as · 58
you did when you sent the letter, we should like permission · 70
to quote your last sentence in one of a series of promotion · 82
pieces. May we have the permission? Very sincerely yours, · 94

JOB 2

Blocked letter
Unarranged
Letterhead
1 carbon
Words: 207
Body: 168

◁ **5 in.** ▷
SS
14/6
▽

Today's date. Miss Jeannette Rawlins, Graham-Jacobs Agency, 5475 Bulwer Avenue, St. Louis 7, Missouri

| 1 | 2 | 3 | 4 | 5 | 6 | 7 | 8 | 9 | 10 | 11 | 12 |

Dear Miss Rawlins: We are very pleased with the plans · 11 · 105
you have developed for the campaign to recruit more dealers · 23 · 117
in the southern states. There are some ideas that we shall · 35 · 129
wish to discuss with you, but the general plan has the very · 47 · 141
enthusiastic approval of the Company's executive committee. · 59 · 153

As you said in your letter, one of the problems is the · 70 · 164
matter of getting quotations that might serve your purpose. · 82 · 176
I found one in a letter from our dealer in Chicago and have · 94 · 188
written to him for his permission to use it; I am enclosing · 106 · 200
copies of our correspondence. His statement is a good one. · 118 · 212

I should like to suggest that you use the statement by · 129 · 223
this dealer in preparing sample ads to show exactly how you · 141 · 235
plan to feature the dealer quotations. Then, if any member · 153 · 247
of our staff or if my correspondent has any doubt about the · 165 · 259
campaign, we can answer him quickly. Very sincerely yours, · 177 · 271

*Placement Plan: Date on line 14 or 2 lines below letterhead, whichever is lower. If letter has under 100 words in body, use 4-inch line and drop 8 lines from date to address; 100-200 words, 5-inch line and 6-line drop; over 200 words, 6-inch line and 4-line drop.

WARMUP *(Each line 2 times)*

◁**60**▷

A blazing jamb quivered as the ax point struck flying blows.
39 28 47 56 10 we 23 you 697 try 546 rip 480 top 590 ore 943
We did not try and will not try to tell them she cannot win.

12-Sec. 5| 10| 15| 20| 25| . 30| 35| 40| 45| 50| 55| 60|

CONTROL PREVIEW *(Each line 2 times)*

aa paragraph bb back cc conservative dd day ee each ff flash
gg zigzag hh other ii lines jj just kk look ll all mm common
nn penned oo tone pp experts qq equaled rr return ss address
tt start uu build vv have ww writer xx extra yy style zz zip

ALPHABET-REVIEW PARAGRAPHS *(Each, 1 time / si 1.30)*

◁**60**▷
DS

3-Min. Writings

	1	2	3	4	5	6	7	8	9	10	11	12

0   Back in the days when a letter had to be penned by the   11

4   writer, it was not common to have extra space between parts   23

8   of a letter; the writer had to use indentions instead. The   35

12   start of each paragraph had to be indented. The lines of a   47

16   return address, of an inside address, and of the close were   59

20   all set up as a series of indentions, just like steps. The   71

24   result was that letters seemed to have quite a zigzag look.   83

28   Letters got a new look when the typewriter came along.   94

31   Because it is a lot faster to block than to indent lines on   106

35   a machine, a letter today is not likely to have many inden-   118

39   tions. The experts say you can build the tone you may wish   130

43   just by the number of indentions in the style of letter you   142

47   use. A lot make your letter seem to be conservative; a few   154

51   make it seem casual; none at all gives a letter a flash and   166

55   a zip, a modern touch, that can be equaled in no other way.   178

Plus ➡   1 | 2 | 3 | 4

PRODUCTION PRACTICE *(Jobs 5-8)*

JOB 5   Review page 82; then address in blocked style a No. 10 envelope for each letter in Jobs 6-8. Use real envelopes, or the ones printed on Workbook pages 63-64, or slips of paper cut to 9½ by 4⅛ inches.

UNIT 26
CORRESPONDENCE

In this unit: (1) copying incoming letters; (2) chainfeeding; (3) typing on index cards; (4) typing display letters; (5) an introduction to "dictation style" letters; and (6) a review of envelope addressing, blocked and semiblocked letters, and letter placement. Read pages 226-233 and answer the study-guide questions on Workbook pages 233-234 before you begin typing the jobs in this unit.

WARMUP (*Each line 3 times*)   ◁**70**▷

```
a;sldkfjghfjdksla; a;sldkfjghfjdksla; a;sldkfjghfjdksla; a;sldkfjghfj
box cog dip elk for his jot lid men new quad rye zoo : 39 28 47 56 10
When they come to us and ask for help, then we will try to help them.
12-Sec.5|   10|   15|   20|   25|   30|   35|   40|   45|   50|   55|   60|   65|   70|
```

RHYTHM PREVIEW (*Each line 3 times*)

```
second copies spare, writer letter played enough carbon assume surely
fail plan find mail when work have load make more it's boss unit job;
says safe for you may lot big one two are the and but did not all too
```

ALPHABET-REVIEW PARAGRAPHS (*2 copies / si 1.29*)   ◁**60**▷
                                                                   DS

3-Min. Writings		
0	Much too frequently, the man for whom you type letters	11
4	forgets to tell you how many carbon copies to make. Or, he	23
8	may not forget; he may assume that you know, for you surely	35
12	should. To start with, you will need a copy for the files;	47
16	and if the firm is large enough to be departmentalized, you	59
si 20	will need an extra copy for each department that might have	71
1.34 24	an interest in the subject of the letter. If the letter is	83
28	about a third person, perhaps he should get a copy. Before	95
32	typing a letter, always plan the number of copies you need.	107

36	If you fail to plan for carbons, you may find yourself	11	118
39	doing a lot of mail a second time, an exasperating thing to	23	130
43	do when you have a big work load. Many typists always make	35	142
47	one or two more copies than are required; then, if the boss	47	154
si 51	wants a spare, it's there. In the second job in this unit,	59	166
1.25 55	for example, the writer says that he is enclosing a copy of	71	178
59	the letter that is to be typed in the first job; there's no	83	190
63	problem if you have played safe and made enough copies; but	95	202
67	if you did not, you will have to type a spare. All typists	107	214
71	must realize that planning the carbons is part of the work.	119	226

Plus ➡   1   2   3   4

COMPUTING WORDS: To the number at the end of the last line you typed completely, add the number (top scale) under which you stopped.
COMPUTING SPEED: Divide words typed by the number of minutes. Or, if your timing is for the minutes indicated in the left margin, add the number (bottom scale) above which you stopped to the number at the start of the line you were typing when time was called.

Semiblocked Letter Style

Closing Lines Start at Center • Date Backspaced from Margin • Paragraphs Indented 5 Spaces

With Date at Right and with a Company Signature

JOB 6

Semiblocked letter
 Shown in pica
 Use letterhead
 Date, right
 Center tab
 Paragraph tab
Words: 164
 Body: 126

December 3, 19-- ◁**5 in.**▷
      6 **SS**
         14/6
          ▽

Miss Lee Ann Sloane
2847 Yates Street
Denver 12, Colorado

Dear Miss Sloane:

    This is a semiblocked letter, which is simply
a blocked letter with the paragraphs indented. As
a rule, the indention is for five spaces; but it is
not uncommon to indent ten, or even more, spaces.

    This letter also shows how and where a typist
reminds himself that he is to send something in the
same envelope with the letter. On the line below
the initials, he types Enclosure; or, if there are
more than one, Enclosures. Some typists prefer to
use the short forms, Enc. and Encs.

    It is important to type that note, for it is
also a reminder for the person who gets the letter
to be sure to see and to note what is enclosed.

                    Very truly yours, 2

                    THE BLACK-GRAY COMPANY 4

                    F. Prescott Taylor
                    Sales Manager 2

FPT:URS
Enclosure

WARMUP: Reach Review *(Each line 3 times)* ◁**50**▷

```
aqa ;p; sws lol ded kik : frf juj ftf jyj fgf jhj
aza ;/; sxs l.l dcd k,k : fvf jmj fbf jnj fgf jhj
ala ;0; s2s 191 d3d k8k : f4f j7j f5f j6j ;0; ;-;
39 39 28 28 47 47 56 56 : 10 10 39 28 47 56 10 39
```

SYMBOL DRILL: Reach Review *(Each line 2 times)*

```
#39 #28 #47 #56 #10  6▸Tab  $39, $28, $47, $56, $10,
39½ 28½ 47½ 56½ 10½          "39" "28" "47" "56" "10"
39¼ 28¼ 47¼ 56¼ 10¼          '39' '28' '47' '56' '10'
39* 28* 47* 56* 10*          -39- -28- -47- -56- -10-
39% 28% 47% 56% 10%          39 & 28 & 47 & 56 & 10 &
39? 28? 47? 56? 10?          (39) (28) (47) (56) (10)
39¢ 28¢ 47¢ 56¢ 10¢          39 @ 28 @ 47 @ 56 @ 10 @
```

NUMBER DRILL: We 23's *(Each line 3 times)*

```
wee 233 root 4995 poor 0994 weep 2330 error 34494
too 599 purr 0744 tree 5433 peep 0330 witty 28556
woo 299 err 344 putt 0755 poppy 09006 troop 54990
```

SYMBOL SENTENCES: ¢, @, $ *(Each line 3 times)* ◁**50**▷

½- and 1-Min.
Writings

| | 1 | 2 | 3 | 4 | 5 | 6 | 7 | 8 | 9 | 10 |

```
He paid 10¢ but charged me 28¢ and John 10¢ more.        10
I feel that 56¢ is steep; 38¢ is more reasonable.        20

I don't know whether he paid $47 or $56 for that.   10 | 30
It is a $39 jacket, but she paid only $28 for it.   20 | 40

He got 56 shares of it @ $10 and 47 shares @ $11.   10 | 50
If you can get 10 @ 39¢ or 28¢, place your order.   20 | 60

We got 1,000 shares @ $2.25 and 200 more @ $2.10.   10 | 70
I quote 5 @ 50¢, 9 @ 75¢, 15 @ $1.39, 25 @ $2.41.   20 | 80
```

CENTURY DRIVE *(1 complete copy, to 100)*

2-Min.
Writings

```
Cut 1 cut 2 cut 3 cut 4 cut 5 cut 6 cut 7 cut 8
cut 9 cut 10 cut 11 cut 12 cut 13 cut 14 cut 15
cut 16 cut 17 cut 18 cut
```
⌈Continue on up to 100. Ultimate⌉
⌊goal is to reach 100 in 2 minutes.⌋

JOB 7

Semiblocked letter
Shown in elite
Letterhead
Date, right
Center tab
Paragraph tab
Words: 176
Body: 141

1 | 2 | 3 | 4 | 5 | 6 | 7 | 8 | 9 | 10 | 11 | 12 |

◁**5 in.**▷
SS
14/6
▽

Mr. Bruce B. Blake
8310 Racine Street
Oakland 9, California

Dear Mr. Blake:

As you see from the date of this letter, we are now well | 11
past the first of the month, when the final payment on your | 23
account was due. I am enclosing a copy of the statement that | 36
was sent you a week ago; you will note that it shows that you | 48
still have one more payment due on your account. | 58

Is there any chance that our record might not be correct | 70
and that you really did mail a check or stop in with the last | 82
payment? Or, might you have simply overlooked the date and | 94
forgotten to send in the final check to close the account? | 105

In any case, Mr. Blake, I know that we both want to get | 117
this matter cleared up; so, within the next two or three days, | 129
will you please telephone us or stop in to see us about it? | 141

Sincerely yours,

THE BLACK-GRAY COMPANY

Ben Dale, Credit Manager

Initials?
Enclosure?

If a name and a
title are both used
and are short
enough to fit on
one line, separate
them by a comma.

JOB 8

Semiblocked letter
Unarranged
Letterhead
Date, right
Center tab
Paragraph tab
Words: 185
Body: 147

1 | 2 | 3 | 4 | 5 | 6 | 7 | 8 | 9 | 10 | 11 |

◁**5 in.**▷
SS
14/6
▽

December 4, 19--   Mr. Marvin N. Maxwell   1039
Clary Street   Fort Worth 11, Texas   Dear Mr. Maxwell:

We have received and noted with interest your let- | 10
ter of application for a sales position with our staff. | 21
We do not have at the present time a vacancy in our | 32
field staff in your part of the state, but we do need a | 43
representative who would make his headquarters in Lub- | 53
bock and cover the northwestern part of the state. | 64

If you are interested in that position, please fill | 74
in and return to me within the next week or ten days the | 86
application form that I am enclosing. I shall be in | 96
your city to attend a convention during the second week | 107
of next month; while there, I should be pleased to talk | 119
with you. If you are truly interested in the job, we | 129
might be able to settle the matter at once and have you | 141
join our staff then and there. | 147

Very truly yours,   THE BLACK-GRAY COMPANY
F. Prescott Taylor   Sales Manager   Initials? Enclosure?

WARMUP: Number-Reach Review *(Each line 3 times)* ◁**50**▷

```
alla ;00; s22s 1991 d33d k88k f44f j77j f55f j66j
als2 d3f4 f5j6 j7k8 19;0 1234 5678 9012 3456 7890
1 2 3 4 5 6 7 8 9 10 11 12 13 14 15 16 17 18 1900
```

NUMBER DRILL: 1, 4, 7 *(Each line 3 times)*

```
1 4 7 1 4 7 111 114 117 141 144 147 171 174 177 1
411 414 417 441 444 447 471 477 711 714 717 741 4
744 771 774 777 1 4 7 1 4 7 111 114 117 141 147 7
```

NUMBER DRILL: We 23's *(Each line 3 times)*

```
we 23 rip 480 rye 463 rut 475 riot 4895 rote 4953
root 4995 rope 4903 rout 4975 ripe 4803 yipe 6803
or 94 out 975 you 697 ore 943 toot 5995 poor 0994
```

NUMBER SENTENCES *(Each line 3 times)*

½-Min.
Writings

	1	2	3	4	5	6	7	8	9	10

```
We need 1 or 2 men, 11 or 12 boys, and 22 others.   10
They had 3 or 4 big ones, 34 small, and 43 large.   20
He got 55 homers, 66 triples, and 156 other hits.   30
He made a 77, a 78, and an 88 in his best rounds.   40
The 90 caddies say 90 boys play 90 games of golf.   50
```

NUMBER DRILL: Cumulative Count *(Each line 3 times)* ◁**50**▷

1-Min.
Writings

	1	2	3	4	5	6	7	8	9	10

```
4001 3902 3803 3704 3605 3506 3407 3308 3209 3110   10
3011 2912 2813 2714 2615 2516 2417 2318 2219 2120   20
2021 1922 1823 1724 1625 1526 1427 1328 1229 1130   30
1031 0932 0833 0734 0635 0536 0437 0338 0239 0140   40
```

NUMBER PARAGRAPH *(3 copies / si 1.29)*

2-Min.
Writings

0	35	In 1955, one 465,000-pound generator went by	9
5	39	rail from New York to Florida. It was mounted on	19
10	44	a 16-wheel car weighing 88,700 pounds--and made a	29
15	49	total weight of 277 tons. This whole unit was 13	39
20	54	feet high, 12 feet wide, and 27 feet long. Also,	49
25	59	it could meet the needs of over 450,000 homes--or	59
30	64	of a community of about 259,000 or so population.	69

Plus ➧ 1 | 2 | 3 | 4 | 5

WARMUP *(Each line 2 times)*

Roxie amazed Jake by pointing to the five bows very quickly.
39 28 47 56 10 we 23 tie 583 toe 593 top 590 two 529 rye 463
They do not think we should try to tell them; nor should we.

12-Sec. 5| 10| 15| 20| 25| 30| 35| 40| 45| 50| 55| 60|

CONTROL PREVIEW *(Each line 2 times)*

aa Atlanta bb about cc Francisco dd paid ee selected ff fact
gg suggest hh other ii file jj join kk talk ll likely mm him
nn Noonan pp prompt qq question rr arrange ss speak tt treat
uu outline vv evening ww answer xx Texas yy frankly zz prize

PRODUCTION PRACTICE *(Jobs 9-11)*

The semiblocked style may be adapted for use in personal business letters by including one's return address, as in Job 9; block the heading lines at the point reached by backspacing from the margin for the longest line. Job 10 reviews the blocked style (page 83). Job 11, shown unarranged, is to be typed in semiblocked form (page 86). Address an envelope for each letter. Use a large envelope if there is an enclosure; use a small envelope if there is no enclosure.

1 | 2 | 3 | 4 | 5 | 6 | 7 | 8 | 9 | 10 |

◁ **4 in.** ▷
SS
12/8
▽

JOB 9

Semiblocked letter
Shown in elite
Use plain paper
Return address
Center tab
Paragraph tab
Words: 132
Body: 88

8310 Racine Street
Oakland 9, California
December 6, 19-- 8 ➧

Mr. Ben Dale, Credit Manager
The Black-Gray Company
1398 Sutter Street
San Francisco 6, California

If a name and title both appear in an address and are short enough to fit on one line, separate them by a comma.

My dear Mr. Dale:

If you will inspect your records closely, you   9
will find that I paid my account in full more than   19
a month ago. You see, I paid the last two install-   29
ments at the same time.   34

As a matter of fact, Mr. Dale, I have on file   44
a very pleasant note from you in which you thanked   54
me for making payments so promptly and offered the   64
kind services of your department any time that I   74
might need them in the future. I am enclosing a   84
copy of your letter. 2 ➧   88

Very truly yours, 4 ➧

Although initials are not used in a personal business letter, an enclosure notation IS used.

Bruce B. Blake 2 ➧

Enclosure

WARMUP: Capitals Review *(Each line 3 times)*

◁ 50 ▷

```
aB cD eF gH iJ kL mN oP qR sT uV wX yZ ;: /? .. -
Adam Babs Carl Dora Earl Fred Gail Hank Inez John
Kane Lida Mary Nate Orva Paul Quen Ruth Sara Tina
Ulla Vera Will Xeno Yola Zora Anna Bill Cain Dale
```

CONTROL DRILL: Individual Finger Reaches, with One-Hand Words *(Each line 2 times)*

Fore-fingers	Left Right Both	

```
target barber tatter garter batter beggar taffeta
Johnny hominy minion phylon unholy unhook minimum
target hominy barber minion tatter unholy taffeta
```

Second fingers	Left Right Both	

```
cedar secede accede exceed recede decease cascade
milky kimono Kokomo minion pipkin minikin million
secede kimono accede minion exceed pipkin decease
```

Third fingers	Left Right Both	

```
waste sweet Warsaw sweats seesaw waxweed westward
Polly onion unhook pompon poplin homonym lollipop
sweet unhook Warsaw pompon seesaw poplin westward
```

Fourth fingers	Left Right Both	

```
daze aware award craze adage zagged fracas savage
pump poppy plump pupil puppy pippin pipkin pompon
daze poopy dazed nippy craze pipkin zagged pompon
```

CONTROL SENTENCES: One-Hand Words *(Each line 3 times)*

◁ 60 ▷

½- and 1-Min. Writings

```
  1 | 2 | 3 | 4 | 5 | 6 | 7 | 8 | 9 | 10 | 11 | 12
Johnny deserted Phillip after Pilkin retreated on Westward.    12
We agreed, as you imply, Polly was only average as a pupil.    24
A million cedar trees were devastated in a warfare barrage.    36
In my opinion, you deserved a better award after my defeat.    48
```

CONTROL SENTENCES: I through R *(Each line 3 times)*

3-Min. Writings

		1 | 2 | 3 | 4 | 5 | 6 | 7 | 8 | 9 | 10 | 11 | 12	
0	40	Ira insisted his item was ideal to include in their digest.	12
4	44	Joseph just joined Jack and John to enjoy a jaunt to Japan.	24
8	48	Ken asked Ike to bank his checks and take Kay the bankbook.	36
12	52	Lucille left Len's letter lying on the mantel all day long.	48
16	56	Mamie married a mean man, and he claimed most of her money.	60
20	60	Nathan didn't know when dinner began and nearly went on in.	72
24	64	Only one or two of those others should come around so soon.	84
28	68	Paul appointed Peter to pick people to promote peace plans.	96
32	72	Quentin quizzed the queen on quick questions quite a while.	108
36	76	Ruth arrived from Rio or Torre by air after a wearing trip.	120
Plus ▶		1 2 3 4	

Blocked letter
Shown in pica
Letterhead
Center tab
Date, right
Words: 162
Body: 131

◁ **5 in.** ▷
SS
14/6
▽

1 | 2 | 3 | 4 | 5 | 6 | 7 | 8 | 9 | 10

Dr. James Kendall
Lake Stone College
Savannah 4, Georgia

Dear Doctor Kendall:

Thank you for your prompt letter in reply to mine.   10
The day and hour that you suggest are fine, and we   21
are more than pleased with the topic that you have   31
selected for your talk. In addition to having all   41
the members of our executive staff at the meeting,   51
we are planning to call in also all our department   61
heads and the managers of our three local stores.   72

I have reserved a room for you at the Piedmont and   82
have arranged for Mr. Verner, whom you know, to   91
meet your train and bring you to the meeting.   101

Mrs. Miller and I should very much like to have you   111
join us for dinner after the meeting if you have   121
made no other plans for your evening in Atlanta.   131

                         Very truly yours,

                         MARTIN MILLER & SONS

Initials?
Enclosure?   Roland I. Miller

JOB 11

Semiblocked
letter
Unarranged
Letterhead
Date, right
Center tab
Paragraph
tab
Words: 173
Body: 136

1 | 2 | 3 | 4 | 5 | 6 | 7 | 8 | 9 | 10 | 11

Placement table
is on page 49.

December 8, 19--   Mr. Patrick F. Noonan   19 Rock-
wood Street   Dallas 3, Texas   Dear Mr. Noonan:

A gentleman whom you know, Mr. Marvin N. Maxwell, is   11
being considered by us for a position as field representa-   22
tive. In his application, he gave us your name as a busi-   33
ness reference. We should be grateful for your telling   45
us what you can about him.   50

I am enclosing a form that outlines the kind of in-   60
formation that we should like to have and an envelope for   72
returning the form to us. It is not likely that you can   83
or would wish to answer all the questions that are given   95
on the form, but we hope that you will answer as many as   106
you can with assurance.   111

We shall treat your comments as confidential, of   121
course; so, we hope that you will speak frankly. We do   132
appreciate your help.   136

Very truly yours,   THE BLACK-GRAY COMPANY   F. Prescott Taylor   Sales Manager   Initials? Enclosures?

WARMUP: 4-Letter Rhythms *(Each line 3 times)*   ◁60▷

```
a b c d e f g h i j k l m n o p q r s t u v w x y z , . / ?
away bank came date even file gave hard into just know last
mail next once part quip read send tend upon very wait year
zest able come deal each form have item jerk kind lent mark
```

CONTROL DRILL: M, R, Y *(Each line 3 times)*

```
made make mean melt mild mine must more most much many mail
came jump home name fame acme clam item calm from them warm

rear raft rail rapt read ream rock rich road rush rope roar
here jury form burn pert from four your fair near hear hour

yank yard year yell yoke your yule yarn yelp yolk yawn eyes
days myth hymn says lays duty very jury only many pity city
```

CONTROL SENTENCES: Alphabet Review *(Each line 3 times)*

½- and
1-Min.
Writings

```
  1 | 2 | 3 | 4 | 5 | 6 | 7 | 8 | 9 | 10 | 11 | 12
Clyde fixed quaint puzzles to give to John, Mark, and Webb.    12
Vike's big squads of experts have won major prizes cleanly.   24
Jacques was amazed by Vi's skill and fixed her a good part.   36
Five or six big comet planes used by Hal Quezz were junked.   48
```

CONTROL PREVIEW *(Each line 3 times)*   ◁50▷

```
type with build reaches hazards relaxed excessive
that your drill errors posture realize techniques
```

ALPHABET-REVIEW PARAGRAPHS *(2 copies / si 1.22)*

5-Min. Writings

		1 | 2 | 3 | 4 | 5 | 6 | 7 | 8 | 9 | 10	
0	40	The two common causes of typing mistakes are	9
2	41	poor posture and excessive pushing for speed. If	19
4	43	you wish to type with few errors, then, you ought	29
6	45	to study these two matters closely. When you try	39
8	47	so hard for speed that a lot of errors show up in	49
si 1.26 10	49	your work, you should realize that you are making	59
12	51	your fingers use techniques that are wrong. When	69
14	53	you wish to build speed, use copy that is so easy	79
16	55	that, as you type it over and over, you find your	89
18	57	speed jumping without your pushing to pull it up.	99

20	59	As to posture, well, remember that your feet	9	108
22	61	must be squarely on the floor; that your arms and	19	118
24	63	elbows must hang relaxed; that your wrists should	29	128
26	65	clear the front of your machine by an inch or so;	39	138
28	67	and that your hands ought to be so close that you	49	148
si 1.18 30	69	could lock your thumbs if you wished. One of the	59	158
32	71	hazards to hand posture is the typing on the keys	69	168
34	73	at the edges of the keyboard. We make few errors	79	178
36	75	on these keys, but the reaches jerk our hands out	89	188
38	77	of position and so invite us to make some errors.	99	198

Plus ➧   1 | 2

UNIT 11
FORMS

In this unit: (1) interoffice memorandums ("memos"); (2) invoices; (3) telegrams; (4) use of the variable spacer to type on guide lines and beside guide words; and (5) use of carbon paper.

Your work will be easiest if, before starting the jobs of this unit, you first read straight through pages 90-98 and then answer the study questions on Workbook pages 73-74.

WARMUP *(Each line 2 times)*   ◁ **60** ▷

```
They requested sixty black jeeps for moving the prizes away.
39 28 47 56 10 we 23 put 075 out 975 wit 285 rue 473 yip 680
If you sell them some more goods, we shall send them a bill.
```
12-Sec. 5| 10| 15| 20| 25| 30| 35| 40| 45| 50| 55| 60|

CONTROL PREVIEW *(Each line 2 times)*

```
aa data bb both cc company dd down ee same ff form gg length
hh help ii time jj jobs kk kind ll lines mm common nn nature
oo routine pp placement qq quick rr standard ss words tt out
uu ruled vv revision ww between xx example yy typist zz size
```

ALPHABET-REVIEW PARAGRAPH *(2 copies / si 1.25)*   DS

3-Min. Writings

| 1 | 2 | 3 | 4 | 5 | 6 | 7 | 8 | 9 | 10 | 11 | 12 |

```
 0        One of the modern touches in office jobs is the use of     11
 4     printed forms that cut down the work load of the typist and    23
 8     the length of time that it takes him or her to get out work    35
12     that is routine or standard in nature or size.  The printed    47
16     letterhead, which cuts out the need for typing a return ad-    59
20     dress, is one good example; another that is quite common is    71
24     a special form for a memo from one person to another in the    83
28     same company, which is quick both to read and to type.  The    95
32     use of forms for bills of all kinds, with key words to help   107
36     the typist fill in the heading and ruled lines to guide the   119
40     placement of other data, saves many hours--and much effort.   131
```
Plus ▶   1 | 2 | 3 | 4

PRODUCTION PRACTICE *(Jobs 1-5)*

Study page 91 and the information in Jobs 2 and 4; then type Job 1 on the workbook page (or, as the directions indicate, on coupons that you bring in); type Jobs 2 and 3 on half sheets of plain paper; and type Jobs 4 and 5 on the workbook forms. If you do not have a workbook, type Jobs 4 and 5 on half sheets of plain paper, like Jobs 2 and 3.

WARMUP: "ME" Drill *(Each line 3 times)*   ◁ **55** ▷

```
aa;;qqppa; ssllwwoosl ddkkeeiidk ffjjrruufj gghhttyygh
mean mesh menu meal meet mere mesa melt mend meld mess
remedy omelet cement camel smear comet amend amen omen
came name same come time fume tame dome lame dime some
```

SPEED DRILL: Common Word Endings *(Each line 3 times)*

```
-ble payable capable trouble liable double table cable
-ify beautify classify certify amplify justify specify
-cle obstacle clavicle article bicycle auricle binocle
-ity locality facility amenity agility ability quality
```

SPEED SENTENCES: Common Word Endings *(Each line 3 times)*

12-Sec. Writings		
The quality of his article is suitable to his ability.	11
Notify her that table fees are payable as you specify.	22
You need ability to ride the bicycle in that locality.	33
The obstacle you told about would justify the amenity.	44

```
12-Sec.5|  10|  15|  20|  25|  30|  35|  40|  45|  50|  55|
```

SPEED DRILL: Rhythm, with 3- and 4-Letter   ◁ **60** ▷
Alternate-Hand Words *(Each line 3 times / si 1.12)*

½- and 1-Min. Writings

```
    1 | 2 | 3 | 4 | 5 | 6 | 7 | 8 | 9 | 10 | 11 | 12
also and both big city cut down did envy end form fit fork    12
girl got half ham jamb jay kept key land lap make man name    24
oboe own paid pay roam rid soap sir than the when wit wish    36

with urn yams yen auto ape busy but chap cot dial due down    48
eyes end firm fix hand hem lend lay melt men nape nay naps    60
odor oak pale pan rich rib sign sob them tow vial vow wick    72
```

SUSTAINED-SPEED SENTENCES *(3 copies / si 1.08)*

3-Min. Writings

```
    1 | 2 | 3 | 4 | 5 | 6 | 7 | 8 | 9 | 10 | 11 | 12
```

0	40	Both the town and city may make the firm fix both big oaks.	12
4	44	They got paid for both the corn and fish but kept the hams.	24
8	48	They may make the busy but also apt chap fix both the urns.	36
12	52	Jane and Maud got half the corn and hams for Lena and Dick.	48
16	56	Dock the maid for half the work she kept and lent the girl.	60
20	60	Both the firm and city own half the lake and half the land.	72
24	64	When the busy men paid the man, the city got keys for them.	84
28	68	Both men paid for half the land and also own half the lake.	96
32	72	They own hens and paid the girl for pans for both the pens.	108
36	76	Alan got both the oboe and auto and paid for half the keys.	120

```
Plus ▶        1    |        2    |        3    |        4
```

HOW TO TYPE ON BUSINESS FORMS . . .

TO   Mr. Walter
        3928 Montc
        Paterson 4

Name................ Mr. Walter
Address.......... 3928 Montc
City................ Paterson 4

.20	1.10
.50	8.00
.35	2.20
	11.30

UANTITY	DESCRIPTIO
5	Dozen ham
3	Dozen dri
12	Pounds so
14	Spools wi

1. Always leave 2 or 3 blank spaces between a guide word (like "To") and the item that is to be typed after it.

2. If there is a series of guides, line up the following items at one point, 2 or 3 spaces after the longest guide.

3. Line up columns of numbers at the right, leaving 1 or 2 blank spaces before the following vertical line.

4. Line up columns of words at the left, leaving 1 or 2 blank spaces after the preceding vertical line.

SHIP VIA   Truck

T PRICE	TOTAL
3.00	18.00
7.25	14.50

To Mr. Walter

Name.. Lt. John

Name.. Lt. John

DESCRIPTION	
	2 ➡
No. 531, Electric	
No. 538, Manual	
No. 337, Electric	

5. When 2 or more items are to line up, set and use a tab stop. If you can, use the same stops in both heading and body.

6. The bottom edge of the typing should line up horizontally with the bottom edge of the printed guide.

7. When typing on any ruled or dotted line, adjust the paper so that the line is in the same position that underscores would be.

8. If a line separates the heading from the body, leave 1 blank linespace between the line and the first line of typewriting.

abcdefghijklmnopqrstu

Address 5647 West Linc

DESCRI
Desks, gray me
Desk chairs, g

9. Note how close the writing line (bottom of typed characters) on your machine comes to the top of the aligning scale. Then—

10. To align typing with printing, adjust the paper so that the bottom edge of the printing comes as close to the aligning scale as your line of writing comes to it.

11. To adjust paper slightly (for exact positioning at the aligning scale), use the variable spacer in the left cylinder knob.

12. Most form work is single spaced, but you can double space if there is room and if you wish to do so.

JOB 1

To gain skill in typing on ruled lines and beside guide words, fill in the practice exercises on Workbook pages 73-74; or, if you do not have the workbook, clip 10 coupons from magazine or newspaper advertisements and fill them in. Use your own name and address. By the time you complete this job, you should be able to position data on lines and after guides quite competently.

WARMUP: Rhythmic-Reach Review *(Each line 3 times)* ◁ **60** ▷

```
aaa ;;; aqa ;p; sss sws lll lol ddd ded kkk kik fff frf jjj
juj ftf jyj fgf jhj fbf jnj fvf jmj dcd k,k sxs l.l aza ;/;
and bit cob due eye fox got hay it, jam key lap men nap owl
pay que row she tot urn vox wit six yap zig boy and the man
```

SPEED DRILL: Word Families *(Each line 3 times)*

```
al along alike alien alert aloft also alto ales alms ale al
ye yellow yeast yearn yelps years yells year yen yes yet ye
ne nerve never news need neck near neat next net new neb ne
```

SPEED SENTENCES *(Each line 3 times)*

12-Sec.
Writings

```
They kept up the usual quantity of fish for the lake visit.
The fight may pay us a profit, and he may risk the auditor.
When did the widow visit with girls of the social sorority?
```

12-Sec. 5| 10| 15| 20| 25| 30| 35| 40| 45| 50| 55| 60|

SPEED PARAGRAPH *(3 copies / si 1.06)*

½- and 1-Min.
Writings

1 | 2 | 3 | 4 | 5 | 6 | 7 | 8 | 9 | 10 | 11 | 12

```
None of us like to think much about the future while we are    12
still training for it, but we ought to know that what we do    24
right now and the habits we make right now may mean much if    36
and when we land the job or post we want.  If we keep right    48
on the ball now, we will be right on it when we have to be.    60
```

SPEED PREVIEW *(Each line 3 times)* ◁ **60** ▷

```
mistakes yourself machine pushing easier trying rusty speed
coast while tense have been from your half long and not too
```

DS

SUSTAINED-SPEED PARAGRAPHS *(3 copies / si 1.16)*

*2-Min.
Writings

1 | 2 | 3 | 4 | 5 | 6 | 7 | 8 | 9 | 10 | 11 | 12

```
0        When you have been away from your machine for a while,    11
6   when you are rusty and not too sure of yourself, it is good    23
12  to type some easy copy like this over and over.  Do not try    35
18  to build up a high speed; just coast through the copy.  Try    47
24  to hold a smooth pace that does not make you feel pushed or    59
30  tense.  Let the ease of the copy bring back your old speed.    71

36       Each time you retype this copy, it will become easier;    82
41  and your speed will begin to climb without your half trying    94
47  to make it do so.  It will, that is, so long as you keep up   106
53  your smooth pace.  If you make a lot of mistakes or jam the   118
59  keys, you are pushing too hard for speed.  Do not push; let   130
65  the ease and smooth typing of the copy sharpen your skills.   142
```

Plus ▶ 1 | 2 | 3 | 4 | 5 | 6

*For calculating speed, see page 226.

JOB 2

Blocked memo
In elite
Half sheet
2 tabs
Words: 125

➥ Set tab 10 spaces from margin

From: Victor R. Kruger   December 10, 19--   **DS**

To: Albert F. Cooke

Subject: Style of a Memo Typed on Plain Paper ₃ ➥

When you type a memo on plain paper, plan for top and side margins of about an   **SS**
inch. Type a heading like the one shown above, using a tab stop that is set
10 spaces from the left margin. Leave two blank lines between the heading and
the message. To position the date, backspace from the right margin.

End the memo by typing the writer's name or his initials a double space below
the body, starting even with the date. Type the usual notations at the left
margin, as shown below. ₂ ➥

                                        V. R. K. ₂ ➥

VRK:URS
Enclosure

JOB 3

Semiblocked memo
In pica
Half sheet
2 tabs
Words: 119

➥ Set tab 10 spaces from margin

From: Victor R. Kruger   December 10, 19--   **DS**

To: The Office Staff

Subject: Extra Typing Job ₃ ➥

        As many of you know, I am now working on a revision of   **SS**
a book that I wrote about five years ago. Much of the revision
is now ready to be typed. Is there anyone on our staff who has
a typewriter at home and who wishes to earn some extra money?

        There will be about 500 pages. I shall provide paper,
carbons, and ribbons. I shall pay 20 cents a page, plus 5 cents
for each of two carbon copies.

        If anyone would like this work, get in touch with me
within the next week or so. ₂ ➥

                                        V. R. KRUGER ₂ ➥

VRK:URS

PART 7: ADVANCED TYPING

This point in a typing course ordinarily marks the start of Advanced Typing—"office-style typing," it may be called.

As you reach this point, you already know how to operate the machine; how to sustain a reasonable rate of typing speed with a reliable degree of accuracy; and how to arrange letters, tables, manuscripts, and business-form materials in the standard designs. Now, new objectives lie ahead of you:

VOCATIONAL SKILL . . .

First and foremost, because all else will depend on this, strive for a truly vocational level of basic operating skill. No college-course graduate should be content with less than 75 words a minute for five minutes, 65 for ten, as a bare minimum.

To help you build such skill and more, if you do not already have it, this book continues the special skill drives that are featured in the preceding Parts. Each Part (25 lessons) begins with 6 lessons in which you do nothing but work for higher skill. Each of the three skill drives ahead (Lessons 151-156, 176-181, and 201-206) provides two lessons of special material for boosting speed, two for improving control, and two for strengthening control of figures. Worth noting:

1. You can profitably repeat each skill-drive lesson many, many times.

2. The directions tell you the *minimum* amount of practice you must undertake to benefit from your practice. Make a point of investing extra practice whenever you can.

3. When you find that you stumble over some particular word or group of words in a drill line or sentence, pause then and there to practice that passage repeatedly — until you can type it fluently — before going on. When taking timed writings (and *do* race the clock frequently), pause between writings to practice every passage that is troublesome. Every repetition should be preceded by some kind of improvement practice that entitles you to expect a better performance when you repeat it.

PROBLEM SOLVING . . .

To this point, most of the copy that you have set up as a letter, table, manuscript, or form was presented to you in what an office typist would call "easy to copy" form.

Somewhere in your training you must learn how many carbons to make, how to analyze data, how to paragraph and capitalize "dictated" material, and so on. It is in this part of the course that you master these things.

To help you in this regard, the remaining lessons (other than the skill drives) are presented in office-style narrative. You receive your material in the form that an office typist would receive it; you get the same directions; you get as little help. The first problems are easy; later ones, more challenging.

For fullest benefit, do not ask for help. Use the index of this book as much as you may wish — but learn to solve your own problems.

SUSTAINED POWER . . .

In addition to higher skill and problem-solving ability, one more ingredient is needed: the power to keep going and going.

To assist you develop this ability, the production lessons (all lessons except the skill drives and tests) are hereafter set up so as to permit you to move quickly from one job to the next. Most jobs are related — in vocabulary, in thought, or form — so that there is logical work flow, as in an office.

The production lessons are in pairs, with each pair of lessons presenting about as much production work as an office typist would accomplish in an hour. Sustained production is hard on skill; do not force yourself to work for a steady hour until you have — with the help of the skill lessons — reached your minimum skill goal. But once you have reached that skill goal, then try to type for a solid hour now and then, just to see how much you *can* produce in an hour and to build your sustained working power.

Now, turn the page and *drive for skill.*

JOB 4

In pica
Workbook
3 tabs

Blocked memo
Words: 135

Interoffice Memorandum

◁ Margins by ▷
alignment

FROM: Victor R. Kruger

TO: Albert F. Cooke

DATE: December 11, 19--

↰ *Tab stop, 2 or 3 spaces after "Date"*

SUBJECT: Style of a Memo Typed on a Memo Form ₃ ➭

↰ *Tab stop, 2 or 3 spaces after "Subject"*

When a memo is typed on a memo form, let the printing at the top serve you as a guide.

1. Set the left margin stop even with the printing and make the right margin the same width as the left.

2. Type the heading lines beside the printed guide words. Use the variable spacer in the left knob if you must adjust the paper so that the typing and printing will be even.

As in the case of a memo on plain paper, end the memo by typing the writer's name or initials a double space below the body, even with the start of the date; and type the usual margin notations. ₂ ➭

V. R. K. ₂ ➭

VRK:URS

JOB 5

In elite
Workbook
2 tabs

Semiblocked memo
Words: 107

INTEROFFICE MEMO

◁ Margins by ▷
alignment

From: Training Director

To: New Employees

Date: December 11, 19--

↰ *Tab stop, 2 or 3 spaces after "Date"*

Subject: Signatures on Memos
₃ ➭
↰ *Tab stop, 2 or 3 spaces after "Subject"*

1. If the signer's name is in the heading, type either his name or his initials below the message.

2. If only the signer's title is used in the heading, type his name below the message, as in this memo.

3. If initials are used as a signature, they do not have to be in the reference initials; if they are left out, the typist's initials should appear, as in this memo. If a signer types his own message, no reference initials are needed. ₂ ➭

J. Kenneth Nash ₂ ➭

URS

Type this contract on legal-ruled paper. Make the corrections indicated. (In this problem, an old contract has been used as a model for drafting a contract for a new employee. Check your dates carefully. Use today's date for the date of this new contract, and be sure that the period covered by the contract begins with the first of next month and ends one year later.) For 11-inch paper, use a 1-inch top margin; for 13-inch paper, use a 2-inch top margin. Do not number the page. Do not type an indorsement.

C O N T R A C T

Use today's date

THIS CONTRACT made and concluded this ~~eleventh day of June, 1956,~~ by and between the Juniper Sales Specialty Company, of 3399 Madison Street, New Orleans, Louisiana, party of the first part, and ~~Charles L. Ferguson, 2828 Ruskin Street, Dallas, Texas,~~ party of the second part. *P. Clarke, 402 Cochran Drive, Pittsburgh, Pennsylvania;*

Article 1. Services. The said party of the second part covenants and agrees to and with the party of the first part, to furnish his services *exclusively* to the said party of the first part as ~~special demonstrator and representative~~ for the period *advertising manager* of one year, or twelve (12) calendar months, beginning ~~July 1,~~ *(start this beginning next month)* ~~1956,~~ and expiring ~~June 30, 1957;~~ and the said party of the sec-*(date this a year later)* ond part covenants and agrees to perform faithfully all duties incident to such employment.

Article 2. Wages. And the said party of the first part covenants and agrees to pay the said party of the second part, for the same, the sum of ~~seven~~ thousand, ~~two hundred~~ dol-*twelve* lars (~~$7,200.00~~), as follows: The sum of ~~eight hundred~~ dollars *1,000.00* *one thousand* ($800.00) on ~~July 31, 1956,~~ and an equal sum on the last day of *(use end of next month)* each succeeding calendar month until the period of one year shall have expired. *12,000.00*

IN WITNESS WHEREOF, the parties to this Contract have hereunto set their hands the day and year first above written.

~~Charles L. Ferguson~~
P. Clarke

Witness to Signature

Bryant Gaynor, Vice-President

Witness to Signature

WARMUP *(Each line 2 times)*

◁**60**▷

```
Six or seven flashing, new jet planes quickly zoomed by him.
39 28 47 56 10 we 23 top 590 yet 635 owe 923 rut 475 ire 843
If you sell them more goods, we shall send them a full bill.
```

12-Sec. 5| 10| 15| 20| 25| 30| 35| 40| 45| 50| 55| 60|

CONTROL PREVIEW *(Each line 2 times)*

```
aa standard bb bills cc carbons dd desk ee realize ff first
gg glance hh helpful ii firm jj judge kk like ll complex mm
minute nn need oo tool pp paper qq equipment rr required ss
save tt telegram vv every ww what xx extra yy many zz sizes
```

ALPHABET-REVIEW PARAGRAPH *(2 copies / si 1.19)*

◁**50**▷
DS

5-Min.
Writings

1 | 2 | 3 | 4 | 5 | 6 | 7 | 8 | 9 | 10 |

0 | 38	Some of the printed forms that save time for	9
2 | 39	you in your job might seem to be complex at first	19
4 | 41	glance, but just a minute of study is required to	29
6 | 43	see how to use them. You will soon see that they	39
8 | 45	do save time as soon as you realize that what you	49
10 | 47	type on a form is like a short letter. A bill or	59
12 | 49	a telegram or a memo is just a short letter--with	69
14 | 51	the greeting and closing left out. If you had to	79
16 | 53	type a whole letter for all bills your firm sends	89
18 | 55	out, you would not have time to do all your work.	99
20 | 57	A tool that will save you time, that is just	108
22 | 59	as helpful as a form, and that is standard equip-	118
24 | 61	ment in the desks of all typists is carbon paper.	128
26 | 63	If you had never heard of carbon paper and always	138
28 | 65	had to type all the copies you need of most busi-	148
30 | 67	ness papers, you would judge carbon paper a great	158
32 | 69	thing as soon as you did hear of it. Carbons may	168
34 | 71	be bought in all sizes, from short to extra long,	178
36 | 73	and in all colors, and in many different weights.	188

Plus ▶

1 | | 2

PRODUCTION PRACTICE *(Jobs 6-9)*

Study about carbon copies, top of the next page; unless your instructor directs otherwise, make a carbon copy with each of the next 4 jobs. Jobs 6 and 7 are telegrams, in two different styles. Jobs 8 and 9 are invoices (bills), both to be set up alike and addressed to the same person, Mr. Kruger. Type Jobs 6-9 on workbook forms or on half sheets of paper ruled to resemble the forms illustrated.

7-Min.
Writing

1 | 2 | 3 | 4 | 5 | 6 | 7 | 8 | 9 | 10 | 11 | 12 | 13 | 14

0   Dear Mr. Clarke: We are pleased to learn that you have accepted   13

2   our offer and that you will be joining our staff on the first of next   27

4   month. We know that you have a big contribution to make to our sales   41

6   effort, and all of us here in the home office will be pleased to meet   55

8   you again and to welcome you to a desk in our Advertising Department.   69

10   We have made a few plans for your first weeks with us. You will   82

12   start, of course, by becoming familiar with the company organization,   96

14   getting to know the persons with whom you will work, and learning all   110

16   you can about our products and our services. The first two days, you   124

18   will report to Personnel for the regular orientation program in which   138

20   you will learn a great deal not only about the company but also about   152

22   all our employee policies--vacations, paydays, insurances, and so on.   166

24   Then, after you have been at your own desk long enough to become   179

26   familiar with the duties that will be yours, you will spend two weeks   193

28   making calls with one of our local salesmen. You will meet customers   207

30   and hear the questions they raise. You will see what features of our   221

32   products interest them and why. You will have a chance to visit some   235

34   workrooms of our present customers and to see how these customers use   249

36   our products; you will see what our merchandising problems are. And,   263

38   you will learn much about the kinds of service we give our customers.   278

40   Our plans indicate that you will be busy with training for quite   291

41   some time before you come to grips with your main duties. We believe   305

43   that the training can be completed, however, several weeks before the   319

45   time when our next promotion campaign, which will be your first major   333

47   assignment, must get rolling. Thus, you will have opportunity to get   347

49   acquainted with all aspects of the job before you start the campaign.   361

51   I am enclosing a contract for your position, Mr. Clarke. Please   374

53   note that it covers all the elements that we talked about. We should   388

55   like to have it back soon. If you would like help in your search for   402

57   your new home, all of us here would be pleased to help. Let me state   416

59   once again, Mr. Clarke, that we are pleased to have you join us. All   430

61   of us are looking forward to working with you. Very cordially yours,   444

Plus ▶   1   2

CARBON COPIES

. . . are made with carbon paper, of course . . .

Carbon paper has a dull side and a glossy side that does the work.

Glossy side is put against the paper on which the copy is to be made.

You always have one more sheet of typing paper than of carbon.

Straighten sides and top of pack carefully before inserting it.

SPECIAL NOTES

1. If pack is thick, hard to start into the machine, depress the paper release long enough to permit the paper to slide easily around the roller.

2. On letters, type "cc" and names under the reference initials (or under the enclosure notation if there is one), to indicate who is to get copies.

3. Type with very firm and even touch.

Use both hands to get pack behind roller for the insertion.

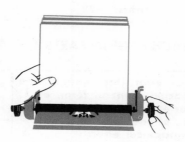

Hold pack with left hand, turn roller smoothly with right hand.

JOB 6

Telegram
Workbook form
Words: 53

◁5 in.▷
SS

Check the class of service desired; otherwise this message will be sent as a full rate telegram

DOMESTIC SERVICE		
FULL RATE TELEGRAM	X	
DAY LETTER		
NIGHT LETTER		

Type "X" to show class of service.

Name of company paying for this telegram, if on charge account.

Check the class of service desired; otherwise the message will be sent at the full rate

INTERNATIONAL SERVICE	
FULL RATE	
LETTER TELEGRAM	
SHIP RADIOGRAM	

NO. WDS.-CL. OF SVC.	PD. OR COLL.	CASH NO.	CHARGE TO THE ACCOUNT OF	TIME FILED

Martin Miller & Sons ₃ ➡

Tab stop, 2 spaces from the bar ➡

Atlanta, Georgia, December 14, 19-- ₂ ➡

Mr. Frederick Williams
1039 Statler Building
Boston 3, Massachusetts ₂ ➡

Before board meets next Monday, I must know whether you can
undertake our building plans. ₂ ➡

Roland I. Miller
Martin Miller & Sons ₂ ➡

RIM:URS

Telegram style is flexible: as above or in all-capitals . . . 5- or 6-inch line . . . single or double spacing.

You will need 3 sheets of plain paper or Workbook pages 219-224. Type Part A on one sheet (use both sides), Part B on a second sheet (use both sides), and Parts C and D on opposite sides of the third sheet. Grading scales:

GRADING SCALE FOR PART A

Step 1: Compute words a minute.	Step 2: Deduct for errors—		Step 3: Grade the remaining words a minute this way:	
	1 error: —1	6 errors: — 9	50 or higher: A	
	2 errors: —2	7 errors: —12	45 to 49 wam: B	
	3 errors: —3	8 errors: —15	40 to 44 wam: C	
	4 errors: —5	9 errors: —18	35 to 39 wam: D	
	5 errors: —7	10 errors: —22		

GRADING SCALE FOR EACH PAGE IN PARTS B, C, AND D

TAKE OFF:	—3 for each major error (top margin, line length, linespacing, general form, etc.). —2 for each minor error (blocking, aligning, indenting, etc., of each part of a job). —1 for each typographical error.	TOTAL TAKEN OFF	10-9	8-5	4-3	2-0
		GRADE	D	C	B	A

PART A: STRAIGHT-COPY TEST (*si 1.35*)

◁**70**▷
DS

Take a 10-minute test on the copy on the next page; or, type it once and grade your work as though you had typed it at 54 words a minute.

PART B: LETTER TEST (*469 total words / si 1.37*)

Type the material on the next page as a 2-page, blocked-form business letter from Bryant Gaynor, Advertising Director, to Charles P. Clarke, 402 Cochran Road, Pittsburgh 28, Pennsylvania.

PART C: TABULATION TEST (*99 total words*)

Type the following financial statement sideways on a full sheet of paper (as in Job 8, page 203), with 10 spaces after Column 1, and 2 spaces between the others.

CORNWALL MANUFACTURING COMPANY
Analysis of Comparative Liabilities and Reserves

ITEMS	1945	1950	1955
Accrued taxes	$ 748,205	$ 931,574	$1,806,293
Mortgage payable	375,150	430,800	715,210
Group insurance payable	1,181	1,790	2,215
Salaries payable	1,975	2,310	5,135
Reserves for contingencies	845,708	1,058,639	1,290,677
TOTALS	$1,972,119	$2,425,113	$3,819,530

JOB 7

Telegram
Shown in elite
Workbook form
1 tab stop
Words: 48

MARTIN MILLER & SONS ₃ ➡

ATLANTA, GEORGIA, DECEMBER 14, 19-- ₂ ➡

DR. JAMES KENDALL
LAKE STONE COLLEGE
SAVANNAH, GEORGIA ₂ ➡

CAN YOU ARRIVE ATLANTA THURSDAY IN TIME TO ADDRESS KIWANIS
LUNCHEON AT 12:30? ₂ ➡

    ROLAND I. MILLER
    MARTIN MILLER & SONS ₂ ➡

RIM:URS

JOB 8

Invoice
Shown in pica
Workbook form
3 tab stops
Words: 76

Note: Review
page 91 before
starting
Jobs 8 and 9.

MEREDITH TYPING SERVICE

305 ROSSLYN STREET • LOS ANGELES 41, CALIFORNIA

TO: Mr. Victor R. Kruger
   1401 West Eighth Avenue
   Los Angeles 17, California

DATE: December 14, 19--   INVOICE

QUANTITY	DESCRIPTIONS	UNIT PRICE	AMOUNT
	₂ ➡ Chapter II--		
14	Pages of straight copy	.20	2.80
6	Pages including tables	.50	3.00
40	Pages of carbon copies	.05	2.00
	Chapter III--		
24	Pages of Straight copy	.20	4.80
2	Pages including tables	.50	1.00
52	Pages of carbon copies	.05	2.60 ₂ ➡
			16.20

⬅ ⬅ 2 or 3 spaces   2 or 3 spaces ➡ ➡

JOB 9

Invoice
Shown in elite
Workbook form
3 tab stops
Words: 59

Note: Address
this invoice to
Mr. Kruger, as
in Job 8.

DATE: December 15, 19--   INVOICE

QUANTITY	DESCRIPTIONS	UNIT PRICE	AMOUNT
	₂ ➡ Chapter IV--		
30	Pages of straight copy	.20	6.00
60	Pages of carbon copies	.05	3.00
	Chapter V--		
18	Pages of straight copy	.20	3.60
12	Pages including tables	.50	6.00
60	Pages of carbon copies	.05	3.00
			21.60

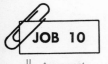

Rough draft
2 pages
Ruled paper
Center tab
Para. tab

2-inch top margin
Center between rules

A G R E E M E N T →

THIS AGREEMENT made the twelfth day of June, 1957, by and between ~~the~~ The Dwyer Construction Company, a corporation under the laws of the state of California, located at 1938 Mills Road, Oakland, California, hereinafter called The Contractor, and the Black-Gray Company, 1396 Sutter Street, San Francisco, California, hereinafter called The Owner.

WITNESSETH that the contractor and Owner, in consideration of the stipulations hereinafter named and made a part hereof, agree as follows:

Article 1. Scope of Work. The Contractor agrees to furnish all the materials and to perform all the works indicated on the drawings and ~~described~~ described in the specifications, entitled, "Specifications, with Accompanying Drawings, describing materials to be used and labors to be performed in constructing an extention to the Garage of the Black-Gray Company at 1932-1934 Sutter Street, San Francisco, California," prepared by Mortimer L. Bell, 209 Ninth St., Sacramento, California, ~~and referred to and~~ acting as Architect in this Agreement, *and referred to as such* the General Conditions of the Contract, the Specifications, and the Drawings.

Article 2. Time for Completion. Work *which is* to be performed under this contract shall be commenced as soon as possible after the singing of this

. . . . After 2 lines
of Article 2,
type leaders
to indicate   omission of
several pages.
Start new page
with Article 8.   . . . .

10   Article 8. The Contract Documents. The General Conditions of the Contract, the Specifications and Drawings, together with this Agreement, constitute the Contract, and are considered as much a part of the Contract as if herein repeated.

← 2 blank spaces here

IN WITNESS WHEREOF the parties hereto have executed this Agreement, the day and Year first above written. *← 2 blank spaces here*

FOR THE BLACK-GRAY COMPANY   FOR THE DWYER CONSTRUCTION COMPANY 3 →

_____   _____
Executive Vice-President   Center titles   President 3 →
                            under lines.

_____   _____
Witness for the Owner   Witness for the Contractor
                                             ← 2 blank spaces here

Page 8 of 8

Do not forget
to type an
indorsement
(page 207).

WARMUP *(Each line 2 times)* ◁**60**▷

We acquired jerky habits from having typed exercises lazily.
39 28 47 56 10 we 23 rot 495 pew 032 toy 596 rip 480 too 599
We shall send them the full bill when he has sold all of it.

12-Sec. 5| 10| 15| 20| 25| 30| 35| 40| 45| 50| 55| 60|

CONTROL PREVIEW *(Each line 2 times)*

AA chapter BB about CC chance DD found EE extremely FF final
GG grateful HH this II list JJ job KK know LL all MM compete
NN interesting OO book PP preparing QQ quoted RR work SS has
TT that UU sure VV invoices WW would XX next YY many ZZ zest

PRODUCTION PRACTICE *(Jobs 10-13)*

Review the semiblocked letter form (page 86) before typing Job 10 on a workbook letterhead. Review the invoice form (page 96) before typing Job 11 on a workbook form. Review the telegram form (page 95) before typing Job 12 on a workbook form. Review the blocked memo form (page 92) before typing Job 13 on a half sheet of plain paper.

JOB 10

Semiblocked letter.
  Shown in elite
  Letterhead
  Date, right
  Center tab
  Paragraph tab
Words: 172
  Body: 135

1 | 2 | 3 | 4 | 5 | 6 | 7 | 8 | 9 | 10 | 11 | 12   ◁**5 in.**▷

December 16, 19--   **SS**
     14/6
     ▽

Mr. Victor R. Kruger
1401 West Eighth Street
Los Angeles 17, California

Dear Mr. Kruger:

    With this letter we are sending you the last part of the   11
book, including the final two chapters and the long list of   23
readings. We are also enclosing an invoice for this work.   35

    We should like you to know that preparing this material   47
has been more to us than just another typing job. Our whole   59
group has found your writing to be extremely interesting; we   71
are sure that the public will read your new book with as much   83
zest as we have.   87

    We are grateful to you for the many kind comments that   98
you made about our work for you. Would you mind if we quoted   110
your last note when next we compete for a typing job? We do   123
hope we shall have a chance to work for and with you again.   135

       Very sincerely,

       MEREDITH TYPING SERVICE

Initials?
Enclosures?

       Jean I. Meredith

JOB 9

Blocked letter
In elite
Table tabs
Letterhead
2 carbons
Words: 220
Body: 200

THE FOSTER INSURANCE COMPANY

123 Lexington Avenue

New York 22, New York

◁ **6 in.** ▷
SS
14/6
▽

June 5, 19--

TO OUR STOCKHOLDERS:

There are shown below the financial results of our operation for the five months ended May 31, with the corresponding figures for the same period last year: ₃ ➡

	This Year January 1 to May 31	Last Year January 1 to May 31
Gross Revenue	$34,559,388	$32,984,787
Operating Expenses	29,653,710	27,402,135
Net Income before Federal Income Taxes	$ 4,905,678	$ 5,582,652
Estimated Federal Income Taxes	2,616,667	3,005,247
Net Income	$ 2,289,011	$ 2,577,405
Earnings per Share (880,000 Shares)	2.60	2.93 ₃ ➡

Position the columns by pivot method (page 197).

Note irregular spacing in first column, to keep spacing consistent in money columns.

Although the earnings figure is lower for the first five months than it was last year, the operating expenses include several appropriations for activities that will continue throughout the year. Accordingly, there is reason to expect that earnings for the year will be equal, or nearly equal, to the record earnings that we enjoyed last year.

Very truly yours,

Some executives prefer their names to be typed in the reference position, like this:

Chairman of the Board

Vincent Young/URS

Any letter is considered a long one when it includes a displayed table or listing.

Invoice to Mr. Victor R. Kruger, 1401 West Eighth Street, Los Angeles 17, California, dated December 16, this year.

SS

Invoice
Unarranged
Check the total
Workbook form
3 tab stops
Words: 76

QUANTITY	DESCRIPTION	PRICE	AMOUNT
	Chapter XIX--		
22	Pages of straight copy	.20	4.40
4	Pages including footnotes	.25	1.00
6	Pages including tables	.50	3.00
64	Pages of carbon copies	.05	3.20
	Chapter XX--		
20	Pages of straight copy	.20	4.00
4	Pages including footnotes	.25	1.00
48	Pages of carbon copies	.05	2.40
			19.00

JOB 12

Day letter
(telegram)
Shown in elite
Workbook form
1 tab stop
Words: 62

◁ 5 in. ▷
SS

Martin Miller & Sons

Atlanta, Georgia, December 17, 19--

Dr. James Kendall
Lake Stone College
Savannah, Georgia

Delighted you can make Kiwanis meeting. Please discuss your incentive plan for sales personnel. Fee $50 for 45 minutes. Will meet your flight.

Roland I. Miller
Martin Miller & Sons

Initials?

JOB 13

Blocked-form
memorandum
Unarranged
Half sheet
2 tab stops
Words: 126
Body: 103

Memo from Victor R. Kruger to Jean I. Meredith on the subject of Payment of My Account, dated December 17, this year.

◁ 60 ▷
SS
7
▽

| 1 | 2 | 3 | 4 | 5 | 6 | 7 | 8 | 9 | 10 | 11 | 12 |

I am enclosing a check for $42.80 to settle my account with   12
you and your Meredith Typing Service for the typing of my   24
book manuscript. You did a fine job for me.   33

I should have no objection to your quoting my many compli-   44
ments on this job. Indeed, I should be very happy to have   56
you use my name as a reference for any kind of typing work.   68

I want you to know, Jean, that I am telling the Personnel   80
Department about the work that you are doing. I know that   92
your superiors would want to know about your initiative.   103

V. R. K.

URS
Enclosure?

JOB 8

Page 2, minutes
of a meeting
Rough draft
Side bound
Center tab
2 carbons
Words: 248

Mrs. Pavlue reported that the material for the mailing to *Wallace* dealers was now on press and than an investment of $970 would be lost if the mailing were not made. Mr. Perkins pointed out that cancelling space in *Premium* would bring our year's space in that magazine under the minimum for the special reates that we have been enjoying. Miss Clarke reported that nearly all mechanicals, art work, and engravings have allready been made for our present advertising schedule and would have to be done over, at an estimated cost of $1500, if the space dimensions were reduced in our advertisements in other magazines. The committee decided to eliminate spcae in the next three issues of *Premium*, with Mr. Perkins demurring.

Wallace

Mr. Starke proposed a study among officers of large companies, to determine how many use our products regularly. He distributed copies of a tentative plan for the survey, which would cost about $750 to conduct. The committee decided that, in view of the budget curtailment, the proposal should be tabled for another month or two.

of the companies

Respectfully submitted,

Marguerite Powell, Secretary

Do not type
an indorsement
on minutes.

Lessons 148-149 : Skill Drills

WARMUP *(Each line 3 times)*   ◁ 70 ▷

a;qpa;z/a;slwoslx.sldkeidkc,dkfjrufjvmfjghtyghbnghfjrufjvmfjdkeidkc,d
visible girls flair throb vials name foam fowl down cod fix owl it is
The one hope that you still have is that they will place a big order.
12-Sec.5| 10| 15| 20| 25| 30| 35| 40| 45| 50| 55| 60| 65| 70|

PUNCTUATION PREVIEW *(Each line 3 times)*

friends. college. course. first. skill. poll. them. Row. too.
yourself, Oakland, Income, Owner, yours, year, jazz, must, then, had,
STOCKHOLDERS: year: too: great? (Shares) night; course; type; is;

PRODUCTION
PRACTICE
(Jobs 9-10)

Notes: The table in Job 9 takes so much space that the letter must be treated as a long one. An agreement is often several pages long; in Job 10, however, you type only the first and last pages of an agreement, since they illustrate all the arrangement problems in it.

UNIT 12
MANUSCRIPTS

In this unit, you will learn (1) how to arrange manuscripts, bound and unbound, with and without footnotes; and (2) how to interpret rough-draft markings. Before starting the jobs, read pages 99-106 and answer the questions on   pages 83-84 of your workbook.

WARMUP *(Each line 2 times)*   ◁**60**▷

```
Liza quit her job, packed six bags, and then moved far away.
39 28 47 56 10 we 23 tip 580 you 697 rye 463 were 2343 2343
There were three of us there, and all three of us were well.
12-Sec.  5|    10|    15|    20|    25|    30|    35|    40|    45|    50|    55|    60|
```

CONTROL PREVIEW *(Each line 2 times)*

```
AA papers BB binding CC inch DD detail EE inserted FF differ
GG page HH the II like JJ just KK kind LL left MM manuscript
NN only OO notebook PP happy QQ equal RR report SS spaces TT
typist UU unbound VV very WW two XX extra YY style ZZ dozens
```

ALPHABET-REVIEW PARAGRAPH *(si 1.30)*   ◁**60**▷ **DS**

5-Min. Writings*

In happy contrast to letters[1] and forms, of which there[2] are dozens of styles[3] and **16** **

kinds, there are just[4] two forms in which a formal[5] paper like a manuscript[6] or report **33**

can be set[7] up. The two forms are very[8] much alike. In only one[9] detail do they differ:[10] **50**

the side margin. On most[11] papers, the side margins[12] are kept even, as in other[13] kinds **67**

of typing. But[14] if the pages are to be[15] bound or to be inserted in[16] some kind of **83**

binder or[17] notebook, a half inch of[18] extra space must be left[19] in the margin on the **99**

binding[20] side. When a report[21] is set up with extra space[22] in the left margin, it[23] is **116**

said to be typed in bound[24] form; when it is typed[25] with equal side margins,[26] it is **132**

said to be in[27] unbound form. The majority[28] of report work in business[29] is, as you **148**

might expect,[30] in unbound form, since[31] most business reports are[32] duplicated. The **163**

fact[33] that report papers may be[34] stapled in a corner does[35] not usually mean you **179**

consider[36] these to be in bound[37] form, although they could[38] be.   (START OVER) **191**

PRODUCTION PRACTICE *(Jobs 1-2)*

Study pages 100 and 101 very closely; then type them as a 2-page, unbound manuscript, as shown. Make 1 carbon copy of each page. The model manuscript is shown in pica; if your machine is elite, you will get about 10 more strokes on each line of typing.

*Your speed on a 5-minute timing is the tiny number nearest where you stop.

**To determine your speed on timings for other than 5 minutes, divide the minutes into the total words typed, which is the number at the end of the last line (above) that you finish, plus 1 word for each 5 spaces you type beyond the end of that line.

JOB 7

Page 1, minutes
of a meeting
Rough draft
Side bound
Center tab
2 carbons
Words: 239

2-inch top margin

Of the Advertising Committee

MINUTES OF THE MONTHLY MEETING

May 18, 19-- ₃

1½-inch margin

1-inch margin

ATTENDANCE:

The regular monthly meeting of the Advertising Committee was held in the office of Mr. Larimore, Advertising Director, who presided at the meeting. The following were present:

put names in 2 columns

Mr. J. Carty	Mr. Fisher	Miss Powell
Miss Clarke	Mr. Larimore	Mr. Stark
Miss Clooney	Mrs. Pavlu	Mr. Wallace
	Mr. Perkins	

The meeting began at two o'clock and adjourned at 4:00.

OLD BUSINESS:

The secretary

~~Miss Powell~~ read the minutes of the last meeting. They were approved as read.

Mr. Stark reported that the show-case cards *that* ~~which~~ had been prepared for dealer's use had proved notably successful. His follow-up survey among 250 dealers indicated:

Dealers wanting additional cards 230 (92%)
Dealers using the cards 180 (72%)
Dealers reporting sales increases .... 215 (86%) ₃

NEW BUSINESS:

Mr. Larimore reported that the Department has been directed to curtail its advertising expenditures by $2,500.00 for the coming quarter. Discussion hinged on these possibilities:

1. Eliminate *ion of the* the June Mailing to dealers.
2. Elimination of the space in <u>Premium</u> magazine.
3. Reduction of space in all magazine ads.

three

(CONTINUED ON NEXT PAGE.)

JOB 1

Page 1, unbound
manuscript
  Shown in pica
  Plain paper
  Center tab
  Paragraph tab
Words: 252

"Main heading" ❯   MANUSCRIPT TYPING ₂ ➠

By Howard T. Richards ₃ ➠

The rules for typing a formal report, such as an article
or term paper, are illustrated on this and the next page. ₃ ➠

THE SPACING TO USE   ❮ A "Subheading"

Use double spacing for the main body of the report. Use
single spacing for footnotes and for quotations that will take
three or more lines. Put one extra blank line after the main
heading or the group of lines that make up the main heading.
Put one extra blank line before each subheading that may be
displayed on a line by itself, blocked at the left margin. ₃ ➠

THE MARGINS TO USE

The top margin should be 2 inches deep on the first page
and 1 inch deep on the other pages. So, typing will begin on
line 13 of the first page and on line 7 of the other pages.

A "paragraph heading" ❯ The bottom margin should be at least 1 inch deep and may
be as deep as 1½ inches. Before inserting the paper, draw a
light pencil mark about 2 inches from the bottom of the paper
as a warning signal. It is later erased, of course.

The side margins should be about 1 or 1¼ inches wide. A
typist sets stops for a line of 6 inches, which is 60 spaces
on a pica machine and about 70 on an elite. Reports are not
usually bound; a clip or staple holds the pages together.

JOBS 5-6

Resolution
In pica
Center tab
Para. tab
2 carbons
Words: 270

Two copies:
1. Double spaced
2. Single spaced

JOHN HERBERT KAUFMANN ₃ →

◁ 6 in. ▷
Center
▽

WHEREAS John Herbert Kaufmann is retiring from his positions as Secretary-Treasurer of this firm and as a Member of the Board of Directors of this firm, having served it and his associates for more than thirty-five years; and

WHEREAS he devoted all his skill and knowledge to the development and expansion of this company, its products, its services, its facilities, and its staff, to the end that today this company is the largest and the most successful in its field of business enterprise; and

WHEREAS he has given generously of himself in the encouragement, inspiration, and assistance of all those who were fortunate enough to work with him personally, to the end that virtually all the executives of this company have, in effect, been schooled by this wise and gentle teacher; and

WHEREAS he has proved himself a generous leader, a warm and thoughtful associate, and a man endowed as much with openness of heart and hand as with wisdom, so that his name is a legend in this industry and that he is loved for what he is more than for what he has done: Therefore be it

RESOLVED, That the Officers, the Members of the Board of Directors, and the Entire Personnel of The Hayes Manufacturing Company do commend, for his devotion to them and his unstinting loyalty and leadership in their behalf, ₃ →

JOHN HERBERT KAUFMANN

Do not type
an indorsement
on a resolution.

JOB 2   Shown in pica
Plain paper
Paragraph tab

Page 2, unbound
manuscript
Words: 109

Page 2 ₃ ➡

    If a report <u>is</u> to be bound (in a notebook, for example),
an extra half-inch space should be left in the left margin. ₃ ➡

THE PLACEMENT OF HEADINGS

    <u>Main headings</u> should be centered.

    <u>Subheadings</u> may be centered or may be blocked at the left,
in capitals or underscored.

    <u>Paragraph headings</u> are indented and underscored.

    <u>The page number</u> is omitted on page 1; on other pages, it
is placed on line 7 at the right margin, with or without the
word "page," and is followed by 2 blank lines.

HOW TO INDICATE REVISIONS . . .   These are the markings or signals used by writers, editors, and typists to revise (to indicate changes or corrections) typewritten work when getting it ready for final retyping. The practical use of many of these rough-draft markings is shown in the next few jobs.

∧	Insert word	and the	
—	Omit word	and so it	
⌇	No, don't omit	and so it	
＼	Omit stroke	and soo the	
/	Make letter small	And so the	
≡	Make capital	it may not	
≣	Make all capitals	It may <u>not</u>	
→⌐	Move as indicated	and so the	
//	Line up, even up	and so the	
≡	Line up, even up	TO: Mr. A.	
ss⌐	Use single spacing . . .	and so the	
↻	Turn around	and the so	
ds⌐	Use double spacing . . .	and so the	
=	Insert a hyphen	red tipped	
5⌐	Indent 5 spaces	It may not	

#	Insert a space	andso the	
⎮	Insert a space	andso the	
⌣	Omit space	the a. m.	
—	Underscore this	It may be	
♂	Move as shown	it is not	
⌣	Join to word	in search	
—	Change word	and if it	
○	Make into period	or to it	
◯	Don't abbreviate	Dr. Wilson	
◯	Spell it out	1 or 2 who	
¶	New paragraph	We can try	
∨	Raise above line	Hale says	
+#	More space here	It may not	
−#	Less space here	It may not	
2#	2 linespaces here	It may not	

| 1 | 2 | 3 | 4 | 5 | 6 | 7 | 8 | 9 | 10 |

46   The weight of a carbon paper is a measure of   9 | 237

47 its thickness and thinness. The more copies that   19 | 247

49 you must make at one time, the thinner the carbon   29 | 257

51 paper must be; if it is too thick, the impression   39 | 267

53 of the type will not show through all the copies,   49 | 277

si 55 just as you'd anticipate. Weight is expressed in   59 | 287
1.28

57 terms of "pounds." Seven or eight pounds is best   69 | 297

59 for making one to four copies; five or six pounds   79 | 307

61 is best for making five to nine copies; for addi-   89 | 317

63 tional copies, use four pounds. Since you cannot   99 | 327

65 wish to stock a dozen different weights, what you   109 | 337

67 do is analyze the paper requirements of your work   119 | 347

69 and choose one or two weights that will fit best.   129 | 357

71   The finish of carbon paper is the measure of   9 | 366

73 the hardness and softness of the coating. If the   19 | 376

75 finish is very hard, not much of the coating will   29 | 386

si 77 come off at one time; so you get more copies, but   39 | 396
1.26

79 none of them is very dark. If the finish is very   49 | 406

81 soft, you will get dark copies--they might be too   59 | 416

83 dark, with some letters filled in--but you cannot   69 | 426

85 use the same sheet many times. There are five or   79 | 436

87 six finishes in most lines of carbon. Again, you   89 | 446

89 must analyze the requirements of your job and se-   99 | 456

91 lect one or two finishes best for your touch, the   109 | 466

93 machine you use, and the blackness you must have.   119 | 476

Plus ▶   1 | 2

PRODUCTION PRACTICE (Jobs 5-8)

The two manuscripts in these jobs, which are usually included in any study of legal papers, show how close manuscript form is to legal form. Jobs 5-6 are simply a display manuscript with two "legal style" flourishes—the deep, 10-space paragraph indentions and the all-cap displays. Jobs 7-8 are a regular, side-bound manuscript; the only legal touches are its formal tone, actual legal status, and use of all-cap sideheadings. The page-2 heading for Job 8 is an adaptation of a "running head" (page 137) and is separated by the ruled line only because the heading is so long that, at first glance, it looks like a sentence.

WARMUP (*Each line 3 times*) ◁ **60** ▷

```
Jack paid for six games, then quit because he was very lazy.
39 28 47 56 10 we 23 try 546 546 woe 293 293 1t 85 85 up 70
The rest of the group had to hike far down the old log road.
12-Sec.  5|    10|    15|    20|    25|    30|    35|    40|    45|    50|    55|    60|
```

CONTROL PREVIEW (*Each line 3 times*)

```
AA space BB problems CC once DD middle EE center FF fraction
GG begins HH their II prize JJ just KK takes LL left MM most
NN note OO total PP split QQ technique RR report SS space TT
title UU rule VV divide WW when XX exactly YY any ZZ realize
```

ALPHABET-REVIEW PARAGRAPHS (*Each, 1 time / si 1.32*) ◁ **70** ▷
DS

5-Min. Writings*

Of the many ways to find[1] the central point of any[2] line or space, the prize[3] winner 16
is the technique[4] of adding and splitting.[5] If a line or space begins[6] at forty and ends 34
at eighty,[7] you realize at once[8] that the middle must be at[9] sixty. You get a rule[10] from 51
that example: Note[11] the points on the scale[12] where the line or space[13] begins and 67
ends; then add[14] the two figures and divide[15] their total by two. The[16] result is the 83
center of[17] the line or space. If[18] you get a fraction after[19] you divide, do not drop[20] 99
it; instead, consider it as a[21] full space. As it happens,[22] this is the one and[23] only time 117
that we don't[24] just overlook a fraction.[25] 125

This procedure is really[26] very helpful in some[27] problems. Suppose that you[28] are 141
typing a report that[29] will be bound at the left;[30] you know that the left[31] margin must 157
be wider than[32] the right. To center a[33] title exactly right, you[34] must locate the center 175
between[35] the margins. Well,[36] you just follow the rule:[37] You note the ends of the[38] 191
writing line, add the[39] figures, then split their[40] total. You can use this[41] same tech- 207
nique to center[42] a number between vertical[43] rules, too, or to center[44] a braced head- 223
ing over[45] two columns. Even a lazy[46] typist can use this procedure.[47]   (START OVER) 236

*See scoring directions on page 99.

PRODUCTION PRACTICE

(*Jobs 3-4*)

Study the list of signs and signals (page 101) used to mark changes and corrections in manuscripts; note how some of these marks are used in Jobs 3 and 4, the manuscript on the next two pages. Study the information in Jobs 3 and 4; then type the material as a 2-page manuscript that is to be bound at the left (as shown, with the left margin ½ inch wider than the right). Be sure to make all the revisions that are indicated.

WARMUP (*Each line 3 times*) ◁**70**▷

```
a;z/a;slx.sldkc,dkfjvmfjghbnghfjvmfjdkc,dkslx.sla;z/a;slx.sldkc,dkfjv
rituals usurps prowls gowns duals theme melt such isle dig rod aid of
The girls wore pale gowns that blended right in with the new rituals.
```
12-Sec.5| 10| 15| 20| 25| 30| 35| 40| 45| 50| 55| 60| 65| 70|

PUNCTUATION PREVIEW (*Each line 3 times*)

```
tissues, worker, sheets, paper, touch, thick, firm, dark, inks, curl,
thinness. quality. pounds. making. used. dark. neat. wax. it.
--without --they --but chemicals; teacher; copies; years; time; done;
```

ALPHABET-REVIEW PARAGRAPHS (*1 copy / si 1.31*) ◁**50**▷
DS

5-Min.
Writings

    1 | 2 | 3 | 4 | 5 | 6 | 7 | 8 | 9 | 10

0	There are a number of things that the typist	9
2	should know about carbon paper, starting with the	19
4	fact that there are hundreds of kinds of it. The	29
6	typing student may simply request the man to sell	39
8	him some carbon paper and takes what is handed to	49
10	him--without realizing that there was a choice in	59
12	the matter. An office worker, however, must know	69
14	how to discuss and describe the carbon paper that	79
16	he needs for his job. The properties of a carbon	89
18	paper are always expressed in terms of its finish	99
20	and its weight and its quality. Let's take a few	109
22	moments for a review of each of these properties.	119

si
1.36

24	The quality of a carbon paper comes from the	9	128
26	things that go into its making. All carbon paper	19	138
28	is made of tissue sheets, coated on one side with	29	148
30	a pliable mixture of dye and wax and oil and some	39	158
32	chemicals; and the quality of the product depends	49	168
34	on that of each of the materials that is used. A	59	178
36	high-grade carbon paper has better tissues, inks,	69	188
38	and wax. It gives you more copies that are clean	79	198
40	and neat. Prize grades of carbon paper will stay	89	208
42	smooth, will not curl, will not smudge, will last	99	218
44	much longer. It is good judgment to buy quality.	109	228

si
1.32

Plus ▶   1   2

(CONTINUED ON NEXT PAGE.)

JOB 3

Page 1, bound
manuscript
Rough draft
Plain paper
Centering tab
Paragraph tab
Words: 249

Reread Jobs 1
and 2, for margins
and spacing.

FOOTNOTES IN MANUSCRIPTS

By J. R. Perkins

◁ Use your name

The main rules ~~that concern the~~ for typing ~~of~~ footnotes in reports and manuscripts are illustrated ~~correctly~~ on this and the next page. The works of Hutchinson,[1] of Gavin and Hutchinson,[2] and of others are authority for the statements made ~~in this~~ here report.

Purpose of Footnotes

1. Footnotes are used to identify a person or other reference mentioned in the body of the report. Example: the footnotes below identify ~~the authors and books~~ references referred to in the first paragraph.

2. Footnotes are used ~~also~~ to give the source of a quotation cited in the report. Examples: Footnotes 3 and 5 ~~on the next page.~~

3. Footnotes are used for explanations that might interest some but not all readers. Example: Footnote ~~No.~~ 4 ~~on the next page.~~

Styling of Footnotes

Set margins for a
6-inch line; then
move the left
margin stop in 5
or 6 spaces, to
provide ½-inch
extra space on this
side, for binding.

4. Each footnote is a separate paragraph. It is indented. It is single spaced.

5. When a footnote gives a book references, it is arranged in the style ~~illustrated~~ shown in the footnotes in this report.

_____

[1] Lois Hutchinson, <u>Standard Handbook for Secretaries</u>, Seventh edition (New York: McGraw-Hill, 1955).

[2] Ruth E. Gavin and E. Lillian Hutchinson, <u>Reference Manual for Stenographers and Typists</u> (New York: Gregg, 1951).

JOB 4

Power of attorney
Words: 397

POWER OF ATTORNEY 3 ▼

DS 13/3 ▽

KNOW ALL MEN BY THESE PRESENTS

THAT I, John R. Appleman, of the City of Elizabeth, County of Union, State of New Jersey, have made, constituted, and appointed, and by these presents do make, constitute, and appoint Frederick N. Bold, of this City, County, and State, my true and lawful attorney for me and in my name, place, and stead to act as my agent in the management of my property, an apartment house situated at 1811 Bergen Road, of this City, County, and State, giving and granting unto my said attorney full power and authority to do and perform all and every act and thing whatsoever requisite and necessary to be done in said management as fully, to all intents and purposes, as I might or could do if personally present, with full power of substitution and revocation, hereby ratifying and confirming all that my said attorney or his substitute shall lawfully do or cause to be done by virtue hereof.

IN WITNESS WHEREOF, I have hereunto set my hand and seal this eighth day of May, 1957. 3 ▼

________________________ (L.S.) 2 ▼

Signed and affirmed in the presence of 3 ▼

________________________ and ________________________

3 ▼

[ACKNOWLEDGMENT]

If the entire acknowledgment will not fit on first page, type it all on second page and number both pages.

State of New Jersey)
County of Union) ss.:

BE IT KNOWN that on the eighth day of May, 1957, before me, Florence L. Baker, duly commissioned and sworn as a Notary Public in and for the State of New Jersey, personally appeared John R. Appleman, known to me to be the same person described in and who executed this Power of Attorney, and he acknowledged this Power of Attorney to be his voluntary act and deed.

IN TESTIMONY WHEREOF, I have hereunto subscribed my name and affixed my seal of office, the day and year last above written. 3 ▼

Do not forget to type the indorsement.

____
Florence L. Baker, Notary Public

JOB 4

Page 2 Page 2 →

Reread Jobs 1, 2, and 3, for margins and spacing.

Page 2, bound manuscript
Rough draft
Plain paper
Paragraph tab
Words: 210

6. Footnotes must be clearly separated from the body or text of the report. One book states: 2 →

Footnotes are separated from the text by a 2-inch line (underscores). Always single space before typing the underscore line and double space after typing it, in order that one blank space will appear above and below it.[3] 2 →

Indent quotations of three or more lines 5 spaces on each side, as shown here.

7. If the last page *of text* is short, insert enough extra space above the ~~underscored~~ separation line to make ~~certain~~ *sure* that the footnotes ~~will~~ appear at the ~~foot~~ ~~bottom~~ of the ~~same~~ page. 3 →

Numbering of Footnotes

8. The points of reference *in a report* are numbered in sequence. The footnotes for a reference must have the same number and ~~appear~~ *be* on the same page as ~~does~~ the reference ~~to it~~.

9. The number ~~always is~~ a superior figure.[4] *close up*

10. The reference number that appears in the body follows the point of reference, without any space, or the punctuation mark that may follow it. In the footnote, however, "Separate a superior figure from the first word of a footnote by one letter space."[5]

To know how much space to leave here, reread paragraph 7.

"Op. cit." in footnote 5 is short way to say "the book already mentioned by the same authorship."

---

[3] John L. Rowe and Alan C. Lloyd, Gregg Typing, New Series (New York: Gregg, 1953), page 89.

[4] A "superior figure" is one raised above the line ~~(by holding the cylinder turned part way while you type the number key)~~.

[5] Gavin and Hutchinson, op. cit., page 143.

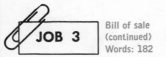
IN WITNESS WHEREOF, I have hereunto set my hand and seal the sixth day of May in the year one thousand nine hundred and fifty-seven. ₂ →

_____ (L.S.) ₂ →

(L.S.) means "place of the seal." It is typed without a space.

Sealed and Delivered
in the Presence of ₃ →

_____ ₃ →

STATE OF ILLINOIS }
COUNTY OF COOK } ss.:

[ACKNOWLEDGMENT]   **ss**

On the sixth day of May, nineteen hundred and fifty-seven, before me did come John Edward Foster, to me known, who, being by me duly sworn, did depose and say that he resides in Illinois; that he is the party of the first part described in, and which executed, the foregoing instrument; and that he signed his name thereto before me and by order. ₃ →

_____
Notary Public ₃ →

Do not forget
to type the
indorsement.

Page 2 of 2

HOW TO "INDORSE" A LEGAL PAPER . . .

Legal papers are usually folded down to a width of 3 or 4 inches—narrow enough to fit in a safe-deposit box. An identification ("indorsement") is then typed in plain view on the back of the paper.

Printed legal papers have a printed panel for this purpose. The typist fills in the obvious data suggested by the guide words; then he folds the document so that the panel is on the back, where it is easily seen.

When a paper is completely typed, the typist makes his own panel, indicating the date and nature of the document. If 8½- by 11-inch paper (which is folded in thirds) is used, the indorsement appears in the middle third, on the back. If 8½- by 13-inch paper (which is folded in quarters) is used, the indorsement appears in the second quarter.

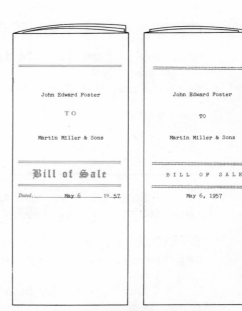

Indorsements on legal papers

WARMUP *(Each line 2 times)*

We promised Jackie eighty--but five dozen equals only sixty.
39 28 47 56 10 we 23 up 70 70 it 85 85 re 43 43 yo 69 69 69
Most of the men were out of the woods before the rain began.

12-Sec. 5| 10| 15| 20| 25| 30| 35| 40| 45| 50| 55| 60|

CONTROL PREVIEW *(Each line 2 times)*

AA Arkansas BB BLACK-GRAY CC facts DD did EE Service FF firm
GG gave HH high II invoice JJ just KK skip LL slowly MM men
NN No. OO order PP shipped QQ quality RR Rural SS Station TT
dictation UU plugs VV value WW well XX XL YY very ZZ EZ line

PRODUCTION PRACTICE *(Jobs 5-7)*

Review the rough-draft markings (page 101); note their use in Jobs 5 and 7. Review the semiblocked form, with date at the right (page 86) before typing Job 5 on a workbook letterhead. Review invoice form (page 96) before typing Job 6 on a workbook form or on a half page ruled to resemble one. Review the manuscript rules (pages 100 and 101) before typing Job 7 as the first page of an unbound manuscript.

JOB 5

Semiblocked letter
Unarranged
Letterhead
Center tab
Paragraph tab
Words: 184
Body: 147

1 | 2 | 3 | 4 | 5 | 6 | 7 | 8 | 9 | 10 | 11 | 12 |

Placement table is on page 49.

January 2, 19--   Mr. E. R. Peebles   Peebles Service
Station   Rural Route No. 2   Hoxie, Arkansas   Dear Sir:

Your letter of December 24, concerning the order that we   11
shipped to you on December 18, arrived here this morning, as   24
did the box of XL spark plugs that you now have returned.   35

When we serviced your order, we should have told you why   47
we sent the XL instead of the EZ line. You see, the firm that 59
has been making the EZ plugs for us just recently went out of 72
business. Because our XL line is nearest the EZ in value and 84
quality, we have been skipping XL plugs in all our recent or- 96
ders that are marked for rush handling. ¶We are very sorry   108
that you are not pleased with the XL shipment and have returned 121
it to us, but we are crediting it to your account, and I am   132
enclosing a revised statement of your account for the month of December.   147

Very truly yours
Yours sincerely,   THE BLACK-GRAY COMPANY   Ben Dale
Credit Manager   Initials? Enclosures?

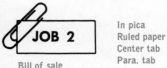

JOB 2

Bill of sale
Words: 245

In pica
Ruled paper
Center tab
Para. tab

B I L L   O F   S A L E ₃

KNOW ALL MEN BY THESE PRESENTS

THAT I, John Edward Foster, of 936 Forest Avenue, Chicago, Cook County, State of Illinois, of the first part, for and in consideration of the sum of One Thousand Dollars ($1,000) lawful money of the United States, to me in hand paid, at or before the ensealing and delivery of these presents by Martin Miller & Sons, of 58 Broad Street, Atlanta, Fulton County, State of Georgia, of the second part, the receipt whereof is hereby acknowledged, have bargained and sold, and by these presents do sell, grant and convey unto the said party of the second part, its executors, administrators and assigns my working model of a machine to simplify the binding of bristles in the manufacture of paint brushes.

TO HAVE AND TO HOLD the same unto the said party of the second part, its executors, administrators and assigns forever. And I do for me and my heirs, executors, and adminis- trators, convenant and agree, to and with the said party of the second part, to warrant and defend the sale of the aforesaid machine hereby sold unto the said party of the second part, its executors, administrators and assigns, against all and every person and persons whomsoever. ₃

(CONTINUED ON NEXT PAGE.)

Page 1 of 2

JOB 6

Invoice
Unarranged
Workbook form
Check total
3 tab stops
Words: 60

Invoice to Mr. Victor R. Kruger, 1401 West Eighth Street, Los Angeles 17, California, dated December 16.

QUANTITY	DESCRIPTION	PRICE	AMOUNT
	Chapter VI--		
25	Pages of straight copy	.20	5.00
50	Pages of carbon copies	.05	2.50
	Chapter VII--		
31	Pages of straight copy	.20	6.20
10	Pages including tables	.50	5.00
82	Pages of carbon copies	.05	4.10
			21.80

JOB 7

Page 1, unbound
manuscript
Rough draft
Plain paper
Center tab
Paragraph tab
Words: 279

Center → THE ART OF ERASING

center → By Ralph Young

Double space all but the footnote

◁6 in.▷
DS
13/2
▽

⑤ Erasing should be done rapidly. It also should be done carefully. The machine ~~should~~ must be protected from erasure crumbs,
and each erasure must be so neat that it is hard to ~~see~~ detect.[1]

A. Simple erasures

Turn the paper so that the point of ~~error~~ correction is on the top
of the cylinder. Move the carriage to one side far enough for
all erasure crumbs to fall outside the machine. If there are
carbon copies, protect ~~them~~ by inserting a stiff card between
the sheet on which you are erasing and the following sheet of
carbon paper.

no ¶ Using a typewriter eraser with a sharp point or edge, erase
~~the~~ the error with light, deft, circular ~~motions~~ strokes. ¶ When erasing
the carbon copies, erase them ① at a time. Use a soft pencil
eraser, and Be sure to place the protecting cards between the
sheet on which you are erasing and the carbon ~~sheet~~.

When all copies are ~~fixed~~ erased, carefully turn back the paper
to the printing point and type the correction. Use very light
strokes (repeating them if ~~it is~~ necessary), trying to match
exactly the shade of ~~ink~~ the typing that appears on the rest of the page.

_____

1 The procedures outlined in ~~the following~~ this material are
explained in detail in Reference Manual for Stenographers and
Typists, by Ruth E. Gavin and ~~Miss~~ E. Lillian Hutchinson (New
York: Gregg, 1951), ~~on~~ pages 5-7.

PRODUCTION PRACTICE *(Jobs 1-4)*

Job 1 requires the special form on Workbook pages 211-212. Jobs 2, 3, and 4 together require four sheets of paper ruled with a double line 1½ inches from the left and a single line ½ inch from the right. Note that Job 1 and Jobs 2-3 are two arrangements of the same material.

HOW TO TYPE LEGAL PAPERS . . .

1. *Basic assumption:* **The paper is to be so arranged that it cannot be altered. Erasures, if permitted, must be initialed by the persons signing the document.**

2. *If paper must be completely typed:*

A. Paper: either 8½ by 11 or 8½ by 13, ruled; double line 1½ inches from the left, single line ½ inch from the right.

B. Margin stops: 2 spaces inside rules.

C. Top margins (for top binding): page 1, 2

inches; succeeding pages, 1½ inches.

D. Page number (if more than one page): centered 1 inch from the foot of the page.

E. Spacing: double.

F. Paragraph indentions: 10 spaces.

3. *If a printed form is used:* **Start each fill-in close to the printing, followed by hyphens to the end of the space. Keep the typing line even with the printing line.**

4. *Indorsements:* **See page 207.**

JOB 1   Bill of sale
Workbook form
Words: 113

BILL OF SALE   𝕶𝖓𝖔𝖜 𝖆𝖑𝖑 𝕸𝖊𝖓 𝖇𝖞 𝖙𝖍𝖊𝖘𝖊 𝕻𝖗𝖊𝖘𝖊𝖓𝖙𝖘,

That I, John Edward Foster, of 936 Forest Avenue, Chicago, Cook County, State of Illinois, ---of the first part,

for and in consideration of the sum of One Thousand Dollars ($1,000) --------------

lawful money of the United States, to me ---- in hand paid, at or before the ensealing and delivery of these presents by Martin Miller & Sons, of 58 Broad Street, Atlanta, Fulton County, State of Georgia, -- of the second part, the receipt whereof is hereby acknowledged, have bargained and sold, and by these presents do sell, grant and convey unto the said party -- of the second part, its --- executors, administrators and assigns my working model of a machine to simplify the binding of bristles in the construction of paint brushes. ----------------

𝕿𝖔 𝖍𝖆𝖛𝖊 𝖆𝖓𝖉 𝖙𝖔 𝖍𝖔𝖑𝖉 the same unto the said party -- of the second part, its --executors, administrators and assigns forever. And I do for me and my -----heirs, executors and administrators, covenant and agree, to and with the said party - of the second part, to warrant and defend the sale of the aforesaid machine ---------------------- hereby sold unto the said party - of the second part, its --executors, administrators and assigns, against all and every person and persons whomsoever.

𝕴𝖓 𝖂𝖎𝖙𝖓𝖊𝖘𝖘 𝖂𝖍𝖊𝖗𝖊𝖔𝖋, I have hereunto set my -hand -- and seal-- the sixth ----- ---------day of May ----------in the year one thousand nine hundred and fifty-seven.

Sealed and Delivered in the presence of

_____ (L.S.)

_____

You will need 2 sheets of plain paper or Workbook pages 93-96. If you do not have the invoice form for Part C, rule paper to resemble the form (page 96). Type Parts A and B (below) on opposite sides of one sheet, and Parts C and D (next page) on opposite sides of the second sheet. Use the scales on this page to grade all your work.

PART A: STRAIGHT-COPY TEST *(si 1.18)*

◁ **65** ▷
DS

Take a 5-minute writing on the *body* of the letter below and grade it on this scale. Or, make 1 exact copy of the body and grade it as though you had typed it at 40 words a minute. Use double spacing and a 65-space line.

Step 1: Compute words a minute.	Step 2: Deduct for errors—		Step 3: Grade the remaining words a minute this way:	40 or higher: A 35 to 39 wam: B 30 to 34 wam: C 25 to 29 wam: D
	1 error: —2 2 errors: —4 3 errors: —6	4 errors: — 9 5 errors: —12 6 errors: —15		

PART B: LETTER TEST *(si 1.31)*

◁ **5 in.** ▷
SS
14/6
▽

Type this 130-word letter in semiblocked form, with date at the right. Use correct form and correct length of line. Grade your work:

TAKE OFF:	—3 for each major error (top margin, line length, line-spacing, general correctness of form, etc.) —2 for each minor error (blocking, aligning, centering, indenting, etc., of individual parts of the job) —1 for each typographical error	TOTAL TAKEN OFF	8-7	6-4	3-2	1-0
		GRADE	D	C	B	A

```
        January 4, 19--    Mr. Gerald Jordan    Acme Drills Company
  3838 Zenith Street    Hartford 7, Connecticut    Dear Mr. Jordan:

     1 | 2 | 3 | 4 | 5 | 6 | 7 | 8 | 9 | 10 | 11 | 12 | 13
```

We were pleased to extend to you in the past month the rare	12
favor of buying from us on credit, although it has long been our	25
firm policy to require payment of all bills within ten days. As	38
you can note from the date on the duplicate bill that I have en-	51
closed, more than four weeks have passed since we shipped to you	64
the goods that you ordered.	70
So that both of us may clear our accounts, we must ask that	82
you pay this bill at once.	87
The low prices for which our firm is known are possible be-	99
cause we do not have to charge for all the credit and collection	112
costs that most firms find so high. May we have your full check	125
by return mail, Mr. Jordan?	130

Yours sincerely,   NELSON HARDWARE COMPANY   Kenneth Zerner
Sales Manager Initials? Enclosure?

UNIT 24
MANUSCRIPTS

In this unit: 1- and 2-page manuscripts, (1) some of which are legal documents, and (2) some of which are regular manuscripts embellished with one or two legal-style flourishes. Your work will be easiest if you (1) review the manuscript-margin rules on pages 100 and 101, (2) study pages 204-215 carefully, and (3) answer the study-guide questions on Workbook pages 209-210.

WARMUP *(Each line 3 times)* ◁**70**▷

```
a;qpa;slwosldkeidkfjrufjghtyghfjrufjdkeidkslwosla;qpa;slwosldkeidkfjr
divisible ritual ivory flake giant lame town burn rush she aid via if
They had to laugh when they found that an auditor would do the books.
12-Sec.5|   10|   15|   20|   25|   30|   35|   40|   45|   50|   55|   60|   65|   70|
```

PUNCTUATION PREVIEW *(Each line 3 times)*

```
executors, Chicago, County, dozen, again, shop, sell, paid, day, all,
whomsoever.  Street.  layman.  tricky.  truth.  often.  order.  form.
ILLINOIS) (L.S.) ($1,000) (or one) margins; forever." letters!  ss.:
```

ALPHABET-REVIEW PARAGRAPHS *(2 copies / si 1.33)* ◁**70**▷
DS

5-Min. Writings

Most of us have a high[1] regard for the law and a[2] feeling that the law is too[3] com- 16
plex for the layman.[4] As a result, there is a[5] tradition (or what amounts[6] to one) that 33
the typing[7] of legal papers is very[8] hard and tricky. Nothing[9] could be farther from 50
the[10] truth. Legal jobs are[11] quite easy to type—much[12] easier, come to think of[13] it, than 67
most other kinds[14] of work that you turn out[15] by the dozen, day by day,[16] on the job. 83

After all,[17] these documents are nothing[18] more nor less than common[19] manuscripts 99
with some[20] fancy flairs to impress[21] folks. One such flair:[22] the antiquated phrasing[23] 115
that is used time and again,[24] such as "and his executors[25] and heirs and assigns[26] for- 131
ever." A wise typist[27] just smiles, knowing[28] that any such phrase becomes[29] easy to 147
type when it[30] is repeated often. After[31] a while, you will zip off[32] such phrases in 164
nothing[33] flat. 167

In some states,[34] another legal touch is the[35] use of vertical lines[36] that mark off the 183
margins;[37] what a help the lines would[38] be on letters! Another[39] note of extra grandeur[40] 200
is the frequent use of solid[41] capitals, just as though[42] a bailiff were shouting.[43] But 217
splendor dims away:[44] You can buy many of[45] these papers in printed[46] form at a dime 233
a dozen in[47] any stationery shop, and[48] you just type a word here[49] and there on the 249
form.[50] 250

PART C: BUSINESS-FORM TEST (48 *five-stroke words*)

Date this invoice December 6 and address it to the Acme Drills Company, 3838 Zenith Street, Hartford 7, Connecticut. Grade your work, using the same scale that you used for Part B of this test. Check all the figures in the Amounts column.

QUANTITY	DESCRIPTIONS	UNIT PRICE	AMOUNT
150	Feet of reinforced hosing	.30	45.00
2	Sets of Farley steel bits	9.90	19.80
2	Farley power drills	7.50	15.00
100	Feet of heavy-duty wire	.12	12.00
			91.80

PART D: ROUGH-DRAFT MANUSCRIPT TEST (264 *five-stroke words*)

Type this report as the first page of a manuscript that is not to be bound. Grade your work, using the same scale that you used for Part B.

◁ **6 in.** ▷
DS
13/2
▽

This is authentic information, well worth remembering.

THE TITLES OF PUBLICATIONS

A Report by J. N. Strong

5] There are two sets of rules for the display of the names of publications, according to a ~~recent~~ article by Hutchinson.[1]

In Formal Manuscripts

In a (formal) report, thesis, term paper, or similar paper typed according to manuscript rules, the name of a publication should be underscored; and the name of any part of the publication should be displayed by quotation marks. ~~Some~~ examples:

I read "Westward Ho," a chapter in My America. *Center the longest line and line up others with it*
I read "Who Will It Be?" in Time.
I read the Daily News editorial, "Now What?"

In Business letters

In letters, the rule is quite different: Enclose book and article titles in quotation marks, but display all other titles (names of magazines, of newspapers, of bulletin, and so on) simply in capitals and small letters. Examples:

I recommend "The Life of Shakespeare." *Line up with the lettering above*
Watch for our ad in the Times-Journal.
I missed "Who Will It Be?" in Time.

There is one exception to this rule. When a publisher writes a letter to sell a book, he may display its name in any way that he wishes. he will probably use all capitals.

---

[1] E. Lillian Hutchinson, "Styles Change in Typewritten English, Too," Business Teacher (April, 1955), page 2.

JOB 8

Wide tabulation
Exact copy
Sidewise
Center
4 tabs
Close leaders
Words: 280

REMEMBER: There are 8½ x 6 = 51 lines when paper is sideways.
REMEMBER: Mark the centering point before inserting the paper.
REMEMBER: Space once before, and twice after, typing a ruled line.

DISTRIBUTION OF INCOME

(Prepared by the Department of Research and Statistics)

How the Sales Dollar Was Applied	This Year Amount	%	Last Year Amount	%
Materials and Services from Others	$512 236 000	54.4	$456 367 000	54.0
Wages and Salaries	298 289 000	31.5	281 769 000	33.0
Pensions, Social Security Taxes, Insurance, and Other Benefits	19 938 000	2.1	18 470 000	2.2
Depreciation and Amortization	17 314 000	1.6	15 174 000	1.8
Interest on Long-Term Debts	4 875 000	.5	4 595 000	.5
Taxes on Income and Property	47 772 000	5.1	41 657 000	4.9
Dividends Declared for the Year	22 052 000	2.3	19 963 000	2.3
Extra Dividend Last Quarter	4 284 000	.5	...	...
Reinvested in the Business	18 480 000	2.0	10 769 000	1.3
TOTALS	$945 240 000	100.0	$848 764 000	100.0

Materials and Services from Others......$945 240 000...4...100.0...6...$848 764 000...4...100.0

PART 4

WARMUP: Flash Phrases *(Each line 3 times)*

```
a;z/ slx. dkc, fjvm ghbn a;qp slwo dkei fjru ghty
if so if it if he if we if in if or if the if she
to go to do to me to us to be to it to the to her
```

SPEED DRILL: Word Families *(Each line 3 times)*

```
anvil antic angry anti ante anon anew any ant and
would worth wore wool wolf worn work word wow won
legal learn lean left leap lead levy leaf led let
```

SPEED SENTENCES *(Each line 3 times)*

12-Sec.
Writings

```
They may go to the lake when she forms the panel.
The profit they make by their fight may go to us.
The form she got for them may also work for this.
```

12-Sec. 5| 10| 15| 20| 25| 30| 35| 40| 45| 50|

SPEED PARAGRAPH *(3 copies / si 1.15)*

1-Min.
Writings

1 | 2 | 3 | 4 | 5 | 6 | 7 | 8 | 9 | 10 | 11 | 12

```
Most of us like to be on a good team and to help it win, if     12
we can.  We get a lot of pleasure from doing our share, and     24
we do not like the fellow who ducks doing his.  That is one     36
thing to remember if you ever go to work on an office team.     48
```

SPEED PREVIEW *(Each line 3 times)*

```
challenge machine victory controls boost rate much note how
supposed progress factors depends number when what that you
```

SUSTAINED-SPEED PARAGRAPH *(2 copies / si 1.13)*   **DS**

3-Min.
Writings

1 | 2 | 3 | 4 | 5 | 6 | 7 | 8 | 9 | 10 | 11 | 12

```
0    You can control the rate at which you build your skill    11
4    in typing.  You may think that your progress depends on the    23
8    kind of fingers you have or on the number of hours that you    35
12   work on the machine.  These things have a place, of course;    47
16   but the big factors, the ones that really boost your skill,    59
20   are the drills you work on and the brain work you do as you    71
24   work on them.  It is not much fun to type a drill; but when    83
28   you study it a bit, to note how it is set up and what it is    95
32   supposed to do to and for you, you will find that there can   107
36   be real challenge and victory in every drill line you type.   119
```

Plus ➡   1 | 2 | 3 | 4

* For a review of directions in this book, see —   Page 5, machine setup   Page 13, meaning of "si"   Page 26, use of speed scales
                                         Page 13, use of black scales   Page 19, use of 12-second scales   Page 41, use of marginal signals

WARMUP *(Each line 3 times)*

```
aassddffgghhjjkkll;;llkkjjhhggffddssaa asdfghjkl;lkjhgfdsasdfghjkl;lk
wieldy flame fiend socks risks eight works sick rush when jam rye pal
The old men on the island had made some handy nets out of old burlap.
```
12-Sec.5| 10| 15| 20| 25| 30| 35| 40| 45| 50| 55| 60| 65| 70|

PUNCTUATION PREVIEW *(Each line 3 times)*

```
stockholders, expectations, Insurance, Vitashine, analysis, pensions,
quarter, weeks, share, study, 10, P. O. Box 100.0 54.0 33.0 54.4 31.5
.5 before. wished. Swensen: year: (Prepared Statistics) Long-Term
```

PRODUCTION PRACTICE *(Jobs 7-8)*

The Job 7 table may be set up by the usual backspacing method (columns 8 spaces apart) or by pivoting (position Column 1 by indenting it 5 spaces; position Column 2 by pivoting from the right margin and allowing 5 spaces for a right-margin indention). Job 8, also, may be set up either by backspacing or by pivoting (on a 90-space line). When planning the top margin of the table, remember that there are 8½ x 6 = 51 vertical lines when paper is sideways. To find where the horizontal center will be, mark the center by a light pencil or crease mark before insertion; then note at what point on the scale that mark appears after insertion.

JOB 7

Blocked letter
Unarranged
Letterhead
Leaders
Words: 240
Body: 203

```
     1  |  2  |  3  |  4  |  5  |  6  |  7  |  8  |  9  |  10  |  11

     Date    Mrs. Wilber Swensen    Executive Director        12
Public Mutual Company    P. O. Box 3755    Cleveland 10,       22
Ohio    Dear Mrs. Swensen:                                     27

     We are always happy to answer an inquiry from one    10 | 37
of our stockholders.  Our report for our operations in   21 | 48
the first quarter, which is being printed now and will   32 | 59
be mailed in about two weeks, shows that our net earn-   43 | 70
ings are $5.04 a share, average for this time of year:   54 | 81

Gross Revenue ............... $55,999,275.00              63 | 90
Net Income before
     Federal Income Taxes ......   9,339,180.00           75 | 102
Estimated Federal
     Income Taxes .............   4,905,227.00            87 | 114
Net Income .................   4,433,953.00               96 | 123
Earnings per Share .........         5.04               105 | 132

     We expect a sharp upturn in our sales in the next  115 | 142
quarter, for we shall be launching Vitashine, the fine  126 | 153
new product that we have been developing for more than  137 | 164
two years.  If Vitashine lives up to our expectations,  148 | 175
based on a careful market study, our sales and profits  159 | 186
will be far ahead of anything that we have had before.  170 | 197

     I trust that this information is what you wished.   181 | 208
If there are other details that you would like to have  192 | 219
for your analysis, we should be happy to provide them.  203 | 230

     Yours very truly,   Orville Mitchell, Treasurer          239
```

WARMUP: "EN" Drill (*Each line 3 times*)   ◁ **50** ▷

```
a;zla; slx.sl dkc,dk fjvmfj ghbngh vmfjc,dkx.slz/
enrich endure enough enter enjoy enemy endow envy
went wend tend lent rent tent send lend mend bent
oven when then open even been yen ten men hen den
```

SPEED DRILL: Doubled Letters (*Each line 3 times*)

```
success account accuse accept accede accord occur
affair effect office differ affix offer staff off
planned connect dinner cannot annual manner funny
suppose appoint shipped appear happen apply happy
```

SPEED SENTENCES: Doubled Letters (*Each line 2 times*)   ◁ **60** ▷

12-Sec.
Writings

Lee Mann cannot accept the offer for cutting apple tariffs.

I approve of his success and applaud his official accuracy.

My office staff is happy to accept any annual dinner offer.

12-Sec. 5| 10| 15| 20| 25| 30| 35| 40| 45| 50| 55| 60|

SPEED DRILL: Common 4-Letter Words (*Each line 2 times*)

1-Min.
Writings

	1	2	3	4	5	6	7	8	9	10	11	12	
	able	busy	days	feel	gave	hear	just	also	call	deal	file	girl	12
	help	keep	away	came	dear	fill	give	here	knew	back	care	does	24
	find	glad	high	know	bank	case	done	fine	gone	hold	last	been	36
	city	down	five	good	home	late	best	come	each	form	half	hope	48
	left	bill	copy	even	four	hand	hour	less	both	cost	from	life	60

SUSTAINED-SPEED SENTENCES (*2 copies / si 1.04*)

3-Min.
Writings

		1	2	3	4	5	6	7	8	9	10	11	12	
0	She said that she would not work with them in their office.													12
4	If he visits with us, we shall call them at once from town.													24
8	The girl is in the third grade and does fine work for them.													36
12	Six men plan to take the boat trip to the side of the lake.													48
16	You will hear from him when he gets down to the lake shore.													60
20	Have you made the best use you could of all that free time?													72
24	She lost all four keys and never did find even one of them.													84
28	He said you might hear from him before the end of the week.													96
32	None of us like the fellow who ducks his share of the work.													108
36	Both men said that they would like to make the trip for us.													120

Plus ▸   1   2   3   4

JOB 6

Second page of
2-page financial
statement
  Exact copy
  Center
  3 tabs
  Open leaders
Words: 199

4. Insert paper for page 1. Pivot the heading lines from the right margin point. Type them. Center the subheading *Assets*.

5. Pivot from the right margin to ascertain the start of each money column (as you did in Job 3). Set tab stops for each.

6. Type page 1. Use the tab stops to locate the column beginnings.

7. Insert paper for page 2. Start the heading lines flush with the left margin, the same space from the top of the page as you provided on page 1. Center the subheading *Liabilities*.

8. Pivot from the right margin to ascertain the start of any money column (in Job 6, the last column is the same as in Job 5).

9. Type page 2. Tape the two pages together, side by side.

Acme Corporation₂ →   ◁**60**▷

DECEMBER 31, 19-- ₃ →

LIABILITIES₂ →

Legal Reserve, Life and Annuity Contracts	$302,514,963.00
Reserve, Disability Policies	2,257,617.00
Reserve for Epidemics and Mortality Fluctuations	2,500,000.00
Investment Fluctuation Fund	5,000,000.00
Gross Premiums and Interest Paid in Advance	1,768,036.00
Taxes Accrued But Not Due	2,078,495.00
Agents' Bond Deposits (By Field Employees)	683,754.21
Reserve for Policy Claims in Process of Adjustment	1,459,619.00
Commission Accrued to Agents, and Miscellaneous Items	936,106.60 ₁ →
	―――――――――₂ →
Liabilities Other Than Capital and Surplus	$319,198,590.81
Capital and Surplus	28,667,602.10 ₁ →
	―――――――――₂ →
TOTAL LIABILITIES	$347,866,192.91 ₁ →

WARMUP: Balanced-Hand Words *(Each line 3 times)*

◁ **50** ▷

```
lm lmn lmno lmnop lmnopq lmnopq lmnop lmno lmn lm
auto body city down elan firm girl hand idle jamb
kale lair make nape oaks pane quay rock sock torn
urns vial worm goal hair iris jape keys lake malt
```

CONTROL DRILL: W, I *(Each line 3 times)*

```
wait wail walk weak weld what whom wide work wish
saws slow owls anew bowl know owed blow owes view

idea ides idle inks idol inch into iron iris inky
kick kind quiz city find give high wise nice sign
```

CONTROL SENTENCES: Alphabet Review *(Each line 2 times)*

◁ **60** ▷

½- and 1-Min. Writings

```
   1 | 2 | 3 | 4 | 5 | 6 | 7 | 8 | 9 | 10 | 11 | 12
Gary Quincy junked that xylophone but won five more prizes.   12
The brown fox jumped easily and quickly over the lazy dogs.  24
Jasper quietly viewed the fox, zebra, kangaroo, and camels.  36
Hazel was quite excited before jumping onto a heavy rocker.  48
```

CONTROL PREVIEW *(Each line 2 times)*

```
tense extra radar escort quarter perched squadron pinpoints
faded watch exact flicker station engines horizon somewhere
```

ALPHABET-REVIEW PARAGRAPH *(2 copies / si 1.21)*

◁ **50** ▷
DS

5-Min. Writings

```
            1 | 2 | 3 | 4 | 5 | 6 | 7 | 8 | 9 | 10
 0  28      As the late dusk slowly faded into dark, the       9
 2  30   squadron went on and on, a long file of shapes on    19
 4  32   all sides of the horizon. Somewhere above us was     29
 6  34   the air escort; we heard the distant whine of the    39
 8  36   jets above the throb of our own engines. A gleam     49
10  38   from the ship ahead became a flicker, a signal to    59
12  40   call up extra hands and eyes for the night watch.    69
14  42   The night was a very tense one, for it was a full    79
16  44   job just to keep in station in a squadron of such    89
18  46   size. The con officer perched by the radar scope     99
20  48   on the bridge, waiting for the exact quarter hour   109
22  50   when he would have to zig or zag between the pin-   119
24  52   points of light on the screen. But the hot night   129
26  54   wore on with no alarms, although few of us slept.   139
```

Plus ▮   1 | 2

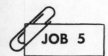

HOW TO TYPE A 2-PAGE FINANCIAL STATEMENT...

JOB 5

First page of
2-page financial
statement
  Exact copy
  Center
  3 tabs
  Open leaders
Words: 195

1. Divide the data into halves of about equal width and depth.

2. Check the vertical spacing of each half, adding or deleting blank spaces, to make both halves even. In this balance sheet, for example, the *Bonds Owned* were single spaced to make page 1 (below) equal the depth of page 2 (next page). Compute the top margin.

3. Select a line length adequate for each half. (A 60-space line is adequate for Jobs 5 and 6.) Set the left margin stop. Set the carriage at the right margin point.

(Continued, next page.)

◁ **60** ▷

The   Providence- ₂ ➡

BALANCE SHEET, ₃ ➡

A S S E T S ₂ ➡

Real Estate Loans	$162,587,305.68
Bonds Owned:	
Government Bonds $45,507,650.33	
Railroad Bonds 4,508,135.65	
Public Utility Bonds . . 62,449,231.34	
Industrial Bonds . . . . 26,878,473.54 ₂ ➡	
Total Bonds Owned	139,343,490.86
Stocks Owned (Basic Industries with	
Dividend Records)	13,129,036.89
Policy Loans Made to Policyholders	11,862,942.16
Net Unpaid and Deferred Premiums	
(Being Collected)	7,099,713.61
Cash in Banks and Offices	6,340,534.93
Real Estate Owned (Including Home	
Office Building)	5,980,846.78
Interest Due and Accrued on Bonds	
and Mortgages	1,412,662.00
Collateral Loans (First Mortgages Only) . .	109,660.00 ₂ ➡
	₂ ➡
TOTAL ASSETS	$347,866,192.91 ₁ ➡

WARMUP: **Right-Hand Security** *(Each line 3 times)* ◁**50**▷

```
lmnopq lmnopq lmnopq lmnopq lmnopq lmnopq lmnopq
llml llnl llol llpl llml llnl llol llpl llml llnl
Lola Maud Nina Mary Paul Lily Mark Noah Pete Nora
```

CONTROL DRILL: **Individual Finger Reaches, with One-Hand Words** *(Each line 2 times)*

Fore-fingers	Left	fat bar garb verb refer great barge target barber
	Right	you hip noun hymn union jumpy mummy hominy unholy
	Both	vat joy art ohm verb hump graft phony after nylon
Second fingers	Left	ace wed edge deed cadet wedge creed secede accede
	Right	in kin ink kim kink pink inky kiln mink link milk
	Both	fed ink dad kin deed milk evade milky cease kinky
Third fingers	Left	was sax saws west sweet vexes asset stress excess
	Right	oil poll loll polo knoll loony jolly Molly Kokomo
	Both	wax oil saw Lon axes look asset holly waxes Polly
Little fingers	Left	zag faze adze gaze raze dazed zebra strata bazaar
	Right	up pop pup pulp pump pomp poppy plump nippy pupil
	Both	zax pip zag pop afar pump graze pupil abate plunk

CONTROL SENTENCES: **One-Hand Words** *(Each line 2 times)* ◁**60**▷

½-Min. Writings

```
 1  |  2  |  3  |  4  |  5  |  6  |  7  |  8  |  9  | 10  | 11  | 12
Polly swears we saw a plump bear in a crate in West Kokomo.   12
You get a minimum trade rate on a seat on my fastest craft.  24
Jill gave my dad a pumpkin after we agreed on a secret bet.  36
Lily saw John in a pool in East Honolulu after you saw him.  48
```

CONTROL PARAGRAPH: **Concentration** *(2 copies)* DS

1-Min. Writings

```
 1  |  2  |  3  |  4  |  5  |  6  |  7  |  8  |  9  | 10  | 11  | 12
     Trondelag, Norway, near Trondheim Fjord, consists of a   11
Nord-Trondelag and Sor-Trondelag.  Skarn Sund connects this  23
Trondheim Fjord with Beitstad Sund.  Hjellebton, Steinkjer,  35
Brekken, and Ogndal are in this vicinity, as well.           45
```

CONTROL DRILL: **Shift Lock and Release** *(Each line 2 times)** SS

½-Min. Writings

```
 1  |  2  |  3  |  4  |  5  |  6  |  7  |  8  |  9  | 10  | 11  | 12
We MUST ship that BLACK-GRAY order by the end of NEXT week.   12
This paper is SECRET and to be handled ONLY BY MR. McGRATH.  24
Here is a can of EASY-WIPE-CLEAN: test it for us BY JUNE 2.   36
MR. JAMES HOWARD-DALE, 3928 MARTIN PLACE, GARY 10, INDIANA.   48
```

* Note: Period and comma can be typed when shift is locked, but shift must be unlocked when hyphen and semicolon are typed.

JOB 4

Financial
statement
  Exact copy
  Center
  3 Tabs
  Open leaders
Words: 401

Use the regular
(backspacing)
method. Put 8
spaces after
column 1. Put
2 spaces between
columns 2 and 3.

The Providence-Acme Corporation₂ ➡

BALANCE SHEET, DECEMBER 31, 19--₃ ➡

A S S E T S₂ ➡

Real Estate Loans		$162,587,305.68
Bonds Owned:		
Government Bonds	$45,507,650.33	
Railroad Bonds	4,508,135.65	
Public Utility Bonds . . .	62,449,231.34	
Industrial Bonds	26,878,473.54	
Total Bonds Owned		139,343,490.86
Stocks Owned (Basic Industries with		
Dividend Records)		13,129,036.89
Policy Loans Made to Policyholders		11,862,942.16
Net Unpaid and Deferred Premiums		
(Being Collected)		7,099,713.61
Cash in Banks and Offices		6,340,534.93
Real Estate Owned (Including Home		
Office Building)		5,980,846.78
Interest Due and Accrued on Bonds		
and Mortgages		1,412,662.00
Collateral Loans (First Mortgages Only) . . .		109,660.00
TOTAL ASSETS		$347,866,192.91

L I A B I L I T I E S₂ ➡

Legal Reserve, Life and Annuity	
Contracts	$302,514,963.00
Reserve, Disability Policies	2,257,617.00
Reserve for Epidemics and Mortality	
Fluctuations	2,500,000.00
Investment Fluctuation Fund	5,000,000.00
Gross Premiums and Interest Paid	
in Advance	1,768,036.00
Taxes Accrued But Not Due	2,078,495.00
Agents' Bond Deposits (By Field Employees) .	683,754.21
Reserve for Policy Claims in Process	
of Adjustment	1,459,619.00
Commission Accrued to Agents, and	
Miscellaneous Items	936,106.60
Liabilities Other Than Capital	
and Surplus	$319,198,590.81
Capital and Surplus	28,667,602.10
TOTAL LIABILITIES	$347,866,192.91

Key: ．³．Public Utility Bonds....⁸....$45,507,650.33.²$162,587,305.68

WARMUP: Keyboard Review *(Each line 3 times)*   ◁ **50** ▷

```
abcd efgh ijkl mnop qrst uvwx yzab cdef ghij klmn
opqr stuv wxyz abcd efgh ijkl mnop qrst uvwx yz,.
alla ;00; s22s 1991 d33d k88k f44f j77j f55f j66j
```

NUMBER DRILL: 1, 4, 7, 0 *(Each line 3 times)*

```
f 4 f4 14 41 144 441 1441 4414 1414 144 441 14 41
j 7 j7 17 71 177 771 1771 7717 1717 177 771 17 71
; 0 ;0 10 01 100 001 1001 0010 1010 100 001 10 01
```

NUMBER DRILL: We 23's *(Each line 3 times)*

```
weep 2330 tour 5974 yipe 6803 pity 0856 wept 2305
riot 4895 your 6974 pipe 0803 wore 2943 were 2343
wiry 2846 true 5473 pout 0975 toot 5995 root 4995
```

NUMBER SENTENCES: Pair Pattern *(Each line 3 times)*   ◁ **50** ▷

½-Min.
Writings

1	2	3	4	5	6	7	8	9	10	
The model plans were on pages 10, 28, 39, 47, 56.										10
They plan on about 2847 to 3956 recruits by 1963.										20
The sum of 821 and 930 and 4765 and 2839 is 9355.										30
The dates are: May 5, 9, 17, 18, 24, 26, and 30.										40

NUMBER DRILL: Cumulative Count *(Each line 2 times)*

1-Min.
Writings

1	2	3	4	5	6	7	8	9	10	
1001	3902	2803	4704	5605	3906	4707	5608	1009	2210	10
1411	4112	1713	7714	4415	1416	1717	4718	7419	7720	20
4021	7022	1023	0124	0425	0726	4127	7728	7029	2130	30
8831	8932	8733	6634	6735	4436	4537	3238	2339	2140	40

NUMBER-REVIEW PARAGRAPH *(2 copies / si 1.12)*   **DS**

2-Min.
Writings

		1	2	3	4	5	6	7	8	9	10	
0	25	When the club was at 39 28th Street, it was known										10
5	30	as the 3928 Club. Now that it has moved to a new										20
10	35	building at 47 56th Street, they have changed the										30
15	40	name to the 4756 Club. The new address is better										40
20	45	located: 10 new men have joined as club members.										50

Plus ▶   1 | 2 | 3 | 4 | 5

WARMUP *(Each line 3 times)* ◁70▷

```
aa ss dd ff gg hh jj kk ll ;; ll kk jj hh gg ff dd ss aa ss dd ff gg
auditor mantle usury blend aisle blame duck pale wick men lap via of
The first firm to come out with a lower price will sweep the market.
12-Sec.5|   10|   15|   20|   25|   30|   35|   40|   45|   50|   55|   60|   65|   70|
```

PUNCTUATION PREVIEW *(Each line 3 times)*

```
brightness, darkness, reserve, hectic, temper, there, stir, you, sea,
expectation. slightly. horizon. winking. still. soft. sea. up.
darkness; switch; moment; night; deep; dawn; you're day's it's owned:
```

ALPHABET-REVIEW PARAGRAPHS *(1 copy / si 1.26)* ◁70▷ DS

7-Min. Writings		1 | 2 | 3 | 4 | 5 | 6 | 7 | 8 | 9 | 10 | 11 | 12 | 13 | 14	
0	40	Of all the moments when peace seems everywhere and a man can let	13
2	41	his soul relax in contentment, the prime one in this sailor's book is	27
4	43	the moment just before dawn when you're a thousand miles at sea. For	41
6	45	an instant the world stands still. You are in darkness, and there is	55
8	47	nothing but the jet quiet of the night around you, except for a hand-	69
10	49	ful of stars that stare down at you without winking. Then the breeze	83
12	51	begins to stir, flapping the signal halyards and making the ship heel	97
14	53	over slightly. You breathe deep; you feel a stirring of expectation.	111
16	55	Then the sun pops up over the horizon. It does not creep up; it	124
18	57	jumps up. Light comes like an explosion. One moment you're standing	138
20	59	in darkness; and the next you are in full brightness, as though some-	152
22	61	one had quietly touched the light switch, but the light is very soft.	166
24	63	It is a good scene to think of when the day's doings get hectic,	179
26	65	when the pressure jangles your temper, when the demands of life press	193
28	67	too insistently. Think of the calmness of the sea, the velvet breeze	207
30	69	on your bare arm, the gentle rock of the ship, the intimate quietness	221
32	71	of the night; and let yourself relax for a moment. And then remember	235
34	73	that a new day will dawn; you can count on it. The sun is there. It	249
36	75	is waiting for the right moment; but it's there, and it will come up.	263
38	77	To know that you can always count on a new dawn is to live with hope.	277
Plus ▶		1 | 2	

PRODUCTION PRACTICE *(Jobs 4-6)*

Jobs 4-6, to be typed on plain paper, illustrate two ways to arrange the same financial statement—on one page and on two pages. Note that you use the regular backspacing method for Job 4 (like Job 2) and the pivot method for Jobs 5 and 6 (like Job 3).

WARMUP: Reach Review *(Each line 3 times)*   ◁**50**▷

aAa fBf dCd dDd dEd fFf fGf jHj kIk jJj kKk lLl

jMj jNj lOl ;P; aQa fRf sSs fTf jUj fVf sWs sXs

jYj aZa s2s d3d f4f f5f j6j j7j k8k 191 ;0; ;-;

NUMBER DRILL: Adjacents *(Each line 3 times)*

;00; s22s 1991 d33d k88k f44f j77j f55f j66j ;00;

1221 1231 1331 1341 1441 1451 1551 1561 1661 1671

1771 1781 1881 1891 1991 1901 1001 1234 1567 1890

NUMBER DRILL: We 23's *(Each line 3 times)*

wet 235 toe 593 pet 035 row 492 owe 923 wort 2945

tow 592 pie 083 rye 463 rot 495 ere 343 were 2343

yow 692 tie 583 pit 085 roe 493 ore 943 pout 0975

SYMBOL DRILL: ' $ *(Each line 3 times)*

If ' is on 8   k8k k'k 8 ' it's dog's Paul's '39 '28 '47 '56 '10

If ' is by ;   ;'; ;'; ;'; it's dog's Paul's '39 '28 '47 '56 '10

1's 2's 3's 4's 5's 6's 7's 8's 9's 10's and 11's

f4f f$f 4 $ $4 $14 $1.44 $144 $39 $28 $47 $56 $10

$1 $2 $3 $4 $5 $6 $7 $8 $9 $10 $11 $12 and $13.00

SYMBOL SENTENCES: ' $ *(Each line 2 times)*   ◁**50**▷

½-Min.
Writings

| 1 | 2 | 3 | 4 | 5 | 6 | 7 | 8 | 9 | 10 |

We lost $39, $28, $47, $56, and $10 respectively.   10

Reunions: Class of '39, in May; of '47, in June.   20

Al's suit cost him $80.95, but Paul's was $95.80.   30

1-Min.
Writings

The lady's little boy didn't lose Mary's $5 cape!   10

John's stocks are worth $7,500; Helen's, $10,000.   20

I'm afraid I get too many D's and not enough A's!   30

NUMBER DRILL: Century Drive *(1 complete copy, up to 100)*   **DS**

2-Min.
Writings

For 1 for 2 for 3 for 4 for 5 for 6 for 7 for 8

for 9 for 10 for 11 for 12 for 13 for 14 for 15

for 16 for 17 for 18 for 19 for 20 for 21 for 22

for 23 for 24 for ┌Continue on up to 100. Ultimate┐
                  └goal is to reach 100 in 2 minutes.┘

HOW TO USE THE "PIVOT" METHOD . . .

It is often necessary to arrange a financial statement so that it is confined to a certain length of line or expanded to fill a particular length of line. Two facts make it easy to contract or expand the width of the statement: The explanations column can be as wide or as narrow as you wish, and leaders carry the eye over wide spaces..

When you wish a financial statement to fill an assigned length of line (for example, Job 3, below, is to fill a 60-space line), follow these steps:

1. Clear machine. Set the left margin stop for the assigned length of line.

2. Set the carriage at the point where you wish the statement to end.

3. Pivot from that point for the width of the last column (that is, backspace from the end point once for each character in the last column), and set a tab stop at the point reached.

4. Pivot from the tab stop (backspace from it)

for the intercolumn blank space and the width of the next-to-last column, and set a tab stop at the point reached.

5. If there are more columns, pivot to their starting point in the same way, always allowing for the intercolumn blank space.

Now you are ready to type the table. As in other methods, you use the tabulator only to locate the first item in each column; after that, you type leaders instead of using the tabulator mechanism.

(This method, incidentally, may be used for any table that appears in running context—in a letter, for example, or a manuscript—where the line length is defined in advance. If the pivoting results in more than six spaces between the first and other columns, use leaders to fill the gap.)

Use the pivot method in Job 3, below. If you are using 50 as a center, Column 1 will begin at 20 and the other columns will be pivoted from 80.

JOB 3

Financial
statement
  Exact copy
  Center
  3 tabs
  Open leaders
Words: 174

The Lincoln Packer Company   ◁ **60** ▷

SUMMARY STATEMENT OF PROFIT AND LOSS

For the Month Ending March 31, 19--   3 ➡

```
SALES . . . . . . . . . . . . . . . . . . . . $27,453.28

COST OF MERCHANDISE
      Starting Inventory . . . . . . . $15,267.00
      Inventory Purchases . . . . . . .   8,476.50
      Total Available . . . . . . . . $23,743.50
      Closing Inventory . . . . . . . . 12,613.50
      Cost of Merchandise Sold . . . . . . . . . . 11,130.00   2 ➡

GROSS PROFIT ON SALES . . . . . . . . . . . . $16,323.28   2 ➡

EXPENSES
      Selling Expense . . . . . . . . . $ 5,425.85
      Rent Expense . . . . . . . . . .   2,500.00
      Heat and Light . . . . . . . . .     620.43
      Depreciation of Equipment . . . .  1,000.00
      Total Expenses . . . . . . . . . . . . . . . 9,546.28

NET PROFIT, BEFORE TAXES . . . . . . . . . . . $ 6,777.00
```

UNIT 14
CORRESPONDENCE

In this unit: (1) postal cards, (2) indented addresses, and (3) indented-style letters. Before typing the jobs, review pages 41, 49, 82, 83, and 86; read carefully pages 115-124; and answer the questions in this unit's study guide on Workbook pages 99-100.

Note: The lessons in this and similar production units are presented in pairs, with Skill Drills and Production Practice provided in each pair of lessons. Two plans for apportioning the time given to these kinds of activities are given on page 41. Review with your teacher the plan that you are to follow.

WARMUP (*Each line 3 times*) ◁**60**▷ SS

```
a b c d e f g h i j k l m n o p q r s t u v w x y z . , / ?
39 28 47 56 10 #39 #28 #47 #56 #10 $39 $28 $47 $56 $10 $.10
Do they or do they not wish to have the lot we are selling?
```
12-Sec. 5| 10| 15| 20| 25| 30| 35| 40| 45| 50| 55| 60|

RHYTHM PREVIEW (*Each line 3 times*)

```
quick might dozen firms cards would start small blank leave
will find that copy five size long just from edge with form
you and are not can two for one use the top set six its get
```

ALPHABET-REVIEW PARAGRAPHS (*2 copies / si 1.25*) ◁**60**▷ DS

3-Min. Writings 1 | 2 | 3 | 4 | 5 | 6 | 7 | 8 | 9 | 10 | 11 | 12

0	You will find that more and more postal cards are used	11
4	in business. They are quick and easy to prepare. They are	23
8	not expensive; you can type two dozen for what might be the	35
12	cost of just one long letter. A card does not require that	47
16	a file copy be made. Some firms use printed form cards for	59
20	many kinds of announcements.	65
22	It is really quite easy to type on a postal card. You	76
25	insert it the long way, just as you would an envelope. You	88
29	start typing two or three lines from the top edge, with the	100
33	margin stops set so as to leave side margins of five or six	112
37	spaces. Despite its small size, you can get as many as 100	124
41	words on the blank side of any Government postal card.	135

Plus ➧   1 | 2 | 3 | 4

PRODUCTION PRACTICE
(*Jobs 1-4*)

Study pages 116 and 117; then type Jobs 1-4 on postal cards or on the postal-card forms on Workbook pages 101-102 or on slips of stiff paper cut to postal-card size (5½ by 3¼ inches).

HOW TO TYPE WITH "OPEN" LEADERS . . .

There are two "styles" of leaders. When periods are typed close together (one in each space), they are called "close." When the periods are spread (each period alternating with a blank space), they are then called "open." Close leaders are normally used, for they are quicker to type. However, when there are a great many leaders and not much other copy, or when the copy is double spaced, the use of open leaders gives a better appearance.

The arrangement of the page is set up the same for both styles. When you type the first line of open leaders, begin with a space first (note, below, the space between *Cash* and the first period). Be sure to stop in time to leave a space at the end of the line of leaders. When you type the first line, note whether the periods fall in the odd or even spaces on the scale; then, use that fact when you start each subsequent leader line. You will often need to space twice (note, below, the two spaces between *Accounts Receivable* and the first period), in order to keep all the periods in line.

When you type Job 2, use the standard back-spacing method to arrange your work. A key line appears below the statement.

JOB 2

Financial
statement
  Exact copy
  Center
  3 tabs
  Open leaders
Words: 137

```
            Elson, Hildreth, and Daucier, Inc.
               CONDENSED BALANCE SHEET
         For the Quarter Ending March 31, 19--

                       ASSETS
     Cash . . . . . . . . . . . $28,750
     Accounts Receivable   . . .  36,391
     Merchandise Inventory  . . .  22,457
     Equipment . . . . . . . . .  25,068
        TOTAL ASSETS  . . . . . . . . .  $112,666


                     LIABILITIES
     Accounts Payable . . . . . . $27,327
     Notes Payable  . . . . . . .     500
        TOTAL LIABILITIES . . . . . . . . .  $ 27,827


                   PROPRIETORSHIP
     Capital, January 1 . . . . . $30,500
     Net Profit . . . . . . . . .  54,339
     Capital, March 31 . . . . . . . . . .  84,839
        TOTAL LIABILITIES
        AND PROPRIETORSHIP . . . . . . . .  $112,666
```

Key: Merchandise Inventory....⁸....$28,750.²$112,666

HOW TO TYPE A POSTAL CARD, BLOCKED STYLE . . .

1. *Address:* Block it. Start on line 11, about an inch before the center (3 lines under the printed word *of*). Double space address of 3 lines; single space address of more lines.

2. *Message:* Set stops for margins of about ½ inch. Set a tab stop at the estimated center; start all the heading and closing lines there. Start on line 3. Use single spacing.

3. *Judgment:* If you ever need to save space, you may use any or all of these procedures:

A. Omit the complimentary closing.
B. Omit the reference initials.
C. Omit space between paragraphs.
D. Omit blank space after the date.
E. Reduce the space for the signature.
F. Type return address on front of card.

Cards holders, down . . .

Card holders, up . . . when typing on cards or envelopes

JOB 1

Postal card
  Shown in pica
  Blocked style
  Center tab
  Workbook form
Words: 85

JOB 2

Postal card
  Send the same
  message to:
Mr. Ralph Drury
28 Alamanda Street
Miami 33, Florida

> THIS SIDE OF CARD IS FOR ADDRESS
> 3

```
        Mr. James L. Benlow
        Benlow Realty Company
        1056 Alhambra Circle
        Coral Gables 34, Florida
```

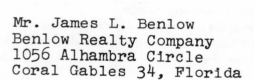

```
                    3

                    3928 East Palm Street
                    Coral Gables 4, Florida
                    February 2, 19--  2

Dear Mr. Benlow:  2

The Executive Committee of the Kiwanis Club
will meet on Friday, February 8, at 12:15 in
the Hastings Room of the Hotel Coral.  If you
cannot attend, please let me know, in order
that I may cancel your luncheon reservation.  3


                    Executive Secretary  1

JK:URS
```

Model postal card in blocked style

PRODUCTION PRACTICE (Jobs 1-3)

The three methods of setting up financial statements, mentioned in the Alphabet-Review Paragraphs, are used in these jobs: Job 1, the "copy" method, with the help of Workbook pages 205-206; Job 2, the regular method; and Job 3, the "pivot" method.

HOW TO USE THE "COPY" METHOD . . .

Most businessmen want the identical form and arrangement used, month after month and quarter after quarter, for their financial statements, in order that each new one may readily be compared with previous ones. One way to assure identical arrangements is to copy exactly the arrangement of a previous statement of the same kind. Steps:

1. Clear your machine.

2. Get a previous statement from the files and insert it in your machine.

3. Turn the paper up, counting and noting the number of lines in the top margin.

4. Note the point on the scale at which each line of the heading begins. (The line with the date in it may need adjustment.)

5. Draw the carriage to the start of the first column; set the margin stop there.

6. Space across the paper, setting tab stops at the start of the other columns.

7. Remove the file copy and insert your paper for the new statement. Type it.

When a statement has leaders, use the tab stops only to locate the first item in each column; thereafter, looking at your paper, type the leaders as you cross the page instead of using the tabulator.

Workbook pages 205-206 provide a "file copy" for you to use in Job 1. If you do not have a workbook, set the statement up by the standard method, the key line for which is shown under the statement below.

JOB 1

Financial
statement
  Exact copy
  Center
  3 tabs
  Close leaders
Words: 190

The Winslow-Halpin Company

SUMMARY STATEMENT OF PROFIT AND LOSS

For the Month Ending March 31, 19-- ₃ ➡

SALES		$48,442.60
DEDUCT COST OF MERCHANDISE SOLD:		
Merchandise Inventory, March 1	$16,495.12	
Merchandise Purchases	35,417.36	
Total Available for Sale	$51,912.48	
Merchandise Inventory, March 31	16,590.70	
Total Cost of Merchandise Sold		35,321.78
GROSS PROFIT ON SALES		$13,120.82
DEDUCT EXPENSES:		
Selling Expense	$ 4,273.54	
Rent Expense	1,044.00	
Heat and Light	273.10	
Depreciation of Equipment	430.00	
Total Expenses		6,020.64
NET PROFIT, BEFORE TAXES		$ 7,100.18

Key: ₃...Merchandise Inventory, March 31.....⁸....$16,495.12.²$48,442.60

HOW TO TYPE A POSTAL CARD, INDENTED STYLE . . .

1. *Address:* Indent it in steps of 5 spaces. Start on line 11, about an inch before the center (3 lines under the word *of*). Double space for 3 lines; single space for more. If a state or city name is long, typing both on one line may bring the state name too close to the edge; in such instances, type the name of the state on a line by itself.

2. *Message:* Set stops for margins of about ½ inch. Set a tab stop for the paragraph indention. Set a tab stop at the estimated center; begin all the heading and closing lines there — it is permissible, but not necessary, to indent them. Start the heading on line 3. Use single spacing.

3. *Judgment:* Same as on preceding page.

Return address is always blocked and single spaced. It starts on line 3, ½ inch from edge.

> 3 ⬅
>
> Mr. Richard Simms
> 5610 Jackson Street
> Philadelphia 24, Pa.
>
> (THIS SIDE OF CARD IS FOR ADDRESS)
> 3 ⬇
>
>
>
> Mr. Thomas Yardley
> 3928 Chelten Avenue
> Philadelphia 26
> Pennsylvania

JOB 3

Postal card
Shown in pica
Indented style
½-inch margins
Tabs every 5
Words: 117

JOB 4

Postal card
Send the same message to:
Mr. George Powers
4747 Frost Street
Philadelphia 36, Pa.

When half way down a card, adjust the paper bail so that its rollers press firmly on the card; then it will not slip as you type near the bottom edge.

> 3 ⬇
>
> February 3, 19--
> Fellow Legionnaire:
>
>   When Bob Lynch steps down from his rank as Post Commander at the March meeting, some kind of honor is due him. So, a committee of us is contacting all members of the Post to invite contributions. If we get enough money, we shall give him a wrist watch.
>
>   If you will contribute a dollar, send a check to me at my home address. Be sure to make the check to the <u>Bob Lynch Fund</u>, not to me personally.
>
>   Dick Simms

Model postal card in indented style

In this unit you will learn (1) how to type financial statements, (2) how to use leaders in tables, and (3) how to solve problems in column headings. Your work in this unit will be easiest if you first (1) review Units 7 and 15, (2) study pages 194-202, and (3) answer the study-guide questions on Workbook pages 203-204.

WARMUP (*Each line 3 times*)   ◁ **70** ▷

```
a s d f g h j k l ; l k j h g f d s a s d f g h j k l ; l k j h g f d
element handle usual corks laugh turns papa wish work may sod pan six
The theme that she worked on had something to do with eight elements.
```
12-Sec.5| 10| 15| 20| 25| 30| 35| 40| 45| 50| 55| 60| 65| 70|

PUNCTUATION PREVIEW (*Each line 3 times*)

```
Instead, machine, example, tables, method, PROFIT, hazard, size, Yes,
statements. quarter. periods. columns. wary. wish. eye. awake!
"money columns" "stub" (first column) --simply --that them; expenses:
```

ALPHABET-REVIEW PARAGRAPHS (*1 copy / si 1.31*)   ◁ **50** ▷
  DS

5-Min. Writings

  1 | 2 | 3 | 4 | 5 | 6 | 7 | 8 | 9 | 10

0	Of all the forms of tables, the ones easiest	9
2	to set up are financial statements. They are al-	19
4	ways in the same form, month after month, quarter	29
6	after quarter. The right way to set up a new one	39
8	is to copy the old one--that is, you get from the	49
10	files the last statement of the same type, insert	59
12	it in the machine, and set up your margin and tab	69
14	stops by eye. If there is none to copy, however,	79
16	you can plan it just as you would any other kind,	89
si 18	size, or shape of table--simply backspace to cen-	99
1.29 20	ter it. There is even a special method, based on	109
22	the fact that the explanations column can be wide	119
24	or narrow, as you may wish. You set your margins	129
26	for whatever line length you wish; you pivot from	139
28	the right margin, backspacing through your "money	149
30	columns" and setting tab stops for them; then you	159
32	use whatever space is left for your first column.	169

34	There are a few things for which to be wary.	9	178
36	For example, all dollar marks in a column must be	19	188
si 38	squared up--and you may overlook that the longest	29	198
1.35 40	number, which makes the dollar sign project most,	39	208
42	may be the one at the bottom of the column. Note	49	218
44	that you do not put six spaces between columns in	59	228
46	a statement; instead, put two spaces between your	69	238
48	money columns and eight spaces between the "stub"	79	248
50	(first column) and the first money column. Still	89	258
52	another hazard, in the use of leaders, is forget-	99	268
54	ting to leave a blank space before and after your	109	278
56	line of periods. Yes, you do have to stay awake!	119	288

Plus ▶   1 | 2

WARMUP (*Each line 3 times*)

◁**60**▷
SS

z y x w v u t s r q p o n m l k j i h g f e d c b a ; : / ?

39 28 47 56 10 39% 28% 47% 56% 10% (39) (28) (47) (56) (10)

They can take away the work we did when they pay us for it.

12-Sec. 5| 10| 15| 20| 25| 30| 35| 40| 45| 50| 55| 60|

RHYTHM PREVIEW (*Each line 3 times*)

taken noted judge their story basic quick would lines short

have ride down such work with true size were tell does sort

the dot how who one get for too can way use any ask not but

ALPHABET-REVIEW PARAGRAPHS (*2 copies / si 1.34*)

◁**60**▷
DS

3-Min. Writings   1 | 2 | 3 | 4 | 5 | 6 | 7 | 8 | 9 | 10 | 11 | 12

0   If you have ever taken a ride down a highway and noted   11

4   the billboards that dot the horizon, you have seen a lesson   23

8   in how to address an envelope. The experts who design such   35

12   displays judge their work by one rule: Make a good impres-   47

16   sion and get the story across in one glance. That is basic   59

20   for envelopes, too. Type the address neatly, so as to make   71

24   a good impression; and type it correctly, so that the post-   83

28   man can read it and understand it in one quick glance.   94

31   The quickest way to type an envelope is, of course, to   105

35   use blocked form, with single spacing. That is true of any   117

39   envelope, of any size. But if you were to ask a postman to   129

43   tell you exactly what he would prefer, he would specify the   141

47   indented form, with double spacing. He does not reject the   153

51   blocked lines, but he can sort indented lines more quickly.   165

Plus ➧   1 | 2 | 3 | 4

PRODUCTION PRACTICE (*Jobs 5-9*)

If you do not have the workbook that provides the envelope forms and letterheads for these and all the other production jobs, always improvise suitable materials. For envelopes, use slips of stiff paper cut to correct size. For letterheads, use plain paper on which you rule or crease a line (to represent the depth of a letterhead) about 2 inches from the top of your paper.

JOB 5

Envelopes

Study page 119; then address in indented style small envelopes (6½ by 3⅜ inches) for the Job 6 and Job 7 letters, and a large envelope (9½ by 4⅛ inches) for the Job 8 letter. Use envelopes on Workbook pages 104, 106, 108.

7-Min.
Writings
si
1.31

Some time ago, we asked you and your[1] staff to take a look at our new[2] garage and | 16
to study its operating[3] methods. We know that your men have[4] been busy in this proj- | 32
ect and are[5] making headway; the manager of the[6] garage has frequently told me of | 48
the[7] visits of men in your squad. | 55

It[8] is our hope that you will soon be[9] able to complete your study and to[10] let us have | 72
your report. There are[11] several urgent reasons why we want[12] you to complete your | 88
study as soon as[13] you can; here are four: | 96

First,[14] there has not been a decrease in the[15] number of complaints that we are[16] | 112
getting from our customers; if anything,[17] we note a slight increase in the[18] number. We | 129
must not delay taking[19] action much longer. | 138

Secondly,[20] our loss from the operation of the[21] garage is mounting. Again, we feel[22] | 154
that some action must be taken. While[23] we wait for the findings of your[24] group, the | 170
balance sheet is going[25] from bad to worse. | 179

Thirdly, the[26] staff at the garage is becoming more[27] and more upset about the work | 195
of[28] your group and the possible outcomes[29] of your study. Rumors of all kinds[30] are fly- | 212
ing about the garage. The[31] men reflect the strain under which[32] they are working. One | 229
foreman has[33] quit, and eight workmen came to us[34] today to ask how much longer the | 245
study[35] will go on. | 248

Fourthly, the agent[36] of the firm that wishes to have the[37] property tells me that | 264
his client[38] has just about given up on this[39] deal and has begun to look at other[40] prop- | 281
erties. The agent may or may[41] not be using the delay to bring down[42] our price, but | 297
his pressure enters[43] the story. | 304

In view of these elements,[44] we should like to urge you to[45] wind up the study as | 320
quickly as you[46] can and to let us have the report[47] of your findings. It would not be[48] | 337
fair—either to our stockholders or[49] to our employees—to extend the[50] duration or the | 354
costs of this investigation.[51] | 360

We do not, of course, want[52] you to delete any detail of the study[53] simply to speed | 376
up the completion[54] of your work. But our officers[55] and board members are no less | 392
eager[56] to see the findings of your work[57] than are the men in the garage. We[58] do hope, | 409
therefore, that you will[59] find you can present your report soon;[60] and we ask that you | 426
let us know[61] how soon you believe that it will be[62] possible to bring your report to us.[63] | 443

HOW TO ADDRESS ENVELOPES IN INDENTED STYLE . . .

1. *Spacing:* Double space a 3-line address; single space 4 or more lines.

2. *Placement:* Begin about ½ inch before the estimated center of envelope. Start on line 14 of a large envelope (9½ by 4⅛ inches). Start on line 12 of a small envelope (6½ by 3⅝ inches).

3. *Arrangement:* Indent lines of an indented address in steps of 5 spaces each.

4. *Long State Name:* If it would come close to the edge of the envelope, type the name of the state on a line by itself.

5. *Special Notations:* Mailing directions ("Airmail," "Special Delivery," "Registered," etc.) are typed under the position of the stamp. Other notations ("Please Forward," "Personal," etc.) are typed at the bottom left, 2 lines below the address and ½ inch from the left edge of the envelope.

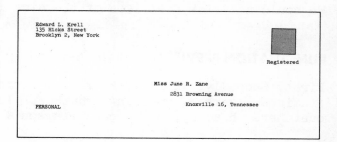

HOW TO ARRANGE LETTERS IN INDENTED STYLE . . .

1. *Spacing:* May be single or double. (If double, be sure to double the word count of the body before using the placement table.)

2. *Placement:* Same as other basic styles.

3. *Date:* Usually blocked at right but may be centered or may be started at the center.

4. *Body:* Indent paragraphs 5 spaces. Some offices indent them 7, 10, or 15 spaces.

5. *Closing Lines:* Arrange them in steps of 5 spaces. If they are short (see page 120), the first may begin at the center. If any closing line might protrude into the right margin, however, start the first line far enough to the left of the center to provide adequate space for even the longest line.

So many tab stops are used that it is common practice to put one every 5 spaces.

Semiblocked:
Inside address is blocked at margin. Closing lines are blocked at center.

Indented:
Inside address is indented in steps of 5. Closing lines are indented in steps of 5.

HOW TO PLACE A LETTER ON THE PAGE . . .

		Under 100	100 to 200	Over 200
STEP **1:**	Drop to date-line position (line 14, or 2 lines below letterhead, whichever is lower).			
STEP **2:**	Estimate number of words in body of the letter	Under 100	100 to 200	Over 200
STEP **3:**	Set margin stops for corresponding line length*	4 inches	5 inches	6 inches
STEP **4:**	Type date; then drop this many lines to address	8 lines	6 lines	4 lines

*Reminder: There are 10 pica spaces to an inch, 12 elite spaces to an inch.

WARMUP *(Each line 3 times)*

```
aa;;ssllddkkffjjgghhffjjddkkssll a;sldkfjghfjdksla;sldkfjghfjdksla;sl
lament enamel icicle sight spend shame duty with sick man pay and fit
We could not risk the lives of the sick men, and so she stayed there.
```

12-Sec.5| 10| 15| 20| 25| 30| 35| 40| 45| 50| 55| 60| 65| 70|

PUNCTUATION PREVIEW *(Each line 3 times)*

```
First, Secondly, Thirdly, Fourthly, course, group, Again, hope, quit,
findings. garage. working. number. longer. report. squad. INC.
customers; headway; soon; can; Pearson & Research & Vice-President J.
```

PRODUCTION PRACTICE *(Jobs 10-11)*

The material on the next page is the body of a 2-page letter. Type it three ways:

1. *Timed Writing.* It has speed markers for a 7-minute writing — the tiny figure nearest where you stop is your speed. The copy may also be used for a 10-minute writing. To compute 10-minute speed: Note the word count at the end of the last line you finish completely; add to it 1 word for each additional 5 strokes you type; then divide the total by 10 (simply mark off one decimal place).

Make a heavy crease about 2 inches from the foot of your paper; as you type near the crease, the change of sound will warn you to type just 2 or 3 more lines on the page.

2. *Job 10.* Arrange the copy as a blocked letter (review pages 186 and 187). Use the workbook form. Use a 3-line page-2 heading.

3. *Job 11.* Arrange the copy as a blocked-style memo (review pages 92 and 187). Use a 1-line page-2 heading.

As a warning signal that you are approaching the bottom of the page, put a light pencil mark about 2 inches from the bottom.

JOB 10

◁ **6 in.** ▷
SS
17/2
▽

Blocked letter
Unarranged
Letterhead
Subject line
Center tab
Words: 488
Body: 442

Type the letter on page 193 as a 2-page letter in blocked form. Use today's date.

Address: Mr. Edward B. Osborne
      Pearson & Osborne
      829 East Sixth Street
      Tulsa 20, Oklahoma
Subject: Request for Your Report
Closing: Very truly yours,
      Gristmeyer Brothers, Inc.
      Richley J. Gristmeyer
      Executive Vice-President

JOB 11

◁ **6 ½ in.** ▷
SS
7
▽

Blocked memo
Unarranged
Plain paper
2 tab stops
Words: 477
Body: 442

Type the letter on page 193 as a 2-page memo in blocked form, on plain paper (see Job 2, page 92). Use today's date. Display the four enumerated paragraphs by using numerals and block-indenting the material in these paragraphs (see Job 4, page 93).

To: Charles F. Hendrickson
      Research & Methods Department
From: Richley J. Gristmeyer
      Executive Vice-President
Subject: Request for Your Report
Closing: Richley J. Gristmeyer

Indented Letter Style

◁ **4 in.** ▷
DS
14/8
▽

JOB 6

Indented letter
Shown in pica
Use letterhead
Tab every 5
Words: 72
Body: 45

February 6, 19-- ₈ ➨

Use today's
date. Type
year in full.

Miss June R. Zane

    2831 Browning Avenue

        Knoxville 16, Tennessee

Dear Miss Zane:

     The indented form is one of the few
letter styles that can be typed in double
spacing. It is good for short letters
that you may wish to spread out.

     Be sure to double the word count in
the body before you plan the placement.

           Yours very truly, ₄ ➨

Standard
punctuation:
colon after
salutation.

Standard
punctuation:
comma after
closing line.

            E. L. Krell ₂ ➨

Type your own
initials in
place of URS.

ELK:URS

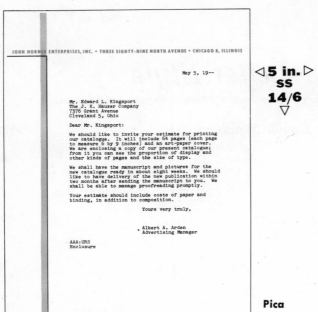

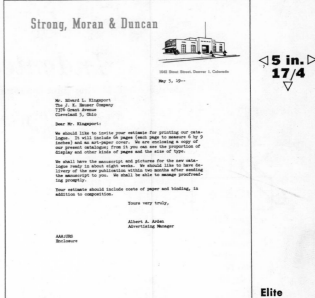

JOB 6: *Left-Weighted Stationery*

When standard 8½- by 11-inch stationery has a band (or list of names) that blocks off the left margin area, shift center point ½ inch to right; then use standard letter placement.

JOB 7: *Right-Weighted Stationery*

When standard 8½- by 11-inch stationery is blocked off at right (here, letterhead is 2½ inches deep), use standard letter placement, but drop 2 less lines after typing the date.

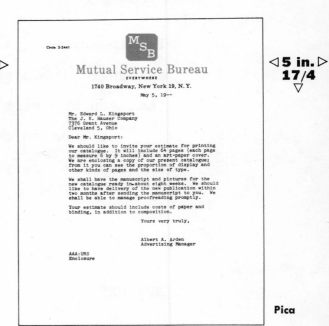

JOB 8: *Stationery for Window Envelope*

When standard 8½- by 11-inch stationery has a special position marked for the inside address, use standard placement for date and body, but type address in the marked area.

JOB 9: *Very Deep Letterhead*

When standard 8½- by 11-inch stationery has a very deep letterhead (here, 2½ inches), use standard placement, but drop 2 less lines after typing the date than you would otherwise.

Indented Letter Style

Address and Closing Lines Indented in 5-Space Steps • Paragraphs Indented 5 Spaces

With Single Spacing

◁ **5 in.** ▷
SS
14/6
▽

JOB 7

Indented letter
Shown in elite
Use letterhead
Tab every 5
Words: 204
Body: 169

February 7, 19-- 6 ➡

Mr. Harold Faunce
    2810 Forest Avenue
        Austin 4, Texas

Dear Mr. Faunce:

    This letter is set up in the indented form, as you will note by a glance at the inside address and closing of this letter. In each of these groups, the lines are indented in steps of five spaces each. Each paragraph is indented five spaces, too.

    The indentions would be slow if you had to tap the space bar five times for each of them, but they are fast if you set tab stops and use them. The office worker who types letters in this style all day long sets a tab stop every five spaces across the paper; then he is sure to have enough of them set to use for any length of letter.

    One care that you must exercise when you use this form is to make sure that none of the closing lines project into the right margin. Start the first of the closing lines far enough to the left to assure that there is room for all the other lines in the closing. 2 ➡

Yours very truly, 2 ➡

Start closing
5 spaces before
the center.

Use the shift
lock for the
company name.

INTERNATIONAL SUPPLY COMPANY 4 ➡

George Chalmers
Training Director 2 ➡

GC:URS

121   **CORRESPONDENCE**

Part 4
LESSON
Unit 14
85

Letter for Mr. John H. Hartwell, Flynn & French, Inc., 9035 Venice Boulevard, Los Angeles 34, California.

	1	2	3	4	5	6	7	8	9	10	11	12	13	14	Cont'd

44   Dear Mr. Hartwell: We wish to learn whether, when our contracts   319

46   come up for renewal in a few more months, there will be any prospects   333

48   of your offering lower prices for the goods that we have been getting   347

50   from your company for the past three years. The answer is important.   361

52   We have two reasons for inquiring about this now. First, we are   374

53   going to press with a new catalogue in about six weeks, by which time   388

55   we should have a firm basis on which to set prices. Second, our com-   402

57   petition is underselling us on six of the items that we get from you.   416

59   We ask that you give this subject close study and tell us within   429

61   three weeks how much of a price reduction, if any, we can expect from   443

63   you on future orders. Very sincerely yours, George K. Brown, Manager   457

Plus ▶   1   2

PRODUCTION PRACTICE
(Jobs 4-9)

Study the miniature letters (below and next page) that show different arrangements when the same letter is typed in blocked form on various designs and sizes of stationery. Then, type the letter above in each arrangement; note that the letter above is not the same as the letter in the illustrations. Use the letterheads on Workbook pages 195-202 or sheets of paper ruled to resemble the stationery.

JOBS 4-9

Blocked letters
Unarranged
Words, each: 165
Body, each: 123

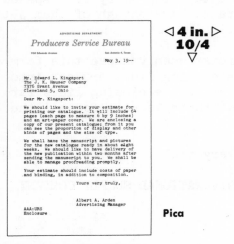

◁ **4 in.** ▷
10/4
▽

Pica

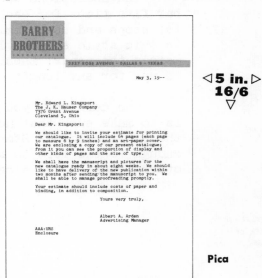

◁ **5 in.** ▷
16/6
▽

Pica

JOB 4: *Half-Page Size Stationery*

This 5½- by 8½-inch paper requires telescoping the letter. Type the date a double space under the letterhead, drop 4 lines to the inside address, and keep the side margins ½ or 1 inch wide.

JOB 5: *Baronial (Monarch) Stationery*

This 7¼- by 10½-inch paper (shown here with a wide letterhead) is given standard letter placement (page 119), except that the limit on the longest line is 5½ inches instead of 6.

JOB 8

Indented letter
Shown in elite
Use letterhead
Tab every 5
Words: 98
Body: 65

◁**4 in.**▷
SS
14/8
▽

February 7, 19--

Mrs. J. Frank Howell
411 North Street
    Milltown, Maine

Dear Mrs. Howell:

    The uniforms that you ordered on January 21   9
will be ready on February 14, as we promised.   18

    At the time you placed your order, you said   27
that you would notify us later whether you would   37
stop in to pick up the uniforms or whether you   46
might prefer to have us deliver them. Please use   56
the enclosed card to indicate your decision.   65

       Yours very truly,

       COMMONWEALTH PRODUCTS

         John E. Burton

JEB:URS
Enclosure

JOB 9

Indented letter

    Type another copy of the letter above, this time using double spacing. Note that this short, 65-word letter becomes an average-length, 130-word letter when it is double spaced.

◁**5 in.**▷
DS
14/6
▽

Lessons 86-87 : *Skill Drills*

WARMUP (*Each line 3 times*)

◁**60**▷
SS

```
aAbBcCdDeEfFgGhHiIjJkKlLmMnNoOpPqQrRsStTuUvVwWxXyYzZ;:/?.,-
39 28 47 56 10 39-- 28-- 47-- 56-- 10-- 39* 28* 47* 56* 10*
How can we pay the man for the job when he has not done it?
```

12-Sec. 5| 10| 15| 20| 25| 30| 35| 40| 45| 50| 55| 60|

RHYTHM PREVIEW (*Each line 3 times*)

```
April honor speak which could title order yours menus world
Year this city does most been like your hold know make duty
Man who has our job may let all its you can ask him did and
```

PRODUCTION PRACTICE (*Jobs 10-12*)

    Type Jobs 10-12 on workbook letterheads. For Optional Job 12-A, use plain paper with a line ruled or creased across the paper 2 inches from the top, to represent a letterhead.

WARMUP *(Each line 3 times)*   ◁**70**▷

aa ;; ss ll dd kk ff jj gg hh ff jj dd kk ss ll aa ;; ss ll dd kk ff
emblem dismal embody right widow blame dish hand paid sow and wit to
The drops of water from the icicle quickly put out the bright flame.

12-Sec.5| 10| 15| 20| 25| 30| 35| 40| 45| 50| 55| 60| 65| 70|

PUNCTUATION PREVIEW *(Each line 3 times)*

reduction, secondly, whether, French, months, Brown, page, wide, now,
distinction. orders. using. years. work. this. him. you. Inc.
Hartwell: typist: plan: paper; wide; narrow; work; (that margins).

ALPHABET-REVIEW PARAGRAPHS *(2 copies / si 1.28)*   ◁**70**▷
                                                                          DS

7-Min. Writing																

1 | 2 | 3 | 4 | 5 | 6 | 7 | 8 | 9 | 10 | 11 | 12 | 13 | 14

0   The size paper that is used for the majority of business letters   13

2 is the common page, eight and a half inches wide, eleven inches long.   27

4 The printing at the top normally takes up about one and a half or one   41

6 and three-quarters inches from the top of the sheet. And right there   55

8 all agreement stops, for each businessman wants his letter to have an   69

10 extra touch of distinction. One man wants colored paper; another has   83

12 to have colored ink on white paper. One man wants a big picture that   97

14 shows his product or his mills. One man wants his printed letterhead   111

16 to be wide; the next wants it to be narrow; a third insists on having   125

18 it lopsided. Some want paper cut in a different size. Now, all this   139

20 has a meaning for the typist: He must adjust his letter placement to   153

22 fit the kind and shape and design of stationery that is given to him.   169

24   It is easy to adjust the placement plan that you know, if you do   180

26 some trial runs and criticize your work. You know that there are two   194

28 expansion joints in a placement plan: the space between the date and   208

30 the inside address, and the length of line (that is, the width of the   222

32 margins). The width of the side margins ought to be just about equal   236

34 to the space between the date and the inside address--plus or minus a   250

36 quarter inch or so. If you are wise, you will test the plan you know   264

38 by trying to use it on some experimental work; then you can judge how   278

40 you need to change the plan, if at all, to make it fit the paper that   292

42 you will be using. The next six jobs will give you practice in this.   306

Plus ▶   1 | 2

⌈Continue with the letter⌉
⌊on the top of next page.⌋

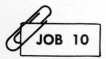

M B C Madison Business Council

120 Monona Avenue • Madison 2, Wisconsin

JOB 10

Indented letter
Shown in pica
Use letterhead
Tab every 5
Address below
Words: 196
Body: 162

February 9, 19-- ₆ ➡

Dear Mr. Hughes:

Each spring the members of the Madison Business Council select and honor at a dinner the member of the Legislature who has done the most to promote the growth of business in our state. I am privileged to inform you that you have been awarded this honor for this year. We should like to invite you to attend and to speak at the dinner in your honor.

We should like to hold the dinner on a Saturday evening in April. If you would let us know which date would be most convenient to you, we could then proceed to make the arrangements for the dinner.

We should also like to know what title you will give your address, in order that we may release it to the papers at the same time we announce your name. We expect to make the news public on April 2, and so we hope to complete all the details by that date. ₂ ➡

Yours very sincerely, ₄ ➡

Executive Secretary ₂ ➡

The Honorable Frederick Hughes
Member of the Legislature
The State House
Madison 2, Wisconsin

Use no reference
initials when an
address is typed
below the letter.

This letter illustrates one "official" arrangement used when writing to public officials and other dignitaries. See page 55 for another "official" form.

8. The page-2 heading is typed on line 7, leaving 6 lines in the top margin. Two blank lines are left between the heading and the material that follows it.

9. The second page of a memo differs in one regard: If it is addressed to a group of people, it is better to identify the page by its subject (example: <u>Personnel Order No. 8</u>) instead of by a listing of the group of addressees.

I hope that this information solves your problem, Mr. Carr. I should be glad to answer any other questions you may have.

Very sincerely yours, 4 ➤

Ralph E. Jones
Training Consultant 2 ➤

REJ:URS

Page 2 of a 2-page letter, with a standard page-2 heading

JOB 2

Letter
Words: 127

Type another copy of Page 2, above. Arrange it with the heading lines blocked at the left, as shown in the illustration below.

JOB 3

Memo
Words: 95

Type another copy of Page 2, above. Arrange it as the second page of a memo, *Personnel Order No. 8*, as shown below. Omit last paragraph, complimentary closing, and the writer's title.

Mr. John Reed Carr
Page 2
May 3, 19--

8. The page-2 heading is typed on line 7, leaving 6 lines in the top margin. Two blank lines are left between the heading and the material that follows it.

9. The second page of a memo differs in one regard: If it is addressed to a group of people, it is better to identify the page by its subject (example: Personnel Order No. 8) instead of by a listing of the group of addressees.

I hope that this information solves your problem, Mr. Carr. I should be glad to answer any other questions you may have.

Very sincerely yours,

Ralph E. Jones
Training Consultant

REJ:URS

Page 2 of a 2-page letter, with heading lines blocked at left

Personnel Order No. 8   - 2 -   May 3, 19--

8. The page-2 heading is typed on line 7, leaving 6 lines in the top margin. Two blank lines are left between the heading and the material that follows it.

9. The second page of a memo differs in one regard: If it is addressed to a group of people, it is better to identify the page by its subject (example: Personnel Order No. 8) instead of by a listing of the group of addressees.

Ralph E. Jones

REJ:URS

Page 2 of a 2-page memo, with a subject line for identification

JOB 11

Indented letter
In elite
Letterhead
Tab every 5
Address below
Words: 153
Body: 122

1 | 2 | 3 | 4 | 5 | 6 | 7 | 8 | 9 | 10 | 11 | 12   ◁ 5 in. ▷
SS

February 9, 19-- 6 ➡ 14/6
▽

Dear Judge Young:

We shall be holding our annual Man-of-the-Year dinner 11
some Saturday evening in April. It will be no secret to you, 23
although it is to the rest of the world, that Fred Hughes is 35
The Man. I am writing to him today to let him know and to 47
ask him to give us the date that is most convenient to him. 59
I shall let you know the date as soon as I get it from him. 72

Can we count on you once more to serve as our toastmaster 83
at the dinner? You did such a fine job at the dinner last 95
year that all of us who are on the committee want you for that 108
honor and duty again this year. We do hope you accept this 120
invitation. 2 ➡ 122

Yours very sincerely, 4 ➡

Executive Secretary 2 ➡

The Honorable Judge John Young
        Federal Court Building
            Madison 2, Wisconsin

JOB 12

Indented letter
Letterhead
Tab every 5
Words: 97
Body: 68

1 | 2 | 3 | 4 | 5 | 6 | 7 | 8   ◁ 4 in. ▷
SS

February 9, 19-- ? ➡ 14/8
▽

Manager, The Blake House
    211 Atwood Street
        Madison 4, Wisconsin

Dear Sir:

Our organization will be holding its 7
annual Man-of-the-Year dinner some Saturday 16
evening in April. Attendance will be about 25
200 or 250 persons. 29

Optional

JOB 12-A

Indented letter
Using double
spacing, send
same letter to:
Manager, Hotel Madison
3338 Winnemac Avenue
Madison 5, Wisconsin

Please let us know for which Saturday 37   ◁ 5 in. ▷
evening your main ballroom will be avail- 45   DS
able and what menus you can provide us at 54   14/6
$5.00 and $7.50 a plate. We shall need 62   ▽
this information by February 17. 68

Yours very sincerely, ? ➡

Executive Secretary, ? ➡

DW:URS

Model 2-Page Letter

Date Backspaced from Right Margin • Closing Lines Blocked at Center • Other Lines Blocked Left

In Blocked Form

JOB 1

Blocked letter
In pica
Letterhead
Words: 448
Body: 398

May 3, 19-- ◁**6 in.**▷
ss
4
▽

Mr. John Reed Carr
Director of Training
Parke-Welles Inc.
1209 Washington Avenue
St. Louis 8, Missouri

Dear Mr. Carr:

This 2-page letter illustrates the guiding rules for letters that take more than one page.   These are the rules:

1.   The line length and top margin are the same as for a long letter: The typist uses a 6-inch line of writing; types the date 2 lines below the letterhead or on line 14, whichever is lower; and drops 4 lines from the date to the inside address.

2.   The bottom margin of page 1 should be 7 or 8 lines deep, so that it will be slightly broader than either side margin; but it can be as many as 10 lines deep or as few as 5.

3.   At least 2 lines of a paragraph should appear at the foot of page 1 and at the top of page 2.   If a paragraph contains 3 lines, they should all be typed on one or the other page.

4.   Page 1 is typed on a letterhead; page 2 is typed on plain paper of the same quality as that used for the letterhead.

5.   Page 2 and each additional page should have a heading that is complete enough to identify the page if it were separated from the rest of the letter.   The heading should include the name of the addressee, the page number, and the date.

6.   The most common arrangement of a page-2 heading is with the name of the addressee at the left, the date at the right, and the page number centered between them.   These items may, however, be blocked at either the right or the left margin.

7.   To make it easier to see the page number, it may be displayed with hyphens, with parentheses, or with the word <u>Page</u>.

UNIT 15
TABULATION

In this unit: (1) ruled tables, (2) boxed tables, and (3) tables with double-column "braced" headings. The jobs of this unit will be easy if, before starting to type them, you first review the tabulation aids in Unit 7, read the pages of this unit, and then answer the study questions on Workbook pages 117-118.

◁ **60** ▷

WARMUP *(Each line 3 times)*

```
cab ade fag ham aim jar kay lax pan oat qua was vat tap zag
39 28 47 56 10 39.0 28.0 47.0 56.0 10.0 3.9 2.8 4.7 5.6 1.0
This is not the time when we ought to mail out their order.
```
12-Sec.   5| 10| 15| 20| 25| 30| 35| 40| 45| 50| 55| 60|

RHYTHM PREVIEW *(Each line 3 times)*

```
about along short count won't until sheet three lines paper
know come into such plan turn easy take time just once page
cut new ran few ago out let try off top now are say get end
```

ALPHABET-REVIEW PARAGRAPHS *(2 copies / si 1.28)*

◁ **60** ▷ DS

3-Min. Writings

	1	2	3	4	5	6	7	8	9	10	11	12

0 Just about the time that we think we know all there is 11
4 to know about typing, along will come somebody with a short 23
8 cut that is new to us. I ran into such a plan a few months 35
12 ago. It is a plan for getting the arithmetic out of verti- 47
16 cal centering. All you have to do is to back down from the 59
20 center of the paper. Let me explain, even though you won't 71
24 quite realize how easy it is until you try it for yourself. 83

28 If you insert your paper far enough for the bottom and 94
31 top to square up at the guide, your line of writing will be 106
35 two or three lines above the middle of the sheet--take time 118
39 to check this, just once, by inserting a page with a crease 130
43 across its center and noting how far it is from the line of 142
47 writing. Well, what you do is insert the paper and turn it 154
51 up to its center; then, you turn the cylinder back once for 166
55 each two lines in the copy, almost exactly the way that you 178
59 center a line horizontally by backing up from the midpoint. 190

Plus ➡ 1 | 2 | 3 | 4

PRODUCTION PRACTICE *(Jobs 1-5)*

Before beginning these jobs, review the topics indicated in the adjacent column; then, analyze Jobs 1-5 carefully and center each on a full sheet of paper (8½ x 11 inches).

HOW TO	PAGES
Use the tabulator	20
Center vertically	29
Center columns	58-59
Center headings	61-62

UNIT 22
CORRESPONDENCE

In this unit : (1) how to type 2-page letters, and (2) how to arrange a letter when stationery is small or when the printed letterhead is unusual in design. The jobs will be easiest if you first read pages 186-194 and answer the questions on Workbook pages 191-192.

WARMUP *(Each line 3 times)* ◁70▷

```
a;sldkfjghfjdksla;sldkfjghfjdksla;s
burlap island auburn their handy tight such they maid aid the for did
They sent him the pair of shoes that he had paid for by working hard.
```
12-Sec.5| 10| 15| 20| 25| 30| 35| 40| 45| 50| 55| 60| 65| 70|

PUNCTUATION PREVIEW *(Each line 3 times)*

```
however, rather, hokum, trap, then, well, name, bad, him, may, 14, 3,
letter.  pages.  Carr.  date.  then.  read.  have.  page.  1.  2.  3.
Page.  Carr:  rules:  me."  (example:  No. 11) lower; course; regard;
```

ALPHABET-REVIEW PARAGRAPHS *(1 copy / si 1.31)* ◁50▷ DS

5-Min. Writings

1 | 2 | 3 | 4 | 5 | 6 | 7 | 8 | 9 | 10

```
 0        Most of us fall into the trap, now and then,         9
 2    of trying to squeeze on one page a letter that is       19
 4    long enough to justify using two pages.  Somehow,       29
 6    we begrudge the extra sheet of paper or the dozen       39    si 1.36
 8    or so seconds involved in inserting one more pack       49
10    of paper and typing a heading on the second page.       59

12        Well, let us not fall into any trap; rather,    9   68
14    let's look for each chance to stretch our letters  19   78
16    into two pages.  Think of the person who gets the  29   88
18    letter.  In one hand he holds a letter that is so  39   98
20    tight that the signer had to squeeze his name, to  49  108    si 1.25
22    get it in.  In the other hand he holds our letter  59  118
24    that has generous margin space and that runs over  69  128
26    to an extra page.  Which letter will impress him,  79  138
28    will please him, will make him feel that the sub-  89  148
30    ject of the letter merits his thoughtful reading?  99  158

32        "When I see a letter that is squeezed," said   9  167
33    a business acquaintance of mine, "I get a feeling  19  177
35    that the writer is going to put a squeeze on me."  29  187    si 1.34
37    That is mere hokum, of course; but it does reveal  39  197
39    that the allover appearance of a letter does make  49  207
41    a general impression that can prejudice, for good  59  217
43    or for bad, the mind of the reader even before he  69  227
45    starts to read.  The investment of an extra page,  79  237
47    plus a few seconds, can pay rich dividends to us.  89  247
```
Plus ➤   1 | 2

PRODUCTION PRACTICE *(Jobs 1-3)*

Read closely the 2-page letter in Job 1 before copying it. Note that Jobs 2 and 3 require that you retype only the *second* page of the two pages in the long letter.

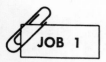

JOB 1

3-column table
Exact copy
Center
Plain paper
Words: 48

ADVERTISING RATIOS 2 →

January, 19-- 3 →

Insertion Order	Number of Readers	Cost per Thousand 2 →
4,534	2,000,000	$4.00
4,535	50,000	3.50
4,536	675,000	3.75
4,537	1,125,000	4.00
4,538	725,000	4.25
4,539	66,000	6.00

Key: Insertion......Number of......Cost per

Columns of numbers must align at right. Set tab stop for longest number; then space in for shorter numbers. Exception: After typing $ sign, shift tab stop over for rest of column.

HOW TO TYPE A TABLE WITH HORIZONTAL RULES . . .

1. *The lines are made* of underscores. A double rule consists of 2 lines: After typing one line and drawing the carriage back by hand, use the variable spacer (in left cylinder knob) to advance the paper about 1/16 inch; then type the second line.

2. *Center the table* just as you would any other table: Backspace from the middle of the paper (centering the key items 6 spaces apart) to reach the position for the left margin stop; then space across the paper, setting the tab stops for the columns.

3. *To position the first rule,* tap the underscore key instead of the space bar when "spacing" across the paper to set the tabs. Be sure to continue the underscoring, however, through the width of the last column.

4. *The correct use of rules:* a double line above the column headings, and a single line under them and at the bottom of the table.

5. *Optional refinement:* Extend the rules so that they overhang the table 3 spaces on each side. This refinement is not essential but is worth the effort for important work.

JOB 2

3-column table
Exact copy
Center
Plain paper
With rules
Words: 71

ADVERTISING RATIOS 2 →

January, 19-- 1 →

2 →

Insertion Order	Number of Readers	Cost per Thousand 1 →

2 →

4,534	2,000,000	$4.00
4,535	50,000	3.50
4,536	675,000	3.75
4,537	1,125,000	4.00
4,538	725,000	4.25
4,539	66,000	6.00	1 →

Key: Insertion......Number of......Cost per

Always single space before and double space after typing a horizontal rule.

WARMUP: Space-Bar Drill *(Each line 3 times)* ◁52▷

a b c d e f g h i j k l m n o p q r s t u v w x y z
z y x w v u t s r q p o n m l k j i h g f e d c b a
1 2 3 4 5 6 7 8 9 0 9 8 7 6 5 4 3 2 1 2 3 4 5 6 7 8

NUMBER DRILL: We 23's *(Each line 3 times)*

We try to tie up our puppy. You tore our property.
23 546 59 583 70 974 07006. 697 5943 974 04903456.

NUMBER DRILL: ½ ¼ *(Each line 3 times)*

;½; ;½; ½½½ 10½ 28½ 39½ 47½ 56½ 10½ 28½ 39½ 47½ 56½
;½; ;¼; ¼¼¼ 10¼ 28¼ 39¼ 47¼ 56¼ 10¼ 28¼ 39¼ 47¼ 56¼

SYMBOL DRILL: / _ *(Each line 3 times)*

/// 1/3 and/or 1/5 and/or 1/6 and/or 1/7 and/or 1/8
_ _ tea rub arc end off lug ash ink awl arm won too
[bracket] [one] [two] [three] [four] [five] [seven]

SYMBOL SENTENCES *(Each line 3 times)*

½-Min. Writings

| 1 | 2 | 3 | 4 | 5 | 6 | 7 | 8 | 9 | 10 |

We divided it, 1/4 to Bob and 3/4 to Joe and/or Al. 11
We divided it, 40¼ to Dick, 29¼ to Tom, 39½ to Dan. 21
We divided it, 49 1/4 to Richard and 49 3/4 to Sam. 32

The linking words to use are and, or, but, and for. 14
Check on your stroking and your carriage returning. 30
Jake was reading to him from The Call of the Yukon. 44

Use underscore to specify or to group words.

NUMBER-SYMBOL PARAGRAPH *(2 copies)* ◁60▷ DS

Some fraction rules: (1) If you build a fraction, you must build all other fractions in the same sentence. (2) If you must build a mixed number [like 19 3/4], a space must separate the whole number and fraction. (3) If you type ½ or ¼ on a stencil or master, type the fraction twice [or, better yet, build it, if you have space] so that it will be clear.

CENTURY DRIVE *(1 complete copy, up to 100)*

2-Min. Writings

Did 1 did 2 did 3 did 4 did 5 did 6 did 7 did 8 did 9 did 10
did 11 did 12 did 13 did 14 did 15 did [Continue on up to 100. Ultimate goal is to reach 100 in 2 minutes.]

JOB 3

3-column table
Exact copy
Center
Plain paper
With rules
Words: 110

AMENDED SALES QUOTAS 2 ➡
Fourth Quarter, 19-- 1 ➡

Name	Quota	Headquarters
Allerton, Fred	$ 7,500	Chicago
Cox, Frances	9,000	New York
Farley, Harold	6,000	Mobile
Jordan, Thomas	8,000	Seattle
Maxwell, Joe	6,500	Las Vegas
Paulson, Henry	7,500	Emporia
Taswell, Leo	8,000	Nashville
Victor, Fred	6,000	Denver
TOTAL	$58,500	....

2 ➡
1 ➡
2 ➡

1 ➡
2 ➡
1 ➡

SPECIAL NOTES:
1. Key items appear here in color.

2. To simplify the centering of column headings, a $ sign may be counted (as in Job 3) or ignored (Job 5, Column 3).

Indent word "Total" 1 space for each column in a table.

JOB 4

4-column table

Center
Plain paper
With rules
Words: 97

REPORT OF SALES 2 ➡
Fourth Quarter, 19-- 1 ➡

Rank	Name	Total Sales	Per Cent of Quota
1	Jordan, Thomas	$10,000	125
2	Cox, Frances	8,500	94 95
3	Paulson, Henry	6,700	89 90
4	Taswell, Leo	6,000	75
5	Victor, Fred	5,880	98
6	Maxwell, Joe	5,200	80
7	Farley, Harold	4,980	83
8	Allerton, Fred	4,500	75 60

2 ➡
1 ➡
2 ➡

1 ➡

Keep headings even at bottom.

JOB 5

5-column table

Center
Plain paper
With rules
Words: 121

ANALYSIS OF SALES REPORT
Fourth Quarter, 19--

Rank	Name	Quota	Total Sales	Per Cent of Quota
1	Jordan, Thomas	$8,000	$10,000	125
2	Victor, Fred	6,000	5,880	98
3	Cox, Frances	9,000	8,500	95
4	Paulson, Henry	7,500	6,750	90
5	Farley, Harold	6,000	4,980	83
6	Maxwell, Joe	6,500	5,200	80
7	Taswell, Leo	8,000	6,000	75
8	Allerton, Fred	7,500	4,500	60

WARMUP: **Reach Recall** *(Each line 3 times)*

◁ **50** ▷

```
aqa ;p; sws lol ded kik frf juj ftf jyj fgf jhj
fbf jnj fvf jmj dcd k,k sxs l.l aza ;/; ;?; ;:;
;0; s2s 191 d3d k8k f4f j7j f5f j6j 234 567 890
```

NUMBER DRILL: **39 28 10** *(Each line 3 times)*

```
3 9 39 139 391 1391 3939 9393 1931 193 931 93 9 3
2 8 28 128 281 1281 2828 8282 1821 182 821 82 8 2
1 0 10 110 011 1101 1010 0101 1011 101 010 01 0 1
```

NUMBER DRILL: **We 23's** *(Each line 3 times)*

12-Sec.
Writings

```
ewe 323 wow 292 eye 363 tot 595 pup 070 tree 5433
were 2343 weep 2330 peer 0334 toot 5995 peep 0330
wiry 2846 pity 0856 pipe 0803 wipe 2803 type 5603
```

| 12-Sec. | 5| | 10| | 15| | 20| | 25| | 30| | 35| | 40| | 45| | 50| |

NUMBER SENTENCES: **Mixed Numbers** *(Each line 3 times)*

½-Min.
Writings

	1	2	3	4	5	6	7	8	9	10	

```
He sold 3204 clips, 1675 pens, and 89 pads today.    10
We did Job 1281, Job 1390, and Job 4756 at night.    20
Team scores were:  90 - 84, 61 - 53, and 73 - 72.    30
Cars 19, 54, and 76 tied at 10:28 in the 3d race.    40
```

NUMBER DRILL: **Cumulative Count** *(3 copies)*

◁ **50** ▷

1-Min.
Writings

	1	2	3	4	5	6	7	8	9	10	

```
4701 3902 2803 5604 1005 1106 2807 6808 9109 3910    10
5611 9812 5913 8814 7615 7816 7617 7418 5519 6820    20
7921 9322 2023 3924 5825 5726 2827 3928 4729 5830    30
5631 1032 8233 4934 7735 6436 7337 9438 6539 9740    40
```

NUMBER-REVIEW PARAGRAPH *(2 copies / si 1.66)*

1- and 2-Min.
Writings

		1	2	3	4	5	6	7	8	9	10	
0	24	The Post Office Department includes not only										9
5	29	15 offices that handle lost packages and articles										19
10	34	but also 325 others that handle the dead letters.										29
15	39	In one annual report, tables show that 22,797,455										39
20	44	letters and 901,231 parcels reached the branches.										49

| Plus ▶ | 1 | 2 | 3 | 4 | 5 |

WARMUP (*Each line 3 times*) ◁ **60** ▷

```
eat bye ice few hex keg jet elm pen roe que set vet use zed
39 28 47 56 10 39 @ 28 @ 47 @ 56 @ 10 @ 39¢ 28¢ 47¢ 56¢ 10¢
They may be able to sell the whole lot before we can do so.
```
12-Sec. 5| 10| 15| 20| 25| 30| 35| 40| 45| 50| 55| 60|

RHYTHM PREVIEW (*Each line 3 times*)

```
model plane being seize every ahead prize quest tasks quota
true test drug shop jugs desk keep beat only dull need dare
job day new lab fix try way who one not can for old any par
```

ALPHABET-REVIEW PARAGRAPHS (*1 copy / si 1.27*) ◁ **50** ▷
                                                           DS

5-Min. Writings		1	2	3	4	5	6	7	8	9	10		

```
        0       Much of the work in any kind of job is about        9
        2   the same, day in and day out.  This is as true in      19
        4   the clouds where you test a new model of a plane,      29
        6   or in a lab where you work with a new drug, or in      39
Very    8   a shop where you design new ways to fix up broken      49
easy   10   jugs as it is at an office desk.  The way to keep      59
si 1.13 12  from being bored is to seize every chance to beat      69
       14   the record, to try the unique, and to find better      79
       16   ways to do all the things you have to do somehow.      89

       18       The only sure way to get ahead in most kinds     9|  98
       20   of work is to gain a reputation for doing good or    19| 108
       22   better work.  If you are the only person who does    29| 118
       24   a certain job, no one knows whether you deserve a    39| 128
Easy   26   prize or not.  Only in the routine tasks that you    49| 138
si 1.28 28  do in common with other people can what you do be    59| 148
       30   compared.  Only in these things can others recog-    69| 158
       32   nize that your work excels.  If you want success,    79| 168
       34   your quest should be for skill in doing the dull.    89| 178

       36       But there is one hazard about which most new     9| 187
       37   workers have to be cautioned, and that is the old    19| 197
       39   danger that the new worker does not know what has    29| 207
Normal 41   already been tried and rejected by the older mem-    39| 217
si 1.43 43  bers of the firm.  A quota of natural mistakes in    49| 227
       45   judgment is permitted to any newcomer, but trying    59| 237
       47   to tell more experienced workers what they should    69| 247
       49   be doing is not included in the newcomer's quota.    79| 257
       51   One has to reach par before he dare coach others.    89| 267
```
Plus ➧   1 | 2

PRODUCTION PRACTICE (*Jobs 6-9*)

After reading closely the explanations on pages 129-130, type Jobs 6-9. Center each on a full sheet of paper. Jobs 7-9 should be ruled after the paper is removed from the machine. Using a contrasting color for the ruling will add to the attractiveness of the tables.

WARMUP: Capital Control (*Each line 3 times*)

◁ 50 ▷

```
Wxyz wXyz wxYz wxyZ Wxyz WXyz WXYz WXYZ WxYz wXyZ
aaGa ;;H; aaFa ;;J; aaDa ;;K; aaSa ;;L; aaAa ;;:;
wWxX yYzZ wWxX yYzZ wWxX yYzZ wWxX yYzZ wWxX yYzZ
```

CONTROL DRILL: Adjacent Fingers (*Each line 3 times*)

RE
```
rent rein remit reign reckon reject report retail
area here bred tire fresh there dream where arena
```

IL
```
ilk ill illegal illicit illness illusion illusive
lily bail mild veil filed broil guilt skill piled
```

ET
```
etch ether ethics ethnic etching eternal eternity
gets meet veto diet jetty comet metal inset meter
```

HI
```
hit hid his high hike hire hide hilly hitch hinge
chip this thief chief shift behind thirty shingle
```

CONTROL SENTENCES: Adjacent Fingers (*Each line 3 times*)

◁ 60 ▷

½-Min.
Writings

| 1 | 2 | 3 | 4 | 5 | 6 | 7 | 8 | 9 | 10 | 11 | 12 |

```
Rex White is ill and failed to get his rent paid this week.   12
Ethel will get a letter that refers to this present record.   24
This report will illustrate how often fires cause failures.   36
The chief idea is to get the basket filled with wet shells.   48
```

CONTROL PARAGRAPH: Concentration (*3 copies*)

1-Min.
Writings

| 1 | 2 | 3 | 4 | 5 | 6 | 7 | 8 | 9 | 10 | 11 | 12 |

Insert accent
marks by pen.

```
       On ne sait comme la bicyclette est en faveur en Paris.   11
Un chemin agréable est souvent le long des rues principales   23
pour éviter des accidents avec la circulation.  Alors, s'il   35
fait beau, les jeunes gens font une promenade à bicyclette.   47
```

CONTROL SENTENCES: A through H (*Each line 3 times*)

½- and 2-Min.
Writings

| 1 | 2 | 3 | 4 | 5 | 6 | 7 | 8 | 9 | 10 | 11 | 12 |

```
 0  Ann Atlas and Gay Adams had a happy day at the last bazaar.   12
 6  Bob Babbitt's boss bought Bob a brown bag and a brief case.   24
12  Chuck could cash that check and pay cash to the city clerk.   36
18  Dad decided to divide the dividend after driving to Dedham.   48
24  Everyone here exerted extra effort or energy every weekend.   60
30  Fay fed five fellows fine food for four or five full weeks.   72
36  Gary got eight good guys to lug over the general's luggage.   84
42  He had high hopes that she had withheld the cash he sought.   96
Plus ➧
```

| 1 | 2 | 3 | 4 | 5 | 6 |

JOB 6

4-column table
Exact copy
Center
Plain paper
With rules
Words: 84

OUR POSITION IN THE AUTO INDUSTRY ₂ ➤

(In Thousands of Units), ➤

Key items are
shown in color.

Year	Industry	Number We Made	Per Cent We Made ₁ ➤
1950	6,666	1,555	23.2
1951	5,339	1,166	21.8
1952	4,321	1,003	23.2
1953	6,117	1,541	25.2
1954	5,559	1,688	30.4
1955	7,908	2,238	28.3 ₁ ➤

HOW TO TYPE A BOXED TABLE . . .

1. *A boxed table* is one with both vertical and horizontal ruled lines, as shown below.

2. *Correct boxing* divides columns and headings but does not close in the sides.

3. *All the lines are drawn* by pencil or pen after the typing is finished.

4. *Procedure:* Type the table as usual, omitting all rules but leaving space for them. The standard 6 spaces between columns provides adequate space for the vertical rules; be sure to leave room for the horizontal rules.

Compare the tables in Jobs 6 and 7. They are to be done alike except that all the rules in Job 7 are to be drawn in — after the table has been typed.

JOB 7

4-column table
Exact copy
Center
Plain paper
Boxed
Words: 45

OUR POSITION IN THE TRUCK INDUSTRY ₂ ➤

(In Thousands of Units) ₃ ➤

Ruled lines on
boxed tables are
drawn. Arrows
here are spacing
guide only for
what you type.

Year	Industry	Number We Made	Per Cent We Made ₃ ➤
1950	1,332	342	25.7
1951	1,417	320	22.6
1952	1,213	235	19.4
1953	1,202	316	26.2
1954	1,038	303	29.2
1955	1,240	374	30.1

WARMUP: Balanced-Hand Words *(Each line 3 times)*

◁ **50** ▷

```
wx yz wxyz wx yz wxyz wx yz wxyz wx yz wxyz wx yz
zig yams when vials usual their shape right quake
pal owl nap mango laity kench Japan icicle handle
got foe eye duels chair burnt audit Zurich wieldy
```

CONTROL DRILL: F, V, U *(Each line 3 times)*

```
file flag face form flat film fast fish flat felt
left beef life half refer stuff knife staff offer

vial vote void view vile volt veil veto very vail
give five even have drive every favor leave heavy

ugly unit upon undo until upset usury under unify
you jury aqua aunt build incur doubt value jaunts
```

CONTROL SENTENCES: Alphabet Review *(Each line 3 times)*

◁ **60** ▷

½- and
1-Min.
Writings

| 1 | 2 | 3 | 4 | 5 | 6 | 7 | 8 | 9 | 10 | 11 | 12 |

```
Why did Professor Black give you a quiz on the major texts?   12
Judy gave a quick jump as the zebra and lynx fought wildly.   24
Jacqueline was very glad the day her film took a box prize.   36
I hope that lazy jack rabbit and quick fox go past my view.   48
```

CONTROL PREVIEW *(Each line 3 times)*

```
are rest hardest peanuts eating exactly squeezed proportion
was hard realize quality figured excelled quantity anything
```

ALPHABET-REVIEW PARAGRAPHS *(2 copies / si 1.28)*

DS

5-Min.
Writings

Once upon a time there was[1] a young parrot that learned[2] how to express one[3] word.   16
We do not know what[4] the word was, but we are[5] told that a peanut was[6] fed to the   32
bird each time[7] that he said it. He[8] figured that he had a pretty[9] good life for a parrot.[10]   50
So, he went on, all his[11] life, eating nothing but[12] peanuts. Lots of people[13] who train   67
for jobs are[14] exactly like that bird,[15] learning just enough to get[16] someone to hand   83
them some[17] peanuts. For the rest of[18] their days, they wonder[19] why they never get   99
anything[20] more. They do not realize[21] that what they receive[22] is sure to be in direct[23]   115
proportion to the quality[24] and quantity of work[25] that they produce, day by[26] day.   131

The hardest lesson[27] in the world to learn is[28] the simple truth that a[29] little of any-   147
thing is not[30] quite enough. There are[31] millions of folks who live[32] on peanuts because   164
they[33] were not willing or able[34] to stay with their training[35] long enough for mastery[36]   181
of the subject; instead,[37] they squeezed out when[38] the going got hard enough[39] to re-   196
veal who excelled.[40]   200

HOW TO TYPE A BRACED HEADING . . .

1. A *braced heading* is one that identifies, and is centered above, two or more columns. Example: *Our Production* (Job 8).

2. *Procedure:* Omit the braced heading (but leave space for it) until the items above which it must be centered have been typed. Then, turn the paper back and insert the braced heading. In Job 8, *Our Production* should be typed after *Number* and *Per Cent* have both been typed.

3. *To center the braced heading,* use any of these methods:

A. SPACING-DIFFERENCE METHOD. Set the carriage at the beginning of the second line of the braced heading. Tap the space bar once for each letter in the first line. When all letters have been spaced out, continue to space to the end of the second line, counting the number of left-over strokes. Indent the braced heading half that many strokes (ignore fractions).

B. COUNTING METHOD. Count the number of spaces and letters in the two typed lines; indent the shorter half the difference.

C. MIDPOINT METHOD. Find the middle of the second line. Set the carriage there. Backspace from that point enough to center the first line.

JOB 8

4-column table
Exact copy
Center
Plain paper
Boxed
Words: 50

OUR POSITION IN THE AUTOMOTIVE INDUSTRY ₂ ⮕

(In Thousands of Units) ₃ ⮕

SS
24
▽

Key items are
shown in color.

Ruled lines on
boxed tables are
drawn. Arrows
here are spacing
guide only for
what you type.

Year	Total Industry Units	Our Production	
		Number	Per Cent ₃ ⮕
1950	7,998	1,897	23.7
1951	6,756	1,466	22.0
1952	5,534	1,238	22.4
1953	7,319	1,857	25.4
1954	6,597	1,991	30.2
1955	9,148	2,612	28.6

JOB 9

5-column table
Exact copy
Center
Plain paper
Boxed
Words: 57

OUR POSITION IN THE AUTOMOTIVE INDUSTRY ₃ ⮕

SS
24
▽

Year	Passenger Cars		Motor Trucks ₃ ⮕	
	Units*	% Industry	Units*	% Industry ₃ ⮕
1950	1,555	23.2	342	25.7
1951	1,166	21.8	320	22.6
1952	1,003	23.2	235	19.4
1953	1,531	25.2	316	26.2
1954	1,688	30.4	303	29.2
1955	2,238	28.3	374	30.1 ₃ ⮕

Center a footnote
if it is shorter than
width of table.

* In thousands of units

WARMUP: "LE" Drill *(Each line 3 times)*   ◁55▷

```
a;sldkfjghfjdksla; a;sldkfjghfjdksla; a;sldkfjghfjdksl
ledge leave least lease learn left leaf lead lean lend
clear clean blend alert bless fled bled flex glen sled
cable ample whole while smile bale mile file able pale
```

SPEED DRILL: Doubled Letters *(Each line 3 times)*

```
robbers bobbin ribbon rubber abbess jobber hobby abbey
braggart sagging baggage suggests beggar bigger begged
commission recommend common summer immune jammed comma
preferred arranged warrant correct arrive borrow error
```

SPEED SENTENCES: Doubled Letters *(Each line 3 times)*

12-Sec.
Writings
```
When summer arrives, mammoth loggers hurry to Hammond.
Bobby suggested a hobby to Larry, and I commended him.
Abbey begged for rubber ribbons to tie to her baggage.
Larry Dobb suggested that his team carry more players.
```
12-Sec. 5| 10| 15| 20| 25| 30| 35| 40| 45| 50| 55|

SPEED DRILL: Common 4-Letter Words *(Each line 3 times)*   ◁60▷

1-Min.
Writings
       1 | 2 | 3 | 4 | 5 | 6 | 7 | 8 | 9 | 10 | 11 | 12
```
long love lose made mind make more most much must name near    12
next nice note once over paid part past play read rest roll    24
said sale same send ship show sock sign size some such take    36
talk tend than that them they this then told town turn used    48
wait want week went what when wish with word work year your    60
```

SUSTAINED-SPEED SENTENCES *(2 copies / si 1.07)*

3-Min.
Writings
       1 | 2 | 3 | 4 | 5 | 6 | 7 | 8 | 9 | 10 | 11 | 12

0	40	She might have a tough time filling the order for the club.	12
4	44	How soon will you be able to write up that report on light?	24
8	48	May sent that gift to them and signed our four names to it.	36
12	52	When the men went to the other parks, they lost both games.	48
16	56	He met them at the corner, and they talked for a long time.	60
20	60	I told her that she must give me more time to do this work.	72
24	64	Did you ever try to get an order out of either one of them?	84
28	68	I felt sure that he would be there in time to see the race.	96
32	72	If they ask for our help, we shall have to give it to them.	108
36	76	It is not fair to ask him to risk cash on such a wild plan.	120

Plus ▶   1 | 2 | 3 | 4

WARMUP (*Each line 3 times*) ◁ **60** ▷

```
aid bit ice fix jig him kin oil rip qui sir via wit yip zip
39 28 47 56 10 39½ 28½ 47½ 56½ 10½ "39" "28" "47" "56" "10"
The boat tied up at the dock just about the time they came.
```

12-Sec. 5| 10| 15| 20| 25| 30| 35| 40| 45| 50| 55| 60|

RHYTHM PREVIEW (*Each line 3 times*)

```
Axion which shows plant stock bring money terms range gains
more than must made good safe some know soon rise near room
Any you let the one own bet and you buy let you can for the
```

PRODUCTION PRACTICE (*Jobs 10-13*)

These jobs require painstaking care: Job 10 requires you to recall the placement and spacing of an indented letter (page 121). Jobs 11 and 12 involve technical revisions of a table. Job 13 involves form postal cards in which, as you type them, you must insert correct dates and addresses.

1 | 2 | 3 | 4 | 5 | 6 | 7 | 8 | 9 | 10 | 11 | 12

Placement plan is on page 119.

JOB 10

Indented letter
In elite
Letterhead
Tab every 5
Words: 182
Body: 147

February 13, 19--

Mr. Paul R. Graham
    4774 Towers Building
        Little Rock, Arkansas

Dear Mr. Graham:

In answer to the inquiries that you raised in your note 11
of February 11, let me suggest: 18

1. There is no reason to believe that Axion Motors is 29
in financial distress. The accompanying table, which shows 41
that Axion has expanded its plant and properties more than 53
a billion dollars in one 10-year period, indicates that the 65
company has tremendous financial reserves. 73

2. Any investment must, of course, be made on the basis 85
of your own decision. I do feel that the stock is a good, 97
safe bet and that money invested in the company will bring a 109
good return in terms of long-range gains. 117

If you decide to buy some shares of Axion, let me know 128
as soon as you can. There is some indication that the market 141
will rise in the near future. 147

Yours very truly,

SPLANE & GARDNER, INC.

Initials? Enclosures?

Benjamin Gardner

PART 6

◁ 55 ▷

WARMUP: Balanced-Hand Words *(Each line 3 times)*

```
aa;; ssll ddkk ffjj gghh ffjj ddkk ssll aa;; asdf ;lkj
eighty girls blend fight firms forms sighs usury angle
lament throe sight soaps their usual whale throw gowns
usurps throb right ivory lairs giant gland towns blend
```

SPEED DRILL: Word Families *(Each line 3 times)*

```
wings wick wide wife wind with wild wink wire wish wit
marsh manor match march maple main malt mark maim maps
mace made maid make mail male mart maw mat mad map man
```

SPEED SENTENCES *(Each line 3 times)*

12-Sec.
Writings

```
The men make signs for us, for she pays them to do so.
Sidney got eight ducks for the girls with a big rifle.
They may risk their right to fish and go to the lakes.
```

12-Sec. 5| 10| 15| 20| 25| 30| 35| 40| 45| 50| 55|

SPEED PARAGRAPH *(3 copies / si 1.16)*

1-Min.
Writings

    1 | 2 | 3 | 4 | 5 | 6 | 7 | 8 | 9 | 10 | 11

```
Time is just the same as money to the man in business.   11
He pays his workers a fair wage and likes to receive a   22
decent return from them.  You should keep this in mind   33
when you take your first job.  Do not get into a habit   44
of watching the clock, but give your best to your job.   55
```

SPEED PREVIEW *(Each line 3 times)*

◁ 60 ▷

```
continuous requires shoulder muscles curved after study act
difference electric remember example manual quiet tired you
```

SUSTAINED-SPEED PARAGRAPH *(2 copies / si 1.20)*   **DS**

3-Min.
Writings

    1 | 2 | 3 | 4 | 5 | 6 | 7 | 8 | 9 | 10 | 11 | 12

0	44	If you feel tired after you have typed for a while, you may	12
4	48	need to study the motions with which you work. The way you	24
8	52	stroke the keys, for example, makes a big difference. If a	36
12	56	lot of arm and hand motions get into the act, you find that	48
16	60	your arm and shoulder muscles get tired from the continuous	60
20	64	strain on them. But if you let your fingers do most of the	72
24	68	work, as they ought, then the arms and hands will be quiet;	84
28	72	and the sinews that control them will not be so tired. The	96
32	76	right way will be the easy way if you remember that you are	108
36	80	to snap the keys on the manual but tap them on an electric,	120
40	84	and that good stroking requires that the fingers be curved.	132

Plus ▶   1   2   3   4

JOB 11

3-column table
Rough draft
Center
Plain paper
Without rules
(as shown)
Words: 73

all caps > A Ten-Year Record of Expansion ← 1#
(In Millions of Dollars) ← 2#

Year	Additions of Materiel	Retirements of Materiel
1946	$ 56.5	$ $18.3
1947	94.4	19.9
1948	79.3	24.7
1949	34.9	23.4
1950	109.7	21.1
1951	217.6	43.1
1952	176.8	32.6
~~1953~~	~~176.8~~	~~32.6~~
1953	151.5	30.5
1954	279.9	58.2
1955	133.6	20.8
TOTAL	$1,334.2	$292.6

JOB 12

3-column table
Working from
your copy of
Job 11 without
changing margin
and tab settings,
retype the table
in boxed form
(like Job 7).
Words: 104

THE PROVIDENCE-ACME CORPORATION

2600 FIFTEENTH AVENUE WEST, SEATTLE, WASHINGTON ₂ ➡

February 14, 19-- ₂ ➡

Gentlemen:

Please reserve a single room, with bath,
for the night of February 25 for Mr. Edward
Perkins, of this company. Please confirm this
reservation and let us know whether we must
make a deposit on the room. ₃ ➡

Secretary to Mr. Perkins

JOB 13

2 indented
postal cards*
Shown in pica
Workbook forms
Words: 65 each

*CARD 1: Mark Hopkins Hotel, 561 Sutter Street, San Francisco 1, California, for February 25
CARD 2: El Capitan Hotel, 2710 Calhoun Street, San Diego 10, California, for February 28

PART C: BUSINESS-FORM TEST *(57 five-stroke words)*

◁ **6 in.** ▷
SS
7
▽

Prepare voucher checks No. 324 and 325 for $100 each "in payment of fee for participating in the sales conference in Atlanta" to enclose with each letter in Part B.

PART D: MANUSCRIPT TEST *(386 five-stroke words / si 1.35)*

Type the following committee report in single-spaced form, with the subheadings centered (as in Job 2, on page 171).

*7-Min. Writings

POLICY ON REPEATING ADVERTISEMENTS

All experts in the field of advertising[1] find that one basic question[2] comes up again and again: Is it wiser[3] to repeat a good advertisement or[4] to keep new ads before the public?[5] The assignment made to our committee[6] was to see whether there is an[7] answer to this question as it applies[8] to the promotion of our products.[9]   17 34 49 64

RESEARCH. We found that a number[10] of good studies have been made on[11] this subject. We took time to review[12] nine such studies. We regret to[13] report that no study deals with a[14] problem just like ours. Each study[15] was concerned with some one phase[16] of the question, and in no case was[17] that one phase the same as the[18] problems that we face in promoting our[19] products. There is a study on the[20] use of color. There is one on the[21] size of the space; two on the position[22] of the ad; two on the use of[23] pictures; four more on the problems[24] of certain types of products, and so[25] on. Although such studies give us[26] broad concepts, they do not add up[27] to an answer.   78 96 112 129 145 161 177 193

RECOMMENDATIONS.[28] We should like to recommend that[29] displays for our products, as a matter[30] of policy, include these features:[31]   206 218

1. If we use a color in any ad,[32] let us always use the same shade or[33] same color in all displays for any[34] one type of product.   235 243

2. Let us[35] design and then use some one signature[36] style for all our ads so that our[37] name and trade-mark may be pounded[38] home.   259 268

3. Let us try to have our[39] displays appear regularly in one[40] position—on the same page and in the[41] same part of the page—for all[42] journals in which we use full schedules.[43] This is secondary; this is not[44] important enough to pay extra to[45] get such positions.   285 301 318 320

The committee[46] feels that no firm policies should[47] be set for other matters; rather,[48] the display staff should have a free[49] hand to use its judgment in[50] deciding when to repeat any display.[51]   336 353 356

*Tiny number nearest where you stop is speed when you type for 7 minutes.

Harold Ewing (Sales)
Martha Holder (Production)
George Lewis (Advertising)
Robert Hess (Agency), Chairman

UNIT 16
MANUSCRIPTS

In this unit: (1) arrangement of news releases, with and without news-release letterheads; (2) arrangement of manuscripts for magazine articles; (3) arrangement of manuscripts for books. Before starting the jobs of this unit, study pages 134-140 and answer the questions on Workbook pages 123-124.

WARMUP (*Each line 3 times*)   ◁ **60** ▷

```
car box cod woe fog how oil jot oak mop son quo vox boy zoo
39 28 47 56 10 39 & 28 & 47 & 56 & 10 & 39# 28# 47# 56# 10#
It is his duty to let us know about it as soon as he knows.
12-Sec. 5|    10|    15|    20|    25|    30|    35|    40|    45|    50|    55|    60|
```

RHYTHM PREVIEW (*Each line 3 times*)

```
product learned package require zippers exactly setting the
you had you and the buy was not the box you may set him but
getting members easiest circuit release spacing perfect for
any buy way his who any you can for the you are use the one
```

ALPHABET-REVIEW PARAGRAPHS (*2 copies / si 1.27*)   ◁ **60** ▷
                                                                                    DS

```
3-Min.
Writings    1 | 2 | 3 | 4 | 5 | 6 | 7 | 8 | 9 | 10 | 11 | 12

  0      If you had some new product that you hoped to sell and     11
  4    learned that the only way the customers would buy it was in   23
  8    green boxes, you would package your product in green boxes,   35
 12    would you not?  You might not like green boxes; but if that   47
 16    was what the customers desired, that is what you would give   59
 20    them.  Good judgment would require that you do so.  If they   71
 24    want zippers or box tops or anything else, you serve it up.   83
 28      That theme is quite important to the typist.  When you     94
 31    type anything for someone else, he is your market.  You may  106
 35    think of him as a customer.  If he is an editor, you set up   118
 39    your product, which is your manuscript, exactly as he wants  130
 43    it to be; there is no point in setting it up any other way.  142
 47    No matter who your customer is, you must adjust your tastes   154
 51    and specialize in giving him what he will buy--a green box.   166
Plus ▶      1    |    2    |    3    |    4
```

PRODUCTION PRACTICE (*Jobs 1-2*)

A news release is a form of unbound manuscript; before typing Job 1, therefore, review pages 100 and 101, for a summary of unbound manuscripts. Be sure to read Job 1 before typing it. Study the revisions in Job 2 (a guide to the marks is on page 101) before you type it.

You will need 3 sheets of plain paper or Workbook pages 183-188. Type Part A on one sheet, the two letters in Part B on opposite sides of the second sheet, and Parts C and D on opposite sides of the third sheet. If you do not have the voucher checks (workbook), rule forms similar to the one on page 165.

GRADING SCALE FOR PART A *(Straight Copy)*

Step 1: Compute words a minute.	Step 2: Deduct for errors—		Step 3: Grade the remaining words a min-ute this way:	
	1 error: —2	5 errors: —11		48 or higher: A
	2 errors: —4	6 errors: —14		43 to 47 wam: B
	3 errors: —6	7 errors: —17		38 to 42 wam: C
	4 errors: —8	8 errors: —20		33 to 37 wam: D

GRADING SCALE FOR PARTS B, C, D *(Production Work)*

TAKE OFF:	—3 for each major error (top margin, line length, line-spacing, general correctness of form, etc.) —2 for each minor error (blocking, aligning, centering, indenting, etc., of individual parts of the job) —1 for each typographical error	TOTAL TAKEN OFF	8-7	6-4	3-2	1-0
		GRADE	D	C	B	A

PART A: STRAIGHT-COPY TEST *(si 1.33)*

◁ **65** ▷
DS
5
▽

Take a 7-minute writing on the *body* of the report on the next page; or, type it once and grade your work as though you had typed it at 52 words a minute.

PART B: LETTER TEST *(total 395 five-stroke words / si 1.38)*

Type *two* copies of this 172-word letter (the first to Doctor Kendall, the second to Miss Thomas). Use full-blocked form (as on page 154) and open punctuation. In each letter, insert *Subject: Payment of Conference Fee.*

1. Date | Dr. James F. Kendall | Lake Stone College | Savannah 4, Georgia — 16

2. Date | Miss Helen Thomas | 16 Myrtle Street | Boston 14, Massachusetts — 16

Dear (insert name) We feel that the contribution that you made to our sales conference — 19
was one of the factors that made it the most successful one we have ever conducted for — 37
our staff. We are deeply grateful to you for taking time from your busy schedule to — 54
join us and to make your fine presentations. — 63

In accordance with the agreement that we had made, we are sending you our check — 79
for your $100 fee. As soon as you send us your statement of expenses, we shall send — 96
you another check for that amount. If it is convenient to you to let us have that state- — 113
ment before the first of the month, by which time we hope to have the accounting for — 130
the sales conference completed, we shall be grateful. — 141

We shall look forward, (insert name), to having you join us for another sales meet- — 158
ing some time in the future. Again, thank you for helping us. — 171

Yours very truly | Roland I. Miller | Enclosure: Check — 183

NEWS RELEASE

From: Jerry McDonald
Chief Wire Editor
Press Syndicate
332 West 42 Street
New York 36, New York ₂ ➧

Release: February 17, 19-- ₃ ➧

JOB 1

News release
Shown in pica
Plain paper
Heading tab
Paragraph tab
Words: 350

"A TYPIST CAN WRECK A NEWS RELEASE" ₃ ➧

NEW YORK CITY, Feb. 17--Many a publicity expert works up a fine publicity release, only to have his typist spoil any chance of its getting attention on an editor's desk. How a release looks may be more important than what it says.

That is what Jerry McDonald, chief wire editor for the Press Syndicate, told members of the New York City Publicity Club at their annual luncheon for news editors, attended by more than 200 publicists at the Statler today. (76 words)

Backspace from margin.

"We receive scores of publicity handouts every day," McDonald said. "Editors are busy people. We might look over the releases to find the most important ones, but it is more likely that we look for the ones that are easiest for us to slap on the circuit or on the press. If you are wise, you make releases easy for an editor to use." (141 words)

McDonald enumerated seven guides for news releases:

A number
counts as
a word.

1. Give a clear title. Be clever if you wish, but be clear. Tell the whole story in one glance.

2. Tell who released the story. Always indicate in the heading to whom the editor can turn for more information.

3. Start the story with a date line.

4. Keep the release down to one page, even if you must use single spacing to do so. If you cannot keep it down to one page, however, then be sure to use double spacing.

5. Never have a margin narrower than a full inch.

6. Give a cumulative word count after every logical stopping point in the story.

7. Be sure the typing is perfect. An error tells the editor that the release is unreliable. (272 words)

Center:

(END)

JOB 9

Personal data
display form
In elite
Plain paper
2 carbons
Outline tabs
Words: 346

Applicant: RICHARD E. JORDAN

Address: 1041 Oaktree Lane
                Park Ridge, Illinois

Telephone: TAlcott 1-4385

Applying for: Junior Accountant

Date: March 21, 19--

A. PERSONAL DATA
    1. Age: 22. I was born March 3, 19--.
    2. Height: 5 feet 10 inches. Weight: 160 pounds.
    3. Military status: Served 3 years in the Navy.
    4. Marital status: Single, but engaged.
    5. Residence: Live with parents.

B. PERTINENT EXPERIENCE RECORD
    1. Maintained storekeeper records and payroll records
        during $1\frac{1}{2}$ years of Navy duty.
    2. Was cashier at Carson's (Chicago) on Saturdays and
        some evenings during last year of high school.
    3. Was bookkeeper for a Junior Achievement Group during
        my first year at Central City College.

C. EDUCATIONAL RECORD
    1. Graduated from Park Ridge High School, May 29, 19--,
        after completing the college-preparatory course.
    2. Will graduate from Central City College on June 3,
        after completing the two-year accounting program.
    3. Academic and skill achievement--
        a. Accounting: 15 semester hours, honor grades.
        b. Business machines: Can use all calculators.
        c. Typewriting: 60 words a minute (10-minute test).
        d. Filing and Systems: Completed 50-hour course.
    4. Have ranked on Dean's list throughout college program.
    5. Extracurricular activities--
        a. Served as business manager for college newspaper.
        b. Treasurer of my church's Youth Group.

D. REFERENCES
    1. Dr. John K. Youngman, Dean of Men, Central City College,
        6 North Michigan Boulevard, Chicago 6.
    2. Mr. Richard Forbes, manager of the Men's Suit Department
        at Carson's, 1 South State Street, Chicago 3.
    3. Mr. Adam Gerhold, director of the Park Ridge Community
        Youth Guild, DeCook Court, Park Ridge, Illinois.

JOB 10

Application
form (workbook)

Page 179-180 in your workbook is an actual employment-application form. Using your personal data, fill it in completely, as though applying for a job for which you are now qualified.

NEWS RELEASE

MARTIN MILLER and SONS
58 BROAD STREET
ATLANTA 1, GEORGIA

RELEASE: February 18, 19--

FROM: William Miller ₃

JOB 2

News release
Rough draft
Workbook form
2 tab stops
Words: 280

NEW USE OF COLOR INCREASE(s) PRODUCTION RATES ₃   ◁ 6 in. ▷
DS

ATLANTA, *Ga.,* ~~Georgia~~, Feb. 18--Painting the work~~i~~ng spaces in
offices and factories ~~with~~ the right color can ~~bring about~~ *result in*
much higher production rates, according to the results of a
practical test recently completed by the Research department
of Martin Miller & Sons, of this city.   (40 words)

"Using the bright color," said William Miller, director
of the MM&S *research* program, "does not make the machinery go faster,
or the mechanic work ~~any~~ harder. But the right color reduces
eyesstrain; and that means much less fatigue, and fewer accidents, and a lessening of tension among workers. ~~Boosts~~ *Increases* in
production rates are an *natural* ~~inevitable~~ result."   (96 words)

The ~~test~~ of "color dynamics" was made in several departments of the Clover Mills Company, Wilmington, Delaware. The
results credited color with reducing absenteeisms by hundreds
of hours and *with* allover production ~~boosts~~ *increases* of 7 per cent in the
factory and 9% in the offices ~~of the firm~~.   (143 words)

The color is applied to walls, to machinery, and to work
areas, *--even* ~~including~~ floors. The plan tested at Clover reduced
~~inside~~ *from outside* glare and, at the same time, provided eye-rest areas
that lessened eyestrain and the tension to which it ~~usually~~
leads. The paints used, manufactured especially for the purpose, by MM&S, is nonreflective and gloss-free.   (200 words)

(END)

135   MANUSCRIPTS

Part 4
LESSON
Unit 16
95

WARMUP (*Each line 3 times*)   ◁ **60** ▷

```
awry bouy cozy duty foxy hymn inky joys quay spry ugly very
we 23 to 59 up 70 or 94 it 85 pity 0856 your 6974 yore 6943
He asked us, "What do you mean when you say, 'Soup's on!'?"
```
12-Sec. 5| 10| 15| 20| 25| 30| 35| 40| 45| 50| 55| 60|

CAPITAL-CONTROL PREVIEW (*Each line 3 times*)

```
K. Inc. Press Martin Applied Residence Telephone Accountant
L. With Place Filing Military Graduated Applicant Gentlemen
Age For Joyce Junior Position Stephens Treasurer Employment
```

PRODUCTION PRACTICE (*Jobs 8-10*)

Jobs 8-10 provide a model letter of application and model personal data form.
If your instructor approves, substitute your own letter and data form.

JOB 8

Blocked letter
Rough draft
Plain paper.
Center tab
Heading tab
Words: 249
Body: 206

1 | 2 | 3 | 4 | 5 | 6 | 7 | 8 | 9 | 10 | 11 | 12 | 13

1041 Oaktree Lane ~~931 Graham Street~~   4
Park Ridge, ~~Lincolnwood 30,~~ Illinois   8
(Use today's date) ~~April 8, 1956~~   12

~~International Supply Company~~ *Martin and Stephens, Inc.*   17
~~463 North LaSalle Street~~ *4652 Chase Avenue*   21
Chicago ~~13~~, Illinois   25
          ↰30

                    ATTENTION: Employment Manager   31

Gentlemen: 34

          wish
I ~~should like~~ to apply for the position of *junior accountant* ~~editorial secretary~~   44
that you advertised in this morning's ~~Daily Times.~~ *Chicago Press.*   55

I was pleased to see your advertisement. I was among the group   68
of seniors from Central City College who were conducted on a   80
tour of your offices a few weeks ago; ever since then, I have   93
hoped that a vacancy might occur for which I might qualify. I   105
shall graduate on ~~May 30~~ *June 3*; my class schedule, however, is such   118
that I could work afternoons from now until then.   128

For this vacancy, you require someone who is both interested in   141
the work and qualified to perform it efficiently. The fact that 154
          an accounting
I am a ~~secretarial~~ major at Central City College is evidence of   166
                              training
my interest in this work and the ~~skills~~ that I can bring to it.   179

With this letter I enclose a personal data sheet that outlines   192
my qualifications in more detail. Won't you please review it?   205
If you will be kind enough to ~~indicate on the enclosed postal~~   211
~~card~~ when I might be granted a personal interview, I shall be   230
grateful for the opportunity to apply in person.   240

let me know by   Very sincerely yours,   244
telephone (TAlcott 1-4385)
                                        Richard E. Jordan
                               Miss Pauline W. ~~Lambert~~   248

2 Enclosures   249

WARMUP *(Each line 3 times)* ◁60▷

```
bud cue fun hug jut auk lux mug wun rut qui sup zut vue you
39 28 47 56 10 "39" "28" "47" "56" "10" 39¼ 28¼ 47¼ 56¼ 10¼
His is the last firm in the city that we could ask to help.
```
12-Sec. 5| 10| 15| 20| 25| 30| 35| 40| 45| 50| 55| 60|

RHYTHM PREVIEW *(Each line 3 times)*

```
heard trick trade often guide under ruled lines pages form
work that have come slip with show type each that show its
zones leave dimly reads favor point every whole write copy
page rule mark stop help term show many more than tell had
```

ALPHABET-REVIEW PARAGRAPHS *(1 copy / si 1.27)* ◁50▷ DS

5-Min. Writings

| 1 | 2 | 3 | 4 | 5 | 6 | 7 | 8 | 9 | 10 |

```
 0           I heard of another trick of the typing trade        9
 2      the other day.  It is a good technique for boost-       19
 4      ing your output on all kinds of work that come up       29
 6      often and have some trick element in the arrange-       39
 8      ment.  It consists of making a guide sheet, which       49
10      you slip under the paper on which you are typing,       59
12      with ruled lines that show exactly where you type       69
14      each portion of any job of similar type and size.       79
```
si 1.31 (lines 4-6)

```
16           For example, suppose that your boss jots off    9 |  88
18      many articles for the same magazine.  They should   19 |  98
20      all be typed the same way--the same margins, same   29 | 108
22      position for the page numbers, and so on.  So, to   39 | 118
24      speed up this job that you do frequently, rule up   49 | 128
26      a sheet of paper with lines that mark off all the   59 | 138
28      key points--where to set margins, where to number   69 | 148
30      the pages, where to start and stop on each sheet,   79 | 158
32      and so on.  Now, put your "visual guide" to work.   89 | 168
```
si 1.23 (lines 22-24)

```
34           The same technique is a big help if you type    9 | 177
35      term papers and theses.  By ruling off the margin   19 | 187
37      zones as are required by the school, and by draw-   29 | 197
39      ing more lines to show exactly how much space you   39 | 207
41      leave for each footnote, you can design a "visual   49 | 217
43      guide" that, showing dimly through the top paper,   59 | 227
45      makes the typing of jobs of this kind very quick.   69 | 237
```
si 1.28 (lines 35-37)

Plus ➧   1 | 2

PRODUCTION PRACTICE *(Jobs 3-4)*

Read Job 3 carefully before typing it; it will take 2 sheets of paper, even though it has been telescoped on the page, to save space. Job 4 illustrates the normal arrangement of book manuscripts, which are usually considered as "unbound" (review pages 100-101).

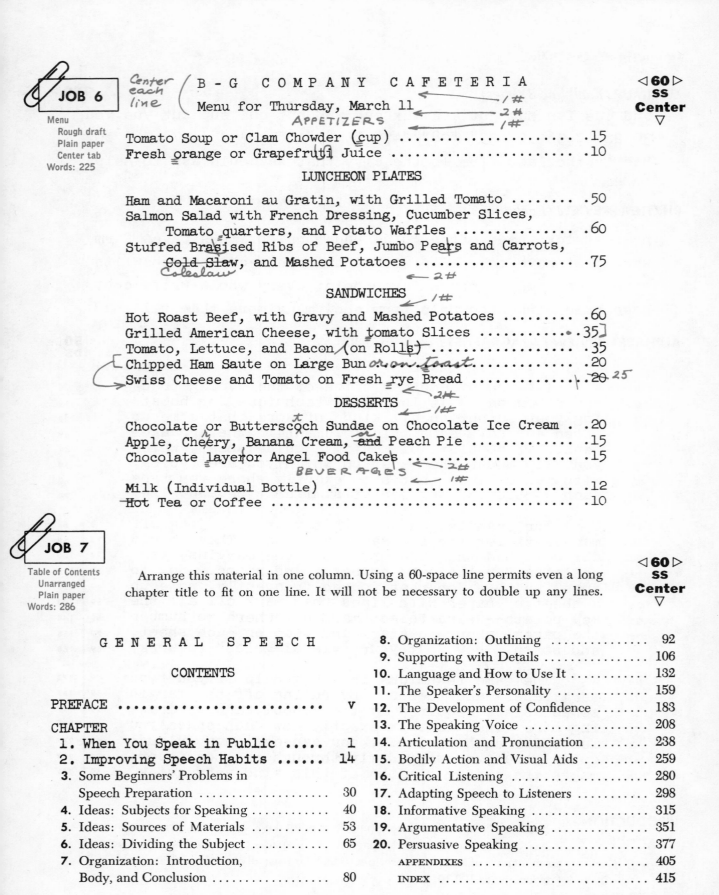

JOB 6

Menu
Rough draft
Plain paper
Center tab
Words: 225

Center each line

B - G C O M P A N Y C A F E T E R I A
Menu for Thursday, March 11
APPETIZERS

Tomato Soup or Clam Chowder (cup) .... .15
Fresh orange or Grapefruit Juice .... .10

LUNCHEON PLATES

Ham and Macaroni au Gratin, with Grilled Tomato .... .50
Salmon Salad with French Dressing, Cucumber Slices,
    Tomato quarters, and Potato Waffles .... .60
Stuffed Braised Ribs of Beef, Jumbo Pears and Carrots,
    Cold Slaw, and Mashed Potatoes .... .75
    Coleslaw

SANDWICHES

Hot Roast Beef, with Gravy and Mashed Potatoes .... .60
Grilled American Cheese, with tomato Slices .... .35
Tomato, Lettuce, and Bacon (on Rolls) .... .35
Chipped Ham Saute on Large Bun or on toast .... .20
Swiss Cheese and Tomato on Fresh rye Bread .... .20 .25

DESSERTS

Chocolate or Butterscotch Sundae on Chocolate Ice Cream . .20
Apple, Cherry, Banana Cream, and Peach Pie .... .15
Chocolate layer or Angel Food Cakes .... .15
BEVERAGES

Milk (Individual Bottle) .... .12
Hot Tea or Coffee .... .10

◁ **60** ▷
ss
Center
▽

JOB 7

Table of Contents
Unarranged
Plain paper
Words: 286

Arrange this material in one column. Using a 60-space line permits even a long chapter title to fit on one line. It will not be necessary to double up any lines.

◁ **60** ▷
ss
Center
▽

G E N E R A L S P E E C H

CONTENTS

JOB 3

2-page magazine article
  Unarranged
  Plain paper
  Paragraph tab
  (3 spaces in)
  1 carbon
Words: 364

MANUSCRIPTS--WITH SALESMANSHIP ₂ ⬎

By Kenneth Willhite
Formerly, Associate Editor
Today's Secretary Magazine ₂ ⬎

(44 Columnar Lines) ₃ ⬎

DS

THE TYPING of a manuscript can help or
hinder its publication. An editor is a
busy person who reads many manuscripts,
many more than he can publish. It is

(Continue in column one, below.)

natural that he should be prejudiced in favor of material that looks as though he had written it himself.

There lies the secret of selling any magazine article: Convince the editor that the article was written especially for him by one who knows his magazine.

#

IT IS NOT enough to tell the editor that such is the case. The typist must prove the point by the form of the manuscript. It must look professional. My advice:

1. Type the article with the same length of line as that used in the columns of the magazine. Type 10 lines from a copy of the magazine. Determine the average line length—and use it. Do not exceed that line length by more than one space on any one line.

2. Precede the page number on every page by the author's name.

3. Indicate how many lines your manuscript will fill in the magazine.

4. Double space the manuscript. If it divides into sections, like this one does, type a number sign in the middle of the blank line, to indicate "insert 1 blank line." It counts as a whole line.

5. Use only 8½- by 11-inch paper.

6. Use touches of the magazine's own style. If it uses sideheads, use them; if it uses short paragraphs, use them; if it uses footnotes, so should you. If it—whatever it does, so should you.

#

MY, WHAT a lot of trouble! Yes, but not as much trouble as it is to write an article and have it rejected because it did not look professional— did not seem to belong in the magazine.

(END)

> Willhite--2
>
> from a copy of the magazine. Determine
> the average line length--and use it. Do
> not exceed that line length by more than
> one space on any one line.
>
> 2. Precede the page number on every
> page by the author's name.
>
> 3. Indicate how many lines your manu-
> script will fill in the magazine.
>
> 4. Double space the manuscript. If it
> divides into sections, like this one
> does, type a number sign in the middle of

Page 2 of a magazine manuscript:
  Same length of line as page 1.
  Type page number on line 7, at the right margin.
  Author's name precedes page number.
  Separate heading from the following text by 2 blank lines.

PIVOTING . . .

When several lines are to end evenly (like the names in Job 4, the hours in Job 5), set a tab stop at the point where they are to end and then backspace from it ("pivot" from it) for each item that is to end at that point.

USING LEADERS . . .

When two items, far apart, are linked by a row of "leaders" (periods), first type the two items and then insert the periods. Leave one blank space before starting the leaders and one blank space after the end of the row of leaders.

JOB 4

Display program
Rough draft
Plain paper
Center tab
Pivot tab
Words: 94

◁ **50** ▷
SS
Center
▽

C O N F E R E N C E   P R O G R A M

Always put 3 spaces between spread-out words. Review page 90.

March 8-12, (Year)   ← 1#
← 2#

Monday: PUBLIC RELATIONS AND ADVERTISING
                Discussion Led by Harvey P. May   ◀ Pivot

Tuesday: INCENTIVE WAGE PROBLEMS   *Hale*
                Discussion led by Emil H. Bender

WEDNESDAY Morning: USING SALESMEN'S REPORTS   *M*
                Discussion Led by William J. Noran

Wednesday afternoon: Luncheon and Excursion

Thursday: ADMINISTERING JOB EVALUATIONS   *K.*
                Discussion Led by ⟨Joseph Strong⟩

Friday: OUR WORK SIMPLIFICATION PROGRAM
                Discussion Led by ⟨John Z. Duncan⟩

JOB 5

Display program
Rough draft
Plain paper
Center tab
Pivot tab
Tab in 10
Words: 103

◁ **60** ▷
SS
Center
▽

THE B-G FOUNDER'S DAY FESTIVAL

Center each line

Saturday, March 13   2#
at
The Golden Bridge Club

BANQUET .... 6:30 to 8:30   ◀ Pivot

big
A once-in-a-lifetime charcoal-grilled
10# steak dinner, complete from soup to nuts,   1#
speaking of which reminds ~~me~~ *us* to mention--   2#

THE SPEAKERS .... 8:30 to 9:00

Toastmaster Harold Freeman is bringing ~~his~~ *an*   1#
alarm clock to make sure that no speakers
talk more than ⟨5⟩ minutes; we want to--   2#

TRIP "THE LIGHT FANTASTIC" .... 10:00 to 12:30

The music is that of Dave Elliott and his   1#
famous band, with vocals by Dora Deevers.

JOB 4

Page of a book
manuscript
Rough draft
Plain paper
Tabs at 5, 10
2 carbons
Words: 337

**SPECIAL
NOTES
ON
JOB 4**

1. Book manuscripts are almost always typed on a 6-inch line.
2. Double spacing is always used for the running text; single spacing is always used for listings and footnotes.
3. Listings are commonly "double indented" 10 spaces.
4. A "running head," giving the title of the book or chapter, appears in all caps on the same line with the page number.

◁ **6 in.** ▷
DS
7
▽

AUTHORS GUIDE   2/ 3 ➤

but whether to use st, d, th, etc., after street numbers will depend on
local preference; they are omitted more and more. ₃ ➤

17. Most Common Uses of Capitals:

We apply some rules about the use of capitals so often that we do not
even think of ~~their being~~ *them as* rules. Every ~~writer~~ *author* knows, ~~we trust,~~ to use
a capital letter--

Indent
10 spaces.

      1) to start a proper name.
      2) to start any sentence.
      3) to start a direct quotation.
      4) to start each line in an outline or poem.

The first rule is used ~~the~~ most often, for there are so many different
~~different~~ kinds of names. We must use a capital for names of--

      1) deity, like <u>God</u> and <u>Holy Spirit</u>.
      2) people, like <u>Joe Brown</u> and <u>Ann Smith</u>.
      3) geographic places, like <u>Los Angeles</u>.
      4) companies, like <u>Gimbel Bros</u>.
    5 6) trade names, like <u>Ivory Soap</u> and <u>Wheaties</u>.
    6 7) days of the week; months; holidays.

Any word substituted for a name begins with a capital, too; like <u>Windy</u>
<u>City</u> for <u>Chicago</u>, <u>Honest Abe</u> for <u>Lincoln</u>, etc.

One rule that is often ~~forgotten~~ *overlooked* is this: Use capitals for family
titles that are used as names but are <u>not</u> preceded by a possessive pro-
noun. Thus: "My aunt ~~will~~ *would* be glad to tell Mother, but I shall ask
Father to speak to my mother first."

When a title is used with a name in a sentence, capitalize the title
if it precedes the name <u>but not if it follows the name</u>. Thus: "There is
Governor Smith with Tom Lake, mayor of our town." Exceptions: <u>Always</u>
capitalize the title of any high government official, *such* as: "Mr. Reed, Secretary of Commerce."

7-Min.
Writings

| 1 | 2 | 3 | 4 | 5 | 6 | 7 | 8 | 9 | 10 | 11 | 12 | 13 | 14 |

0   Go to a library, and you will find a full shelf of books written 13

2 on the technique of having a bright, clean, and jolly face. You will 27

si 4 find more theses on what to do with your hair and your hands and your 41
1.26

6 feet, how you should stand and sit and walk, how you should dress for 55

8 different affairs of the day, and so on. Millions of words have been 69

10 printed on the why's or how's of grooming, all of which emphasize the 83

12 personal value of building as handsome an exterior as the pocketbook, 97

14 good sense, and the gifts of Nature permit. A few facts stand out in 111

16 all that maze of words. All agree that the important things are good 125

18 taste, the size of the person, and the basic demands of the occasion. 139

20   These factors of taste, size, and occasion are just as important 152

22 in dressing up your typing as in dressing up a person. For a moment, 166

si 24 think of taste by itself. You know, of course, that there is quite a 180
1.31
26 difference between a daring scheme for a new product, which can stand 194

28 an exciting flair, and a quarterly report in which it looks as though 208

30 the department were about to lose its shirt or its head. You have to 222

32 know the difference between a new plan being readied for an important 236

34 customer, on whom it is good sense to spend some time and effort, and 250

36 one that will soon be presented to the board of directors, who always 264

38 fuss over costs, down to the last cent and the last minute you spend. 278

40   In a like vein, the size of your report makes an obvious differ- 291

42 ence, too. It is not wise to place a fancy cover on reports that are 305

si 44 only two or three pages long. On the other far extreme, you would be 319
1.36
46 quite alert and get a pat on the back if you went to some pains for a 333

48 cover that does justice to a report that has a hundred pages and con- 347

50 veys a pretty rosy hue. The matter of occasion is quite similar. Do 361

52 not make an elaborate cover for regular reports; for, if you begin to 375

54 do so, you have to keep it up month after month. Save special covers 389

56 for exceptional occasions. Do not let your pride in pleasing the man 403

58 who wrote the report weaken your senses of taste, size, and occasion. 417

Plus

    1   2

**PRODUCTION
PRACTICE**
(*Jobs 4-7*)

Jobs 4-7 are each to be centered vertically on full sheets of plain paper. Before starting these jobs, review the directions for vertical centering that were given on page 29.

WARMUP (*Each line 3 times*)   ◁ **60** ▷

busy city edgy fray hazy joys quay yank yelp wavy waxy yams
39 28 47 56 10 39, 28, 47, 56, 10, (39) (28) (47) (56) (10)
We shall not be able to say a single word about it to them.
12-Sec. 5| 10| 15| 20| 25| 30| 35| 40| 45| 50| 55| 60|

RHYTHM PREVIEW (*Each line 3 times*)

rates table judge exact speed cares short great sixth tenth
such part four fine wish work talk than hard time slow news
Dr. and the few ago all who say man use one was his are had

CAPITALS PREVIEW (*Each line 3 times*)

I The Elm Most Texas Dallas Street Editor Journal Executive
H. By It Dr. Yours Green Young Thomas Pittsburgh University
It It He He His Most When About State Tempe College Arizona

PRODUCTION PRACTICE (*Jobs 5-7*)

Before typing Job 5, review page 121. Before typing Job 6, review page 137. Before typing Job 7, review pages 126 and 129. The material for Job 6 is shown on a 50-space line, with scales, so that you may use it for an extra 5-minute writing practice (si 1.42) if you wish.

Placement plan: See page 119.

JOB 5

Indented letter
Unarranged
Letterhead
Tab every 5
Words: 143
Body: 115

| 1 | 2 | 3 | 4 | 5 | 6 | 7 | 8 | 9 | 10 | 11 |

Today's date

        Editor, Executive Journal   505 Elm   **11**

Street   Dallas 2, Texas   Dear Sir: **18**

     Most of your readers are executives who have   **27**

secretaries and who give dictation regularly. I believe   **38**

that your readers would be interested in an article that   **49**

discusses the dictation rates of businessmen.   **59**

     I have prepared such an article. I enclose the   **68**

first part and a table from the manuscript. The entire   **80**

article includes 266 columnar lines and four tables. The   **91**

article is based on the fine study conducted a few years   **103**

ago by Dr. H. H. Green, at the University of Pittsburgh.   **114**

     I should appreciate learning from you whether   **123**

you would wish me to submit the entire manuscript. Yours   **135**

very truly, Thomas Young   **143**

PERSONAL TITLES IN BUSINESS CORRESPONDENCE

The committee appointed by Mr. Wilson to study the use
of personal titles in business correspondence found that the
subject is amply treated in many reference sources. It was
also found that the references are in complete agreement.

Definition

This report deals only with personal titles; it does not
concern business titles (such as Sales Manager) or honorary
expressions (such as The Hon. or Esquire).

Findings

1. In business correspondence, every personal name used
in a salutation or address (both in the letter and on the envelope) is preceded by some kind of personal title.

2. Mr. and Mrs. are always abbreviated. Other personal
titles are not abbreviated unless a first name or at least one
initial precedes the last name. Examples:
Right: Dr. E. G. Doe, Doctor Doe, Dear Doctor Doe:
Wrong: Dr. Doe, E. G. Doe, Dear Dr. Doe:
Right: Col. E. Doe, Colonel Doe, Dear Colonel Doe:
Wrong: Col. Doe, E. Doe, Dear Col. Doe:

3. When a title is used with a name in the letter body,
the rule (No. 2) about abbreviations applies. Example: "We
saw Mr. Jones talking with Doctor Doe at the meeting."

Page 1 of a 2-page committee report

Retype Job 2 as a 2-page *unbound* manuscript
(review rules on pages 100-101) with *centered* subheadings. Your work will be similar to these illustrations.

PERSONAL TITLES   2

4. Personal titles are not commonly typed in signatures,
although women may type Miss or Mrs. before their typed names
if they wish. Some doctors like to have M. D. typed after
their names when writing on professional matters. Military
officials, if writing in an official capacity, require their
rank and branch of service after their names (like business
titles). Few businessmen have personal titles typed before or
after their typewritten names.

Thomas Allerton
Ruth Ellen French, Chairman
Virginia F. Saxon

Page 2 of a 2-page committee report

NOTES: 1. Any report may be typed as a regular manuscript, in bound or unbound form.
2. Many experts recommend using an abbreviated title (like Personal Titles),
called a "running head," in the heading of all pages after the first page.

Lessons 121-122 : *Skill Drills*

WARMUP *(Each line 3 times)*   ◁ **60** ▷

bout crux duet fuzz hung junk quip suit swum taut vuln ugly
were 2343 tree 5433 prey 0436 your 6974 wipe 2803 pipe 0803
We had been told that he was "tough"; he was not so at all.
12-Sec. 5| 10| 15| 20| 25| 30| 35| 40| 45| 50| 55| 60|

CAPITAL-CONTROL PREVIEW *(Each line 3 times)*

A These Strong Bender Monday Thursday Afternoon Toastmaster
On Save Golden Harvey Friday Wednesday Excursion Discussion
All May Duncan Bridge Tuesday Morning Saturday Butterscotch

JOB 6

2-page magazine manuscript
Unarranged
Plain paper
Paragraph tab (3 spaces in)
2 carbons
Words: 227

HOW BUSINESSMEN DICTATE

◁ 40 ▷ SS

By Thomas Young
Arizona State College
Tempe, Arizona

(27 Columnar Lines)

1 | 2 | 3 | 4 | 5 | 6 | 7 | 8 | 9 | 10 DS

5-Min. Writings

0 ONE OF THE TOPICS most frequently talked about by 10
2 all who work in offices is the rate of dictation. 20
si 1.41 4 Most men feel that they dictate at a modest pace, 30
6 while most secretaries say that the dictators ac- 40
si 1.46 8 tually talk much faster than they realize. It is 50
10 hard to judge the exact speed of dictation unless 60
12 you have, and use, special devices to measure it. 70

14 A short time ago, a man who cares about this 9 79
16 matter made such a machine and measured the speed 19 89
18 of dictation as it was going on in a great number 29 99
si 20 of offices. When he analyzed the results, he had 39 109
1.38 22 quite a good picture of dictation and the jolting 49 119
24 news that no one has such a thing as an "average" 59 129
26 rate of expressing himself. His speaking varies. 69 139

◁ 40 ▷ DS 7 ▽

28 He found that businessmen have four paces of 9 148
30 speaking. About a sixth of the dictation is very 19 158
32 slow, about half is fairly fast, about a third is 29 168
si 1.39 34 fluent, and about a tenth is very rapid. He also 39 178
36 found that there is no routine pattern--dictation 49 188
38 speed is jumbled. It zigzags from fast to rapid, 59 198
40 from slow to extreme speed. It is quite a story. 69 208

Plus ➧ 1 | 2

JOB 7

3-column table

Full sheet
Boxed
2 tab stops
Words: 40

EVERY DICTATOR'S CHANGE OF PACE

Single spacing

Dictator's Manner	Dictation Pattern	Per Cent of Time
Groping	Very slow	15.0
Thoughtful	Steady	45.0
Confident	Fluent	30.0
Sprinting	Very fast	10.0
TOTAL	....	100.0

Double spacing

JOB 2

1-page report
by a committee
In pica
Plain paper
Center tab
Para. tab
Words: 351

Any report (any length) may be single spaced on
a 6-inch line, with top margin of 1 or 2 inches.

PERSONAL TITLES IN BUSINESS CORRESPONDENCE ₃ →   ◁ **6 in.** ▷

7
▽

The committee appointed by Mr. Wilson to study the use
of personal titles in business correspondence found that the
subject is amply treated in many reference sources. It was
also found that the references are in complete agreement. ₃ →

Put 2 blank lines before,
and 1 after, a subheading.

Definition ₂ →

This report deals only with personal titles; it does not
concern business titles (such as <u>Sales Manager</u>) or honorary
expressions (such as <u>The Hon.</u> or <u>Esquire</u>). ₃ →

Findings ₂ →

1.   In business correspondence, every personal name used
in a salutation or address (both in the letter and on the envelope) is preceded by some kind of personal title.

2.   <u>Mr.</u> and <u>Mrs.</u> are always abbreviated. Other personal
titles are not abbreviated unless a first name or at least one
initial precedes the last name. Examples:

<u>Right</u>: Dr. E. G. Doe, Doctor Doe, Dear Doctor Doe:
<u>Wrong</u>: Dr. Doe, E. G. Doe, Dear Dr. Doe:

<u>Right</u>: Col. E. Doe, Colonel Doe, Dear Colonel Doe:
<u>Wrong</u>: Col. Doe, E. Doe, Dear Col. Doe:

3.   When a title is used with a name in the letter body,
the rule (No. 2) about abbreviations applies. Example: "We
saw Mr. Jones talking with Doctor Doe at the meeting."

4.   Personal titles are not commonly typed in signatures,
although women may type <u>Miss</u> or <u>Mrs.</u> before their typed names
if they wish. Some doctors like to have <u>M. D.</u> typed <u>after</u>
their names when writing on professional matters. Military
officials, if writing in an official capacity, require their
rank and branch of service after their names (like business
titles). Few businessmen have personal titles typed before or
after their typewritten names. ₂ →

Chairman's name may
be first, last, or
in alphabetic order.

Thomas Allerton
Ruth Ellen French, Chairman
Virginia F. Saxon

You will need 2 sheets of plain paper or Workbook pages 131-134. Type Parts A and B (below) on opposite sides of one sheet, and Parts C and D (next page) on opposite sides of the second sheet. Use these scales to grade your work:

GRADING SCALE FOR PART A *(Straight Copy)*

Step 1: Compute words a minute.	Step 2: Deduct for errors—		Step 3: Grade the remaining words a minute this way:	
	1 error: —2	4 errors: —10		45 or higher: A
	2 errors: —4	5 errors: —14		40 to 44 wam: B
	3 errors: —7	6 errors: —18		35 to 39 wam: C
				30 to 34 wam: D

GRADING SCALE FOR PARTS B, C, D *(Production Work)*

TAKE OFF:	—3 for each major error (top margin, line length, line-spacing, general correctness of form, etc.) —2 for each minor error (blocking, aligning, centering, indenting, etc., of individual parts of the job) —1 for each typographical error	TOTAL TAKEN OFF	8-7	6-4	3-2	1-0
		GRADE	D	C	B	A

PART A: STRAIGHT-COPY TEST *(si 1.30)*

Take a 5-minute writing on the copy below; or, type it once and grade your work as though you had typed it at 47 words a minute.

◁**50**▷ DS

PART B: NEWS-RELEASE TEST *(si 1.33)*

Type the material below as a news release authorized by William Miller. Entitle it MM&S TO OPEN SCHOOL FOR COLOR ENGINEERS. Date line should be ATLANTA, Ga., Feb. 22___. Use workbook form or the heading style on page 134.

◁**6 in.**▷ DS

5-Min. Writings				
0	40			

1 | 2 | 3 | 4 | 5 | 6 | 7 | 8 | 9 | 10 |

0	40	The first special school for engineers to be	9
2	42	trained in how to use color to help production in	19
4	44	plants and offices will open here within the next	29
si 1.28 6	46	six weeks. The new school will be sponsored by a	39
8	48	local paint firm that has set the pace in the new	49
10	50	field of color dynamics. Head of the school will	59
12	52	be Dr. William Martin. (61 words)	64
13	53	Announcement of plans for the new school was	9	73
15	55	made by Martin Miller, head of the firm of Martin	19	83
17	57	Miller & Sons, who pointed out that the company's	29	93
si 1.36 19	59	research in the use of color had not only created	39	103
21	61	a new field of study, but also stirred up demands	49	113
23	63	for experts who could serve as color consultants.	59	123
25	65	Only by setting up the new school could the local	69	133
27	67	firm serve its patrons. (130 words)	74	138
28	68	Men enrolled for the training will be put on	9	147
29	70	the MM&S payroll in return for a pledge to remain	19	157
31	72	with the firm for two years. They must be twenty	29	167
si 1.27 33	74	or older, must be single, and must have completed	39	177
35	76	two or more years of college. The training is to	49	187
37	78	be a six-month program in the "color kitchens" of	59	197
39	80	the firm's Atlanta plant. (192 words)	64	202

Plus ▶   1   2

JOB 1

Manuscript
display
  Exact copy
  Plain paper
  Center
  3 tabs
  Words: 450

Suggestion: Have you wondered how many clear, readable carbon copies you could possibly type at one time? Or, have you wanted to try your hand at preparing a stencil or spirit master? The material below, which is especially valuable as a reference, would be worthy of multicopy production.

THE WRITING OF NUMBERS

Write in Words--

a. <u>Ten</u> and the numbers below:

The plane has four jet engines.
She had five dogs and two cats.

b. Round numbers, in general:

About ten thousand should come.
I expect nearly twelve hundred.

c. Numbers that start a sentence:

Twenty-eight players took part.
Two hundred twelve were needed.

d. Indefinite amounts of money:

They gave thousands of dollars.
He had several hundred dollars.

e. Numbers that are ordinals:

It is their second anniversary.
It's his twenty-first birthday.

f. Ages and years, when general:

He must be seventeen years old.
He worked here for eight years.

g. Names of centuries, decades:

Back in the nineteenth century.
He told about the gay nineties.

h. Street names, <u>ten</u> and below:

The store is near Fifth Avenue.
She lives at 191 Second Avenue.

i. Time, informal and <u>o'clock</u>:

Come over at a quarter to nine.
My plane leaves at ten o'clock.

j. Military, political divisions:

With the Forty-second Regiment.
The Fortieth Election District.

Write in Figures--

a. Exact numbers above <u>ten</u>:

The airplane had 36 passengers.
He has 367 or 368 Irish stamps.

b. Round numbers in advertising:

We have sold over 10,000 books.
We get nearly 500 orders a day.

c. Numbers in a series:

Get 8 bags, 4 boxes, 28 crates.
I saw 6 men, 11 boys, 14 women.

d. Exact amounts of money:

They gave $1,000 to the school.
He had either $1,500 or $2,000.

e. Numbers used with percentages:

No discount is over 8 per cent.
Sales: shoes, 6%; coats, 7.3%.

f. Ages and years, when exact:

John is 17 years 11 months old.
He worked 21 years and 3 weeks.

g. Graduation, historical years:

He belongs to the class of '56.
The fine spirit of '76 and '98.

h. Street names above <u>ten</u>:*

The store is near 188th Street.
He lives at 919 East 22 Street.

i. Time with minutes, <u>a.m.</u>, <u>p.m.</u>:

I expect Ralph at 8:45 tonight.
The planes depart at 10:35 p.m.

j. Dimensions and measurements:

The back room is 14 by 25 feet.
The pail holds 2 quarts 1 pint.

---

* Whether to use <u>st</u>, <u>d</u>, <u>rd</u>, or <u>th</u> after street-name numbers depends on local preference. More and more businessmen prefer not to use them.

PART C: LETTER TEST (*si 1.53*)

Type this average-length letter on a workbook letterhead. Use indented form and single spacing. Make all the corrections and changes indicated.

| 1 | 2 | 3 | 4 | 5 | 6 | 7 | 8 | 9 | 10 | 11 |

Today's date   Manufacturers' Assurance Company

19 (So.) Wabash (Ave.)   Chicago 3, Illinois   Gentlemen:

We believe that it is time that we review the   9
accident insurance rates that we are now paying your firm   20
in behalf of our six factories.   27
The rates we are now paying were set up in 1944   36
on the basis of our accident records for a four-year period that 49
began in January, 1940. Since we made our arrangements with   61
with your firm, the number of accidents and the extent of   72
damages have decreased so much that we feel a rate adjustment is due us. 87
I am enclosing a table that gives the accidental   96
figures for the six factories concerned. Those that in-   107
volve damages are, of course, already in your own records.   119
The details of the accidents are all on the a matter of record, 130
and the record is at your disposal. We sincerely hope that   142
your underwriters will restudy our rates and that we shall   153
have action on them before the start of the next quarter.   165

Yours very truly,   Southern States Corporation

C. D. Ferry, Treasurer   Initials? Other notations?

PART D: TABULATION TEST (*116 five-stroke words*)

Center this ruled table on a full sheet of paper, columns 6 spaces apart.

SOUTHERN STATES CORPORATION

Average Number Accidents Per Month

Factory Location	1945 to 1949	1950 to 1954	1955 to Date
Chattanooga, Tennessee	18.3	16.5	10.8
Fort Worth, Texas	12.4	10.3	8.7
Greensboro, North Carolina	31.7	24.9	18.7
Little Rock, Arkansas	15.0	12.1	10.3
Memphis, Tennessee	9.0	6.4	6.3
Montgomery, Alabama	. . .	4.5	3.4
Totals	86.4	74.7	58.2

UNIT 20
MANUSCRIPTS

In this unit: (1) committee reports; (2) display arrangements; (3) "pivoting"; and (4) the use of "leaders." The work will be easiest if, before starting the jobs, you first read pages 169-176 and answer the study questions on Workbook pages 177-178.

In this unit: (1) committee reports; (2) display arrangements; (3) "pivoting"; and (4) the use of "leaders." The work will be easiest if, before starting the jobs, you first read pages 169-176 and answer the study questions on Workbook pages 177-178.

WARMUP (*Each line 3 times*)   ◁ **60** ▷

```
body crow foam fogs hock jolt mope oxen quod upon void zone
wey 236 out 975 rot 495 rip 480 pot 095 try 546 our 974 974
We finally got "the good news":  The regiment would not go.
12-Sec. 5|    10|    15|    20|    25|    30|    35|    40|    45|    50|    55|    60|
```

CAPITAL-CONTROL PREVIEW (*Each line 3 times*)

```
It Good Round Number Esquire Personal Military Twenty-eight
On Mrs. Exact Thomas Example Allerton Definition Indefinite
All True Write Saxon Virginia Colonel Dimensions Graduation
```

ALPHABET-REVIEW PARAGRAPHS (*2 copies / si 1.31*)   ◁ **50** ▷
                                                                    DS

5-Min. Writings		1 | 2 | 3 | 4 | 5 | 6 | 7 | 8 | 9 | 10	
0	47	The person who wants to get ahead on the job	9
2	49	has to learn how to use common sense. It is fine	19
4	51	to know and to be able to quote the rules, but it	29
6	53	is better to know when the exact rule ought to be	39
si 1.29 8	55	set aside. You have to analyze the situation. A	49
10	57	report can be set up in manuscript style, for ex-	59
12	59	ample; but if you have to duplicate it, you might	69
14	61	be smarter to use single spacing so that you will	79
16	63	get the report on fewer stencil or master sheets.	89
18	65	On the other hand, the saving of paper might	9 | 98
20	67	not be as important as making a better impression	19 | 108
22	69	on the executives to whom you will send copies of	29 | 118
si 1.36 24	71	the report; you must use your judgment. You must	39 | 128
26	73	choose between the quick short cut and the longer	49 | 138
28	75	method that gives a more attractive product. You	59 | 148
30	77	must realize that there is a right time for each.	69 | 158
32	79	Good judgment in such matters might not come	9 | 167
34	81	until you have risked a few mistakes. You should	19 | 177
35	83	repeat some of your jobs, when time permits, try-	29 | 187
si 1.30 37	85	ing to arrange them in a different way, or trying	39 | 197
39	87	to fit them on a smaller size of paper, or taking	49 | 207
41	89	other liberties with the exact directions. True,	59 | 217
43	91	you must be quick to do what you are told to do--	69 | 227
45	93	but you must nurture your judgment skill as well.	79 | 237
Plus ➡		1 2	

PRODUCTION PRACTICE (*Jobs 1-3*)

Jobs 1 and 2 contain information you should study and remember. Ask your instructor whether you should make either job into a multicopy project. Jobs 2 and 3 illustrate two ways to prepare a report of an investigation. Use plain paper for all three jobs.

PART 5

WARMUP: Flash Phrases *(Each line 3 times)*

◁ **60** ▷

```
a;qpa;z/a; slwoslx.sl dkeidkc,dk fjrufjvmfj ghtyghbngh a;a;
of the or the if the so the in the at the by the and to the
this is what is that is when is why is who is she is now is
```

SPEED DRILL: Word Families *(Each line 3 times)*

```
approach applaud appeal appear apple append apply apron apt
sound solve sober soak soup soda soft sort soil son sod sow
where whole which while whose whirl when what whip whim who
```

SPEED SENTENCES *(Each line 3 times)*

12-Sec.
Writings

```
If it is their turn to go, they may find the work cut down.
The profit of eighty bushels of corn may pay for their men.
Rickey may throw the fur pelt down and pay the duty for it.
```

12-Sec. 5| 10| 15| 20| 25| 30| 35| 40| 45| 50| 55|

SPEED PARAGRAPH *(3 copies / si 1.11)*

1-Min.
Writings

1 | 2 | 3 | 4 | 5 | 6 | 7 | 8 | 9 | 10 | 11 | 12

```
One of the fine traits that we ought to form while young is   12
the habit of being nice to others.  We ought not to have to   24
make an effort to be nice.  But if it takes an effort, then   36
we should make it.  It is too bad that so many of us do not   48
learn how to grin while we are still young enough to learn.   60
```

SPEED PREVIEW *(Each line 3 times)*

◁ **60** ▷

```
maintain checking without habits doubt bring help copy keep
carriage minutes someone failing speed rings eyes shoe rate
```

SUSTAINED-SPEED PARAGRAPH *(2 copies / si 1.15)*

3-Min.
Writings

| | | | | | | | | | | | | DS |
| 1 | 2 | 3 | 4 | 5 | 6 | 7 | 8 | 9 | 10 | 11 | 12 | |

```
 0        If you are trying, as you should, to maintain for many   11
 4    minutes the same rate of speed that you are able to get for   23
 8    a minute or two, you will find it a big help to keep check-  35
12    ing on your motions.  Ask someone to watch you as you type.  47
16    It takes just one or two bad habits to bring on fatigue and  59
20    cut down your speed.  One of the most common of all the bad  71
24    habits is failing to keep the eyes on the copy.  There seem  83
28    to be some who doubt that their arm is strong enough to get  95
32    the carriage back without help from the eyes.  If that shoe  107
36    fits you, better get rid of it.  It is a bad habit to have,  119
40    one that rings up a lot of errors and cuts down your speed.  131
```

Plus ▶   1 | 2 | 3 | 4

Part 5
LESSON **101**
Unit 17

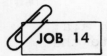

Form: 4 fill-in
postal cards
  Shown in pica
  Workbook forms
Address cards
  to list below
Words, total: 121

THE CENTURY INSURANCE COMPANY
255 Broadway
Buffalo 4, New York

March 19, 19--

Dear Mr. Quinette:

We have received your request for a copy of:

"How Much Insurance Should I Have?"

We are sending it today, with our compliments. We hope
that it will prove to be of interest and value and that
we may have the pleasure of serving you again.

SERVICE MANAGER

Fill-in postal card is used for routine acknowledgments.

Mr. Charles L. Quinette, 2839 Fairfield Avenue, Fort Wayne 6, Indiana
Mrs. Katherine Newman, 475 Haledon Avenue, Paterson 2, New Jersey
Mr. Theodore Chadwick, Brent Lighting Company, 562 West 65th Street, Chicago 38, Illinois
Miss Freda J. McLellan, Hobart Metal Company, 109 Locust Street, St. Louis 3, Missouri

JOB 15

Form: 4 labels
  Shown in pica
  Workbook forms
Use addresses
  listed above
Words, total: 61

As when addressing an
envelope, use double
spacing for a 3-line
address; single spacing
for a 4-line address.

Labels come singly
or in perforated
rolls or sheets.

THE CENTURY INSURANCE COMPANY
255 Broadway • Buffalo 4, New York

Mr. Charles L. Quinette

2839 Fairfield Avenue

Fort Wayne 6, Indiana

THE CENTURY INSURANCE COMPANY
255 Broadway • Buffalo 4, New York

Mr. Theodore Chadwick
Brent Lighting Company
562 West 65th Street
Chicago 38, Illinois

Labels are easy to type.

WARMUP: "AL" Drill *(Each line 3 times)*

◁ **60** ▷

```
a;qpa;z/a;slwoslx.sldkeidkc,dkfjrufjvmfjghtyghbngh
alarm alone alert alien alike alibi alto also ales
half pale sale male fall talk walk malt salt walls
signal moral final usual trial peal meal real seal
```

SPEED DRILL: Manipulative Techniques *(3 copies)*

➤ Move margin stop so that it locks here. Set a tab stop at every tenth space across the line.

Margin Release	for them	for them	for them	for them	for them	for t---
Tabulator	the	the	the	the	the	the
Tab and Backspacer	the	them	them	them	them	them
Tabulator	the	the	the	the	the	the

SPEED DRILL: One-Hand Words *(3 copies)*

12-Sec. and ½-Minute Writings

```
     1   2   3   4   5   6   7   8   9   10  11  12
add bag cat egg fed gas red sad tab vat ate ewe sat age was    12
joy lip oil you ply ink inn him pup hip ill kin pun yon mum    24

adze babe cafe dare edge face gave race save tact vast vest    12
loom lull kill nook pill mill noon hook hoop null poll look    24
12-Sec. 5|  10|  15|  20|  25|  30|  35|  40|  45|  50|  55|  60|
```

SPEED-UP SENTENCES: One-Hand Words *(Each line 3 times)*

◁ **60** ▷

1-Min. Writings

```
     1   2   3   4   5   6   7   8   9   10  11  12
My case was deferred after John agreed on greater tax fees.    12
In my opinion, Lynn was dazed after severe stress in water.    24
Phillip was my best pupil after we defeated Joplin in polo.    36
You gave Johnny a great scare after you faced a grave test.    48
```

SUSTAINED-SPEED SENTENCES *(2 copies / si 1.27)*

3-Min. Writings

```
      1   2   3   4   5   6   7   8   9   10  11  12
 0  Both boys were busy with very good news from some book club.    12
 4  Will they give much help when that girl goes away from home?   24
 8  That same call came when they were away from work last week.   36
12  Your real wish will come true many days from this very hour.   48
16  This last plan that they said they made does seem very good.   60
20  Those older folks often spoke about their never being early.   72
24  Party music often makes folks happy after being extra tired.  84
28  Those seven girls wrote every month after their awful fight.  96
32  These women think those dress sales might bring extra value.  108
36  Keith might stamp these first sixty short forms twice again.  120
Plus ➧      1           2           3           4
```

WARMUP (*Each line 3 times*)   ◁ **60** ▷

```
axis bird film high jilt pain pick pity quiz riot view size
wept 2305 tire 5843 tore 5943 trip 5480 pity 0856 your 6974
He had the gall to sit there and say, "I refuse to answer!"
```
12-Sec. 5| 10| 15| 20| 25| 30| 35| 40| 45| 50| 55| 60|

CAPITAL-CONTROL PREVIEW (*Each line 3 times*)

```
Mrs. Case Yours Newman Should Charles Quinette Pennsylvania
The How Much Freda March Angelo Chadwick Insurance McLellan
If Miss Have Rocca Sixth Avenue Theodore Benjamin Katherine
```

PRODUCTION PRACTICE (*Jobs 13-15*)

Type Jobs 13-15 on the workbook forms or on sheets of paper of appropriate size. Note particularly the marginal notation about addressing labels; apply this information also to the envelope you address for Job 13 and to the postal cards you address in Job 14.

JOB 13

Hanging-indented
letter
  In pica
  Letterhead
  Para. tab
  Center tab
Words: 154
  Body: 125

```
        1 |  2 |  3 |  4 |  5 |  6 |  7 |  8 |  9 | 10
                                          March 18, 19--        4

Mr. Benjamin Case                                              8
1935 Sixth Avenue                                             11
Altoona, Pennsylvania                                        16

Dear Mr. Case:                                               19

If you type many sales letters, this letter form is          29
        a good one to use now and then.  The letter          38
        must be planned for it, of course, so that           47
        the starting words that "hang" in the margin         56
        will have some common point of interest.             64

If you wish to use this form, which is known as the          74
        hanging-indented form, you indent all lines,         83
        except the first, in each paragraph, letting         92
        the key words project into the margin.              100

If you do try this form, you will wish to remember          110
        that you may indent as many or as few spaces        119
        as you wish.  In this letter, the indentions        128
        are for seven spaces--just enough to make the       137
        words "If you" stand out clearly.                   144

                        Yours very sincerely, 4 ➧            149


                        Angelo della Rocca 2 ➧               153
AR:URS                                                      154
```

WARMUP: Balanced-Hand Words *(Each line 3 times)*

◁ **50** ▷

```
rs rst rstu rstuv rstuvw rstuvw rstuv rstu rst rs
aid bog coal dish eight fight gland icicle handle
jay ken lair maid neigh oriel panel quench ritual
sod tug urns vial whale works yamen visual Zurich
```

CONTROL DRILL: D, J, E *(Each line 3 times)*

```
dawn dike dock drop dwarf drain ditch delay daily
glad edit kind idea bread grade heard index salad

jack jury jilt jowl jaunt jewel joint judge juice
joys ajar eject banjo reject object rejoin abject

each else envy spic equal eject elect eight ember
anew life item have debit alone clerk cause refer
```

CONTROL SENTENCES: Alphabet Review *(Each line 3 times)*

◁ **60** ▷

½- and
1-Min.
Writings

```
     1 |  2 |  3 |  4 |  5 |  6 |  7 |  8 |  9 | 10 | 11 | 12
On his way here, that quick fox jumped back over a gazelle.    12

My fine black ax just zipped through the wood quite evenly.    24

The six zebras jumped out of the winter glare very quickly.    36

Max worked quietly, alphabetizing the cards for vital jobs.    48
```

CONTROL PREVIEW *(Each line 3 times)*

```
10 to 15 ice crawl extent uneven slowly "control jeopardize
rate judge speed" expert inching hazards question situation
```

ALPHABET-REVIEW PARAGRAPH *(2 copies / si 1.23)*

◁ **60** ▷
DS

*5-Min.
Writings

There are some who feel[1] that the way to type with[2] good control is to type[3] slowly, 16

as though typing[4] in second gear; they are[5] wrong. There is more to[6] it than that. It is 34

true[7] that you cannot type with[8] expert control if you are[9] zipping along at your[10] 50

very top rate; it is true[11] that you must relax the[12] speed drive to some extent.[13] But 66

the situation is[14] quite a bit like walking[15] on ice. If you race, of[16] course you lose your 84

balance[17] and fall; but if you[18] just crawl along, inching[19] your way, you skid more[20] 100

than ever, for all the[21] uneven spots jeopardize your[22] footing. There are more[23] haz- 116

ards in walking too[24] slowly on ice, as many a[25] limping old man has found;[26] and 131

there is such a thing[27] as going too slowly when[28] typing, too. The question[29] is, "What 148

speed is the[30] one for control?" Most [31] experts judge that the[32] "control speed" is 10 to 165

15[33] per cent under the top[34] speed rate for 5 minutes.[35] 175

*See scoring directions on page 99.

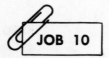

JOB 10

Forms: 2 receipts
Model, reduced
Workbook forms
Words, total: 90

**Illustration of a
typewritten receipt**

```
                                              March 17, 19 57
Received from    John Sandusky - - - - - - - - - - - - - - -
                 Three Hundred Fifty and no/100 - - - - - - - - - - - Dollars
                 On Account - - - - - - - - - - - - - - - - - - - - - - -
                                              THE BLACK-GRAY COMPANY

$ 350.00
```

No. 3-66: From The Black-Gray Company to John Sandusky, for $350, in full payment on account.

No. 3-67: From The Black-Gray Company to Cyril W. Maud, for $189.65, on account.

JOB 11

Forms: 2 notes
Model, reduced
Workbook forms
Words, total: 96

**Illustration of a
promissory note**

```
$625.85                              March 17, 19 57
Thirty days - - - - - - - - - - - after date  we  promise to pay to
the order of  The Black-Gray Company - - - - - - - - - - - - - - -
Six Hundred Twenty-five and 85/100 - - - - - - - - - - - - - Dollars
at  United Fidelity Company, Los Angeles, California - - - - - - -
    Value received                   ROGERS WHOLESALE COMPANY
No. 183      Due  April 16, 1957
```

Promissory Note No. 183: The Rogers Wholesale Company promises to pay $625.85 to the order of The Black-Gray Company, at the United Fidelity Company, of Los Angeles, California, 30 days from today.

Promissory Note No. 184: The Ford-Bart Company promises to pay $900.00 to the order of The Black-Gray Company, at the Second National Bank, of Bakersfield, California, 60 days from today.

JOB 12

Forms: 2 drafts
Model, reduced
Workbook forms
Words, total: 120

**Illustration of a
commercial draft**

```
$1,500.00           San Francisco, California, March 17, 19 57
At sixty (60) days' sight - - - - - - - - - - - - - - - - - Pay to
the order of  The National Trust Company, San Francisco, California
One Thousand Five Hundred and no/100 - - - - - - - - - - Dollars
Value received and charge the same to account of  THE BLACK-GRAY COMPANY
To  The Crest Corporation
    Bakersfield, California
No. 341
```

Draft No. 341: The National Trust Company, of San Francisco, is to deposit $1,500.00 to the account of the Crest Corporation, of Bakersfield, California. The Black-Gray Company, of San Francisco, guarantees to repay the bank within 60 days from today.

Draft No. 342: The Southern Trust Company of Los Angeles is to deposit $750.00 to the Account of Swem & Swem Co., 87 Spring Street, San Jose 10, California. The Black-Gray Company, of San Francisco, guarantees to repay the bank within 30 days from today.

WARMUP: Left-Hand Security *(Each line 3 times)* ◁ **50** ▷

```
rs tu vw rstuvw rs tu vw rstuvw rs tu vw rstuvwvu
ssts ssrs ssvs ssws ssts ssrs ssvs ssws ssts ssrs
rRsS tTuU vVwW rRsS tTuU vVwW rRsS tTuU vVwW rRsS
```

CONTROL DRILL: Adjacent Letters *(Each line 3 times)*

AS
```
as ask ash aster asked ashes ascend aspect aspire
last alas past bias hash peas task seas mash case
```

ER
```
era ere err erase erode erupt ergot eraser ermine
germ ever were veer where infer exert never every
```

WE
```
web wed wet wept weak weld wend weary wedge weird
awe owe tower lower showed grower newest dwelling
```

OI
```
oil boil oily soil coin choice doing point enjoin
coil join loin spoil joist boiler jointly invoice
```

CONTROL SENTENCES: Adjacent Letters *(Each line 3 times)* ◁ **60** ▷

½-Min.
Writings   1 | 2 | 3 | 4 | 5 | 6 | 7 | 8 | 9 | 10 | 11 | 12

```
Cass Baker erected a vast dwelling just west of that point.   12
The soil west of Boise was choice, and we offered him cash.   24
Web may join Ashley's choir after he has all his work done.   36
The weather may often cause soil erosion on the West Coast.   48
```

CONTROL DRILL: Alphabet-Review Lines *(Each line 3 times)*

½- and
1-Min.
Writings   1 | 2 | 3 | 4 | 5 | 6 | 7 | 8 | 9 | 10 | 11 | 12

```
many worth seized expect quiver jacket gentle almost before   12
warm quote church hazard expend bridge stroke verify jungle   24
next puzzle because history jonquil damaged knowing favored   36
work chives expert morning against banquet justify realized   48
Maxwell binding skeptic anything frequent organize juvenile   60
```

CONTROL PARAGRAPH: Concentration *(3 copies)*

1-Min.
Writings   1 | 2 | 3 | 4 | 5 | 6 | 7 | 8 | 9 | 10 | 11 | 12

```
    Appropriate knowledge concerning those qualitative and    11
quantitative characteristics and qualities of individuality   23
ameliorating ambidextrousness, transmuted those individuals   35
into unctuous hypocrisy.                                      40
```

JOB 8

Forms: 2
voucher checks
Model, reduced
Workbook forms
Words, total: 82

This is one of many forms of voucher checks. All are double. One part (top, bottom, or side) is a standard check. The other part tells what the check is for.

To type on ruled lines, use variable spacer to adjust form so that line is in the position that underscore would be. Review page 91.

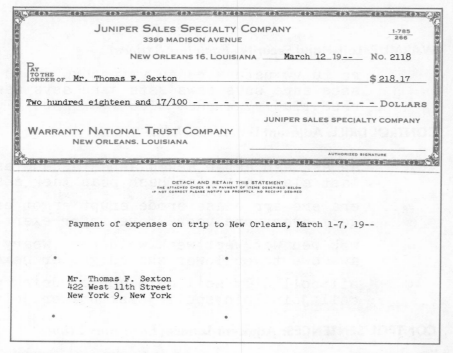

JUNIPER SALES SPECIALTY COMPANY
3399 MADISON AVENUE

NEW ORLEANS 16, LOUISIANA ____March 12__ 19 -- ___ No. 2118

PAY
TO THE
ORDER OF Mr. Thomas F. Sexton $ 218.17

Two hundred eighteen and 17/100 - - - - - - - - - - - - - - - - - - DOLLARS

JUNIPER SALES SPECIALTY COMPANY

WARRANTY NATIONAL TRUST COMPANY
NEW ORLEANS. LOUISIANA

AUTHORIZED SIGNATURE

DETACH AND RETAIN THIS STATEMENT
THE ATTACHED CHECK IS IN PAYMENT OF ITEMS DESCRIBED BELOW
IF NOT CORRECT PLEASE NOTIFY US PROMPTLY. NO RECEIPT DESIRED

Payment of expenses on trip to New Orleans, March 1-7, 19--

Mr. Thomas F. Sexton
422 West 11th Street
New York 9, New York

Illustration of a voucher check

Courtesy Dennison & Sons

Voucher Check No. 2118: Pay $218.17 to Mr. Thomas F. Sexton, 422 West 11th Street, New York 9, New York, in "Payment of expenses on trip to New Orleans, March 1-7, 19___."

Voucher Check No. 2119: Pay $15.50 to Mrs. Helen W. Jackson, 148 Clinton Avenue, Minneapolis 8, Minnesota, in "Payment of personal services and expenses as a member of the Minneapolis Juniper Club."

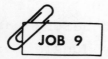

JOB 9

Forms: 2
standard checks
Model, reduced
Workbook forms
Words, total: 37

JUNIPER SALES SPECIALTY COMPANY   No. M-15
3399 MADISON AVENUE

NEW ORLEANS 16, LOUISIANA ___March 12__ 19 --

PAY
TO THE
ORDER OF Cox-Marley Company $ 139.00

One hundred thirty-nine and no/100 - - - - - - - - - - - - - - - - - - DOLLARS

JUNIPER SALES SPECIALTY COMPANY

WARRANTY NATIONAL TRUST COMPANY
NEW ORLEANS. LOUISIANA

AUTHORIZED SIGNATURE

Illustration of a standard check

Courtesy Dennison & Sons

Check No. M-15: Pay $139.00 to the Cox-Marley Company.
Check No. M-16: Pay $37.44 to the Brougham Delivery Company.

WARMUP: Keyboard Review *(Each line 3 times)*

```
abc def ghi jkl mno pqr stu vwx yz- , . / ? ; : !
111 s2s d3d f4f f5f j6j j7j k8k l9l ;0; ;-; ;½;¢;
111 s"s d#d f$f f%f j_j j&j k'k l(l ;); ;*; ;¼;@;
```

NUMBER DRILL: 1, 5, 6 *(Each line 3 times)*

```
f 5 f5 15 51 155 551 1551 5515 1515 155 551 15 51
j 6 j6 16 61 166 661 1661 6616 1616 166 661 16 61
15 16 56 156 651 516 1561 5161 6156 615 156 61 51
```

NUMBER DRILL: We 23's *(Each line 3 times)*

```
rout 4975 your 6974 pure 0743 writ 2485 prey 0436
tort 5945 rote 4953 yipe 6803 wept 2305 true 5473
wiry 2846 wipe 2803 pity 0856 trow 5492 pout 0975
```

NUMBER SENTENCES: Pair Pattern *(Each line 3 times)*

½-Min. Writings

1	2	3	4	5	6	7	8	9	10	11	12

```
He assigned us pages 10, 28, 39, 47, and 56 for our lesson.   12
She scored 100, 93, 82, 74, and 65 on that series of tests.   24
He grossed 63, 60, 59, 56, 52, 51, 48, and 47 on the tests.   36
See pages 28, 39, and 47, in Booklet #1056, for new models.   48
```

NUMBER DRILL: Cumulative Count *(Each line 2 times)*

1-Min. Writings

1	2	3	4	5	6	7	8	9	10	11	12

```
2801 3902 4703 5604 1005 6606 7707 8208 9309 6710 1611 1712   12
1013 7414 6515 6716 7617 2618 3919 4720 5621 6722 8623 9724   24
1625 1726 1627 2828 3929 4730 5631 1032 6133 7134 6735 7636   36
8237 9338 6539 7440 1041 2742 9643 8744 7245 6346 7247 6748   48
```

NUMBER-REVIEW PARAGRAPH *(2 copies / si 1.41)*   DS

2-Min. Writings

1	2	3	4	5	6	7	8	9	10	11	12

```
 0 | 35     John's company now has 56 stores, located in 30 cities   11
 6 | 40   in the West.  They employ 147 women and 138 men, or a total  23
12 | 46   of 285 workers, in these stores.  The various products they  35
18 | 52   sell are supplied by over 90 different firms, located in 26  47
24 | 58   states.  This is an amazing set of figures when you realize  59
30 | 64   that this company opened its first store in 1947.            69
```

Plus ▶ | 1 | 2 | 3 | 4 | 5 | 6 |

feeds paper,[41] dampened by a chemical "spirit,"[42] against the master; and the sheet 300

rolls[43] out, a copy of the master. You can[44] get the carbon in all sizes and[45] in four 317

colors—purple and blue and[46] red and green. The purple carbon[47] is used most; it will 333

give the most[48] copies—up to 200, if you use quality[49] carbon. 345

STENCIL COPIES. The[50] fact that liquid will always leak[51] through holes is the 360

root of the stencil[52] process. Stencils are just thin[53] sheets of tissue, coated with wax[54] or 378

plastic. When you type your master[55] copy on a stencil, you make holes[56] in the coat- 394

ing. Then, when the[57] stencil is put on a machine with a[58] drum full of ink, the ink 410

seeps[59] through the openings you have made and[60] prints a copy of the typing on each[61] 427

sheet that passes through the[62] machine. There are always jobs for[63] typists who spe- 443

cialize in stencil work.[64] 448

PRODUCTION PRACTICE *(Jobs 7-12)*

Type Jobs 7-12 on workbook forms or on similar forms that you may be able to
obtain from a local business house. Only Job 7 will take more than a few minutes;
the others are brief. Each workbook form is given in duplicate (printed on both
sides of the paper) so that, after you have typed each job once, you may start
them over in the time that you will have left.

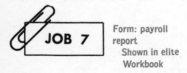

JOB 7

Form: payroll
report
Shown in elite
Workbook

Words: 86

JUNIPER SALES SPECIALTY COMPANY
PAYROLL

OFFICE OR DEPARTMENT Advertising   FOR PERIOD March 6   THROUGH March 10   19 --

EMPLOYEE	NO.	HOURS WORKED	COMPENSATION			DEDUCTIONS		PAID
			Regular	Extra	Total	FOAB	Income Tax	Net Amount
Barkley, Ellen	1	45	56.67	11.39	68.06	1.36	10.10	56.60
Dodge, Victor L.	2	40	85.00	.....	85.00	1.70	13.00	70.30
Graham, Karl	3	$42\frac{1}{4}$	52.50	6.50	59.00	1.18	8.20	49.62
Morton, Annette	4	44	87.50	10.47	97.97	1.96	15.20	80.81
Thompson, Fred T.	5	40	75.00	.....	75.00	1.50	11.20	62.30
Upton, Robert D.	6	vac.	90.00	.....	90.00	1.80	14.10	74.10
TOTALS	7	$251\frac{1}{4}$	446.67	28.36	475.03	9.50	71.80	393.73
	8							

WARMUP: Reach Review *(Each line 3 times)* ◁50▷

```
Aaa Bff Cdd Ddd Eee Fff Gff Hjj Ikk Jjj Kkk Lll
Mjj Njj Oll P;; Qaa Rff Sss Tff Ujj Vff Wss Xss
Yjj Zaa 2ss 911 3dd 8kk 4ff 7jj 5ff 6jj 0;; ½;;
```

NUMBER DRILL: Adjacents *(Each line 3 times)*

```
1231 1231 1341 1341 1451 1451 1671 1671 1781 1781
1891 1891 1901 1901 10-- 10-- 1091 1091 1981 1981
1871 1871 1761 1761 1541 1541 1431 1431 1321 1321
```

NUMBER DRILL: We 23's *(Each line 3 times)*

```
we 23 yow 692 tip 580 pep 030 ripe 4803 poet 0935
up 70 rep 430 tut 575 rut 475 wiry 2846 trey 5436
or 94 yip 680 wry 246 wit 285 poor 0994 pour 0974
```

SYMBOL DRILL: % - * *(Each line 3 times)*

```
                f5f f%f f%f 5% 5% 5% 4% 3% 2% 39% 28% 47% 56% 10%
                ;-; ;-; ;-; -- -- bric-a-brac -39 -28 -47 -56 -10
If * is on -     ;-; ;*; ;*; -* -* -*- -*- -*- 39* 28* 47* 56* 10*
If * is on 8     k8k k*k k*k 8* 8* 8*8 8*8 8*8 39* 28* 47* 56* 10*
If * is on 6     j6j j*j j*j 6* 6* 6*6 6*6 6*6 39* 28* 47* 56* 10*
```

Type whichever
of these 3 lines
is appropriate
for your machine.

SYMBOL SENTENCES: % - * *(Each line 3 times)* ◁60▷

½-Min.
Writings

| 1 | 2 | 3 | 4 | 5 | 6 | 7 | 8 | 9 | 10 | 11 | 12 |

```
If our coach* quits--and we hope he doesn't--we might lose.    12
Savings of 10%, 28%, 39%, and 47% were offered at the sale.    24
* John Black--football coach--asked for a 20% salary boost.    36
```

1-Min.
Writings

```
A dash is made of two hyphens--like that.  But use just one    12
hyphen--with or without spacing--for each number-span dash*    24
because, as in 19--, hyphen pairs can mean missing figures.    36
* Thus, 10 to 28% is 10-28% or 10 - 28%, but never 10--28%.    48
```

CENTURY DRIVE *(1 complete copy, up to 100)* DS

2-Min.
Writings

```
Did 1 did 2 did 3 did 4 did 5 did 6 did 7 did 8 did 9 did 10
did 11 did 12 did 13 did 14 did 15 did 16 did 17 did 18 did
19 did 20 did 21 did 22 did 23
```

⌈Continue on up to 100. Ultimate⌉
⌊goal is to reach 100 in 2 minutes.⌋

WARMUP *(Each line 3 times)*

◁ 60 ▷

```
bead flee grew help jerk next peck quip seem they vein zero
wee 233 too 599 pow 092 two 529 rue 473 rye 463 pie 083 083
You should have seen how the sheriff put them "in the jug"!
```

12-Sec. 5| 10| 15| 20| 25| 30| 35| 40| 45| 50| 55| 60|

CAPITAL-CONTROL PREVIEW *(Each line 3 times)*

```
W. Karl There Sexton Stencils Sandusky Thompson Corporation
Upton Rogers Spirit Graham Wholesale "Business" Bakersfield
Dodge Carbon Victor Delivery Brougham Cox-Marley California
```

ALPHABET-REVIEW PARAGRAPHS *(1 copy / si 1.32)*

◁ 60 ▷
DS

*7-Min. Writings

One of the firms that sell duplicators[1] has an eloquent slogan that is[2] worth examin- 16
ing: "Business runs on[3] copies." The fellow who made up[4] the phrase hit the nail on 33
the head;[5] business does run on copies—lots[6] of them. There is hardly anything[7] that is 51
typed in an office without[8] having at least one copy; there are[9] dozens of jobs for which 68
you well[10] might make hundreds of copies.[11] Copies are important to a typist.[12] 83

CARBON COPIES. Of all the methods used[13] to make copies of what is typed,[14] the 99
most common is with the use of[15] carbon paper. If you need up to a[16] dozen copies, you 116
can type them all[17] at the same time by using thin paper[18] and thin carbons— 130
even more if[19] you have an electric machine. The[20] number that you need most fre- 146
quently[21] is two or three—one for the files[22] and one for your follow-up folder,[23] and 162
perhaps an extra one to send[24] along to someone else. Many typists[25] judge it wise, and 179
perhaps it is,[26] always to make an extra, "just in[27] case." 190

SPIRIT COPIES. When you were[28] eight or so, you enjoyed writing[29] with a purple 206
pencil; you knew that[30] you could press wet paper against[31] the writing and get an 222
exact copy of[32] what you had written down. That[33] pencil contained a certain dye, 237
and[34] the fact that that dye will transfer[35] is the whole basis of the spirit[36] duplicating 255
process. You type a[37] master copy, using special carbon[38] paper that contains the dye. 272
Then you[39] put the master on a machine made[40] for the purpose. It 284

(TURN PAGE)

*The tiny number nearest where you stop is your speed on a 7-minute writ-
ing. For writings of other lengths: (1) Note number at the end of the last
full printed line you copied; (2) add 1 for each additional 5 strokes (letters
or spaces) you typed; (3) divide by number of minutes for which you typed.

UNIT 18
CORRESPONDENCE

In this unit, special problems and procedures involving:

1. The three punctuation styles—standard, full, and open.

2. Special displays—subject lines, attention lines, "blind" carbon-copy notations, postscripts, listings, etc.

3. Three new (but very much alike) letter styles —the full blocked, square blocked, and "NOMA Simplified" blocked. Before starting the jobs, read pages 149-158 closely and answer the study-guide questions on Workbook pages 137-138.

WARMUP (Each line 3 times)

◁ **60** ▷

```
back deft high joke lazy loam next nope pour quit rest wavy
were 2343 wept 2305 tour 5974 your 6974 tire 5843 trip 5480
Have you never read a story that began, "Once upon a time"?
```
12-Sec. 5| 10| 15| 20| 25| 30| 35| 40| 45| 50| 55| 60|

CAPITAL-CONTROL PREVIEW (Each line 3 times)

```
St. Some Jones Louis Bache Rhode Richmond Whenever Virginia
Now But Ralph Young Filene Thomas Training Kennard Missouri
One Ruth West Blvd. Savard Island Journal Houston Gentlemen
```

ALPHABET-REVIEW PARAGRAPHS (2 copies / si 1.31)

◁ **60** ▷
DS

3-Min. Writings | 1 | 2 | 3 | 4 | 5 | 6 | 7 | 8 | 9 | 10 | 11 | 12 |

```
 0     The other day I saw a short letter with, I judge, only      11
 4   55 or so words in the body.  But, you know, that letter had   23
 8   so many extras tacked onto it--there must have been a dozen    35
12   of them--that it took as much space as a long letter would.    47
16   It had an attention line, a subject line, a table, a quota-    59
20   tion, all three signature lines, a postscript, and a carbon    71
24   notation with six names.  It lacked only an enclosure note.    83
28       Now, the reason I mention this is that the typist must     94
31   exercise some judgment when he plans letter placement.  The   106
35   guide that we memorize is, and must be, flexible.  A change   118
39   you will need to make frequently is this one:  Whenever you   130
43   have an extra display line, such as a subject line, put one   142
47   less space after the date than you would without that line.   154
```
Plus ➡ 1 | 2 | 3 | 4

PRODUCTION PRACTICE
(Jobs 1-4)

Type Jobs 1-4 on the workbook letterheads (or, if you do not have a workbook, on plain paper on which you have ruled or creased a line about 2 inches from the top, to represent the depth of a letterhead). Note that Jobs 3 and 4 are arranged in the *style* of Job 1, but with the *punctuation pattern* of Job 2. Note also that carbons are directed for Jobs 2, 3, and 4.

JOB 5

Form: monthly
statement
  In pica
  Workbook form
  4 tabs
Words: 53

MARTIN MILLER & SONS   58 BROAD STREET
                                     ATLANTA 1, GEORGIA

Statement of Account

WITH   The National Company   DATE   April 1, 19--

           6 North Michigan Avenue

           Chicago 2, Illinois

			AMOUNT ENCLOSED
			$ . . . .

PLEASE RETURN THIS STUB WITH YOUR CHECK

DATE	REFERENCE	CHARGES	CREDITS	BALANCE
Feb 26	Brought Forward			130 00
Mar 2	Payment on Account		130 00	00
Mar 12	Invoice No. 2913	255 05		255 05
Mar 17	Invoice No. 3122	188 14		443 19
Mar 20	Payment on Account		400 00	43 19

JOB 6

Form: credit
memorandum
  In elite
  Workbook form
  5 tabs
Words: 31

MARTIN MILLER & SONS   58 BROAD STREET
                                     ATLANTA 1, GEORGIA

Credit Memorandum

TO   The National Company   DATE   April 3, 19--

      6 North Michigan Avenue   CREDIT MEMO NO.   CM4-13

                                  ORDER NO.   3-12/8

      Chicago 2, Illinois

YOUR ACCOUNT HAS BEEN CREDITED AS FOLLOWS:

QUANTITY	DESCRIPTION	CAT. NO.	UNIT PRICE	TOTAL	NET AMOUNT
1	Steel file cabinet	FF19	35 25	35 25	34 54
					34 54

JOB 1

Blocked letter
 Shown in pica
 Letterhead
 Enumeration tab
 Center tab
Words: 264
 Body: 181

◁ **6 in.** ▷
SS
14/5
▽

March 2, 19--

Use today's date.
Type year in full.

Mr. B. Frank Thomas,
John Bache & Company,
1028 Goodfellow Blvd.
St. Louis 21, Missouri

Dear Mr. Thomas:

I am pleased to answer your inquiry about punctuation styles
for business letters. There are three patterns:

1. The "full" or "closed" pattern requires that every line
    in the letter, other than those in the body, be ended by
    a punctuation mark. This letter illustrates the "full"
    pattern. You rarely see this form today.

2. The "standard" pattern requires only that two display
    lines be ended by punctuation: the salutation, which is
    followed by a colon; and the complimentary closing, fol-
    lowed by a comma. Most letters are in this pattern.

Example:
page 155

3. The "open" pattern eliminates punctuation marks after all
    display lines, except the period after an abbreviation.
    Not even the salutation or complimentary closing end with
    punctuation. This pattern is new, but becoming popular.

Example:
page 151

This letter also shows, as you requested, one of the several
methods of arranging an enumeration in the body of a letter.

Yours sincerely,

If a letter seems long,
type reference initials
without dropping down,
or drop only 1 line.

Ralph E. Jones,
Training Consultant   1 or 2 ➡

REJ:URS   2 ➡

P. S. A postscript is simply another paragraph. It is set
up like any other paragraph--blocked or indented, as the case
may be. The initials are usually as I have shown, but using
"PS:" or "PS--" is also acceptable.

JOB 3

Form: purchase order
In pica
Workbook
4 tabs
Words: 57

PURCHASE ORDER

THE NATIONAL CO.

6 North Michigan Avenue • Chicago 3, Illinois

TO Martin Miller & Sons

58 Broad Street

Atlanta 1, Georgia

DATE March 11, 19--

NO. C-34876

QUANTITY	DESCRIPTION	CAT. NO.	UNIT PRICE	TOTAL
3	Steel files, gray	FF19	35 25	105 75
1	Steel desk, gray	ED12	75 50	75 50
1	Steel desk chair, gray	EC18	34 00	34 00
2	Steel chairs, olive green	GC37	22 50	45 00
				260 25

JOB 4

Form: invoice
In pica
Workbook
5 tabs
Words: 59

MARTIN MILLER & SONS

58 BROAD STREET • ATLANTA 1, GA.

INVOICE

2913

CUSTOMER'S ORDER NO. C-34876

DATE March 12, 19--

SOLD TO

The National Company
6 North Michigan Avenue
Chicago 2, Illinois

SHIP TO

Same

SHIPPED VIA Collect Freight   TERMS 2/10, n/30   SALESMAN None

QUANTITY	DESCRIPTION	CAT. NO.	UNIT PRICE	TOTAL	NET AMOUNT
3	Steel files	FF19	35 25	105 75	
1	Steel desk	ED12	75 50	75 50	
1	Steel desk chair	EC18	34 00	34 00	
2	Steel guest chairs	GC37	22 50	45 00	
				260 25	255 05

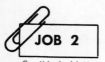

JOB 2

Semiblocked letter
Shown in elite
Letterhead
Paragraph tab
Center tab
3 carbons
Words: 230
Body: 188

Semiblocked Letter Style

Closing Lines Start at Center • Date Backspaced from Margin • Paragraphs Indented 5 Spaces

With Attention Line, CC Notation, and Open Punctuation

◁ **6 in.** ▷
SS
14/5
▽

March 3, 19--

Savard & Company
171 Westminster Street
Providence 3, Rhode Island ₂ ➧

                    ATTENTION: TRAINING DIRECTOR ₂ ➧

Gentlemen ₂ ➧

     The attention line is used when you wish to make sure that some
particular department or official gets your letter. An attention line
is typed a double space below the inside address. It always precedes
the salutation.

     The attention line is typed on a line by itself. It may be cen-
tered, or it may be blocked at the left margin. It may be arranged in
many styles, some of which are: ₂ ➧

               Attention: Training Director
               Attention: Training Director   Center longest line;
               Attention: Training Director   set tab; begin all
               Attention of the Training Director   lines at tab stop.
               ATTENTION: Training Director
               ATTENTION OF THE TRAINING DIRECTOR ₂ ➧

     Some other points of style in this letter are: (1) correct form
for a listing, in which the longest line is centered and the others
are blocked with it; (2) correct form for indicating, below, who will
receive a carbon copy (cc) of this letter; and (3) correct punctuation
in the "open" pattern. ₁ or ₂ ➧

                                                      When last line is short,
                                                      you may save a line, if
                    Yours very truly ₄ ➧   you wish, by dropping
                                                      only 1 line to closing.

                    Ralph E. Jones
                    Training Consultant ₀, ₁, or ₂ ➧

REJ:URS
cc Mr. Filene
   Miss Young

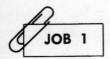

JOB 1

Form: 2 stock
requisitions
  Reduced model
  Workbook forms
  1 tab
Words: 73

First stock requisition: Ann Jessmore, of Billing Department, needs for tomorrow 1 ream of half-sheet letterheads; 1 ream of interoffice letterheads; 600 half-sheet billheads; 2 boxes of paper clips; and 2 short-hand notebooks.

Second stock requisition: John Deer, Shipping Department, needs for next Monday 6 rolls of No. 14 twine; 5,000 shipping tags; 500 No. 7 cardboard cartons; 3 Underwood black ribbons; 2 Royal black ribbons; and 5 shorthand notebooks.

JOB 2

Form: purchase
requisition
  Shown in pica
  Workbook
  2 tabs
Words: 65

```
S T O C K   R E Q U I S I T I O N

Today's Date   February 27

Deliver to___Ann Jessmore

Department___Billing

Date Needed   March 1


QUANTITY           ITEMS


1 ream          Half-sheet letterheads

1 ream          Interoffice letterheads

600             Half-sheet billheads

2 boxes         Paper clips

2               Shorthand notebooks


Signed_____
```

Typical stock requisition

PURCHASE REQUISITION
THE NATIONAL COMPANY • CHICAGO 2, ILLINOIS

DELIVER TO   T. M. Winters   DATE OF REQUEST March 10, 19--
            Executive Offices   DATE WANTED April 1, 19--
                           WHY WANTED Replacements, as
DEPARTMENT Sales   already budgeted
REQ'N NUMBER M-1-R   APPROVED

QUANTITY	DESCRIPTION
3	Steel file cabinets, 4-drawer, 13 inches, gray
1	Steel desk, executive, gray*
1	Steel desk chair, executive, gray
2	Steel chairs, guest, arm olive gray
	* See item ED12 MM&S catalogue, for style of desk

PURCHASING DEPARTMENT INFORMATION

ORDER FROM ....   PURCHASE ORDER NUMBER ....
....   DATE ORDERED.................................
....   DATE RECEIVED ....

A purchase requisition is a request, not an order.

JOB 3

Blocked letter
Unarranged
Letterhead
Use open
punctuation
1 carbon
Words: 168
Body: 132

Date | The Training Journal | 1000 Hanover Avenue | Richmond 26,   15   Placement plan is on page 119.
Virginia | ATTENTION: ADVERTISING MANAGER | Gentlemen   25

I am considering placing an advertisement in your publication.   38
Please send me the following information about your rates and cir-   51
culation: 53

1. An analysis of your circulation, with particular attention to the   67
number and type of training directors who subscribe to your publica-   81
tion.   82

2. An enumeration of other advertisers who, in the past five years,   96
have offered their services to the training directors of large companies.   111

3. Your rate card and whatever literature you have that tells the   124
relative merits of occasional large displays versus frequent small dis-   138
plays.   140

I should appreciate an early reply, for I need this information within   154
a week or ten days.   158

Yours very truly | Ralph E. Jones | Training Consultant   170

JOB 4

Blocked letter
Unarranged
Letterhead
Use open
punctuation
1 carbon
Words: 190
Body: 154

Date | Mrs. Ruth L. Kennard | Stephen Sampson & Sons | 1216 Com-   14   Placement plan is on page 119.
merce Street | Houston 2, Texas | Dear Mrs. Kennard   24

I am pleased to receive your invitation to work with you in revising   38
the training program for SS&S office workers. I shall come to Houston   52
about the tenth of next month, expecting to stay and work with you   66
until the job is completed. In order that I may become oriented to the   80
work you are already doing, please send the following materials to me: 95

1. A copy of the training guide that is now being used in your in-   109
service courses.   112

2. An outline, no matter how brief, of those aspects of the program   126
with which you are not satisfied.   133

3. A set of your printed stationery—the billing forms, letterheads,   147
and so on.   150

I hope that sending these materials will not be an inconvenience to   163
you. I am looking forward to meeting you and to working with you on   177
this project.   180

Yours sincerely | Ralph E. Jones | Training Consultant   192

UNIT 19
FORMS

In this unit, to develop a broad understanding of the general arrangement and use of printed business papers, you will type on a wide variety of them —14 altogether. Before starting the jobs, read pages 159-168 and answer the study-guide questions on Workbook pages 153-154.

WARMUP (*Each line 3 times*)   ◁ **60** ▷

```
aims axes bask flag hazy jazz plan quay riot save scad what
weep 2330 peep 0330 peer 0334 pyre 0643 pout 0975 pipe 0803
I said that the famous saying is, "Never give up the ship!"
```

12-Sec. 5| 10| 15| 20| 25| 30| 35| 40| 45| 50| 55| 60|

CAPITAL-CONTROL PREVIEW (*Each line 3 times*)

```
One But Sons Invoice Brought Illinois Jessmore Replacements
In Some Rolls Forward Georgia Michigan Shipping Interoffice
All Here True Every National Executive Shorthand Department
```

ALPHABET-REVIEW PARAGRAPHS (*2 copies / si 1.28*)   ◁ **60** ▷
DS

*7-Min. Writings

One of the most thriving kinds of[1] business in this day and age is the[2] business of designing business forms.[3] True, almost all stationers[4] have standard forms on their shelves;[5] but it is true, too, that most big[6] firms bring in an expert who will[7] analyze all the forms they use and[8] then design new ones that are easier[9] to use and that save time for the[10] persons who use them. You would not[11] suppose a firm that sells jars of[12] medicine would use the same billhead[13] as a firm that sells steel beams.[14] In the same sense, the requisition[15] form for office supplies would[16] not serve the needs of a factory.[17]

16
33
50
67
84
100
117
119

But even though forms will vary from[18] office to office, all forms are[19] organized on principles that you, the[20] typist, should know. Here are some[21] examples: All forms should use[22] standard typewriter spacing; you[23] should never have to shift a tab stop,[24] squeeze a number, or adjust the[25] variable spacer after you have once[26] set up the machine. A form should[27] have guide words or signals to show[28] what should be typed in each part[29] of the form; you should not have to[30] guess. Every form must resemble a[31] letter; that is, you should be able[32] to type the entries on the form in[33] almost exactly the same sequence[34] that you would if it were a letter.[35]

136
153
169
185
201
218
234
246

*How to measure your speed if you have taken writings of other lengths? See page 163 footnote.

PRODUCTION PRACTICE
(*Jobs 1-6*)

Type Jobs 1-6 on workbook forms or on papers ruled to resemble the illustrations. If correct procedures are used (page 91), none of these jobs will take more than 5 minutes. Most of the workbook forms are in duplicate (printed on both sides of the paper) so that, after you have typed each job once, you may start them over in the time that you will have left.

WARMUP *(Each line 3 times)*

◁ **60** ▷

```
badge dizzy fight jacks lemon pique rusts vixen where woven
weepy 23306 pouty 09756 write 24853 wrote 24953 witty 28556
He kept asking us, "Why can't an old dog learn new tricks?"
```
12-Sec. 5| 10| 15| 20| 25| 30| 35| 40| 45| 50| 55| 60|

CAPITAL-CONTROL PREVIEW *(Each line 3 times)*

```
If Phi Mrs. Truda State Subject Jenkins College Fraternally
Pi One This Omega Kansas Because Detroit Western Cincinnati
Full Tracy Elsie George Blocked Emporia President Patterson
```

ALPHABET-REVIEW PARAGRAPHS *(2 copies / si 1.28)*

◁ **50** ▷
DS

5-Min. Writings		1 2 3 4 5 6 7 8 9 10	
0	47	One of the tricks used by most of the expert	9
2	49	typists in placing letters is to judge that their	19
4	51	letters are average in size. They make an excep-	29
6	53	tion only for a very short or a very long letter.	39
si 1.26 8	55	Then, as they near the bottom of the letter, they	49
10	57	spread or squeeze the ending, to make it come out	59
12	59	right. For instance, you may leave as few as two	69
14	61	or as many as six lines for the penned signature.	79
16	63	The notations at the end of a letter are an-	9 88
18	65	other point of expanding or squeezing. They need	19 98
20	67	not always begin two lines below the signature or	29 108
22	69	title line. They may start even with it when you	39 118
si 1.30 24	71	need to save space. They may start several lines	49 128
26	73	down when you need to take up space. You can use	59 138
28	75	single spacing or double spacing. You can double	69 148
30	77	up the cc listing. If you have an enclosure, you	79 158
32	79	can list what it is. You must use your judgment.	89 168
34	81	Some firms, but not all, allow the typist to	9 177
35	83	use the company name as an expansion point, also.	19 187
si 1.28 37	85	Some letters require a company name, but most can	29 197
39	87	have it or omit it at will. The subject line may	39 207
41	89	be an option, too; but you will have whizzed past	49 217
43	91	it before you know whether you need to save space	59 227
45	93	or fill it up. Apply your judgment in this unit.	69 237
Plus ➡		1	2	

PRODUCTION PRACTICE *(Jobs 5-8)*

Type Jobs 5-8 on workbook letterheads. Note that the "bcc" notation on Jobs 6-8 will be typed at the top of the *carbon* copies, not on the original (letterhead) copies. Note also that Jobs 7 and 8 are identical "form letters" in which only the inside address is changed.

DIRECTIONS FOR REVIEW OF LETTER STYLES

Use same letter (below) for all jobs. It contains:
Letter, 177 words, si 1.34. Body, 137 words, si 1.26.

JOB NO.	LETTER STYLE TO BE USED	EXAMPLE ON PAGE —	PUNCTUATION PATTERN	SPACING TO USE	SPECIAL DIRECTIONS
10	Indented	120	Full	Double	Center subject line.
11	Semiblocked	151	Standard	Single	Block subject line.
12	Blocked	150	Open	Single	Insert: bcc Mr. Ellis.
13	Full-Blocked	154	Standard	Single	Block subject line.
*14	NOMA Simplified	157	Open	Single	Omit salutation and closing.
*15	Square-Blocked	155	Standard	Single	Center subject line.

Optional jobs—do not type them unless your instructor tells you to do so.

5-Min. Writings				◁50▷ DS
0	35	Type today's date. Mr. Frank A. White, 3928		9
2	37	Anderson Avenue, Grand Forks, North Dakota. Dear		19
4	39	Mr. White: SUBJECT: NEW REPRESENTATIVE. In the		29
6	41	past, Mr. White, you have been so kind as to help		39
8	43	us many times. We hope that you can do so again.		49
10	45	Among the many young men you know in or near		58
12	47	Grand Forks, is there a young man who might prove		68
14	49	eligible to represent our firm in your state? We		78
16	51	are looking for a personable young man. He ought		88
18	53	to be 25 or so years old. He should have had two		98
20	55	or three years of sales experience, and he should		108
22	57	have finished at least one year of college train-		118
24	59	ing. He must be interested in a lifetime selling		128
26	61	career. The job will pay $4,200 a year to start.		138
28	63	If you know of someone who would be suitable		147
29	65	for this opening, please suggest his writing soon		157
31	67	to me. I should appreciate your help. Cordially		167
33	69	yours, Alvin L. Lake, Personnel Manager. ALL:URS		177
Plus ➧		1	2	

Full-Blocked Letter Style

Every Line Begins at the Left Margin

With a Subject Line and Open Punctuation

JOB 5

Full-blocked
letter
  Shown in pica
  Letterhead
  No tab stops
Words: 217
Body: 179

March 6, 19--

◁ 5 in. ▷
SS
14/5
▽

Mr. Roger Patterson
Western Life Company
2856 East Fourth Street
Cincinnati 2, Ohio

Dear Mr. Patterson

Subject: Form of a Full-Blocked Letter

This letter is set up in the full-blocked style, in
which every line begins at the left margin. Some
companies modify it by keeping the date at the right,
but most firms use it as shown here. Because this
style is the fastest to type, it is considered very
modern. It is natural, although not necessary, to
use "open" punctuation with this style of letter.

This letter also illustrates one arrangement of the
subject line, which may be used with any style of
letter. A subject line, like an attention line, may
be typed with underscores or capitals. In a full-
blocked letter, it must be blocked; in other letter
styles, it may be blocked or centered. It always
appears after the salutation and before the body,
for it is considered a part of the body.

Some companies, notably law offices, prefer to use
the Latin terms Re or In Re instead of Subject.

Yours very truly

PARKER-LEHIGH COLLEGE

Elsie Frost

Mrs. Elsie Frost, Dean

EF:URS

A woman is assumed to be
Miss unless Mrs. is either
typed as shown here or included parenthetically in
the pen signature.

NOMA Simplified Letter Style

All Lines Begin at Left Margin • Punctuation is Open • Subject Line and Name in all Capitals

A Modification of the Full-Blocked Style

JOB 9

NOMA Simpli-
fied letter
In pica
Letterhead
Aligning tab
1 carbon
Words: 193
Body: 163

⊲**5 in.**⊳
SS
14/6
▽

March 8, 19--

Mr. Richard Humphrey, Jr.
Humphrey Lumber Company
520 S. W. Park Avenue
Portland 5, Oregon ₃ ➧

A WORD ABOUT THE SIMPLIFIED LETTER ₃ ➧

A few years ago, Mr. Humphrey, the National Office
Management Association designed a new letter form
that they called the "NOMA Simplified Letter." It
is illustrated by this letter. Its main features:

Note the
omission
of periods.

1 It uses the efficient full-block letter style.

2 It contains no salutation or closing (NOMA feels
   these expressions are meaningless).

3 It tells in all capitals what you want to know
   as you pick up the letter: what the letter is
   about and from whom it was received.

4 It tries to convey a brisk but friendly tone,
   with the addressee's name used in the message.

Despite obvious merit, Mr. Humphrey, this form has
not proved popular. Perhaps habit is too strong.
Perhaps this form looks, as some say, too much like
a circular. Anyhow, why not try it yourself? ₄ ➧

Ralph E. Jones

RALPH E. JONES, TRAINING CONSULTANT ₂ ➧

Initials in
small letters.

urs
Enc.

bcc Evans
    Forest
    Miller

◄ To indicate distribution of carbon copies without revealing it to the addressee:
1. After finishing letter, remove whole pack.
2. Take off original copy and first carbon paper.
3. Reinsert the rest of the carbon pack.
4. In the open space at the top, type "bcc" (blind carbon copy) followed by appropriate names, titles, or initials.

JOB 6

Square-blocked
letter
  Shown in elite
  Letterhead
  No tab stops
  4 carbons
  Use standard
  punctuation
Words: 283
Body: 242

Mrs. Truda Tracy George   March 6, 19--   ◁ **60** ▷
President, Phi Omega Pi   **SS**
Kansas State College   **18**
Emporia, Kansas   ▽

My dear Mrs. George:

        SUBJECT: THE SQUARE-BLOCKED LETTER

A square-blocked letter like this one is simply the familiar
full-blocked letter with (1) the date moved to the right and
typed on the same line with the start of the inside address,
to "square off" that corner; and (2) the reference initials
also brought to the right, to "square off" that corner.

This letter style does have one disadvantage: If the letter
is very short, the date and inside address will bump into one
another; so, most persons who use this letter style make it a
rule not to use less than a 50-space line. You have to remind
yourself to start lower on the page, too; that is, start the
first line about half way between where the date and inside
address would be in any other letter style.

But this arrangement does have many advantages, too. It is
almost as quick to type as the full-blocked style. It saves
the space that is otherwise lost by dropping after the date
and after the signer's identification, so that you may type
a longer letter on one page. It makes any letter seem much
shorter. It permits any kind of display you wish, whether it
is blocked or centered. It is very flexible. And, it is so
new that it looks smartly different.

        Fraternally yours,

A married woman's
typed signature
shows form she   *Elsie Frost*
wants in reply.
        Mrs. George W. Frost   EF:URS
                                                    2 Enc.

JOBS 7-8

Full-blocked
letters (2)
  In elite
  Letterheads
  2 Carbons
  "bcc" notation
  Use open
  punctuation
Words: 184
  Body: 145

March 7, 19--

Personnel Department [No. 7]
Jenkins-Acme Company
2228 Griswold Street
Detroit 26, Michigan

Gentlemen

SUBJECT: INTERVIEWS FOR JUNE GRADUATES

You will recall that a member of your department came to our
school and interviewed a number of our students just prior to
graduation last year. As a result, you were able to select
several fine young prospects for your company. Do you wish
to arrange a similar interview plan this spring?

If you do, please let us know what date during the first two
weeks of June would be preferable to you. Perhaps you could
give us two dates, in order that we may be able to avoid con-
flicts in scheduling the interviews. Because graduation will
not occur until June 25, interviewing during the early part
of June might be well timed both from your point of view and
from that of the students.

Yours very truly

PARKER-LEHIGH COLLEGE

(Mrs.) Elsie Frost

Elsie Frost, Dean

EF:URS

March 7, 19--   4

[No. 8] Personnel Department   8
Davis-Wilson Company   12
1318 Griswold Street   17
Detroit 26, Michigan   21
                                       23

                                       31

                                       43
                                       55
                                       67
                                       79
                                       89

                                      102
                                      114
                                      126
                                      138
                                      150
                                      162
                                      168

                                      171

                                      176

                                      179

[bcc Miss Wiley]   184

◁ **60** ▷

Lessons 111-112 : *Skill Drills*

WARMUP *(Each line 3 times)*

```
cabled flight jumper kindle lazily mosque votive mixed whom
wet 235 pet 035 yet 635 rue 473 pit 085 tip 580 top 590 590
Why did they not know that the signal was "Who goes there?"
```
12-Sec. 5| 10| 15| 20| 25| 30| 35| 40| 45| 50| 55| 60|

CAPITAL-CONTROL PREVIEW *(Each line 3 times)*

```
We Jr. Frank Perhaps Portland Humphrey National Association
In The Forks Dakota Richard Consultant Personnel Management
I Road White Anyhow Despite Simplified Cordially Consultant
```

PRODUCTION PRACTICE *(Jobs 9-15)*

    Type Job 9 on a workbook letterhead; but type Jobs 10-15 (which review letter
styles and will take about 5 minutes each) on plain paper, on which you have
ruled or creased a line about 2 inches from the top to represent the depth of a
letterhead.